Advanced Use Case Modeling

The Addison-Wesley Object Technology Series

Grady Booch, Ivar Jacobson, and James Rumbaugh, Series Editors

For more information, check out the series web site at www.awprofessional.com/otseries.

The Component Software Series

Clemens Szyperski, Series Editor

For more information, check out the series web site at www.awprofessional.com/csseries.

Advanced Use Case Modeling

Software Systems

Frank Armour
Granville Miller

✦ Addison-Wesley

Boston • San Francisco • New York • Toronto • Montreal
London • Munich • Paris • Madrid • Capetown
Sydney • Tokyo • Singapore • Mexico City

The publisher offers discounts on this book when ordered in quantity for bulk purchases and special sales. For more information, please contact:

U.S. Corporate and Government Sales
(800) 382-3419
corpsales@pearsontechgroup.com

For sales outside of the U.S., please contact:

International Sales
(317) 581-3793
international@pearsontechgroup.com

Visit Addison-Wesley on the Web: www.awprofessional.com

Library of Congress Cataloging-in-Publication Data
Armour, Frank.
    Advanced use case modeling : software systems / Frank Armour, Granville Miller.
        p.   cm. — (Addison-Wesley object technology series)
    Includes bibliographical references and index.
    ISBN 0-201-61592-4 (alk. paper)
      1. Computer software—Development.   2. Use cases (Systems engineering) I. Miller,
Granville. II. Title. III. Series.

QA76.76.D47 A74 2000
005.3—dc21

                                          00–042102

Text printed on recycled and acid-free paper.
ISBN 0201615924
6 7 8 9 1011 EB   07 06 05 04
6th Printing   November 2004

This book is dedicated to my parents,
Joan and Frank E., to whom I owe everything.

—Frank

This book is dedicated to Zina,
who makes life worthwhile and puts it all in perspective.

—Randy

Contents

Foreword

When I came up with the use case concept in 1986, it was based on many years of work in component-based system development. We had had many other different techniques to do the job, techniques that were overlapping and had gaps. With use cases we got a tool with many facets. Some of them are:

- Use cases are the requirements capture vehicle.
- Use cases are the base for defining functional requirements.
- Use cases facilitate envisioning applications.
- Use cases assist in system delimitation.
- Use cases are the means to communicate with end users and customers.
- Use cases provide the dynamic, black-box view of the system.
- Use cases are the base for object derivation; objects naturally fall out of use cases.
- Use cases provide a tool for requirements traceability.
- Use cases are the base for user interface and experience design.
- Use cases facilitate moving from functional requirements to object and component structures.
- Use cases are the base for allocating functionality to components and objects.

- Use cases are the mechanism to define object interaction and object interfaces.
- Use cases define access patterns to a database.
- Use cases help us with dimensioning of processor capacity.
- Use cases are the base for integration testing.
- Use cases define test cases.
- Use cases are the base for incremental development.
- Use cases help us with estimation of project size and required resources.
- Use cases provide a base for user documentation and manuals.
- Use cases are a tool for controlling a project.
- Use cases drive the development activities.
- Use cases have become the standard way of representing business processes.
- Use cases are used to describe what a legacy system is doing in a reengineering activity.
- Use cases are used when reengineering a business to become an e-business company.

And the list goes on. Of course, I certainly recognize that use cases are not the snake oil or the silver bullet of software development. However, the development of the use case idea has just started.

Advanced Use Case Modeling provides a set of guidelines for developing a use case model for software systems. It provides a toolkit of techniques to be utilized by experienced use case modelers. As with any toolkit, each tool has an intended purpose and the right tool should be selected for each job. Frank and Randy have done an excellent job of providing techniques that reflect their vast experience in the industry.

The use case continues to drive business processes, software systems, and component engineering projects. Some of the original concepts behind this modeling technique have evolved through the work of researchers, practitioners, and the standards bodies, but the fundamental ideas remain the same. The use case is an elegant way of communicating the needs of a business or software system. I am sure that, over time, new communication needs will lead to other ways of employing use cases; the possibilities are endless.

Ivar Jacobson

Preface

The use case approach is increasingly popular with our customers, to
an extent that some will only specify systems using them.

—Anthony Heritage and Phil Coley [Heritage 1995]

In this rapidly changing business and technological environment, use case modeling has emerged as one of the premier techniques for defining business processes and software systems. Business engineers now employ use cases to define complex business processes across lines of business and even to define entire businesses. Use cases are also the standard for defining requirements for the software systems created using today's object-oriented development languages such as Java, Smalltalk, and C++. In the field of software components, a very young industry whose market is estimated to be more than $12 billion in 2001 [Hanscome 1998], use cases are rapidly becoming a method of communication between suppliers and vendors.

The users of this technique for defining systems are as diverse as its uses. Use case modeling is already being employed by most Fortune 1000 companies and is being taught at many academic institutions all over the world, and the popularity of this modeling technique continues to grow.

Business process and software requirements engineering are rapidly evolving fields. Research in these areas continues to propose new methods of dealing with potential problems, even while actual practice is slow to adopt only a fraction of those proposed. This slow-moving partial adoption has been termed the "research–practice gap" [Berry 1998]. Creating yet another use case book without an extensive experience base would merely add to this gap. Our approach is significant because we present a practitioner's approach firmly grounded in the real world.

Goals

Over the past six years, we have worked on some large, ambitious projects involving software development and business engineering. To create the best possible use case models, we found it necessary to extend the seminal work of Ivar Jacobson in certain areas. This book details our extensions, which complement Ivar's ongoing work. The flexibility of use case modeling and the Unified Modeling Language, which we use to describe these models, allows us to produce extensions to solve real-world problems successfully.

The goal of this book is to further the advancement of use case modeling in software and business engineering. To achieve this goal, the book provides a comprehensive yet readable guide to use case modeling for the practitioner. Specifically, it explains advanced use case modeling concepts, describes a process for implementing use case modeling, and discusses various use case modeling issues.

Audience

The audience for this book is anyone involved in the conceptualization, development, testing, management, modeling, and use of software products and business processes. Although it contains a sizable amount of content related to business processes, this book is geared toward all of us in the software industry. Software professionals are the largest body of use case engineers because use case development was first introduced as a software requirements vehicle.

Business analysts will agree that use case engineering has undergone the greatest transformations on their front. Business analysts and their software process brethren are quickly learning that automation via software is not the only reason for employing use cases. In fact, more and more of business process modeling using use cases is not geared toward the generation and production of new software but is being done to understand, and in some cases, standardize and optimize key business processes across multiple lines of business.

Many of the techniques described in this book transcend the software or business arenas of the reader community. The well-established link between business use cases and software system use cases is described as we illustrate the ways in which software systems can be derived from a business process. The only thing we ask is that our business readers be patient as we start on the software side.

Academic institutions will also find this book useful. This book can be used as a text in an object-oriented analysis (OOA) course in which use cases play a key role.

How to Use This Book

The theory of use case development often differs from the actual practice of use case development. One reason for this difference is that very few software development projects are "green fields"; most are started with a preconceived notion of a legacy process for successfully creating software. We are not advocating the removal of the legacy processes. In fact, many of the artifacts involved in these processes may be necessary due to the nature of the problem that is being solved through software development. Some of these artifacts may also be mandatory for getting the necessary approval to begin a software development project.

Use case modeling cannot be successful in isolation. The process of creating use case models must be put in the context of the specific organization. Every organization has unique cultural aspects. Luckily, we find some commonality as well as differences in nearly every facet of the business engineering and software development processes across organizations.

Experience in one organization can often be useful in another. When patterns of failure have emerged from our use case adventures, we have attempted to capture the factors that have been directly responsible. The pitfalls of use case modeling generally fall into two categories: those in the use case development process itself and those found when use cases are integrated with commonly used software development practices. Some of the pitfalls are so significant that they can stop the development of a system dead in its tracks.

This book provides a process framework for creating models of software systems. A **process framework** is a set of activities used to develop a process. Our frameworks should be customized specifically for your organization. This book describes the second of the three process frameworks (Figure P-1), the conceptualization and specification of software systems.

Each process framework is independent and fully defined. They may all be performed in concert or separately. For example, software system and component engineering may be used together to provide requirements for software system development using components. The combination of business process and software system engineering creates an understanding of the elements necessary for business process automation. A business process is not usually completely automated via software systems. The requirements for the business process, therefore, become a superset of those of the software systems used by people carrying out the business process.

The three frameworks provide a means for specifying the requirements for engineering all of the systems required for business process automation, incorporating software building blocks. When process frameworks are combined, the outputs created during the previous framework may be utilized as inputs to the next.

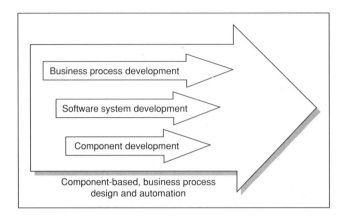

Business process development

Software system development

Component development

Component-based, business process
design and automation

FIGURE P-1   Process frameworks of the advanced use case modeling process

To make the most of this book, we recommend following an established software development process. We respect the notion that not all companies are capable of following a software development process in exactly the same way. The **ceremony**, or amount of formality, involved usually differs dramatically from company to company and even from project to project [Booch 1996].

Ceremony helps define how much of a process framework to use [Miller 2000]. High-ceremony projects tend to utilize more of the activities, perhaps adopting advanced use case modeling wholesale. Low-ceremony projects use only a portion of the material described. Regardless of the level of ceremony, you will certainly find use cases in some form useful for the definition of requirements for a project.

Organization and Content

There are many books on use cases available on the market today. Ours is unique in its coverage of the role of use cases in software development. We also present some substantially new material not found in any other paper or book. We balance this new material with a comprehensive survey of the existing work in the field of use case modeling.

To allow this book to stand on its own, we present two chapters of fundamental material. These two chapters begin after an introduction to advanced use case modeling. Chapter 1 discusses the conceptual role of actors in the use case model. A detailed account of how to recognize actors is provided to prepare the use case modeler to discover use cases. Chapter 2 discusses the general format and proto-

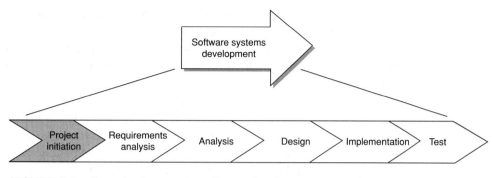

FIGURE P-2 Generic phases of a software development process

col for creating use cases. The Unified Modeling Language, the Object Management Group (OMG) standard for use case modeling, is explained.

  Part 2 starts with the first phase of software development, project initiation (Figure P-2). Chapter 3 focuses on this phase by looking at the things that define the system scope—the problem that is to be solved and the business opportunity created by the new or improved system, and the financial feasibility of building a software system to address this opportunity.

  Chapter 4 describes use case modeling in the requirements analysis phase of the software development process (Figure P-3). Use cases help to describe the functions

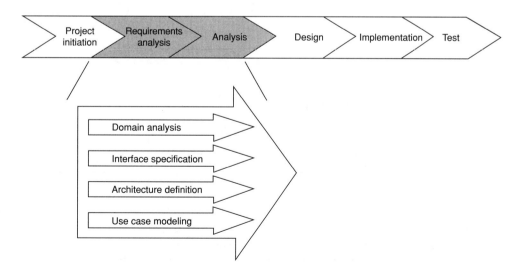

FIGURE P-3 Decomposition of the requirements analysis and partial analysis phases

of the system and to balance the use case model; form is provided with a well-designed architecture that can enhance the use case model.

In Part 3, we introduce a bank loan application example that is used throughout the book to illustrate the concepts of use case modeling. The example does not represent any actual loan system. The necessary functionality for an actual loan application has been streamlined for purposes of the example.

In Part 3 we also describe the advanced use case modeling process framework. Chapter 5 decomposes use case modeling into activity groups, or groups of logically related activities (Figure P-4). The chapter describes a framework for use case modeling that is used to describe system use case modeling through Chapter 15.

Chapter 6 describes the initial steps in setting up a use case modeling effort. The selection and customization of use case frameworks, the selection of standards and techniques, and the consideration of training and mentoring needs are outlined.

Chapter 7 discusses the initial steps of creating the use case model. The outcome of this activity group is a use case model that captures a "conceptual" picture of what the system will need to do.

Part 4 focuses on expanding the use case model. Chapter 8 begins the discussion of how initial use case descriptions are expanded to become base use cases with more detailed requirements and how this increased complexity is modeled. Chapter 9 discusses the practice of placing conditional and iterative logic within a use case's flow of events. Two techniques for modeling these concepts are presented.

Chapter 10 describes the use of extend, include, and generalization relationships to model the alternatives, variations, and commonality in the use case model.

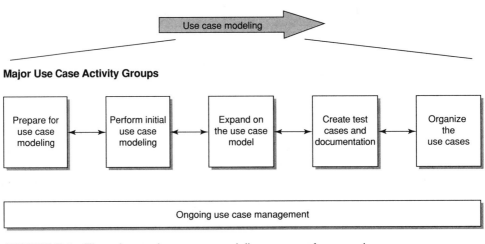

FIGURE P-4   The advanced use case modeling process framework

Chapter 11 discusses the capture of additional or supplemental information associated with an individual use case. Chapter 12 discusses the importance of mapping the use cases to the analysis object model. Techniques such as CRUD matrixes, object to use case tables, and sequence diagrams are outlined. Chapter 13 discusses the concept and utilization of scenarios to complement the use case model.

The final phase of any software engineering process is testing. Chapter 14 discusses testing and documenting the system and the role use cases play in driving these activities. Chapter 15 examines organizing use cases by business functional packages and by dependencies based on use case preconditions and postconditions. A discussion of various views of the use case model is presented. A wrap-up of key use case artifacts is also presented.

Part 5, Additional Topics, begins with Chapter 16. This chapter examines the effect of use cases on user interface design. Transactions are used to segment the use case model to provide elements for conceptual user interface development. Grouping techniques allow screens to be built from the transactions.

Chapter 17 examines the effect of change on the use case model. In successful software systems, changes that affect the functionality of the system are inevitable. Change may occur during the project or after it has shipped.

Chapter 18 discusses some of the necessary considerations for deploying advanced use case modeling. All or part of the process framework may be utilized depending on the needs of the project. This chapter outlines the elements that determine how much to use. It also describes how to document this process.

The final chapter, Chapter 19, discusses the quality attributes of a good use case model. It also describes the various roles that use case modeling can play within a system analysis effort. Finally, iterative and incremental development with advanced use case modeling is briefly outlined.

Complementary Works

This book stands on its own and can be read without referring to other works. However, quite a bit of helpful material is available on requirements engineering, use case development, and process improvement.

Software system requirements engineering

- Ivar Jacobson, Grady Booch, and James Rumbaugh, *The Unified Software Development Process*, Addison-Wesley, Reading, MA, 1999.

- Ivar Jacobson, Magnus Christerson, Patrik Jonsson, and Gunnar Overgaard, *Object-Oriented Software Engineering: A Use Case Driven Approach*, Addison-Wesley, Reading, MA, 1992.

- Dean Leffingwell and Don Widrig, *Managing Software Requirements: A Unified Approach,* Addison-Wesley, Reading, MA, 2000.
- Geri Schneider and Jason P. Winters, *Applying Use Cases: A Practical Guide*, Addison-Wesley, Reading, MA, 1998.
- Rational Software Corporation, *Rational Unified Process.* 2000.

Business process engineering

- Ivar Jacobson, Maria Ericsson, and Agneta Jacobson, *The Object Advantage: Business Process Reengineeering with Object Technology,* Addison-Wesley, Reading, MA, 1995.
- Michael Hammer and James Champy, *Reengineering the Corporation*, Harper Business, New York, 1993.
- Rational Software Corporation, *Rational Unified Process.* 2000.

Component development

- Ivar Jacobson, Martin Griss, and Patrik Jonsson, *Software Reuse: Architecture, Process, and Organization for Business Success*, Addison-Wesley, Reading, MA, 1997.
- Clemens Szyperski, *Component Software: Beyond Object-Oriented Programming*, Addison-Wesley, Reading, MA, 1998.

You may notice a number of references to other works in the body of this book. We did an extensive survey of the use case literature that predates the publication of this book and found many ideas worthy of inclusion. We also found many areas where we had developed solutions independently that were similar to those found in the literature. In these cases, we refer to the work in which the idea originally appeared. This gives the reader the flexibility to explore these references to get other viewpoints and gives credit to the other deserving authors.

For the latest information on use cases, supplemental and additional material, or how to contact the authors, visit us at our website, www.advancedusecases.com.

Acknowledgments

Much of this book is based on the work of Ivar Jacobson, inventor and visionary in the field of use case engineering. We have attempted to remain true to his original work throughout this book. We thank Zina Znayenko Miller for tirelessly editing the book, often on very short notice. We would also like to thank our reviewers, who provided valuable feedback in the various stages of the book, especially Monica Gupta, Todd Hansen, and Karin Palmkuist. This book would not be where it is today without them.

We thank American Management Systems and its clients for many use case modeling opportunities and experiences. We would also like to thank the following individuals: Andy Baer, Chris Ball, Jeff Bitner, Susan Bowler, Lorrie Boyd, Mike Bradley, Bob Brodd, Bill Catherwood, Judy Cohen, Dennis de Champeaux, Peter Dimitrious, Sean Furey, Mary Gorman, Kevin Heineman, Peter Knowles, Steve Larue, John McGregor, Les Moore, Perri-Ann Sims, Mark Schroeder, Chris Tatum, and Patrick Wall. We would also like to thank Brenda Damario, Christine Milliken, and Nora Parker from the U.S. Census Bureau.

Thanks also to these Addison-Wesley reviewers: Jeff Bitner, Senior Principal, Corporate Technology Group, American Management Systems; Maria Ericsson; Monica S. Gupta, former Director of Middleware and Web Integration Lab, AMS Center for Advanced Technologies; Todd Hansen, Senior Architect, Make Systems; Karin Palmkuist, Enea Data; Mark Schroeder, Folio[*fn*]; and Sam Supakkul, Senior Architect, Digital Pockets.

We would like to thank all the students of the systems and requirements analysis courses at American University and George Mason University, whose experiences and insights helped refine the book. An early version of this work was presented at a tutorial at OOPSLA '98. The attendees of this tutorial asked some very thought-provoking questions that influenced this book. We would also like to thank Sarah Alijani from American University and Steve Kaisler of the Sergeant of Arms of the U.S. Senate for their contributions.

Thanks also go out to those involved in the publication of this book, Kristin Erickson, Krysia Bebick, Carter Shanklin, and all the folks at Addison-Wesley. Special thanks to Diane Freed, project manager, and Kim Arney, who typeset the book. And finally, we thank all the people in the industry who have been willing to share their experiences.

We hope this book is as useful to you and your organization as it has been to ours.

Frank Armour
Granville Miller
November, 2000

Introduction

The productivity of knowledge is going to be the determining factor in the competitive position of a company, an industry, an entire country.

—Peter F. Drucker [Drucker 1993]

The nature of business has changed, and the signs of this change are all around us. Fundamental methods of business, forged during the industrial revolution and perfected over the last 300 years, have now been forever replaced. The new methods are primarily based on information and technology and driven by global competition. This era, in which production methods are based on knowledge rather than labor and competition, has been coined the *information age*. The pioneers of this age have created new companies so powerful that they can rival or threaten the powerhouses of the established business world.

There is much more to these new business methods than meets the eye. Information and technology are critical but not necessarily sufficient to foster a change of this magnitude to the business landscape. A small start-up company such as Amazon.com is not capable of challenging a Barnes and Noble with technology alone. It has been able to *use* technology and information to create productivity increases and competitive advantage. And it has created competitive advantage in a very organic and imaginative way.

The news of productivity increases and competitive advantage has not been lost on those of us who have not been the actual pioneers of the information age. The rapid acceleration of computer and telecommunications technology has generally resulted in a significant boost in the velocity of business [Greenspan 1999]. It seems that most of us have benefited, even if we don't ourselves use the ad hoc methodologies that propel 10 percent of the start-ups to success. It is, however, important to understand the critical factors that contribute to the general well-being that we are all currently experiencing. We must also understand the factors that can allow us to be more competitive.

Role of Information Technology

One thing is certain: there is no longer any doubt about the role of information technology in today's companies. It is a fundamental part of the operations of every company. The relationship between business and computers, albeit tumultuous at times, has solidified. The result is a partnership that fosters or enables true business change.

As information technology has focused on business change, so has business itself. Business engineering and automation are no longer synonymous with layoffs [Hammer 1995]. In many cases, automation can be used simply to handle the mundane work, allowing us humans to focus on the more interesting areas of our jobs. Interestingly enough, there are also cases where automation cannot be used. In these cases, automation has been found to create more problems than it solves. Many health care claim systems have been fully automated, only to find that combatting fraud requires human intervention. The result has been a harmonious combination of humans and technology in today's claim systems. However, the point is that we now realize that change is inevitable. If we do not change when competitive advantage can be increased, our competitors will, and we will lose the market position for which we have worked so hard.

Information technology is an essential enabler of this business change [Hammer 1993]. However, technology initiatives cannot be performed in a vacuum. They must be completed as part of a bigger ambition: the changing of a business system. This change must occur in organizational, process, and people initiatives. Technology can then be *used* to enable the change.

Enabling Change through Information Technology

Nowhere is the partnership of information and technology exemplified more than in the World Wide Web. Very few companies that wish to remain in business can afford to ignore this medium. The Internet, as an avenue for sales, marketing, and support, continues to be very lucrative. In fact, the number of businesses with Web sites on the Internet surpasses the number of businesses with toll-free phone numbers! Web sites are only one of many ways that software automation can increase efficiency.

A popular view is that all business change projects utilizing information technology should have a measurable result [Thorp 1999]. Certainly a measurable result, commonly known as return on investment, is important to any business.

However, using only the bottom line as an indicator of the value of any project misses some of the key lessons of the twentieth century. Creating Web-based technology centers initially was not thought of as yielding tangible value for companies. You never know when an important technology change may occur. Businesses that are ready for change do better than those that are not.

Another intangible benefit of information technology is the potential for innovation. Innovation is key to the information age, yet very little instruction is offered on how to encourage innovation in a systematic way. Peter Drucker, who correctly predicted in 1993 [Drucker 1993] from an economic and sociological perspective much of what we are seeing today, described the dynamics of what we now know as knowledge management. He claimed that the way to encourage the productivity of knowledge is

> . . . to focus on the end result, on the task, on the work. "Only connect" was the constant admonition of the great English novelist, E. M. Forster. It has been the hallmark of the artist, but equally of the great scientist—of a Darwin, a Bohr, an Einstein. At their level, the capacity to connect may be inborn and part of the mystery we call "genius." But to a large extent, the ability to connect and thus to raise the yield of existing knowledge (whether for an individual, for a team, or for the entire organization) is learnable. Eventually, it should become teachable. It requires a methodology for *problem definition*—even more urgently perhaps than it requires the currently fashionable methodology for "problem solving."

What Peter Drucker is describing is the need for a methodology to systematically define problems that occur in business. Without this methodology, we cannot make the connections required for innovation. A methodology is needed that ingrains the ability to consistently *use* technology and information to create productivity increases and competitive advantage. Some of the values of these increases may be tangible, others intangible (at least by strict accounting rules).

Our ability to define problems gives us three very important pieces of the productivity puzzle. The first and most important is the ability to focus on the result that we are attempting to achieve. The second is the realization of the need and the desire to continuously learn. Finally, there is the gratification of solving a worthwhile problem. A motivated, learning organization is a worthy adversary in the competitive battles of a global economy and technological paradigm shifts.

Software Industry

The software industry has proven to be a lucrative business all on its own, producing wealth without compare for a few individuals. Perhaps this wealth and opportunity come from the role this technology plays in the change of business. Certainly all software is not aimed at business. Some is aimed at the consumer and some is written just for fun.

Regardless of who the audience may be, building software that meets their needs is critical to the success of the system. Therefore, in software as in business, problem formulation is very important. It is also very difficult. Fred Brooks [1987] wrote in a landmark article:

> The hardest single part of building a software system is deciding precisely what to build. *No other part of the conceptual work is as difficult as establishing the detailed technical requirements, including all the interfaces to people, to machines, and to other software systems.* No other part of the work so cripples the resulting system if done wrong. No other part is more difficult to rectify later.

Brooks stated then what is still true today. The most difficult aspect in the successful delivery of software solutions is the *precise conceptualization and specification* of the system to be built. To create the conceptualization and specification requires not only an in-depth understanding of the problem to be solved but also an understanding of how the computer can be used to help solve the problem.

The problem with the conceptualization and specification of software applications is the invisibility factor [Brooks 1987]. Invisibility means that it is very difficult to visualize a new software function. The customer tries to describe what he wants done; the requirements are then gathered, and all is passed along to the eager developer. Unfortunately, during this process, something often gets lost in translation (Figure I-1). This imperfect communication may also be one reason why the process of specifying an application is so hard and takes such a long time. New applications may be useless because they are not what the customer asked

FIGURE I-1   Exact software function is difficult to visualize and communicate

for. The complexity involved in this understanding naturally increases with the size of the system, with the innovation involved in the problem and the solution, and with the number of interfaces that the system has.

Software Component Industry

Because of the competitive nature of the software industry, time to market is often the most critical element in the success or failure of a system. Components are a promising technology capable of increasing software development productivity. Components make it possible to assemble software systems from building blocks. System developers build a basic system using these building blocks and add their own elements for competitive advantage.

Certainly the technology for capturing the building blocks is available. One example of a component technology that is widely used is JavaBeans. The critical element necessary to create components is the distillation of requirements to the level of detail that allows them to be useful to a component creator [Finch 1998]. Distilling requirements to this level also creates a focus on solving the problem instead of on overengineering.

Measurable Value

The focus of an engineering effort using advanced use case modeling is on the development of a complex system. This complex system is called the **final deliverable** (Figure I-2). The value of the final deliverable should be quantifiable so that the return on investment for the project may be understood. Along the way to achieving this final goal, models are created to better understand the goal. These models are called **artifacts**.

The people to whom we are delivering a system of measurable value are called stakeholders. A **stakeholder** is someone who is directly affected by the delivery of the complex system. Some stakeholders may directly interact with the proposed system; they may be users, operations people, installers, and so on. These stakeholders belong to a group known in use case modeling as **actors**. An actor is an entity (some of which may be human) that interacts with the system. We examine actors of software systems in detail in Chapter 1.

Others may be affected indirectly by the delivery of the system. These stakeholders may be customers (who do not use the system), management, developers, and so on. Whether a stakeholder is direct or indirect, the satisfaction of this diverse group of people is important to the success or failure of a project. However, each of these groups may have a very different idea of what they want from the system and a very different point of view.

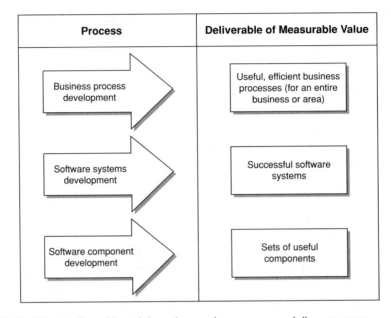

FIGURE I-2   Final deliverables of the advanced use case modeling process

Advanced Use Case Modeling

Advanced use case modeling is a systematic process for formulating problems for business engineering, software engineering (Figure I-3), or component engineering. This process is extremely powerful, yet it is easily understood by people whose focus is either business or software. The technique targets the *uses* of systems and so focuses attention directly on the problem to be solved. The methodology describes how to create models that specify interactions in a business, software system, or component system. Modeling interactions allows us to obtain tangible and measurable value in whatever area we are in. We reap the intangible benefits (such as innovation and the ability to deal with the unexpected) as well.

Use cases are the fundamental unit of modeling in the advanced use case modeling process. Use cases drive the activities performed within the process and also the activities that happen next. Most important of all, they provide a common language in which all parts of an organization (business, software system, and component engineering) can communicate.

Use cases provide an incremental and "modular" way to describe a system. A **use case** describes a way in which a complex system is employed by its users. Additions or changes to system functionality are easy to make to models. Since a

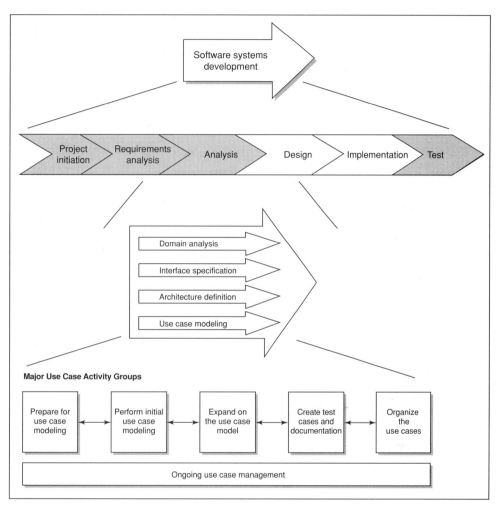

FIGURE I-3   The advanced use case modeling process framework

use case merely describes one way to use a system, the complete description of a system requires many use cases. The combination of the use cases and the actors in a given system forms its use case model. The **use case model** describes the composite behavior of a system.

Use cases provide representations of system requirements that can be easily understood by the different stakeholders. Each use case is described using narrative text. The use case model is described with a combination of narrative text and a small subset of easy-to-learn symbols called the Unified Modeling Language (UML).

Advanced use case modeling is a methodology applicable to a wide range of problems in business, software, and component engineering. The successful use of the methodology requires an environment in which the end result is understood to be of value.

Conclusion

Advanced use case modeling grew out of the many productivity initiatives that began in the late 1980s: business processes, object-oriented systems, and software component engineering. This methodology is a systematic technique for defining, conceptualizing, and specifying problems in these domains. Formulation and subsequent solution of problems in these areas often yields tangible benefits: a more efficient business process, a new software system, or a component library.

It is our belief that use case modeling provides intangible benefits as well. We offer use cases as a user-friendly and systematic way of achieving innovation and productivity gains. The goal of the methodology is to increase productivity through a single, unified communication vehicle that branches from business to systems to components. Certainly the groups responsible for these deliverables are very different. However, a common language facilitates the business change required to compete effectively in any arena.

Part 1
Fundamentals

What's in this part?

This part presents some of the fundamentals of use case modeling: actors and use cases.

Creating a use case model seems deceptively easy, yet many find it difficult. The traditional use case process involves three steps:

1. Find the actors.
2. Find the use cases.
3. Describe each use case.

A few other steps are implied or optional. For people who are new to use case modeling, they are spelled out as follows in an extended use case process:

1. Define the system boundary.
2. Find the actors.
3. Find the use cases.
4. Describe each use case.
5. Refactor the use case model (optional).
6. Prioritize use cases (optional).
7. Add future requirements (optional).
8. Organize the use case model (optional).

Advanced use case modeling uses the extended use case process. In small systems, such as those typically described in textbooks, a simplified version of the extended use case process is enough to create a use case model. In larger or more complex systems, a more elaborate process is needed (see Chapter 20). To illustrate the difference between the fundamental use case process and advanced use case modeling, let's examine the first step, defining the system boundary.

Part of use case modeling involves creating a use case diagram. A **use case diagram** is a pictorial representation of the model (Figure P1-1). It is a concise way of showing use case models without getting into the detail of the use cases themselves. The UML defines a use case diagram as a graph whose nodes are actors and use cases and whose links are the relationships among use cases, among actors, and between use cases and actors [UML 1999]. The use case diagram is examined in Chapter 3.

A use case diagram visually presents these relationships at a *very high technical level*. However, the elements of the use case diagram are not detailed enough to create a system. They only represent the text-based definitions of use cases and actors that model the real abstractions of the system. With the amount of material that can accumulate in the text-based definitions, getting the "big picture" can be quite a task. The use case diagram summarizes the documents and makes them easy to navigate and understand.

The first step of the extended use case process, "Define the System Boundary," is often assumed but not necessarily achieved. Use case modeling is often started without consensus on what is to be built. This is not necessarily bad for experienced use case modelers, but it can be disastrous for inexperienced ones.

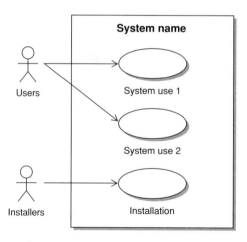

FIGURE P1-1   Use case diagram

There are many ways to "focus" on the scope of the system, and they are discussed in Chapters 1, 3, and 4. Here we briefly present the simplest way.

The system is often depicted in a use case diagram by a rectangle with the system name in the upper left corner. The rectangle is called the **system boundary**. Elements that are part of the system are placed within the rectangle. External entities that are not part of the system and that interact with the system are shown outside the rectangle.

A system name is needed to complete the first step. A name is usually self-evident when all stakeholders can easily define what they want from the system and where the system starts and ends. But before patting yourself on the back for having completed in a couple of minutes what takes several weeks in many projects, ask yourself a few questions.

First, do you know all the stakeholders in the system? If not, you may need to perform a stakeholder analysis (Chapter 6). Do all stakeholders agree on the name? Do you know all of the system's intended users (Chapter 1)? Is the system worth building (Chapter 3)? Do you know the responsibilities of the external systems with which your system may interact (Chapter 4)? Do all stakeholders know which functions are to be performed by the system and which ones are to be performed manually (by people)? For some projects, these are not simple questions—this is only the first step.

Part 1 looks at the fundamentals of use case modeling. In Chapters 1 and 2 we examine the various elements of the use case model.

- *Use Cases*. A use case is a sequence of actions required of the system. It defines a functional stripe through the system and is shown as a horizontal ellipse with the name of the use case appearing either inside or below the ellipse.

- *Actors*. Use cases provide observable or measurable value to one or more actors. Actors may be anything outside the system that exchanges information with it, including users and other systems. Each actor is represented by a stick figure labeled with the name of the role the actor plays.

- *Containers*. A container may contain use cases in the case of a system boundary. Packages, another form of container, can hold use cases and/or actors. Packages may also contain other containers.

- *Relationships*. Relationships link two elements—use cases, actors, or packages. Associations link use cases and actors to show how the two interact. Dependencies may exist between two packages indicating (in the use case view) a relationship between a use case or actor in one and a use case or actor in another. The "extend" and "include" relationships are relationships between two use cases. An actor may inherit behavior from another actor using the generalization relationship.

Chapter 1

Actors

The actors represent what interacts with the system.

—Ivar Jacobson [Jacobson 1992]

What's in this chapter?

This chapter discusses the conceptual role of actors in the use case model. A detailed account of how to recognize actors is given.

The modern approach to software engineering is to build models of the real world in a given problem domain. However, a software system is much more than a set of cooperating objects or code modules. The value of a software system lies in its behavior. This behavior often manifests itself in the interaction with entities (such as users and other software systems) outside the system. The system perceives the interaction between it and these external entities as events that it must acknowledge in some way.

When an event occurs that causes interactions between a software system and its environment, entities in the environment are involved in the interaction. Some of the entities initiate the event, others interact with the system as a result of the event. In use case modeling, these entities are known as actors. Actors help us to find use cases by helping us to understand what interactions will occur in a system. This chapter describes these external entities. Throughout this chapter, we use descriptive graphics to represent actors; we return to the use of standard UML notation for actors in the next chapter.

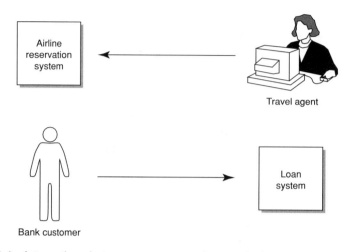

FIGURE 1-1   Interactions between systems and actors in the environment

What Is an Actor?

An actor is an entity that interacts with the system for the purpose of completing an event [Jacobson 1992]. Examples of actors include a bank customer submitting a loan application to a bank and a travel agent determining seat availability using the World Wide Web to access a reservation system (Figure 1-1).

Actors aren't necessarily human users of the system. They can be other systems, external organizations, external devices, and other external entities that interact with the system—anything external that interacts with the system (Figure 1-2).

When an actor is human, it is a role played by a user interacting with the system. An actor is not a single individual or a specific entity. For example, an actor is modeled by the concept of customer, not by Jane Smith the customer (Figure 1-3).

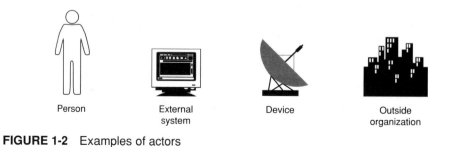

FIGURE 1-2   Examples of actors

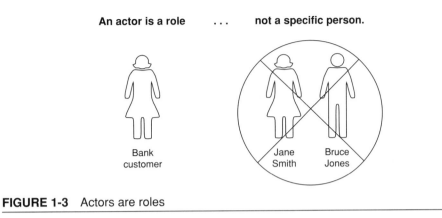

FIGURE 1-3 Actors are roles

Just as an actor can model many people or instances of the role, an individual person can play more than one role: bank manager Jane Smith can also be a customer of the bank. Specifically, an actor can be thought of as a tangible external entity that has some interaction with system and that plays a role. There are some exceptions to these guidelines. When there is a specific physical entity, such as an existing inventory system or temperature sensor that is known to have interactions with the system, that entity can be explicitly modeled as an actor.

Why Define Actors?

The roles actors play provide perspectives on why the use case is needed and on its outcome. For example, the reason a particular actor initiates a use case is almost always a major factor in why the use case is needed in the first place. The actor's role in the environment and the unique behaviors and system responsibilities will provide stong influences on the use case. Subtle differences in the role an actor plays can produce variations in the use case interactions. For example, determining that a loan processing system needs to respond to both business and individual customers identifies the need to model unique use cases on the specific needs of both business and individuals.

By focusing on the actors, you can concentrate on how the system will be used instead of how it will be built or implemented. Focusing on the actors helps to refine and further define the boundaries of the system. Actors also determine the completeness of the system requirements. That is, given a role, you can ask, "What other system interactions will this role require?" Finally, the actors can be a factor in deciding whether to have complete and independent subsystems and/or increments that deliver business value (Figure 1-4).

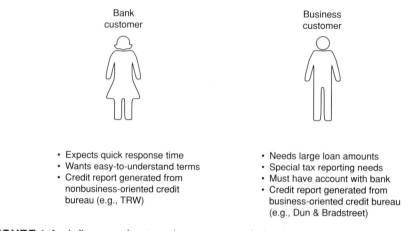

Bank
customer

Business
customer

- Expects quick response time
- Wants easy-to-understand terms
- Credit report generated from
  nonbusiness-oriented credit
  bureau (e.g., TRW)

- Needs large loan amounts
- Special tax reporting needs
- Must have account with bank
- Credit report generated from
  business-oriented credit bureau
  (e.g., Dun & Bradstreet)

FIGURE 1-4   Influence of actor roles on system behavior

Defining the actors helps to identify potential users that need to be involved in
the use case modeling effort. For example, when modeling the interactions
between a customer service representative and a telephone customer care system, it
is very important to understand the customer service representative's perspectives,
needs, and desires. Without knowing whom to talk to concerning the behavior specific to a use case, how can we understand system requirements? Identifying the
actors explicitly helps to direct us to the individuals we need to engage in the modeling effort. It also helps to direct us to the individuals who will need to validate the
behaviors defined in the use cases (such as users and customers). Even if the
requirements are "already specified," many questions will need to be answered as
the details of the system unfold.

How to Find the Actors

When performing use case modeling, review the following sources of information
for potential actors of the system.

- Existing context diagrams and other models that describe the boundary of
  the system with its environment. Look for external entities that have
  interactions with the system.

- The stakeholder analysis that determines which group of people will
  interact with (champion, develop, use) the system (discussed in more detail
  in Chapter 6).

- Written specifications and other project documentation, such as memos about meetings with users, help to identify users who may be potential actors.
- Minutes of requirements workshops and joint application development (JAD) sessions. Participants in these sessions may be important because the roles that they represent in the organization may interact with the system.
- Training guides and user manuals for current processes and systems. These guides and manuals are often directed at roles representing potential actors.

When looking for actors, ask the following questions:

- Who or what initiates events with the system?
- Who or what interacts with the system to help the system respond to an event?
- Are there any reporting interfaces?
- Are there any system administrative interfaces?
- Will the system need to interact with any existing legacy systems?
- Are any actors already defined for the system?
- Are there any other hardware or software devices that interact with the system that should be modeled during analysis?
- If an event occurs in the system, does an external entity need to be informed of this event? Does the system need to ask an external entity a question to help it perform a task?

Since an actor is any entity that interacts with the system, it is helpful to understand, within a specific use case, how the actor interacts with the system. Does the actor initiate the event, or does the actor's interaction involve helping the system respond to the event? Identifying how the actors interact helps to organize the actors and clarify the interactions and interfaces defined in the use case. Actors can participate in the use case in different ways. One actor can expect measurable value from the use case, while another is involved only to "help" the system provide the measurable value. Different requirements are associated with each kind of actor.

Primary and Secondary Actor Types

A use case is not limited to a single actor; any number of actors may be participating in the case. However, a use case exists to provide value to at least one actor. The actors that participate in a use case themselves have different roles and responsibilities to play: some will receive value, others will provide a service, others will help trigger or initiate the use case.

Ivar Jacobson [1992] has categorized actors into two types: primary and secondary. A **primary actor** is a user who will obtain value from the system. The needs of the primary actors drive the behaviors or functionality represented in the use case. If their needs or roles change, significant modification to the system will have to occur.

As an example, imagine that a loan processing system is in use by internal bank employees. A new Web-based loan application system is being considered for business reasons. While we may be able to adapt certain business rules from the original system, we cannot just slap a Web-based interface on the existing system. Bank employees will have different system privileges than external loan applicants. Access to other loan information is generally available to members of the loan department but not to the Web applicants. Usability requirements are also different. Loan department employees can take classes on how to use the system. The Web applicant must be able to navigate the system with no training at all.

We recommend that you start with primary actors when developing use cases. When identifying primary actors, consider the following questions.

- What business function does the actor perform for the business or organization?
- What is the measurable value of the roles and responsibilities achieved by the actor? The answer will drive much of the behavior and requirements defined in the use case. Any change to this value can significantly affect these behaviors.
- What behaviors must the system provide to satisfy this value?
- What business needs or requirements are associated with the value?
- Are there timing, performance requirements, or other interface requirements associated with the value?

Secondary actors provide service in the use case and would not exist if there were no primary actors. Secondary actors typically participate in the use case to support creating value for other actors. Examples of secondary actors in a loan processing system include operations personnel who install a system or provide backups of the loan information. When identifying secondary actors, ask the following questions.

- What value is this actor supporting in the use case? Will changes or refinements to the value as the system is developed affect this actor?
- Are there timing, performance, or other interface requirements associated with the service?

Actor Personalities

Actor personalities can be used to guide the process of discovering and identifying actors who can participate in a use case. An actor can have multiple personalities within a use case and across multiple use cases, depending on the specific interactions they are involved in. Actor personalities are summarized in Table 1-1.

An **initiator** is an external entity that initiates a behavior of the system for the purpose of completing an event. An initiator can request a service or otherwise trigger the event. A customer applying for a loan at a bank is an initiator of the event "apply for loan." An initiator may or may not be a primary actor. When identifying an actor with a initiator personality, ask the following questions:

- What event does this actor initiate? Does this event start the use case?
- Is the event based on time? In many cases, the initiator of a use case is the actor that receives some value from the system (primary actor). However, in the case of batch processing or other time-dependent situation, what triggers the use case?
- What are the requirements for the way the actor interfaces with the system? This question often discovers information, timing, and capacity requirements.

An external **server** personality is an external entity (person, organization, or external system) that responds to a request by the system. External servers assist the system in satisfying its responsibilities by providing a service. For example, in the "apply for loan" use case example, the loan processing system queries a credit bureau for information on the customer's credit worthiness. The credit bureau is an external server, since it responds to a request for a service. A server personality

TABLE 1-1 Summary of actor personality types

Personality Type	Behavior
Initiator	Initiates the use case
External server	Provides a service to the system in the use case
Receiver	Receives some information from the use case
Facilitator (proxy)	Supports another actor's interaction with the system

is almost always a secondary actor. When identifying an actor with a server personality, ask the following questions.

- What service does the actor provide? How is it related to the value the use case provides to another actor?
- What are the interface requirements associated with this actor— information, timing, capacity?
- If the server actor is another system, will behaviors of that system need to be modified or developed to support its role in this use case? (We have seen that requirements for other systems interfacing with the system to be built tend to be overlooked, resulting in unexpected and additional work on the project.)

External **receiver** personalities receive information from the system. An example of an external receiver would be a data warehouse that is outside the system and receives information from the system. When identifying an actor with a receiver personality, ask the following questions.

- What information does this actor receive? Why does this actor need the information? An enterprise data warehouse, for example, would need information for customer analysis.
- What specific data format requirements does this actor have? Receivers usually need information in specific data formats.
- What are the interface requirements associated with this actor— information, timing, capacity?

When a primary actor needs to access service performed by the system but does not always interact with the system directly, the interaction can be carried out for the primary by another actor that acts as **facilitator**. For example, a loan request can be submitted directly to the system by the customer either via the Web or via a paper loan application that is then entered by a data entry clerk. The data entry clerk actor can be viewed as having a facilitator personality; it helps the customer submit a loan. (See the Interesting Issue box on page 13 for a detailed discussion of this topic.)

When identifying an actor with a facilitator personality, ask the following questions.

- What services does the facilitator perform?
- What restrictions does the facilitator place on the primary actor's interactions with the system?
- Does a special interface have to be built to accommodate this actor?
- Is there is a possibility that the facilitator will be replaced or complemented in the future with automation such as a GUI interface?

INTERESTING ISSUE: WHICH ACTOR INITIATES THE USE CASE?

Sometimes a use case is triggered by the need of an entity that may not actually physically interact with the system. For example, when analyzing a "Make airline reservation" use case, who is the actor? Is it the customer who requests the reservation or the travel agent who directly interacts with the reservation system to create the reservation? Both are outside the system. A simple means of resolving this issue would be to rename the use case "Enter reservation request"; clearly, the travel agent would be the actor. However, the organizational reason for creating the original use case—that of a customer submitting a reservation request for processing—may be lost. Also, modeling both the customer and the travel agent might be important, since a simplified and restricted customer interface might be created in the future.

Business and System Actors

In use case modeling, these two different types of actors are referred to as business and system actors. A *business actor* is defined in business use case modeling and represents the business entity that interacts with the business environment. The *system actor* is defined in system use case modeling and normally has a direct interaction with the system. In the example, the customer would be the business actor and the travel agent would be the system actor.

If both business and system use case modeling are being performed (highly recommended), then in the business use case the customer would be the actor and in the system use case the travel agent would be the actor. Sometimes an actor is both a business and system actor. For example, the customer could interact directly with the system to make travel reservations via the Web.

If business use case modeling is not being performed (a common practice due to time constraints, limited resources, and so on), then how does a project identify the business actor? There is no easy answer to this question. A lot depends on the level of analysis. Selecting the actor that participates in the system use case depends on several criteria:

- Does the entity primarily just relay information? Or is significant value added?
- Does the definition of the actor provide critical context for the use case?
- Is it likely that the actor will be replaced by automated interface? For example, Web interfaces are often used for direct interaction.
- Is the event, from the actor's perspective, focused just on this system, or does it encompass multiple systems?
- At the current level of analysis, is the focus on the business requirements of the system or the specific physical interface requirements?

Continued on next page.

The level of analysis being performed will probably help define the actors. For example, high-level actors that help model business needs are probably more useful early in the analysis. As the system interfaces become more clearly defined, the physical interactions become more important, and therefore defining the actors engaged in them also becomes more important.

For example, early in system definition it may not be known whether the customer's interface to the system will be through a travel agent, the Web, or both. In this case, it may be too soon to have a travel agent as the actor, even if ultimately the travel agent does enter the information.

Possible Solution

Sometimes in a single use case modeling effort it is difficult to make a clear distinction between two entities. Nevertheless, it is important to document the involvement of both entities in the use case, regardless of who the actual actor is. A possible solution is to identify both the entities as actors during the system use case model effort, with one of the entities as the primary actor and the other acting as *facilitator*. For example, if a customer submits a reservation request, the travel agent who enters the information into the system may be a facilitator. If the facilitator is a Web interface, the primary actor remains the same.

Early in the process, we like to think of the business user as the actor, with the actual entry being recorded by a facilitator. However, our system boundary cannot be considered fully defined until we understand who the true users of the system will be. Software developers cannot enter the next phase of development until they know for whom the system is to be written. Ultimately, there may be no single, perfect answer to this question. When you decide to model the actors, the important aspect is that you retain both these perspectives, as they are meaningful for the use case.

Be very careful, however, not to indiscriminately mix business and system use case modeling. They serve two different purposes and, in many cases, two different audiences. Mixing business and system use cases can confuse the readers and make the system boundary convoluted. The best way to handle this problem, of course, is to do both business and system use case modeling and provide traceability between the two models.

Facilitators can be easily confused and misused. A facilitator should be restricted to a specific entity (person or software system), not to general tools or utilities such as a POP3 mail server or paging system. Selecting these general tools as facilitators will hide the actual actors who use the system.

One way to distinguish between initiators and servers/receivers is to determine the direction in which the interaction is occurring. If the actor is initiating the interaction, then the actor is probably an initiator, and this is the start of the

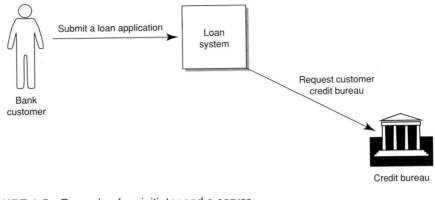

FIGURE 1-5   Example of an initiator and a server

use case (Figure 1-5). If the system initiates the interaction, then the interaction is probably taking place to support an event initiated by an another actor. If an actor both initiates and responds to subsequent requests of the system for more information within the same use case, consider that actor to be an initiator. However, if the direction in which the interaction will occur is not clear, do not spend too much time worrying about these relationships. The actor relationships aid in understanding the external entities. However, the system is the important element and should be the subject of concentration.

It should be noted that there is discussion within the use case modeling community about the level of detail needed to define an external server or receiver. The discussion centers on whether the information in a use case should be only that which is visible to the user. (The pros and cons of this issue are discussed later.)

When finding actors, it is important to identify and understand the different personalities an actor can have so that the requirements for interfacing with external entities can be defined, evaluated, and specified. It is not, however, a good idea to try to rigidly classify each actor into a predefined personality type; instead, use personalities to help you identify actors and their participation in the use case.

Abstract Actors

Some actors play a conceptual role, others a more concrete one. For example, the model of a bank might have in it the role of customer, which takes advantage of a variety of services. The model of a loan processing system, on the other hand, might include a more concrete role, such as applicant or borrower. In a sense, an applicant and a borrower share the properties of being a bank customer. However, the customer role may not be specific enough to capture all the elements necessary to describe a user of a loan processing system.

In this case, the customer is the "superrole" and the borrower or applicant are the "subroles." The relationship between these two types of roles is *generalization*. In modeling actors, generalization is used to represent the commonality and differences between two entities. The purpose of this representation is to develop a use case model with as little redundancy in actor communication with the system as possible [Jacobson 1992].

An abstract actor represents shared or common behavior between two or more actors. Abstract actors always perform a superrole. An abstract actor, however, may not be apparent during the process of finding actors. Instead, abstract actors are created to factor out the common behavior resulting from two concrete actors interacting in the same way with the same use case or use cases. An abstract actor differs from the actors (often called concrete actors), and this becomes apparent in system analysis. An abstract actor is made up, so the system has no actual entities that play that role. This concept is similar to the concept of the abstract superclass in object-oriented languages.

Early in the process of finding actors, it may be difficult to determine the abstract actors. However, as the analysis progresses and interactions between system and actors become more detailed, the interaction between the actors and the system will become clearer. Abstract actors typically evolve as the model is refactored and commonalities are discovered.

Actor Notation

We recommend using the UML notation for actors. As an extension to UML, following is a customizable template for actor specification. The template contains fields for the actor's name, the actor's description, and whether the actor is abstract. Obviously, an integrated CASE tool to capture the actors and to link them to the use cases is optimal. The set of actor definitions for a use case model is called the **actor glossary**.

Actor Specification	
Actor Name: <name> **Abstract:** <Yes, No>	
Description: <Description of Actor's Role>	

Conclusion

Actors are a core concept in use case modeling. There is no more important phrase than "Know thy user." Actors are means to identifying and documenting the users of the system so that the users' needs can be modeled and validated. The goal is to ensure that the system ultimately will meet their needs.

Finding and representing actors can be a challenge in a large system development effort. When identifying actors, remember that they can have different personalties when interacting with the system. Some will initiate use cases; others will provide service. Each use case will have an actor that receives observable value from the system. Additionally, look for those external entities (secondary actors) that support the system.

Chapter 2
Use Cases

Engineering is the application of science and mathematics by which the properties of matter and the sources of energy in nature are made useful to people.

—*Webster's New Collegiate Dictionary* [Webster 1999]

What's in this chapter?

This chapter discusses the basic format and protocol for finding and creating use cases. It also discusses and defines the basic UML notation for diagraming the use case model.

In the last chapter, we showed how external entities called actors play a role in the development of a system. The next element in the development of our model is the use case, the central modeling construct of the process. A **use case** describes the way a system is employed by its actors to achieve their goals. It is quite literally "the act." Formally, a use case is

> a description of a set of sequences of actions, including variants, that a system performs that yield an observable result of value to an actor. [Booch 1999]

A use case describes a single goal and all the possible things that can happen as the user attempts to reach the goal. Regardless of the type of complex system being described by the use cases—business, business process, software system, framework, or component library—the definition is the same.

Finding Use Cases

To understand how we find use cases, let's start with the loan processing use case diagram that was begun in the introduction to Part 1. In the first step we defined the system boundary (denoted by a rectangle) for a loan processing system. Now we add the actors (denoted by stick figures) outside the system boundary (Figure 2-1) and begin to fill in the system boundary with use cases to model the functionality of the system.

To find the use cases for a given system, we must examine the goals of the system [Cockburn 1997a]. The goals of a loan processing system might include the following.

- *Apply for loan.* The applicant submits the information necessary to apply for a loan. The information is checked for completeness by the system.

- *Check status of loan.* The applicant may query the system for any status changes in the loan as it proceeds through the acceptance process.

- *Submit additional loan information.* If the loan request requires additional information, such as an explanation of a problem in a credit record, the applicant must provide the information for the loan process to proceed.

- *Accept loan.* When the loan is approved, the applicant must agree to all conditions under which the loan is issued.

Enumerating goals helps us find use cases. Each general goal that yields observable value corresponds to a use case (Figure 2-2).

Use cases provide observable (sometimes called measurable) value to an actor. Therefore, use cases always describe an interaction between a system and at least one actor. This relationship between an actor and the use case is called an **association**. When an actor is associated with a use case, it is said that the actor **communicates** with the use case.

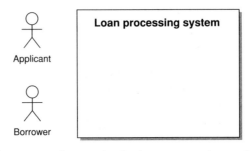

FIGURE 2-1   Partial use case diagram for the loan processing system

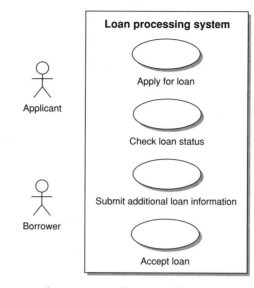

FIGURE 2-2   Loan processing use case diagram with use cases

Associations may be bidirectional or unidirectional. Unidirectional associations are represented by a line from the initiator of the communication with an arrowhead printing in the direction of initiation [Quatrani 2000]. An association may reflect behavior of the actor or of the use case. When an actor initiates the communication with a use case, it is called an initiator (Chapter 1). However, use cases can initiate communications with actors, as well.

A good example of a unidirectional association would be the association between the applicant and the "Apply for loan" use case (Figure 2-3). The applicant always initiates the communication, so the association between applicant and the "Apply for loan" use case is unidirectional with the arrow pointing to the use case. However, if the system required functionality to notify an applicant of the need for additional loan information (such as the reason for a credit record blemish), the "Request additional loan information" (not shown in Figure 2-2) use case might initiate the communication.

Understanding who initiates communications can be helpful when starting to write a use case. Most use case modeling tools, such as Rational Rose, support unidirectional associations. Still, many use case modelers choose not to use unidirectional associations because it is often evident from the use case who the initiator is.

A well-formed use case model must show associations (either unidirectional or bidirectional) between each use case and some actor. Although we will see exceptions when we refactor the use case model, use cases are usually triggered by some

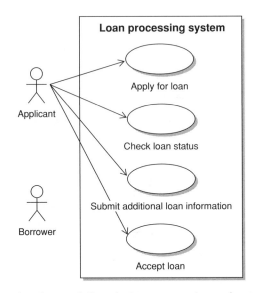

FIGURE 2-3   Unidirectional associations between an actor and use cases

event that is initiated by an actor. Therefore, if unidirectional associations are used, most use case models should have a unidirectional association originating from some actor to each use case. Use cases that do not communicate with at least one actor are suspect since every use case, by definition, provides value to an actor.

Associations between actors and use cases logically lead to a discussion of interfaces. **Interfaces** are a vital part of any complex system. An interface is the protocol and medium by which actors interact with a complex system. In business systems, call centers may provide billing information or technical support via the telephone. In software systems, there are interfaces to the user and to other systems. In component systems, interfaces may be CORBA IDL, the definition of interface class methods, or framework hotspots [Pree 1995].

Each association contributes to an overall interface between the system and its actors. An interface is the composite of the elements necessary to facilitate the interactions between an actor and the system. Interfaces should be documented in interface specifications (see Chapters 5 and 17).

Describing Use Cases

Once we have identified the goals of the system and placed them inside the system boundary, we must describe how we intend to reach each goal with our system. A use case is much more than an oval in a use case diagram. A use case is a narrative representation of the behavior of the system. A use case is composed of a name and a description (often called the body of the use case) of the many ways to achieve the goal.

We named our use cases in the last section when we enumerated the goals of our system. The name should describe the desired goal. For example, "Rent video" would be a logical candidate for the name of a use case where the video clerk rents a video to a customer. Naming use cases will be described in more detail in Chapter 7.

Once a use case is named, the description must be written in narrative text. However, simply writing a use case without an outline can make the use case difficult to understand and change, especially when it describes a system of substance. To permit any stakeholder to understand the use case quickly, the body of the use case must be carefully structured.

The use case structure divides the use case body into logical pieces (Figure 2-4). Structure ensures that use cases are consistent across the entire system by showing writers what details to consider when writing a use case. Structure also helps the readers find the element of the use case that they are looking for.

There are probably as many variations of use case structure as there are organizations doing use case modeling. The requirements for what should be included in a use case may be outlined in the development case (see Chapter 19) and captured in a use case template (see Chapter 8). A **use case template** defines the structure of the use case body for all use case developers on a given project. A use case template for all projects may be difficult to standardize, but most normally include at a minimum the following:

- *Actors.* Description of the actors involved in the use case.

- *Preconditions.* Constraints on the state of the system before the use case can be triggered.

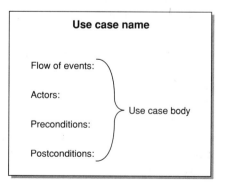

FIGURE 2-4   Use case format

- *Flow of events*. Activities that occur as the actors and system attempt to reach a goal. The activities can include the interactions between system and user. They may also include transactions the system performs in response to or to support these interactions, and any initial setup steps that an actor or system must perform prior to an interaction but that directly affect the interaction.
- *Postconditions*. Constraints on the state of the system after the use case has successfully completed.

Preconditions and postconditions describe the state of the system or, more appropriately, the state of the elements of the system, before and after a use case has run its course. A use case cannot be started until its preconditions are met. For example, the loan must be approved before the applicant may accept (sign for) the loan. Some use cases may not have constraints (and thus have no preconditions) on their ability to be started. The "Apply for loan" use case may not have any restrictions on its ability to be started.

A use case that has run its course may have postconditions, certain things that are always true if the use case was successful. For example, once an applicant accepts a loan, the applicant is now a borrower and must pay back the loan. A new loan has been created and money moves from the lending institution to the borrower. Other use cases may not change the state of the system and so have no postconditions. An example of this form of use case is "Check loan status."

The flow of events describes all of the many ways that a desired goal may be reached (or in some cases, fail to be reached). It can take many forms. In free-flowing text form, the goals are described in a narrative. Free-flowing text is one of the two most popular forms; the other popular method of describing use cases is the step method, an annotated form. In the step method, each step toward the goal is consecutively numbered.

The aim of the flow of events is to describe all the ways a system may behave as an actor attempts to reach a goal. On route to the goal, there will presumably be several decision points (Figure 2-5). A decision point is an area where the system, or in some cases the actor, must decide if it is proceeding along the expected path to the desired goal. The expected path of "Rent video" involves moving the video copy off the shelf (the inventory), validating the membership, and receiving money equal to or greater than the rental cost. At these decision points, the system responds as expected and the experience for the video clerk (and hopefully the customer) is routine.

But what happens when the video appears to be already checked out, the membership has late fees on it, or the credit card is denied? These exceptions or alternate paths must also be captured in the use case. In some cases, these contingencies can be resolved and the goal may be achieved. In other cases, an unsuccessful outcome may result.

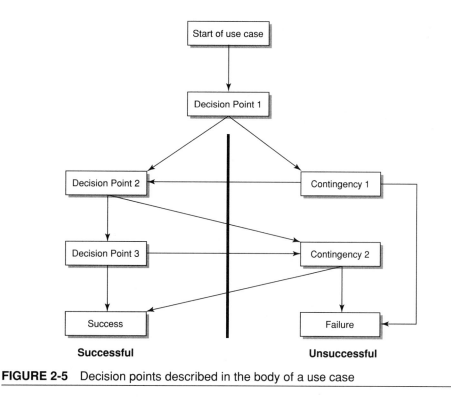

FIGURE 2-5 Decision points described in the body of a use case

Refactoring the Use Case Model

A system may be defined as the sum of its use cases. When attempting to capture a complete set of behavior, a use case model can become overly complex because it contains redundancy; that is, parts of two or more use cases may describe the same functionality. Extend and include relationships are a way of refactoring, or structuring, the use case model to deal with redundancy. These relationships help eliminate commonality across use cases.

An **extend** relationship (Figure 2-6) allows a use case to be "extended" with additional behavior and variations. An extend relationship is useful when one use case has all the behaviors of another. For example, a three-way telephone call requires that a basic telephone call be made first. The call originator must dial the first party and then dial the second party. Therefore, the "Originate three-way call" use case extends the "Originate basic call" use case.

A use case can have many extend relationships. The extending use case can also choose when to use the functionality of the use case that it extends. The extend relationship between use cases is represented by a directed line from the use case providing the extension to the extended use case.

Chooses when to use the functionality of the extended use case

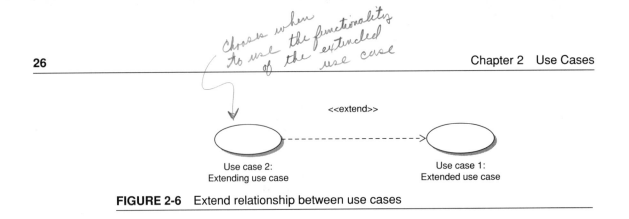

<<extend>>

Use case 2:
Extending use case

Use case 1:
Extended use case

FIGURE 2-6   Extend relationship between use cases

An **include** relationship (Figure 2-7) allows a use case to access a set of behaviors defined in another use case. It is a good mechanism for capturing and representing common behaviors used by multiple use cases. This functionality can be factored into **abstract use cases** included in use cases. An abstract use case is simply a reusable piece of functionality. Abstract use cases have the unique characteristic that they do not need to be directly associated with an actor.

One of the most common abstract use cases is "Authorize user" (also known as "Login"). Since many systems require a user ID and password (or some other form of authorization) to enter the system, this use case is found in many use case models. The include relationship between use cases is shown by a directed line from the use case that is using the abstract use case.

Include and extend relationships can be confusing to new use case developers. Many use case experts recommend avoiding discussion of these refactoring techniques until a use case development group is very comfortable writing use cases. Writing good use cases can be tricky enough for those new to use case modeling; refactoring cases can be downright frustrating. We discuss this confusion in more detail in Chapter 10.

As demonstrated in Chapter 1, actors may share the behaviors of an abstract actor. This relationship is known as **generalization** (Figure 2-8). Generalization is especially common when one actor may become another (such as an applicant becoming a borrower after a loan is made). In the use case diagram, inheriting behavior is depicted by the type of arrow shown in Figure 2-9.

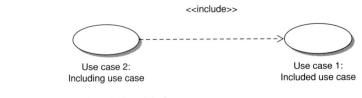

<<include>>

Use case 2:
Including use case

Use case 1:
Included use case

FIGURE 2-7   Include relationship between use cases

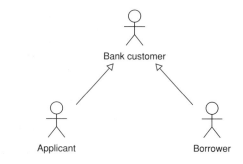

FIGURE 2-8 Applicant and borrower inherit from bank customer

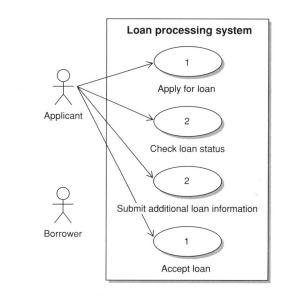

FIGURE 2-9 Development priorities for the loan processing system

Extending the UML Use Case Process

All of the fundamentals we have described thus far are part of the Unified Modeling Language specification. However, advanced use case modeling enhances the basic use case process and its symbol language to describe elements necessary when building complex systems (Table 2-1). We describe two forms of the use case beyond the canonical form found in the UML: prioritized use cases and change cases.

TABLE 2-1   Elements of the UML and advanced use case modeling

System Boundary	System name	Defines the limits of the system and contains the use cases for the system. Actors are placed outside the boundary.
Association	———————	Relationship between an actor and the use case with which it directly interacts. An actor may be associated with more than one use case and vice versa.
Unidirectional association	——————→	Association that shows the initiator of the communication (arrow).
Include relationship	<<include>> ‑ ‑ ‑ ‑ ‑→	Directed relationship between two use cases in which one use case uses the behavior of another.
Extend relationship	<<extend>> ——→	Directed relationship between two use cases in which one use case adds to the behavior of another.
Generalization relationship	——————▷	Directed inheritance relationship among actors.
Actor	(stick figure)	External entities representing users, systems, and other elements interacting with the system.
Package	Use cases	Container of use cases (and other UML elements beyond the scope of this book). Can be used to organize the use case model on any number of different properties.
Change case	Change case name	Potential future use case. Change cases carry a certain amount of risk and are not part of the current development or business model.
Prioritized use case	1 Use case name	Use case to which a priority is attached for the purposes of differentiating the more urgent or important use cases.

Prioritized Use Cases

Basic use cases are **prioritized** to define the order in which functionality is needed (Figure 2-9). Prioritized use cases allow the definition, development, and/ or deployment phases of the engineering process to proceed in an orderly fashion. For example, the deployment of the automation of a business system may be planned to be carried out in phases. Prioritized use cases allow recognition of the aspects of the system that must come first and those that can be delayed.

A prioritized use case is represented by the regular use case oval with a number inside (see Table 2-1). The lower-priority use cases, indicated by a larger number, may be delayed in its definition, development, or deployment.

Priorities and the properties that lead to prioritization are described in Chapters 4, 15, and 19.

Change Cases

Another form of use case outside the canonical form is used to describe potential changes. **Change cases** document potential future behavior of the system [Ecklund 1996]—behavior that is outside the scope of the current project, perhaps to keep the scope of the project manageable, but that may have to be incorporated into the system in the future without reengineering or designing the system.

A well-known axiom of system development is that the architecture of systems tends to be more resilient to change if the change is anticipated when the architecture is created. It is also well known that some change in systems can be anticipated. Change cases allow us to anticipate future requirements and build a better system architecture.

Change cases are represented by an oval with a triangle (delta) inside (Figure 2-10). The black triangle lets everyone know immediately that this functionality is outside

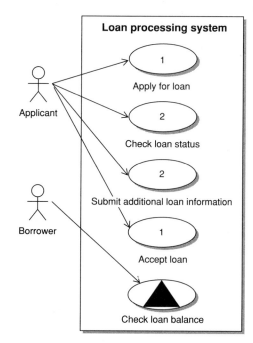

FIGURE 2-10 Potential future functionality for the loan processing system

the scope of the current system. Because change cases are a special form of prioritized use case, some developers use the symbol of a prioritized use case (see
Table 2-1) with a special priority signifying that the use case is beyond the scope
of the project. Regardless of how they are symbolized, they should be clearly dif-
ferentiated so that they do not become a distraction. This form of use case is
described in more detail in Chapter 17.

Organizing the Use Case Model

Large use case models may result in information overload. Even the use case diagrams may not allow stakeholders to quickly understand which use cases they
need to read. Hence use cases must be organized into logical groupings. These
groupings are called **packages**. A package looks like a folder in a use case diagram and contains use cases (Figure 2-11). A package name should reflect the
properties common to its contents. The many ways to organize the use cases in a
use case model are discussed in Chapter 15.

Another Approach to Building a Use Case Model

The steps we have just described represent a top-down approach to building a use
case model. The top-down approach assumes that you understand enough about

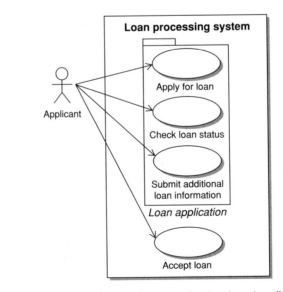

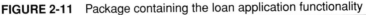
FIGURE 2-11   Package containing the loan application functionality

your system to provide general descriptions. A bottom-up approach can also be used to build use case models [Regnell 1996]. A use case model built from the bottom up starts with the specifics of the problem and generalizes them to create use cases (Figure 2-12).

To understand how the bottom-up approach works, we need to understand the difference between a scenario and a use case. The use case contains all the paths, both successful and unsuccessful, in our attempt to reach a goal. A **scenario** is one of these paths with specific information included in it [UML 1999]. For example, Tom attempts to place a voice call to Sally, who is already talking to someone else, so Tom receives treatment (a busy signal). This example path is a scenario in the use case "Originate basic call."

Scenarios can be used to structure use cases. A popular technique for creating the flow of events description is to start with the "sunny day" or "best way" scenario—that is, what happens when everything goes perfectly. General terms are used to describe this initial flow; specific details (such as "Tom" and "Sally") are not used. Creating this scenario can be an easy way to get started when writing use cases for the first time.

Of course, there are usually a large number of potential scenarios for a given goal. Some will yield successful outcomes, others will not. Other successful scenarios will deviate at some point from the "best way" scenario. The deviations can be recorded as substeps. If we collect a group of scenarios that address the same goal and record them in a general form, thus capturing a complete class of scenarios, we create use cases. This is the second step in the bottom-up process.

Finally, we can generalize the roles of the participants to create actors. Once we draw the associations between the actors and the use cases, we have completed the last step in the bottom-up approach to creating use case models. All the optional steps, such as prioritizing, adding future requirements, refactoring, and organizing the model, can then be added.

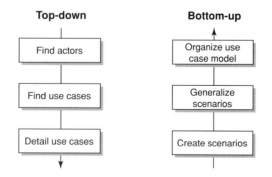

FIGURE 2-12   Top-down and bottom-up approaches to use case modeling

Running through scenarios allows us to determine the completeness of use cases. Simply reverse the process of recording scenarios and use them to test use cases. Since the use case must contain all the goals of our system, missing scenarios means incomplete use cases. The point is that we can use scenarios to create use cases or validate them. Using scenarios in this manner ensures that the use case covers all of the possible attempts to reach a goal.

Conclusion

The extended use case modeling process is useful for describing very simple systems. However, the complexities of most of today's software systems require more than the simple steps of the fundamental process. These systems require an advanced use case modeling process.

In advanced use case modeling, each step of the extended use case modeling process is enhanced to provide a process framework that may be customized to fit the project; detail and steps are added to allow scalability.

Part 2
Project Initiation

When developing use cases it is extremely important that the use case model's place in the overall system development effort be well understood. When embarking on the system development effort, it can be tempting to jump in and start use case modeling right away. Although use cases were created to be applied in the early stages of system development, and although they are a very flexible technique, they are not the only technique that can be used to understand and model the system.

One of the greatest areas of both leverage and risk when developing a software system is in the initial scope of effort. This is where the overall concept of how the system will operate and support the business environment evolves. The objectives for a system are defined, key risks are discovered, and the overall direction of the system development is set. Before modeling how individual actors will interact with the system, it is critical to understand what business problem the system is addressing and its overall size and boundaries.

Second, placing the use case model within the context of the overall development effort is important in understanding and analyzing the system's requirements and behaviors and the role of the use case. Developers need to understand the other techniques that will be used to "balance" the complete system picture and how the techniques can be drawn on to fill in the picture.

Because we feel it is so important for the use case modeler to be alert to these issues, this part presents two short chapters on scoping the system and balancing the use case model.

Chapter 3

Scoping the System: Vision Document and Business Case

Further, for those of you who are really serious, if you can't link the application to new customers, happier customers, and fatter bottom lines, you shouldn't even think about building it.

—Steve Andriole [Andriole 1998] (© 1998 IEEE)

What's in this chapter?

Before we start to develop a use case model, we must first identify the problem that we are intending to solve. What is the business opportunity created by the new or improved system? Is it financially feasible to build a software system to address this opportunity?

We are about to begin the task of building a software system by employing use case modeling. One of our first tasks will be to ask the users what they want in the system, and then ask our software developers to provide an estimate on it. Chances are that this task will be no small feat.

Before we embark on the task, we should ask some important questions. What is the system that we intend to build? Do all of our stakeholders, especially those who will fund and use the product, agree on this? If so, how much is it going to cost? Is it worth building?

Answering these questions is the purpose of two artifacts: the vision document and the business case. These two artifacts are complementary. The **vision document** qualifies the problem to be solved and the **business case** justifies the amount of effort involved in its solution. Therefore, the vision document must be developed first so that an assessment of the work involved may be completed in the business case.

Describing the Problem: Vision Document

In the early stages of software development, an idea for a software system is conceptualized. This conceptualization may come from the development of a business process that identifies an opportunity to computer-assist the workers involved in the process or perhaps an opportunity to completely automate several steps. It may have just been somebody's good idea.

Regardless of the origin of the need to develop a software system, the idea must be captured and elaborated on. This is the purpose of a vision document. This document has been called many other names: a problem statement [IBM 1997], statement of work [Donaldson 1997], system concept, and concept of operation (see the Interesting Issue box on page 37). We call it the vision document to be consistent with the terminology of the Unified Process [Leffingwell 2000]. The document contains an initial "cut" at the problem the software system is intended to solve.

Often the understanding between those who dwell in the problem domain and those who live in the solution domain is imperfect. This is precisely because the groups approach the problem from two different viewpoints. The vision document begins the process of understanding and communicating the needs of the problem formulator to the solution provider. The ensuing activities will investigate and communicate the costs back to the problem formulator. A business case will measure the costs against the benefits of solving the problem. The project will continue if the benefits outweigh the costs.

Tackling the Dark Side

Is creating a vision document as easy as answering the question "What is the problem?" Certainly the world is full of problems just waiting for us to solve. Most IT and software development organizations are not lacking in this area. However, the knowledge that we must next create a business case to show the value of the project to the organization prevents us from selecting just any random problem. We know that finding the project that will truly solve a business problem or make a software product competitive is not easy. So how do we cut through all the noise to find the one project that everyone can agree on and that makes existing customers happier or brings in new customers?

Sorting the "good" projects out from the "bad" projects is usually done politically, not technically [Andriole 1998]. Different groups have their agendas and therefore ideas on what a "good" project should be. Executives generally want the most value for the dollar. Project managers want a project whose expectations align with reality. Software developers want to use the latest software technologies and techniques. And the users? Has anyone asked them what they want? With

INTERESTING ISSUE: WHAT IS A CONCEPT OF OPERATIONS AND HOW DO USE CASES FIT INTO IT?

Conceptual analysis is an approach for analyzing the problem that will be solved by the system. This approach focuses on defining the high-level behaviors of the system and its place within the operational (business) environment. A conceptual analysis provides an overall picture of the purposes of the system and should be performed before a detailed requirements effort is embarked on. The goal of the analysis is to understand how the system will meet its objectives within the organizational or business context. If a detailed requirements analysis is performed without first considering and validating the conceptually larger picture, there is a risk that while individual functions of the system may meet individual user needs, the system will fail to meet the overall organizational needs.

A conceptual analysis should consider and include the following elements [Fairley 1996] [IEEE 1998c]:

- Description of the current system or manual processes
- Description of the organizational needs that are motivating the system development
- User types and characteristics
- High-level features of the new system(s)
- Development priority of the features
- Scenarios describing the operations of the system for each user type
- Limitations of the proposed system
- Analysis of the relationship of the proposed system with its environment

The resulting conceptual operations (conops) document presents these elements in a fashion that is understandable and comprehensible to key decision makers and stakeholders. Most of the conops efforts we have been involved with have been short (between 50 and 100 pages) and developed quickly (one or two months). After the conops document has been validated and revised, a detailed requirements analysis is then embarked on. Conops documents go by a number of other names, including vision document and system concept document.

Use case techniques can be used to model a number of conops elements. The scenarios describing the operations of the system can be modeled with the initial use cases described in Chapter 7 (or if more detail is needed, the base use cases described in Chapter 8). The user types and characteristics can be modeled with actors. Development priorities of the system can be stated by prioritizing the use cases. The analysis of the impact of the proposed system on its environment can be represented by a before-and-after set of use cases. One set shows how things happen now, the other shows how things will be performed with the new system in place.

all these sometimes contradictory viewpoints and the difficulty involved in conceptualization (described in the Introduction), is it any wonder that this task is so arduous?

Several questions should be answered in the vision document. Some of these questions provide a political litmus test [Andriole 1998] by which the initial value of projects can be judged. Others are information required as a basis for future engineering activities.

1. What is the problem we are attempting to solve?

   The answer provides a product overview. Additional information might include the version number and some of the features that distinguish this new product or version.

2. Who are the customers of this solution? Who are the other major stakeholders?

   Identifying potential users is a very important part of understanding the value of a project.

3. "What is the project's purpose? If completed, what impact will the new or enhanced system have on organizational performance? On profitability? On product development? On customer retention and customer service?" [Andriole 1998]

   The logical next question asks what value the system brings to its users, to the organization, and to its creators. The intangible benefits, such as the developers becoming proficient in a new technology, should be listed along with the tangible ones.
      This value of the benefits does not have to be quantified. That is done in the business case. However, the answers to the questions will be used for the quantification.

4. Where would this solution be positioned relative to our business and our other products? What are alternatives or competing products? [Leffingwell 2000]

   Understanding how a solution affects the business is critical to building a business case. Since the vision document is an input to the business case, a good description of the business impact in the vision document can often be the difference between a "go" and a "no go." This is the part of the vision document where a detailed business use case model and activity diagrams from the business use cases play a key role. These documents provide context for the role of the project in a "total" solution.

5. What are the differentiating functional and nonfunctional requirements? What are their priorities? What are the risks? What other systems will this system interact with?

The answer to these questions starts to define the system boundary and should provide the minimum information necessary to cover the needs of all of the stakeholders. More detailed information will be discerned in the various use case models developed later in the project. Thus, the system boundary is refined as future activities such as use case modeling and system interface specifications (see Chapter 4) are performed.

6. What future directions might the product have to take to keep up with trends in the domain? What new technologies might need to be integrated with the project in the future?

Keeping an eye to the future is always prudent when formulating a project. Understanding where change can turn into risk means thoroughly understanding why the system is necessary. The project will take some time to materialize. We must understand that the business or domain will probably change in the time it takes to produce the system.

The many techniques with which to gather the information necessary to answer the questions are beyond the scope of this book. The reader is referred to Gause [1989].

The first thing to do when creating a vision document is to name the project. This may be more difficult than it sounds. The final act involved in creating the vision document is to ensure that it is agreed on (and sometimes signed) by the major stakeholders. This gathers the commitment necessary to see the project through as it passes through the sometimes smooth, sometimes troubled waters ahead.

Just as the vision document has many names, it also has many forms. Most organizations have a form in which they expect information to appear. They may also have requirements for the information they expect. Some of the preceding questions may be part of this required information, others may not. If any of the preceding questions are missing from the version of the document you are dealing with, you might want to ask these questions of yourself before you commit tne resources, agree to project manage, sign off as a user of, or develop a new project. If the organization does not have a vision document template, we recommend the one found in Leffingwell [2000].

Determining Project Feasibility: Business Case

The purpose of a business case is to justify the undertaking of a project. The need to develop a business case varies from organization to organization. Most organizations like to know that they are getting their best return on any investment—and software development is an investment. Therefore, it makes sense to see either a tangible or an intangible return on this investment. The job of the business case is to specify the expected return as accurately as possible.

There are many forms of a business case. Most people think of it as a lengthy financial document whose required creation is a bureaucratic block to creativity. In organizations where this a true statement, it is safe to say that most software projects are started and finished without such a document. However, these organizations may be operating under a business case without knowing it.

Suppose you understood the benefits of (or the amount of revenue you would receive from) a software system. You might fix your costs by setting a deadline, using a fixed team of software developers (and managers), and buying the expected equipment necessary to build the system. Sound familiar? You are operating under an informal business case.

Even with the availability of a form, many software development organizations undertake projects without much thought about the full business implications of the projects. This attitude can be attributed to the competitive and entrepreneurial spirit of today's software market. But whether an organization requires a formal business case or not, the concepts are important, even if they are never written down.

Writing the Business Case

Writing a business case is like writing a use case: it is always difficult at first but becomes easier with experience. The best place to start is with the vision document, in which the expected benefits of the project should be captured. Potential benefits include increased or new sources of revenue, increased productivity, increased reliability, goodwill, accomplishment of an organizational mission, increase in development capability through experience gained, and assets such as reusable components [IBM 1997]. Quantifying these benefits, especially the intangible ones, may not be easy.

The project costs are also difficult to quantify, especially at the outset of the project. We may be able to achieve ballpark figures based on a single person's experience. Less subjective estimates may come out of a group technique, such as the Wideband Delphi Technique [Boehm 1981], where several people meet and discuss estimates until they agree. When using a technique like this, keep in mind that software developers notoriously underestimate a project's needs. A common way to improve the accuracy of a software developer's estimate is to multiply the amount of time (and/or money) predicted by two.

At this point, we do not have all the facts, so the business case will probably characterize the benefits more accurately than the costs. Even without reliable cost estimates, completion of this level of information in the business case is a key decision point. We can see if the costs and the benefits (as depicted in Table 3-1) are in the same ballpark. This comparison allows us to understand whether the benefits warrant further elaboration of the business case and the software project.

There are many ways to document the value of a software system. A complete list requires quite a bit of accounting knowledge and is beyond the scope of this book. A simplistic way, which does not reflect the time value of money (e.g., interest rates and other potential investments) is the cash flow method. Using the cash flow method, the costs are subtracted from the benefits to show how cash is accumulated and spent across the life of the project.

A summary of the cash flow (see Figure 3-1) can help to quickly print out whether a project is worth undertaking. The actual business case should break down the costs and benefits in more detail. For example, the benefits might be three payments from a customer of $1.8 million each. The payments might be contingent on the product passing certain acceptance criteria of functionality and performance. These criteria may be documented somewhere else (such as in a contract), but they must also be listed in the business case.

A detailed analysis of the costs of the software project must also be included. Costs for personnel, capital (hardware, software, and infrastructure), and other things such as travel should be itemized so that they may be understood by the decision makers. References to the requirements described in the vision document help to amplify the expected cost of each new feature and permit decision makers to understand where choices may be made to reduce the price tag of the project at the expense of removing a feature.

Finally, documenting financial risks is critical. Is the "sunny day" scenario projected the most likely outcome? If something goes wrong, what will the impact be? Is a technology new or unproven? What is the experience level of your team? Are the benefits based on a projection or a fixed price contract? What are the contractual or market effects of delivering late? Risk analysis can set expectations for

TABLE 3-1   Cash flow analysis of a proposed software system (thousands of dollars)

	1Q00	2Q00	3Q00	4Q00	1Q01	2Q01	3Q01	4Q01	1Q02
Benefits	0	0	0	0	0	0	1800	1800	1800
Costs	120	240	600	600	600	600	240	120	120
Flow	−120	−360	−960	−1560	−2160	−2760	−120	480	2160

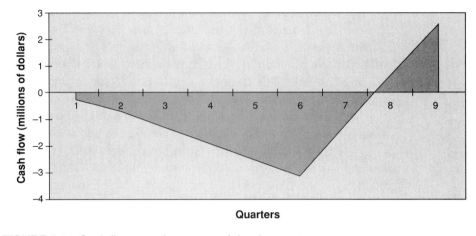

FIGURE 3-1   Cash flow over the course of development

things that go wrong. And following Murphy's Law, if something can go wrong, it usually does.

One risk not usually anticipated by a business case is the effect of the departure of a critical staff member. Smaller companies may be unable to afford a staffing model that provides the redundancy necessary for complete backup. When these companies lose a key person, the effect can be additional, unanticipated cost. The business case is an appropriate place to document risks such as minimal redundancy in the staffing model.

Each risk should be quantified with a percentage chance of occurrence and a cost of dealing with the problem. The best way to compute these values is through history. For example, if the organization averages 5% turnover per year, this information may be used to quantify the expected likelihood of losing a staff member. In addition, the cost of losing such a staff member may be quantified by the cost of finding a replacement and getting the new person "up to speed." Staffing models that favor redundancy decrease the costs of turnover and overall personnel costs for the project. Of course, the best case is always when a project does not encounter any problems.

Revising the Business Case

Since the vision document contains only a cursory explanation of the project, revision of the business case will be necessary as more information about the scope of the system is determined through use case analysis and architectural design and prototyping. We therefore recommend at least one revision of the cost analysis after the completion of the project plan. The project plan provides more detailed information on the length of time necessary to complete the project and the amount of staff, materials, and equipment involved. As a result, a detailed cost model may be added to the business case. This detailed cost model can be reevaluated if necessary to ensure that the expected value of the project will still be achieved. Should the evaluation reveal that the costs are starting to outweigh the benefits, the project can be evaluated to see whether reduced functionality can allow the project to remain feasible.

Risks may also be updated in the revised business case as a result of the project plan. Architectural prototypes may have been created, which should eliminate many of the risks documented in the earlier business case. The result is a cost model in which the engineering risks are all but eliminated and the software production risks, usually smaller, are left.

The business case remains a living document throughout software development. Other checkpoints should follow any deviation from the project plan or when a significant problem is encountered. The business case should also be updated to reflect new risks as soon as they are identified.

Building a business case requires accounting knowledge far beyond the scope of this book. For more information about building this complex document, see Schmidt [2000].

Conclusion

The vision document and the business case are tools for determining the scope of a software project. The vision document creates a system boundary for the project by setting expectations for what the system will and will not do. The stakeholders of the system are identified and are expected to reach consensus with respect to the expectations stated in the document.

The business case sets expectations for the benefits and risks associated with the project. The business case attaches financial value to the project defined in the vision document.

Each document marks a key decision point in the project's ability to move from the inception phase to the elaboration phase. Formulating these documents and successfully passing through the decision points represents the transition from a viable concept to a software system project.

Chapter 4

Balancing the Software System Use Case Model

> Use cases alone are not enough to carry you into design. The temptation is to base development on use cases, especially to developers who come from a transaction-oriented background. The results are usually enormous control objects, no reuse of functionality, and duplication of objects.
>
> —Anthony Heritage and Phil Coley [Heritage 1995]

What's in this chapter?

Use cases can describe the functionality of the system, but form is necessary to balance functionality. Form is provided with a well-designed system architecture. In this chapter, we discuss the ways that architecture can enhance the use case model.

Use case modeling, when used in isolation and performed incorrectly, may lead to certain types of problems. First, use cases can be utilized to specify many different kinds of software systems; they are a conceptualization of the way a particular system will be used. The specified system can then be implemented using a variety of programming languages such as object-oriented (Java, C++, Smalltalk, or Eiffel), structured (C, Pascal, or COBOL), or functional (Lisp or Prolog). Use cases are most often used to describe systems created using object-oriented technology; after all, use cases were invented in the context of an object-oriented methodology.

The ability to represent many different software technologies presents a problem. While the world is full of objects and they represent a nice way to categorize software elements, traditional work is done in a more functional manner. As use cases map work onto a model of cooperating objects, they represent functional stripes across the objects. Representing systems as functional stripes maps well to the structured and functional programming paradigm but could drive an object model in the functional direction. A potential risk of utilizing the use case model to drive object-oriented development is the possibility of ending up with a functional model instead of an object model [Firesmith 1995]. This risk is greater for developers with less experience with object-oriented development. However, experienced software developers have fallen prey to the problem as well.

A second problem arises in modeling large systems with use cases. Developing large use case models can be a lesson in understanding how many different views of a system there can be. As the number of use case developers increases, so does the number of natural deviations from a common vocabulary and common understanding. Each developer approaches the description of a system with individual bias. Use cases authored by different developers may describe the same thing differently. Synonyms and homonyms requiring interpretation by the original author creep in. The result is a disjoint use case model and frustration in realizing the system in subsequent steps.

Finally, defining the task of the system is a common problem in the conceptualization and specification of systems [Jacobson 1992]. There can be many different ways users can sort through the system (see the Interesting Issue box on page 47). Another common difficulty is understanding where to stop. An inconsistent or undefined system boundary is the number one problem in use case modeling [Lilly 1999].

Jacobson realized the possible problems when he introduced use case analysis [Jacobson 1992]. He advocated three concurrent initiatives to balance the use case model (Figure 4-1). The first is the use of **domain analysis**, a technique for developing an initial object model.

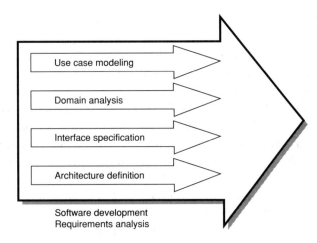

FIGURE 4-1   Three concurrent initiatives to balance the use case model

Interesting Issue: What to Do When Lost in Functionality

Most software development projects can define a set of processes that the user follows when using the system. Defining these processes is straightforward. Watch a user do work manually, capture these processes, and then automate or reengineer them. In these cases, following your use case development process should be relatively easy. But what should you do when you get lost?

A developer of a word processor wanted to develop a use case model for his project but was worried because of the amount of functionality and possible relationship combinations. He was building a system for which he felt large functional stripes were impossible and small functional stripes would make the description too complicated. Systems where the user can combine many different elements are extremely complicated. A well-known problem in this area is telecommunication feature interaction. It is easy to get lost in an attempt to describe each feature and its interaction with others.

The answer to finding the "right" level of detail lies in the object model. In a word processor, users manipulate objects such as documents, paragraphs, tables, pictures, and so on. However, the user does not tend to interact with all these objects at the same time. Using domain analysis to create a partial object model can often allow use case developers to understand the right level of detail. This information can then become the vocabulary of the use cases.

Beware! Developing use cases around low-level objects such as words and characters can lead to use case explosion. It is important that each object in the domain analysis be evaluated in the context of the user. Will a user see more measurable value from "Create a word" or "Create a paragraph?" Is one perhaps just part of the other?

Domain analysis is not meant to drive use case modeling; it is meant to balance it. If you get lost in domain analysis, move back to use case modeling. Look at the processes from an actor perspective as they interact with the objects.

The second technique is **interface specification**. Interface specification documents the interactions with external entities, the actors. Finally, **architecture definition** allows us to logically decompose systems into subsystems and components. Nonfunctional requirements can also be addressed in this definition. This chapter examines each of these activities and their ability to reduce some of the possible risks in use case modeling.

Analyzing the Domain

Creating a common vocabulary to be used across the use case model is a very important task. A common vocabulary keeps use case developers focused on the right level of use case to be written. The vocabulary should reflect tangible objects in the domain germane to the system being developed. For example, in the loan application system, possible objects are "loan application," "applicant," "loan agreement," and "credit history." As there may be many semantic pitfalls in creating this vocabulary (such as differentiating between a loan application and a loan request), domain understanding is critical to the success of this activity.

The result of this activity (called **domain analysis**) is a **system glossary** or **domain object model**. What's in the system glossary can range from a simple name–definition format (Figure 4-2) to a full-fledged analysis object model complete with associations between the objects. Creating the glossary is an iterative process. As new use cases are found, new entries may be made in the glossary. Similarly, the glossary should serve as a reference for writers of use cases. When changes are made in use cases, the glossary should be updated for accuracy and completeness.

A good way to start a system glossary is to extract the applicable objects from the business glossary,[1] if one exists. This is one way that advanced use case modeling for business process development feeds the software system development process. Using the terms from the business glossary ensures consistency between the business and the systems that aid it. Other inputs to the system glossary might include the vision document, interviews, other required documents, domain experts, and discussions.

The system glossary can also contain information about objects beyond the information in a use case. It might contain formulas, calculations, or business rules that would not be found in a use case but might constrain the way the use case is written. For example, certain personal information (name, social security

Domain object	Description
Loan application	Request to borrow money for a given period of time. The application must contain a name, address, social security number, principle, and term.
Applicant	Potential customer who applies for a loan.
Loan agreement	Contract between the lender and the borrower on the terms of the loan.
Credit history	Information regarding a customer's financial responsibilities. Credit history is used to determine the worthiness of an applicant.

FIGURE 4-2   Simple system glossary for a loan application system

---

[1] A business glossary is to the modeling of business processes what a system glossary is to modeling software systems.

number, and address) is mandatory on all loan applications. This requirement could be spelled out in each use case or found in the glossary.

When domain analysis is performed in conjunction with use case modeling, it reduces the risk of a functional design. (See the Interesting Issue box on page 47.) Domain analysis pinpoints the language to be used to create textual descriptions in the use cases. It enforces, in some sense, an object-oriented approach by calling out the objects as the use cases are written. We will discuss the glossary and its role in use case development further in Chapter 8.

Domain analysis is one of many techniques designed to aid in the definition of the system boundary. Since objects in the system glossary have tangible value in the system domain, it is easy to see whether they are germane to the problems the system attempts to solve. Reviewing the system glossary can yield objects that fall outside the scope of the system. Objects outside the system boundary may appear in the system glossary, but it should be noted that they are outside the system boundary. These objects may be part of the services that other systems provide or part of a larger business process. When writing a use case, be careful with these objects, as they may cause you to increase the scope or build a solution that encompasses an area greater than necessary.

For traceability reasons, a third column may be added to the simple system glossary with the names of use cases that act on the object (Figure 4-3). Use case names can be added to this column as the use cases are identified (if it is obvious) or when the base or initial use case descriptions are written (see Chapters 7 and 8). Traceability can be helpful in the later stages of architectural development and design when objects are partitioned into logical groupings called **subsystems**. The

Domain object	Description	Use case
Loan application	Request to borrow money for a given period of time. The application must contain a name, address, social security number, principle, and term.	Apply for loan, Check loan status
Applicant	Potential customer who applies for a loan.	Apply for loan, Check loan status, Submit additional loan information
Loan agreement	Contract between the lender and the borrower on the terms of the loan.	Accept loan
Credit history	Information regarding a customer's financial responsibilities. Credit history is used to determine the worthiness of an applicant.	Apply for loan

FIGURE 4-3   Simple system glossary with use case traceability

impact of a use case on the subsystem can be easily understood simply by examining the impact on the objects within it.

Domain analysis is a form of object modeling, a complete description of which is outside the scope of this book. This brief discussion of domain analysis is included because it is important to the proper development of object-oriented software systems. More information about domain analysis can be found in [Jacobson 1992].

Documenting the Interfaces

Another element that helps demarcate the system boundary is interface specifications. Interface specifications delineate the responsibilities of the system to the external entities interacting with the system, its actors. For every actor, there is by definition an interface.

Interface specifications come in two flavors: user interface and system interface specifications. User interface specifications document interactions with human users. System interface specifications document interactions with other systems. These specifications may be created prior to actual use case modeling in some cases, but they are usually created in conjunction with writing the actual use cases.

User Interface Specification

The most common of the interface specifications is the user interface specification. While the use case model specifies who the users are and what they need the system to do [Jacobson 1999], a user interface specification describes the system experience ("look," "feel," "sound,") of its users. Therefore, these specifications are necessary when one or more of the actors of the use case model are people.

User interfaces should be separated from the business logic of the system. This allows a user interface to maximize its versatility in the presentation of the business logic to the user. The specification of the user interface is no different. User interface logic should, in most cases, be left out of the use case and captured in the specification.

User interface specifications should be developed from the use cases. Therefore, a user interface specification should usually be crafted after the use case is written to ensure that the "use" of the system is correctly portrayed to the user. In this way, we specify the needs of the intended system before trying to realize the needs for a potential user [Ahlqvist 1996], following well-accepted software system design principles.

While the user interface specification is written after any given use case, the specification can, in turn, help clarify the system boundary of the use case model and verify the use case. One common problem in a use case is the loss of under-standing of what information the user can and cannot provide. This is a system boundary problem. Since user interface specifications live in the concrete world, it is easy to detect these mistakes.

Modern technology has created tools for quickly developing user interfaces. As a result, a user interface prototype can be created as simply as any presenta-tion. In fact, the Unified Process no longer calls for user interface specifications [Jacobson 1999], opting for user interface prototypes instead. However, you may find prototypes difficult to distribute to the users of your system for validation. If this information needs to be distributed, prototype the user interface and create the specification using screen capturing tools. The user interface specification will be examined in greater detail in Chapter 16.

System Interface Specification

Software systems often need to communicate with other external software sys-tems. External systems often provide services to or request services from the system defined by the use case model. To facilitate the requests, interfaces need to be developed or may already exist. Interfaces must be very precise (as sys-tems are less adaptable than people) so that correct information is communi-cated between the two. The system interface specification documents machine interfaces.

Two types of external systems are found when developing the use case model of a software system. One is the "legacy" system, the system that is already up and running, capable of providing services to our new system. Legacy systems affect a use case model by defining part of the system boundary. System speci-fications for these systems should be written prior to the development of use cases associated with them to ensure a complete understanding of the services provided by the systems so that use cases are well defined.

The second type of external system is one that will be built concurrently or following the development of the new system. Negotiation must be performed to ensure a complete understanding of the system boundaries. These interfaces are often subject to change during development. Protocols, the way in which machines communicate, enhanced or reduced as a clearer picture of the informa-tion needed, are formed during software development. The specification of these protocols may be ongoing during use case modeling and into later stages of soft-ware development.

Systems communicate in many different ways. A popular method is byte streams through communication protocols such as TCP/IP and CORBA (Figure 4-4). Documenting services requested or provided may be as simple as documenting the byte streams (position of bytes in the communication stream) or

```
//IDL for Loan class
interface Loan {
        float balance();
        float principle();
        float interestRate();
        long termInMonths();

        void makePayment(in float payment);
};
```

FIGURE 4-4   CORBA IDL definition of an applicant

CORBA IDL.[2] On the other hand, the document can also be extremely complex, and include state information, handshaking, "keep-alives," and more. Some amazingly complex system interface documentation can be found in the telecommunications industry, where it is common to find the equipment of multiple vendors communicate routinely.

Defining a Software Architecture

Defining software architecture is very important in the early stages of software development as the architecture specifies what is and what is not possible with the system. To understand this impact, ask yourself how many times you have heard it said, "To add that new feature, we are going to have to redesign the whole system."

What is system architecture? There is no single industry standard definition of this concept, but many definitions are similar to the following:

> The software architecture of a program or computing system is the structure or structures of the system, which comprise software components, the externally visible properties of those components, and the relationships among them. [Bass 1998]

Software architecture has roots in building architecture (hence the name) [Coplien 1999]; there are many similarities. Both are crafts, although the craftsmen are becoming increasingly more formal. Both are influenced by their environments and driven by their requirements. They are not so much about technology, although technological capability plays a big role in what can and cannot be done, as they are about the architects and the builders who take advantage of technology.

---

[2] There is more to this documentation, such as port numbers, error conditions, and so on.

To develop a software architecture requires identification and prioritization of the important use cases. "Important" use cases are those in which the users derive the most benefit. In a video store use case model, "Rent video" is an important use case. "Withdraw cash" is an important use case in an ATM example. Important use cases may be significant for other reasons, such as real-time constraints, reliability, and other system qualities.

To build software architecture, you need the smallest set of use cases necessary to cover the important architectural aspects of the software system. To choose the cases, ask yourself whether each use case is going to have a significant impact on the way you structure your software. If so, is the impact already addressed by a use case in the set? Is another use case in the model more representative of the impact?

Another area to consider is the future requirements of the system. What future changes are likely to have an architectural impact on the system? Will portability—that is, the ability to change from one platform or operating system to another—be necessary in a future release? We should already understand many of these requirements as a result of building our vision document. If these requirements are functional in nature, we can create **change cases** (discussed in Chapter 18) or use cases to reflect these changes for consideration in our architecture. Don't discount the future. Planning for change may be as important to creating a robust architecture as any of our current requirements.

Once you have created the set of important use cases, you can plan and describe the system architecture. Important use cases can be given a priority of 1 and become the focus of an iteration (see iterative development, Chapter 19) of the software development process, where a system limited to the architecturally relevant functionality in the identified use cases will be created. This tends to take more time than most are willing to spend at this stage.

Alternatively, an architectural prototype may be created that considers prioritized use cases but does not build production code. The purpose of an architectural prototype is to validate the architecture with the minimum amount of functionality. Considerations in an architectural prototype may be performance, scalability, ability to distribute the system, and reliability. The goals of an architectural prototype should be clearly outlined, as this form of architectural development can overlook details that would be found in actually building the system.

Once the architecture is complete, a description of the architecture should be captured in a software architecture document. This document describes the technologies and patterns [Gamma 1994] used to realize the use cases. To achieve the qualities necessary to implement this set of use cases, as well as achieving cost effectiveness and adhering to a schedule, decisions may have to be made that constrain other qualities. These decisions should be documented as well.

Another part of the software architecture definition is **subsystem decomposition**. In subsystem decomposition, the system is partitioned into logical subsystems. Each subsystem contains semantically similar entities. A subsystem is a subclass (in UML) of Package that represents "an independent part of the entire system being modeled" [Booch 1999]. Subsystems may be dependent on other subsystems and overlapped to form layered architectures.

For example, a subsystem decomposition of a video store example may include the subsystems "rental" and "membership" (and many more). Use cases for membership activities such as "Create new membership" would fall into the "membership" subsystem. Use cases such as "Rent Video" may be part of the "rental" subsystem. However, "Rent video" requires membership services, so there is a dependency between the "rental" and "membership" subsystems.

Not all subsystems are as concrete as the ones in the two examples. Use case assortment may create new subsystems to capture common, abstract behavior between use cases [Miller 1999]. Use case assortment develops use cases to serve as requirements for framework development. These new use cases may abstract behavior across subsystems to form new behaviors. Use case assortment is discussed in [Miller 1999].

Subsystems impose organization on the development team. Responsibilities are created as subsystems are identified. A software development team is often dedicated to a subsystem, creating team dynamics. Some subsystems, however, may be bought rather than developed. Integration will need to occur between the built and the bought pieces. Therefore, all subsystems should be documented.

Software architecture tends to be a living thing. It is enhanced over time as new system requirements are generated by new and changing use cases. Good software architecture is malleable and resistant to breakage as the changes occur.

Packaging the Architecture

Domain analysis, interface specification, and subsystem decomposition, as parts of software architecture [Jacobson 1999], can be combined into a single document or broken out into separate documents (as is described in Chapter 19). The value of separate documents is that they can address different purposes and potentially different stakeholders. Essentially, these documents represent different points of view (see Chapter 3). In some cases, the same people need all the information. In these cases, a single software architecture document is more useful.

Deciding whether to build a single software architecture document or a separate software architecture document, a system glossary, and various interface specifications should be part of the development case. The development case should explain who the stakeholders are for each document and what they intend to achieve.[3] This is one of the many reasons why a single, one-size-fits-all process is not possible.

Conclusion

The use case model must be balanced with software architecture. An unbalanced use case model can result in

- A functional model (which is fine for structured or functional programming approaches)
- A disjoint or noncohesive use case model because of differing vocabularies and understandings of the system
- A fuzzy system boundary (this can also result in nonexistent or poor system scoping, see Chapter 11)

Domain analysis serves to create the vocabulary of the use case (and later subsequent object models) and help define the system boundary. Interface specifications also define system boundaries. Architecture definition serves to document the technology and patterns to used in the system development as well as ensure certain performance, availability, and quality aspects.

---

[3] For example, you may not want to distribute an architecture document externally, but may need to distribute interface documents to other vendors who will interface to your system.

Part 3
Advanced Use Case Modeling Framework: Initial Use Case Model

What's in this part?

This part presents the process framework for advanced use case modeling.

In Part 3 of this book (Chapters 5–7) we introduce and describe a framework for applying use cases—first the preparatory steps for use case modeling, then key use case concepts and a process framework for applying use case modeling. In a large development effort—with many developers, a large size, and an extended time frame, possibly interspersed with incremental and iterative deliveries of functionality—a use case modeling effort should be approached in a disciplined, organized manner, not as a short, ad hoc activity with few rules. The use case model and its approach should always be friendly to stakeholders, particularly nontechnical customers and clients, and it should be performed with forethought.

A key aspect of successful modeling on large projects includes preparing for the use case effort—arranging training, setting standards, selecting tools, and customizing the overall approach to fit the business domain and organizational culture. The actual use case modeling effort itself involves discovering and defining the actors and use cases, and documenting the descriptions.

The example of a bank loan processing system will continue to be used in this part. The example is fully outlined as follows.

Loan Processing System Example

A small bank currently performs loan processing primarily as a manual process. To reduce costs and improve customer service, the bank wants to automate and integrate key aspects of its loan processing activities. The types of loan programs the bank currently makes are individual consumer loans and business loans.

Currently, for each loan type, the loan applicant fills out a paper loan application, attaches supporting documents (such as personal financial statements, company financials, projections, and so on), and submits it to the bank. The information on the loan request is manually reviewed for errors and validated by a loan assistant.

The loan assistant then requests a credit report from a credit bureau. A hard copy of the credit report is reviewed by the loan clerk for a complete credit history, and the loan assistant verifies the applicant's credit standing, income, and/or collateral. The loan clerk also accesses the existing account management system to gather any account or loan history the applicant has with the bank.

The information is packaged into a loan request and forwarded to a loan officer for evaluation. If the loan request is approved, the loan officer then determines the best loan conditions and notifies the applicant. The time it takes to process a loan request is typically a minimum of two weeks for both consumer and business loans. If the applicant accepts the loan, the loan is then extended and documented (booked). The bank also handles the loan payments and interacts with the loan account management system.

The bank wants to automate as much of the loan processing as possible. The bank wants to reduce the turnaround time to 48 hours for consumer loan requests and 72 hours for business loan requests. The bank also wants to reduce the number of personnel involved in the loan process and increase the number of loan requests that can be processed in a given period of time.

The bank would like to improve the efficiency of its current loan service activities, such as payment and loan account management, the bank's loan portfolio management, and late loan collection (collection of past due loans). The bank also wants to offer lines of credit to existing bank customers who have been good customers.

To support these business needs, the bank would like the system to validate the loan application for missing or incorrect information, automate providing a loan officer with details of the loan request including information on the loan application and the results of an automated credit analysis, as well as generating a credit score and initial recommendation on the loan request.

The system should allow the loan officer to accept or override the system's recommendation to either approve or disapprove the request. If needed (based on the size of the loan requested), the system should forward the loan request to the loan committee for credit review and approval/disapproval.

The system needs to be able to automate loan billing, notify the loan officer of delinquent loans, and report on the status of the loan portfolio (the set of loans that are currently active at the bank). The bank also wants to be able to share data between the loan processing system and other bank systems including the existing accounts management system and data warehouse.

Assumptions

The loan accounting functions will be performed by the existing accounts management system, but the loan processing system will interface with the accounts management system to generate billing, perform portfolio analysis, and so on.

The developed system should be able to initially handle individual consumer and business loans. It is envisioned that the system will be extended in the future to handle mortgages and student loans as well.

The 48-hour and the 72-hour time constraints are for loan requests that meet the bank lending requirements. If more evaluation of the loan request is needed, additional time will be needed.

The bank places greatest priority on streamlining the loan request process and lesser priority on the loan billing and accounts management aspects.

Chapter 5

Introduction to the System Use Case Modeling Process Framework

What's in this chapter?

This chapter presents a framework for use case modeling.

When we the begin to develop a use case model, we need to understand what we want to accomplish, what our end result will look like, and how we are going to get there. Although use case modeling can appear to be very simple at first, it becomes clear during a project that use case modeling must be performed in a disciplined, well thought-out manner. This chapter introduces a process framework for applying system use cases.

The answers to many questions may help you build a process framework:

- What are the goals of your use case modeling project?
- What outcome are you expecting from the effort?
- How do you ensure that the use case model is developed in a consistent manner across multiple analysts, customers, and users?

- How does use case modeling fit into the larger systems development picture?
- What level of formality is your organization comfortable with?

As mentioned earlier, use case modeling is an extremely flexible technique that can be customized and applied in an almost unlimited number of ways. However, with this advantage comes a challenge: use cases can be applied in almost any way you like. This means that to be successful, standards need to be in place. The project must determine the common templates to be used. It must also define the applicable models and techniques. These are placed in a document called a development case (see Appendix B). The development case is a customized description of a process tailored to fit your development project.

In Chapters 5–15, we present a use case process modeling framework and describe how it generally fits into the software system development process. In Chapter 18, we study a specific development process model, the Rational Unified Process, and show how the process framework fits into it. Then you should be able to integrate the use case process framework into other development process models.

Need for a Software Development Process

In any system development effort, a process is performed, whether the developers are aware of it or not. The developers perform a set of activities that will have a definite outcome. Problems arise when the developers are making up the process as they go along. When this occurs developers are reactive, responding to development crises without having a clear development objective or a defined path for getting there and then monitoring or adjusting the approach as needed.

Without a well-defined process, developers find it difficult if not impossible to know what they are doing and why. They have difficulty achieving consistent results across the project, monitoring the progress, and diagnosing and adjusting the process when needed.

All software development projects need to start with a process framework. A process framework is a set of activities, approaches, models, and techniques for achieving the outcome of the development effort—a working system that meets customer needs in a timely manner and within an agreed-on budget. To achieve these goals, projects must be planned and scheduled. Without a process in place, reliable scheduling is impossible. A process framework includes the following elements:

- People involved
- Models, techniques, and notations

- Process activities
- Automated tool support

When embarking on a use case modeling effort or any system development effort, it is important to first identify the individuals who will be involved in the effort, the models and techniques that will used, the standards to be enforced, and the process that will integrate all the elements to the development objectives. It is equally important that each member of the development team understands the value of the models and techniques that will be used.

The use case modeling process and the concepts utilized in the process are briefly described next. We then introduce a process framework for applying use case models. Some of the initial activities in the framework are presented; the definition of activities continues in subsequent chapters.

Advanced Use Case Modeling Process Framework

This section introduces the advanced use case modeling process framework and its key activities. An organization will need to modify and customize the framework for its own use. Although some use case activities naturally occur before others, the process is not meant to be linear. Developers will need to iterate throughout the process.

System Use Case Model: Modeling and Relationships

When creating use cases for a large system, particularly during an iterative development effort, the use case diagrams, descriptions, and other models will be evolving and will be refined as the use case modeling effort progresses. We refer to the complete set of diagrams and descriptions needed to represent the use cases and actors as the **use case model**. In addition to the use cases themselves, the use case model includes supporting text, glossaries, diagrams, and other documentation used in specifying the use cases.

The basic use case notation and concepts described in Chapter 2 provide a starting point for documenting the use case model. However, performing an extensive use case effort on a large system requires a more complete and robust set of diagrams, descriptions, and notations. In this section we introduce and describe the additional documentation used to represent use cases and their relationships with one another. Typically, use cases are first used to model the system at a conceptual level, focusing on the primary behaviors of the system, and they are refined to describe the increasing levels of detailed requirements information.

What Are System Use Cases?

This section discusses the role of use cases in the development of a single system. These use cases are referred to as **system use cases**. The following are key aspects of system use cases.

- During requirements analysis, a system use case models a business event, for example, a customer withdrawing funds from an ATM machine.
- A system use case is a descriptive "abstract scenario" of how an actor interacts with a system and how the system responds to the interaction.
- A system use case is a broad behavior of the system initiated by actors.
- A system use case constitutes a complete flow of events.
- A set of system use cases collectively describes system functionality.
- A use case model represents a complex reality and is developed iteratively.

A complete system use case model does not occur at once. Each use case typically goes through a process of refinement as more information is learned about the system requirements. In addition, the larger the system, the more complex are the requirements for the system. As the requirements analysis process proceeds, the use case descriptions go through a series of abstract levels, with more details added to the descriptions as more is learned about the problems.

For these reasons, a single, flat level of detail is normally insufficient to support an ongoing and evolving analysis process and also to provide the ability to robustly and effectively capture, partition, and represent the vast functionality of a large system. It is necessary, as the use case descriptions are progressively defined, to represent them at higher levels of detail. As more about the requirements is learned, more details are added to the use case descriptions. Details can be added by

- expanding information within a specific use case, that is, adding to its description,
- finding additional use cases as the requirements become clearer,
- extending the details of the use case model, through extend, include, and generalization relationships, and
- integrating multiple use cases to define larger system processes and functions and the bigger picture.

A system use case model can include the following (Figure 5.1):

- *Initial system use case descriptions.* Use case descriptions developed during the beginning of the requirements analysis identify and broadly describe

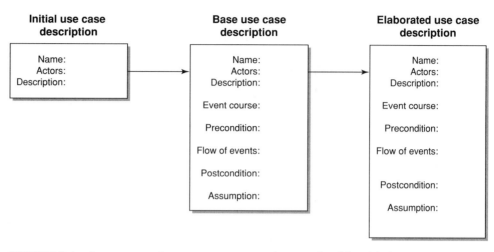

FIGURE 5-1 As more requirements are captured, more detail is added to the use case descriptions

system behaviors initiated by actors. They provide a conceptual representation of the system.

- *Base system use case descriptions.* Base system use case descriptions expand on the initial system use case descriptions by documenting use case behavior in greater detail. Base use cases focus on the "ideal" behaviors and paths of use cases and avoid documenting exceptions or alternatives.

- *Elaborated system use case descriptions.* In elaborated descriptions, details of behavior such as condition logic and alternative flows are added to the base use case descriptions.

In addition to the use case descriptions, the system use case model can include other elements:

- *Use case diagrams.* Diagrams provide a high-level visual representation of the actors, the use cases, and the relationships between them.

- *Extend, include, and generalization relationships.* These relationships document extensions and commonality in use cases and also the major exception conditions and alternative flows of events that can occur in a use case. In an include relationship, a use case includes the behavior defined in another use case or behaviors that are included in multiple use cases. Extend relationships document extensions in the use case flow of events.

Generalization relationships are similar to those in object modeling and document the relationship between an abstract or more general use case and more specific sub cases. (*NOTE*: As of UML 1.3, the extend and use relationships have been updated and replaced with the extend, include, and generalization relationships).

- *Instance scenarios*. These scenarios describe instances or examples of how use cases are executed. They are useful as a validation mechanism and to generate test cases.

- *Analysis object models*. These are models that map the use cases to the objects needed to realize the behaviors in the use case. They help to identify more detailed requirements and to map the use cases to the design. The use case to object model mapping activity can normally be performed using mapping tables, UML sequence, or collaboration diagrams.

- *Dependency streams*. These diagrams capture the dependencies between the various use cases and show how groups of use cases are tied together in larger process flows.

- *Business function packages*. When several use cases are part of a large business process, these packages group the use cases by common business functions or areas.

There are a number of reasons to describe use cases at various forms and levels of abstraction. First, as mentioned earlier, a complete use case model is not built in just one step. The model is built progressively and iteratively, as a natural result of the process of analysis, discovery, and modeling of system functionality. As more knowledge is acquired, the model is elaborated; the representations capture this progress as it occurs.

Second, the use case model has several audiences—customers, users, analysts, designers, and systems architects, to name a few. The different audiences view the use cases in different ways. Different stakeholders of the system have different viewpoints from which they examine and validate the use case model. Multiple representations help facilitate their understanding and their validation of the model. The use case model has a diverse audience, ranging from customers who are interested in functionality at a high level and users who need to validate the detailed functionality of a specific use case to the object designers who need enough information to map the use cases into an object model. A use case model must be complete and robust enough to accommodate the needs of the CIO or customer of the system who wants to review the use case diagrams and conceptual descriptions in order to understand the system concept and a system designer who wants to review the lowest level of detail in order to understand the implications of object design.

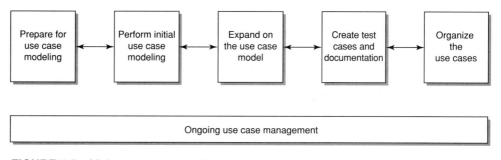

FIGURE 5-2 Major use case activity groups

Third, multiple representations allow use cases to be more easily partitioned for development. A model containing only initial and base use case descriptions can be created for a system concept or concept of operation document. Elaborated use case descriptions and a comprehensive set of extend and include use cases can be developed during analysis activity. Incremental delivery is also supported, as entire system functionality can be modeled as a set of initial and base use case descriptions. As each increment is developed, the use cases selected for development in that increment are further refined.

Fourth, multiple use case representations are an organizational technique for adding order and understandability to a large use case model. (Further organizational techniques are discussed in Chapter 15.)

It is important to remember that use case modeling is not a linear process. Use cases are discovered, elaborated with detail, rethought, reworked, and revised as the use case modeling effort progresses.

Use Case Modeling Activities

The major activity groups in system use case modeling include the following (Figure 5-2).

Prepare for use case modeling and determine use case approach.

- Create a glossary of system vocabulary.
- Perform a stakeholder analysis; select team members and identify involved customers and users.
- Select and customize a use case process framework.

- Select use case modeling standards, templates, and tools. Agree on granularity, voice, and style.
- Determine training and mentoring needs.

Perform initial use case modeling.
- Create initial use case diagram and/or context diagram.
- Identify the major actors.
- Discover the use cases (Initial descriptions).
- Start to identify/refine candidate business (domain) objects.

Expand on the use case model.
- Develop base use case descriptions.
- Iteratively elaborate the base use cases descriptions and determine extend, include, and generalization relationships.
- Map use cases to object models.
- Develop instance scenarios.

Organize the use cases.
- Develop business functional packages.
- Identify use case dependency streams.
- Organize the use cases by stakeholder views.
- Refactor the use case model.

Ongoing use case management.
- Validate use case model with users.
- Define and execute training plan.
- Track ongoing use case modeling progress.
- Update and customize framework, based on stakeholder feedback.

The Interesting Issue box on page 69 discusses the dangers and challenges of mixing system use case definition and GUI design too early in requirements processing. The Interesting Issue box "Is There Only One Right Way to Model with Use Cases?" (page 70) talks about how different approaches can be used when performing use case modeling.

INTERESTING ISSUE: SYSTEM REQUIREMENTS VERSUS GUI DESIGN

System use cases are similar in concept to what Larry Constantine calls essential use cases [Constantine 1999, 1995]. We agree with Constantine that use cases at the system or essential level need to be carefully focused in order to understand the business requirements. It is too easy with use case modeling to slip into GUI design too early and lose sight of the big picture.

For a small system or a prototype of a piece of a large system, early GUI modeling can be effective. However, GUI modeling with a large system without a clear understanding of the overall scope can be very dangerous. A large system will include many, many requirements, not all of which would appear in a GUI design. Also, when designing GUIs it is a good idea to consider the implications to the system and data architecture. You can develop a gorgeous GUI design working with the users and end up finding out that it requires a five-table relational database join.

In addition, we have seen efforts when the requirements capture breaks down because the team starts to argue over GUI design aspects, such as where to place an OK button, and loses focus on the essential requirements. GUI design and prototyping are a great and necessary step in system development and are sometimes critical to stimulating the user's thinking about the system. But separating the business requirements from the user interface requirements is important to a successful project. We discuss the development of conceptual user interface designs from system use cases in Chapter 16.

Creating or Customizing a Process Framework for a Specific Project

When a project is first conceived, the developers should select, refine, or create a process framework for the project. A number of commercial processes, such as the Rational Unified Process, are available for use and refinement on an object-oriented project.

Process frameworks normally need to be adjusted based on a number of project-specific factors:

- *Size of the project.* Large projects typically require much more process and guidance then smaller projects, where the overhead of following a rigorous process can sometimes outweigh the benefits.

- *Domain.* Although all software development processes involve many of the same key activities—analysis, design, and testing, for example—the specifics can vary greatly depending on whether the system is a business system, a real-time military system, or a systems application such as a compiler or operating system.

INTERESTING ISSUE: IS THERE ONLY ONE RIGHT WAY TO MODEL WITH USE CASES?

Use cases are a very flexible and extendable software development technique. Use case modeling concepts may be applied very informally and loosely or very rigorously and formally. Factors of length, terminology, organization, and structure can be markedly different from one use case effort to another. All of these various approaches have strengths and weaknesses; none is carved in stone. This has the advantage that individuals and organizations can apply and customize use case modeling to suit their needs.

The relative merits of such concepts as conditional logic and level of formality are still being debated in the use case community. A use case modeler should understand the issues associated with each approach and determine the best approach to solve a specific problem. Various differences between use case approaches include:

- Level of problem at which use case modeling is applied
- Formality and complexity of the use cases (we will discuss this in more detail in Chapter19)
- Organization and structure of the use cases (we discuss this in more detail in Chapter 15)
- Inclusion or exclusion or system behavior in the use case flow of events
- Integration and participation of the use case modeling in the larger development process

Regardless of what approach a project decides to take, everyone needs to agree on it and use it consistently throughout the effort. There is nothing worse than sending several teams out to perform use case modeling and getting back results that are unusable because the techniques were not applied consistently. For a good reference on the common pitfalls of use case modeling see Lilly [1999].

An entire book would be needed to perform a detailed survey of the multitude of use case interpretations and applications. Here we present an approach to use cases that we have found works with repeated success. It is grounded in basic use case and extends modeling concepts. We attempt to point out strengths and weaknesses in different approaches and techniques. Different approaches to defining and formalizing use cases are surveyed in Hurlbut [1997].

- *Use of incremental or iterative development.* When using an iterative or incremental development approach, the leaders of the project need to clearly think out its strategy for tracking progress, revisiting deliverables, and so on.
- *Experience of the team.* An inexperienced development team will typically need more structure and guidelines than an experienced one.

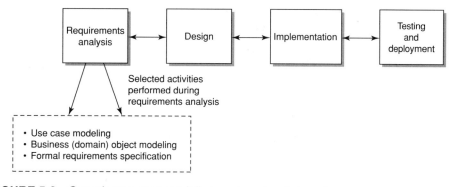

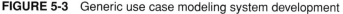

FIGURE 5-3　Generic use case modeling system development

This generic use case process framework is meant only for system use case modeling and should be refined and modified into the overall systems development process (Figure 5-3).

Almost every systems development effort varies in its specifics, so any use case process framework almost always needs to be customized. As Ivar Jacobson [1998] has stated, "There is NO universal process." We have not seen a process framework for any systems development effort that did not need some form of adjustment or customization. However, it's a lot easier to customize an existing framework that is based on project experience than to develop your own from scratch.

When customizing a use case modeling framework, the framework's process, activities, and tools can be adjusted. An existing process, whether it is commercial or developed in-house for internal use, is simply a starting point. A single specific use case framework can be customized or multiple frameworks can be combined to fit in with the larger development process. Figure 5-4 shows three dimensions in

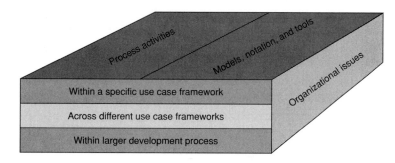

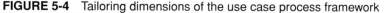

FIGURE 5-4　Tailoring dimensions of the use case process framework

which a framework can be tailored. First, the specific activities to be performed and models, notations, and tools can be customized. Second, the relation and dependencies of activities and models can be adjusted. In addition, the framework itself can be fitted into the larger development process. Finally, the organizational cultures and issues need to be considered.

Conclusion

This chapter outlines a use case process framework, with a clear definition of goals, objectives, and considerations. Use case modeling for a large iterative development requires multiple models and a well-thought-out process for applying the models. Use case modeling may seem simple at first, and for small projects it can be. However, for large efforts, the activities, models, and notations, as well as the stakeholders involved, need to be clearly defined in the use case process framework, and the framework must fit into the larger development picture.

Chapter 6

Preparing for Use Case Modeling and Determining Use Case Approach

> When schemes are laid in advance, it is surprising how often
> the circumstances fit in with them."
>
> —Sir William Osler (1849–1919), Canadian physician

What's in this chapter?

This chapter describes the initial steps in setting up a use case modeling effort. Selecting and customizing use case frameworks, selecting standards and techniques, and consideration of training and mentoring needs are outlined.

This chapter discusses some of the activities that need to be performed when setting up a use case modeling effort, activities in the first major use case activity group, "Prepare for use case modeling and determine use case approach" (Figure 6-1). The activities are identification of stakeholders, selection and customization of a process framework for use case modeling, and selection of standards, templates, and tools to support the effort. Finally, mentoring and formal training need to be planned and put in place.

Perform a Stakeholder Analysis

A number of different "stakeholders" are involved in the use case modeling process. A stakeholder is defined as any individual who has a "stake" or interest in the use case model. The stakeholders must be identified and engaged in the use case modeling effort as early as possible and their feedback must be solicited and incorporated into the use cases. Only with active participation of all the stakeholders

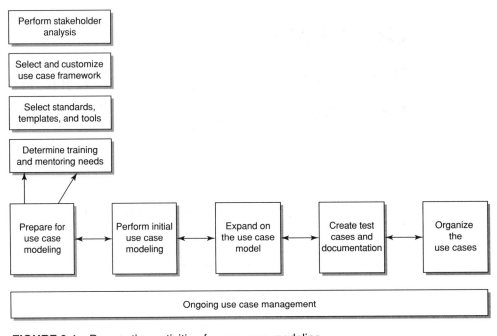

FIGURE 6-1   Preparation activities for use case modeling

can a use case effort—and the system—be successful. Although this task can seem time-consuming and difficult, the payoffs for all the stakeholders are great. For example, the customer that is paying for the information systems development efforts and the project manager responsible for developing the system can use the use cases to agree on system scope and then estimate the schedule and budget. The users will use the system use cases to identify and validate the system requirements, thus reducing the "surprise" factor when the system has been developed ("That's not what I thought the system would do"). The system developer and architects utilize use cases to help drive the analysis and design of the system.

A **stakeholder analysis** should be performed as part of the system development process. A stakeholder analysis normally identifies the key stakeholders, what organizations they are with, their overall organizational responsibilities, their relationship to the project, and any issues or concerns that are associated with the individual. Following are categories of stakeholders who are involved in a use case modeling effort.

- Customers
- Users
- Project managers

- System analysts
- System architects
- System developers
- Testers
- System operators and maintainers

Each stakeholder has different needs and perspectives (Table 6-1). The different attributes of a system (such as requirements, schedule, progress, budget) are of concern to different categories of stakeholders.

It is critical that each system stakeholder be involved in the use case modeling effort. Without this involvement, it is extremely difficult to get buy-in for the system and the development approach that is being taken. If the stakeholders are not involved early in the system development effort, not only does the project team have a difficult time capturing the system requirements, the stakeholders do not feel a sense of ownership. Then, if things don't go quite as planned during the development

TABLE 6-1   Stakeholders and use case modeling

Stakeholder	Benefits of the use case model
Customer	<ul><li>Provides customer requirements for validation</li><li>Helps determine overall system scope</li><li>Helps in estimating schedule and budget</li><li>Acts as basis for acceptance testing</li></ul>
User	<ul><li>Provides user requirements for validation</li><li>Models the user's interaction with the system</li></ul>
Project manager	<ul><li>Helps in estimating schedule and budget</li><li>Assists in assessing the feasibility and the risk of the project</li><li>Helps in tracing requirements</li><li>Helps in tracking the progress of system development</li></ul>
System architect	<ul><li>Drives the system architecture</li><li>Helps in tracing architectural requirements</li><li>Supports trade-off analyses for technology selection</li><li>Helps in assessing completeness, consistency, and coherency of architecture</li></ul>
System developer	<ul><li>Provides models of the requirements for system design</li><li>Acts as a means for system documentation</li></ul>
System maintainer	<ul><li>Provides guidance for system modification</li><li>Provides guidance for architecture evolution</li></ul>

effort (e.g., delays, cost overruns, demands for changing requirements), the stake-holders will be far less likely to understand, support, and champion the effort.

Select and Customize a Use Case Process Framework

Before jumping into use case modeling, you will need to create or select and cus-tomize a use case process model.

First, determine the role of use case modeling within the overall system development process context. Define how use cases will fit in and relate to the other analysis models, such as object models, architectural models, formal writ-ten requirements, and designs. If you are adapting a preexisting process frame-work, determine what modifications you will need to make:

- Modifying existing methods or process activities
- Integrating activities or methods from different use case frameworks or approaches
- Adjusting activities for use within the overall system development process

When customizing a framework, consider the size of the project. Smaller projects typically need much less structure than large ones. Some organizations like a lot of structure, while others prefer a less structured approach. Be sure you are tuned in to the culture of your organization. Consensus is critical. A large, estab-lished company with thousands of IT professionals in a traditional industry may like and want a significant amount of structure, or what Booch refers to as "ceremony" [Booch 1996]. A small Internet startup will probably want just enough structure to "get it done." If possible, test the framework on pilot projects and refine it before deploying it to the rest of the organization. Have the participants on the pilot project act as champions and mentors to the rest of the organization. This will help build consensus and provide critical hands-on support.

We recommend starting with an existing object-oriented framework such as the Rational Unified Process and customizing it as needed for your effort.

Select Use Case Standards, Templates, and Tools

When many individuals work on a large project, use case modeling standards must be established that will provide guidelines, such as the appropriate represen-tations for use case text descriptions and use case models. Standards dictate com-mon approaches and representation for development of the use cases—what models will be developed and how they will look—and the level of detail a model will define and how will it fit in with the other models.

To ensure and encourage a common and consistent approach, standards should be supported by common templates, such as use case templates, use case diagram templates, and so on, along with guidelines for using them and checklists to ensure that they are completed and validated correctly.

Not only do standards help to ensure that the use case model is developed consistently, they help to educate developers as to how the process will proceed. If the developers are experienced and have been on previous use case modeling efforts, the proposed standards can generate healthy debate and result in a useful refinement of the approach before the project begins.

The easiest and best approach to creating standards is to select already developed industry standards such as the Unified Modeling Language as your starting point. But be careful: UML is very large and will need to be customized and modified for most project efforts.

Computer Automated Software Engineering (CASE) tools should be selected that will support your models, descriptions, templates, and processes. Although it is highly unlikely that one tool will meet all your project needs, it is critical for large projects, particularly projects with lots of iteration, that tool support is provided. CASE development tools can vary from Rational Rose for large-scale development to Visio for simple projects. Be prepared to supplant a primary tool with other tools and manual processes to support your effort.

Normally, it is a good idea to define and tailor your processes, models, and templates first, and then look for a CASE tool that supports them. The CASE tool tail should not be permitted to wag the process dog.

Tailoring your use case modeling approach can complicate CASE tool support. Since the tool may not be able to "adjust" to customization, some revisions to templates and approaches can be made to facilitate the integration of a good CASE tool into the project. Remember that any changes or tools should support your final objectives.

It is easy to oversell the benefits of a CASE tool to upper management and the development team. No CASE tool will meet all your documentation and communication needs. A CASE tool supports the analysts; it does not do the thinking for them. An inexperienced analyst with a CASE tool is still an inexperienced analyst: "A fool with a tool is still a fool."

It is imperative that the organization evaluate any tool in-house. While this can be time-consuming, it is virtually impossible to plumb the depth and abilities of CASE tools without an extensive review.

Determine Training and Mentoring Needs

There cannot be enough said about the role of formal training and mentoring in the success of a use case modeling effort. Everyone who works on the project should be expert in what they're doing.

Formal Training

When providing training for individuals involved in the use case modeling effort, it is important to focus on more than simply how to "do" good use cases. Elicitation techniques (e.g., requirements analysis, interviewing skills), interpersonal skills, overall requirements management, and an understanding of systems development are also important, as use cases do not stand alone. Keep in mind the following points:

- Use case training should be synchronized with the process framework.
- Provide formal training courses on use case modeling.
- Have team members participate in training programs that involve a workshop setting and simulated or real-life examples. This gives the team members some hands-on experience before attempting the project.
- Use immersion courses or boot camps that provide intense, long-term (several weeks to several months) instruction.
- Make sure the training is available "just in time."

Also consider whether training will be provided by an in-house or an outside vendor. If an outside vendor is being considered, they will need to know whether the training will help drive the process (i.e., you are looking for process support guidance as well) or whether it will need to map to a development approach that has already been selected.

Mentoring

Formal classroom training and written documentation are great tools for providing the basics of the technology. However, experienced individuals can analyze the specific needs of the project and customize the training approach. Experience needs to be shared and shared quickly across the organization. Build a network within the company of people with similar experiences who can draw on each other for guidance and advice. Cross-pollination of experience across multiple projects can go far to supplement documentation and formal training that may be limited by rapid change and busy instructors.

What makes a good use case mentor? What are the characteristics for an ideal mentor? When we select individuals to act as mentors, we look for the following characteristics.

Knowledge and Information Technology Skills.   Obviously, good mentors must have experience in the areas they are mentoring. For example, a use case mentor must have both the practical experience and the theoretical knowledge to guide the team effectively through difficult analysis decisions. Mentors are able to take lessons learned on one use case modeling effort and make them available to the next project team(s) across the organization.

In addition, the mentor should be able to keep up with the latest and greatest the industry has to offer, distill all that information, and filter from it what is important for the project. Many times, due to project deadlines, members of project teams will not have time to explore the latest ideas and industry experiences and then determine how to integrate them into the industry effort.

Ability to Instill Confidence. Mentors need the respect, trust, and confidence of the team and the team needs to feel comfortable asking questions and accepting advice. Not only should a mentor have knowledge of the specific use case approach, but the team should feel that the mentor has experienced firsthand some of the issues with which they may be struggling.

Mentoring Personality. A mentoring personality includes the following traits:

- Teaching and coaching skills
- Communications and facilitation skills
- Approachability
- Ability to deal with difficult personalities
- Ability to juggle priorities. Mentors are pulled in many directions.
- Ability to work under stress and pressure. Mentors generally find themselves putting out brush fires and working with people who are struggling to make deadlines.
- Ability to recognize their limitations with regard to time and skills.

Ability to Adjust to the Context of the Project. Mentors must have the ability to adjust to a specific project context. They are not always injected into the project at the same stage. Therefore, they must be able to assess the environment and the needs of the project quickly and then act accordingly. Mentors need to have enough experience to generalize use case modeling techniques and methods and apply them to new situations. They must also be open to new approaches and be willing to adjust and modify the approaches they have taken on a particular project in the past.

Ability to Analyze Team Member Experience and Abilities. Good mentors need to be able to evaluate the different talents and capabilities of the team and capitalize on the strengths. The job of mentor is to try to find a role for everyone.

Commitment to Project Objectives and Goals. Mentors need to view their success as the success of team. They must be aligned with project objectives and goals and be effective in establishing buy-in from the team to achieve the goals.

Mentors can be selected from in-house staff or they can be external consultants. An external mentor may bring a new perspective, knowledge, and experience from outside development efforts to the effort; an internal mentor may feel more commitment to the project and understand the internal culture much better.

Conclusion

Preparation is a key for successful use case modeling on a large project. A stakeholder analysis should be performed to identify all interested parties. A framework for applying use cases is developed and put in place. The standards, approaches, and techniques to be used are chosen and planned. Finally, to ensure a knowledgeable project team, training and mentoring are put in place.

Chapter 7

Performing Initial Use Case Modeling

What's in this chapter?

This chapter discusses the initial steps in creating the use case model. The outcome of this activity group is a use case model that captures a conceptual picture of what the system needs to do.

This chapter outlines the initial activities for creating the use case model, a process we refer to as *initial use case modeling*. The outcome of this activity group is a use case model that captures a "conceptual" picture of what the system needs to do. During initial use case modeling, the key behaviors of the system are defined, the major actors are identified, and an initial mapping to high-level business objects is performed.

As shown in Figure 7-1, the activities in this group include the development of a context diagram and descriptions of the major actors and primary use cases. Once again, although the activities are presented in a linear order, there will be a large amount of parallelism and iteration among them.

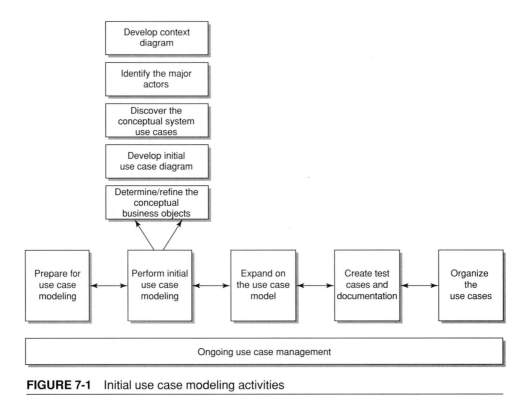

FIGURE 7-1   Initial use case modeling activities

Develop Context Diagram

Sometimes people develop a traditional context diagram before developing a formal use case diagram. A context diagram is a very quick and focused representation of the system boundaries, entities that interact with the system, and the nature of the interaction. Since the context diagram is a little less formal than a use case diagram, analysis can start very early on without formally defining use cases or actors. It also has a long history in system development analysis [DeMarco 1979] [Yourdon 1989], so users and systems analysts may already be comfortable with it. Although this activity is not traditionally used in use case modeling, it can be a quick and easy way to get started with the analysis when you are dealing with an unclear problem or working very early with a customer or users.

The context diagram (Figure 7-2) represents the system as a big circle with external entities surrounding it. In the traditional context diagram, directed lines (arrow) indicate the flow of information between the external entities and the system. In a use case modeling content diagram, the arrows show interactions that

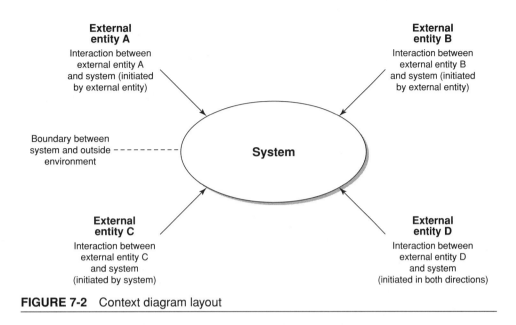

FIGURE 7-2 Context diagram layout

will potentially map to use cases. Under normal circumstances, the external entities will serve as input into the identification of the actors.

In a context diagram, everything inside the circle is "inside" the system and everything outside the circle is "outside" the system. An external entity can be a person providing information to or receiving information from the system or an external system receiving information from or sending information from the system. Any interaction and/or information shared between the system and external entities should be documented as directed lines, but their descriptions should be kept at a high level. For example, the need for reports can be captured on the context diagram as a general interaction without listing every report. There is no hard and fast rule on the number of external externals and interactions that can be shown in a context diagram, but remember that this is a one-page overview of the system, not a detailed description. As the analysis proceeds, the external entities and arrows will map to more detailed actor and use case descriptions.

When developing a context diagram, review such documents as business use cases, Business Process Reengineering (BPR) results, existing requirements, the stakeholder analysis, enterprise IT architecture descriptions, and strategic planning documents. Start by asking the stakeholders to list the external entities in the system environment that will interact with the system. Place these external entities around the system and describe the interactions between the external entities and

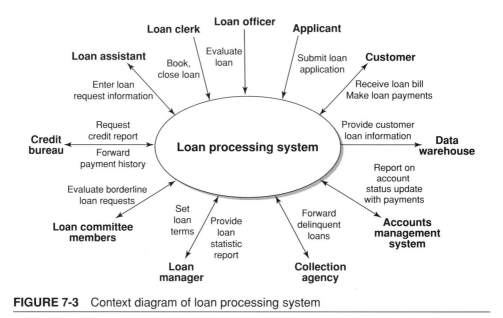

FIGURE 7-3   Context diagram of loan processing system

the system. There is no need to be formal; more formality will be introduced in the following activities that define actors and the initial use cases.

Drawing a traditional context diagram can be skipped if there is sufficient information or experience to start formally defining the use cases and actors. However, it is a quick way to get started scoping the system.

The context diagram for the loan processing example is shown in Figure 7-3.

Now is a good time to start to create a glossary similar to the system glossary of domain object definitions in (Chapter 4) of standard terms and definitions that will be used during the use case modeling. The glossary will continue to be updated as the use case modeling progresses, but the initial glossary should be created before the initial use case models so that all participants agree on a common terminology to use in describing the actors and use cases. A glossary helps to improve the readability of the use case modeling artifacts and can reduce rework.

Identify the Major Actors

During this activity the project team starts to identify and document the actors. (Actors were defined in Chapter 1.) Look for the major or primary actors that interact with the system. As the use case analysis proceeds, more actors will be found, and the level of detail on each actor will be refined. Remember that an actor is a role, not a specific individual. The role should reflect the responsibilities the actors have in the environment within the context of how they interact with the system. For example, in a travel management system, a good role name for the actor who submits a travel voucher would be "Employee." A bad name would be "User," since a user could be anyone who uses the system. The more precise the actor name, the better.

When looking for the actors, look for individuals, other systems, or other organizations that will interact with the system. In addition to brainstorming with users and customers, look at these documents and deliverables:

- Draft context diagrams and other models that describe the system within its environment (e.g., BPR results, existing system models, strategic plans, and so on)
- Stakeholder analysis that has identified the stakeholders and their roles
- Written specifications and other project documentation, such as memos about meetings with users, to help find users who may be potential actors
- Individuals who participated in requirements workshops or joint application development (JAD) sessions
- Training guides and user manuals for current processes and systems
- Organization charts

Finally, and most important, elicit from the key users in the use case modeling process the names of people whom they think may interact with the system.

Involving the users and customers does not mean that they should write the use cases unassisted. If a project lets the users write the use cases, then the use case model will almost always be inconsistent, incomplete, and overscoped. In addition, since the users wrote the use cases, they will feel that they "own" them. It can be very difficult to get the users to agree to a major reworking, if needed.

It is the job of the project's use case modelers to work with the users and customers to elicit and gather the appropriate requirements information, transform this information into a quality use case model, and have the users review and validate the use case model. Most of the time we like to discover the actors first, and then define the use cases (see the Interesting Issue box on page 86).

The initial primary actors who were identified for the loan processing use model are shown in Figure 7-4.

Once the primary actors have been identified, it is useful to select and talk to representative members of each actor role. During these interviews, try to determine what interactions the actors will need to have with the system to meet the system objective and goals. Consider the level of computer experience that may

INTERESTING ISSUE: WHICH COMES FIRST—THE ACTOR OR THE USE CASE?

Typically we look for actors as the first step to discovering a use case. Remember that Jacobson's definition of use cases includes the phrase "measurable value to an actor"; it is therefore very difficult to discover a use case without first determining who or what in the system's external environment needs measurable value from the system.

We normally start by trying to define the primary actors or the actor that initiates the use case. The primary actors are the reason a use case will exist. Secondary actors and external servers are discovered after the use case's flow of events is developed in more detail. Since we normally start looking for the primary actors and then detail and elaborate the use cases, new actors can just be added to the documentation as they are found.

We were once involved in a system development effort in which the proposed functionality was so different and new we were unable to find actors until we had documented the systems functions using use cases. We then went back and created new actor roles for each use case. So if you are having a hard time finding actors, try to find some use cases first; that should help identify the actors.

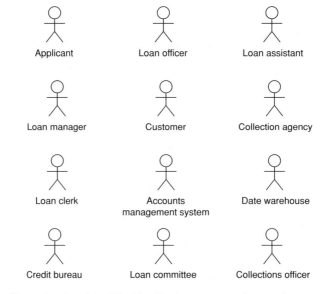

FIGURE 7-4   Several actors identified for the loan processing system

span an actor role. Normally, we like to speak with at least three individuals for each human actor role:

- one who is very experienced with the role
- one who is a novice at the role
- one who is considered to be representative of the role

Also, if the role is played in different geographical locations, including different countries, talk to a representative in each location. Sometimes system behaviors will need to be different in other locations or cultures.

If the actor is another system, try to contact someone knowledgeable about that system's functionality, such as a user or system maintainer, to discuss the other system's capability to carry out the behaviors expected of it.

We document actors with the actor specification forms shown in Chapter 1, and we record the actor description in what we call an actor glossary. The glossary is the list of actors and their descriptions. At this time, document the actor's name and include a short description of what the actor does. The rest of the actor templates will be filled in as more is discovered about the use cases. Sample actor specifications follow for the applicant, customer, loan officer, and accounts management system.

Actor specification
Actor name: Applicant   **Abstract:** <No>
Description: An applicant is an individual or organization who submits a request for a loan to the bank. The applicant will utilize the system primarily to submit loan requests.

Actor specification
Actor name: Loan officer   **Abstract:** <No>
Description: A loan officer is an officer of the bank who has the designated responsibility of evaluating requests for a loan. A loan officer has the power to grant a loan or, depending on the size of the loan request, refer the requests to the loan committee for a decision. A loan officer uses the system for such activities as evaluating loan requests and reviewing outstanding loans.

Actor specification
Actor name: Customer   **Abstract:** <No>
Description: A customer is an individual or business that currently has a relationship with the bank. For the purposes of the loan management system, a customer is someone who holds an active loan account or has been extended credit.

Actor specification
Actor name: Accounts management system   **Abstract:** <No>
Description: The accounts management system is an existing legacy system that maintains information on the status of a customer's existing accounts with the bank, such as checking, savings, and money market. This system will hold the loan account information for a loan customer that will be needed by the loan management system.

Discover the Conceptual System Use Cases

Obviously, one of the most important activities in use case modeling is identifying the use cases! In this activity, the initial set of high-level use cases is identified and documented. The initial use case descriptions document the major interactions that actors will have with the system; they model the primary requirements that will drive the system developments.

The set of initial use case descriptions, along with the use case diagram discussed in the next activity and the major business objects, should give the stakeholder a conceptual picture of what the system will look like. This level of detail is commonly referred to as a *concept of operation* or *system concept*.

One way to start to identify the initial system use cases is to examine the list of actors and ask the following questions:

- What measurable value is needed by the actor?
- What business event might this actor initiate based on the actor's role?
- What services does the actor need from the system?
- Does the actor need to receive information from the system?
- What type of service does the actor provide?

When performing this step it is important to keep the actor's perspective in mind. Each use case discovered should represent some responsibility of the system that supports an actor's business needs. As you conduct this process, you will discover many possible interactions that users can have with the system. It is important to make sure that the use cases are driven by system objectives and goals, and when the use cases have been defined, make sure that they trace to at least one system objective and goal; for large systems, it is easy to overidentify use cases. Cockburn [1997a, 1997b] describes the use of goals to try to help identify use cases.

Naming Conceptual Use Cases

Name the use cases to reflect, as precisely as possible, the reason for the primary actor's interaction with the system.

- The use case name should provide a short description of the actor's interaction with the system.
- The use case name should reflect the actor's goal in interacting with the system.
- The use case name should be stated from the perspective of the actor.
- The use case name should be an active verb–noun phrase. The verb should be in the imperative mood to denote an action that the actor should perform; a use case is an event, not a process or information flow. For example, a good use case name for submitting a travel voucher is "Submit travel voucher." A not-so-good use case name is "Travel voucher submission." "Submit travel voucher" implies an event and is much more specific; "Travel voucher submission" implies a process and could involve far greater functionality than the event of submitting the voucher. (See the Interesting Issue box below for another approach to naming use cases.)

In naming the use cases in the loan processing system example, the following questions might be asked. The answers suggest good names.

- For the loan applicant, what value is needed from the system? The ability to submit a request, receive notification, and so on.
- For the loan officer, what support is needed from the system? Loan request information captured in a form that is ready to evaluate.
- For the customer, what services are needed? The receipt of timely billing.

INTERESTING ISSUE: ANOTHER APPROACH TO NAMING

Most people utilize a verb–noun phrase to name their use cases, but some use a transitive gerund or verb of continuing action rather than the second person imperative form [Constantine 1999]—"Renting video" instead of "Rent video." The reason given for this approach is that the behavior of the system is ongoing.

Some people reserve the imperative mood to describe the steps within the use case and the transitive gerund for naming the use case. For example, the use case "Purchasing products" might have the following steps: "Total items, calculate applicable discount, calculate applicable taxes, calculate grand total, charge customer, make change for customer, thank customer, and give customer purchased products [Ambler 1997]." Both approaches are equally acceptable.

Example use case names might be "Submit request," "Evaluate loan request information," and "Receive timely billing."

Don't be afraid to move quickly when brainstorming the use cases. Use case modeling is very iterative. You will have plenty of opportunity throughout the process to find new use cases, merge use cases, and throw out irrelevant use cases.

Documenting Conceptual Use Cases

An initial use case description documents an individual use case at a high level of abstraction. This normally involves a couple of sentences or a free-form paragraph outlining the purpose of the use case and the activities in the use case. This level of use case description allows for a quick understanding of the interactions between the actors and the system and the system responsibilities and behaviors in response to the interactions. Figure 7-5 shows a sample template for capturing a high-level use case.

Conceptual use case descriptions can be developed quickly and provide a focused overview of the major behaviors of a system. They are intended as a starting point for understanding and modeling the final use cases. They are also an excellent means for presenting the system to high-level decision makers in a compact and understandable fashion. Furthermore, they must be done in order to locate an initial use case diagram. Even short use case descriptions ensure that all the stakeholders have the same broad behavior in mind when referring to a specific use case.

The description should provide a reader with a complete, high-level understanding of the use case. Guidelines for writing a conceptual use case description follow.

- Summarize the business goal motivating the use case.
- Describe the purpose of the use case.
- Summarize the major behaviors that occur in the use case (the use case's scope).
- Write no more than several sentences or a paragraph.
- Use the present tense and the active voice.
- Include a final sentence that describes the result of the action.

Use Case: Name of the use case
Actor (s): Names of the actor or actors who interact with the system
Description: Description of the way the actor(s) and system interact and the system responsibilities

FIGURE 7-5   Initial use case template

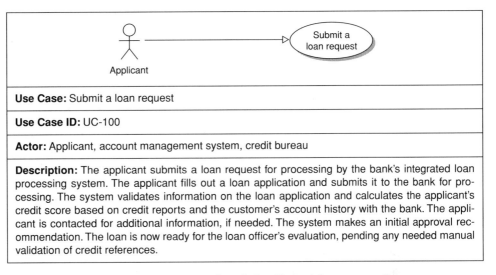

Use Case: Submit a loan request

Use Case ID: UC-100

Actor: Applicant, account management system, credit bureau

Description: The applicant submits a loan request for processing by the bank's integrated loan processing system. The applicant fills out a loan application and submits it to the bank for processing. The system validates information on the loan application and calculates the applicant's credit score based on credit reports and the customer's account history with the bank. The applicant is contacted for additional information, if needed. The system makes an initial approval recommendation. The loan is now ready for the loan officer's evaluation, pending any needed manual validation of credit references.

FIGURE 7-6   Sample initial use case description "Submit loan request"

Figures 7-6 through 7-9 are a set of initial use case descriptions and graphics for the loan management system that provides a high-level understanding of the basic functionality of the loan processing system.

Finally, when identifying and documenting the initial use cases, remember the following:

- Focus on the actor's perspectives by asking what the actor expects from the interaction.
- Make sure the use case is initiated by a business event and is expected to provide value to some actor. If a use case does not provide value to any actor, challenge its existence.

Use Case: Enter validated credit references

Use Case ID: UC-110

Actor: Loan assistant

Description: The loan assistant enters any credit reference information that needs to be validated manually. This information can include such information as external bank accounts and repayment sources (i.e., income) that cannot be validated automatically.

FIGURE 7-7   Sample initial use case description "Enter validated credit references"

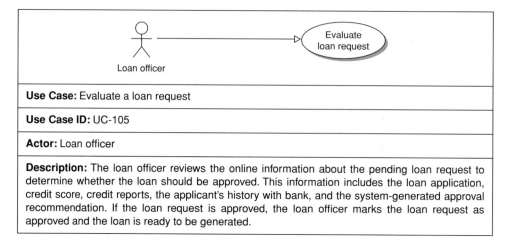

FIGURE 7-8   Sample initial use case description "Evaluate loan request"

- The user should be able to identify the use case as a business event that will occur within the user's role.
- Capture each use case at the same level of granularity.
- When an actor is another system (e.g., a credit reporting or payment gateway), it can be valuable to consider a number of systems so that you can generalize the interactions using abstract actors. This can add to the flexibility of the model.

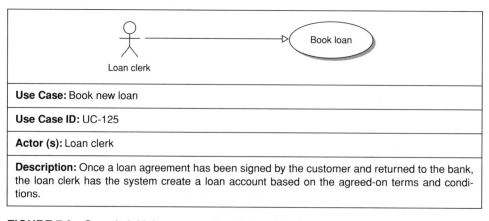

FIGURE 7-9   Sample initial use case description "Book new loan"

- Try to keep design decisions out of the conceptual use case model. A common problem with use case modeling is the baggage associated with preconceived notions of how the system should work. Always ask, "Is this functionality really required, or am I assuming a solution?"
- Don't get bogged down in details, but do validate the use cases and their descriptions with actors and other stakeholders after completing this activity and creating the use case diagram.

Developing Conceptual and Base Use Case Descriptions as One Deliverable

Some organizations combine the modeling of conceptual descriptions with the base use case descriptions, discussed in the next chapter, into one deliverable that they present to the stakeholders. In many cases, it is an easy step to a "basic" base use case description once the conceptual descriptions are complete. A lot depends on the users' involvement and their expectations of the use cases. If users are intimately involved in the project and want regular deliverables to review, conceptual descriptions are the first set of use case descriptions to present to them. Also, if the system is very large, both sets of use cases for the entire system may be impractical to do in one step. However, if the system is smaller, consider combining the conceptual step with base use case description.

Using Workshops to Identify Conceptual Use Case Descriptions

When developing conceptual descriptions, we prefer to generate them in use case modeling workshops involving key users, customers, and analysts. The high-level nature of conceptual use cases facilitates brainstorming and discussion among the team. If the system is very large, consider breaking use cases down into known functional groups and holding individual workshops on each area.

A workshop group should brainstorm and reach consensus on the conceptual use cases, which may be as simple as the use case name and a short sentence or phrase representing its goal. Then, in small teams or as individuals, the group can write the formal conceptual use case descriptions. The group should then come back together as a whole to review and, if needed, rework and regularize the conceptual use cases. If several use case workshops are occurring simultaneously, they should all follow this process.

It is important to have a skilled use case facilitator running the sessions and to have written guidelines that everyone observes. It is also important to provide at least minimum use case training to all participants. We find that beginning the session with an hour or two of formal use case training is a good way to get everyone on the same page and to provide the training at just the right time. For a good generic resource on facilitation, see Schwarz [1994]. It is important that everyone agree on whether the current "what is" situation or the desired "what will be" is being modeled. See the Interesting Issue box below for further discussion on this topic.

INTERESTING ISSUE: USE CASE POINTS OF VIEW

The first thing that we must decide when describing a system using use cases is the point of view we will take. We have two choices in this matter: "what is" or "what will be." Are we attempting to describe an existing process or to describe reengineering that will make the process more efficient? The choice greatly affects how we write the use cases and ultimately how we engineer the system. The choice should be clear from the description of the intended system in the vision document.

To describe "what is," or baseline, we use the **system interaction approach** [Fowler 1997]. With this approach, we describe what the actors do with the system rather than what they want to do with the system. This approach can be used to capture existing processes and describe "legacy" software systems or exact component specifications. The problem with this approach is that it does not encourage innovation, one of the keys to success in this information age. However, there are times when we want to describe "what is" and innovation is not warranted.

To describe "what will be," or target, we use the **system goal approach** [Fowler 1997]. With this approach, we describe what the user wants to do with the system. This is especially important for new systems, such as new or reengineered processes, new software systems, or component systems that drive system architecture. This approach defines the problem to be solved, not an implementation of a solution. It describes "what will be." As a result, it encourages innovation.

Both approaches have merit. We tend to use the system goal approach in most cases, as it describes the problem in a way that gives us maximum solution flexibility. However, we may wish to constrain our solution to a certain field of possibilities. In these cases, the system interaction approach provides these limitations. Combining the two techniques creates hybrid use cases that allow maximum flexibility in some areas and constraint in others.

Hybrid use cases may be dangerous, as they promote an illusion of allowing flexibility. However, the writers of hybrid use cases may be unaware of their assumptions. If you are concerned about unwanted bias entering your use case model, employ someone outside the domain or organization to perform an evaluation of the model. The use of an outsider is a common technique employed in the development of business process models [Hammer 1993].

Initial use case modeling provides a conceptual understanding of the system, its major behaviors, and its primary actors. Use the conceptual use cases to validate with the customer and user that the system analysis is on the right track. A good way to proceed through the development of initial use case modeling is to schedule several days of off-site workshops that include the different stakeholders. Use these workshops to develop drafts of the use case model and object model. The project team can then more formally document the results and validate this information with the stakeholders. After this validation occurs, the project will be ready to proceed with the next set of activities.

Initial Use Case Descriptions and Extreme Programming

Extreme programming is a new approach to developing software that stresses small teams of paired programmers working closely with the customers to develop software quickly and to be able to respond to changing customer requirements during development. Extreme programming utilizes the concept of *user stories* to start to capture user requirements. User stories are somewhat similar to initial use case descriptions; they are typically short (about three to four sentences), informal, and written using the customer's terminology. In an extreme programming approach, each user story should be able to be implemented within one to three weeks. When the story is ready to be implemented, the developers work directly with the customer to gather a more detailed description of the requirements. While there is some similarity between the initial use case descriptions and user stories, there are some critical differences as well. If the reader is interested in extreme programming see Beck [1999] and Jeffries [2000].

Develop Initial Use Case Diagram

A use case diagram provides a visual representation of the participation of the actors in the use case. On a system of any size, there will be multiple use case diagrams. Some may show the relationship between the actors and the system, while others may show the base use cases and their extends, includes, and generalization relations (discussed in Chapter 11). A use case diagram also may focus on clusters of related use cases and show all the relationships the use cases have—includes, extends, generalizations, and actor. Initial use case diagrams are developed concurrently with conceptual use cases and continue to be detailed as the use case modeling evolves. Sample use case diagrams for the loan processing system are presented in Figures 7-10 and 7-11.

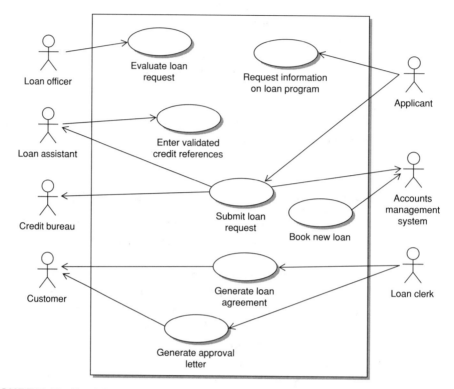

FIGURE 7-10   Partial use case diagram for loan submission use cases in the loan processing system

Determine/Refine the Conceptual Business Objects

The purpose of the "Determine conceptual business objects" activity is to further refine the glossary and to start defining the conceptual relationships between the objects. As discussed in Chapter 4, the system glossary contains objects representing major business entities or events. The glossary includes a description of each object and its conceptual relationships with other objects. Defining entities in the glossary and the relationships between these entities is often called **domain object modeling**.

Object modeling is an activity that continues throughout the development process. As development proceeds, objects that will be realized in the system are discovered and refined. That is, the object model is at different levels of abstraction and completion at various stages of development. Three well-defined levels of object modeling are domain, analysis, and design. The glossary looks at an

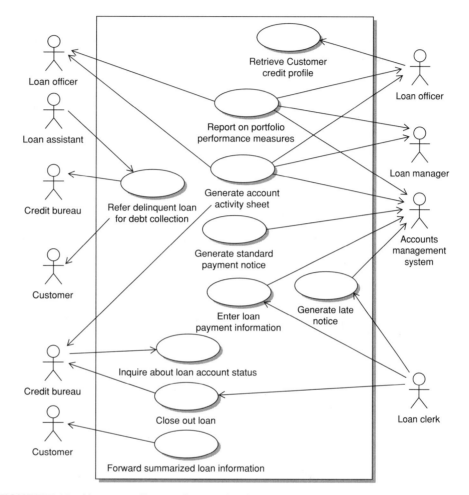

FIGURE 7-11 Use case diagram for ongoing loan management use cases in the loan processing system

object model at the domain level. In other words, the glossary contains definitions of objects that make sense to a business (e.g., loan, application, terms, and so on).

Relationship of Use Cases and the Object Model

The relationship between use cases and object modeling is a strong one. A discussion of use case modeling without including its relationship to corresponding object models would present only a partial picture of the role use cases play during requirements analysis.

Use cases can serve as a validation vehicle for the domain object model by ensuring that all the necessary abstractions have been found. In this capacity, use cases can help identify additional objects and validate existing ones. Use cases can also help control the scope of the object model by clearly identifying the interactions between the system and its environment. When objects are modeled via use cases, they are associated with the event described by the use cases and are therefore traceable to higher-level objectives, functions, and work flows. Modifications to objects can be validated by determining whether the modifications are within the scope of the use cases. Use case and object modeling complement one another and are usually performed as parallel activities.

When discovering the objects at this level of analysis it is effective to apply the following guidelines to each system use case.

- Walk through the use case to identify the objects that participate in it.

- Look for nouns. Many times nouns represent objects, but nouns can be "verbed" and verbs can be "nouned." Also, many nouns in a large document may not be objects or be interesting from a system perspective.

- Ask what products are "produced" by the use case and what the inputs are.

- Ask which actor initiates a event and which other actors participate in the use case.

- Group candidate objects into categories. Categorization techniques can be found in Booch [1994] and Coad [1991].

- Try to brainstorm for "candidate" objects; don't try to eliminate objects too early.

- Look for objects that have different names but are really synonyms and choose a common name for them.

- If an object is ambiguous (does not map cleanly to a business concept), try to map it more cleanly or else eliminate it.

- If the object appears to be atomic—that is, it represents a single simple value—it may be an attribute of another object (e.g., first name or birthdate).

The following is an example set of known categories that typically represent objects, based on several categorization techniques.

- Tangible things   (e.g., car, boat)
- Concepts   (e.g., checking account)
- Events   (e.g., sale, withdrawal)

- Outside organizations (e.g., supplier)
- Roles played   (e.g., customer)
- Other systems   (e.g., admissions system)

Start to document each object with its high-level characteristics and create a business or high-level object model with relationships such as associations, generalization, and aggregation. Although some people like to perform very detailed use case modeling before attempting object modeling, we have found that the object model provides perspective on the system requirements that is difficult to represent in the use case, such as the number of accounts a customer can have. An object model can elegantly represent this fact as an association (with multiplicity) between a bank account object and a customer object. Defining use cases and objects tends to go back and forth; that is, use cases are defined to a level of detail and then objects are found. Next, more details are added to the use case model, and additional objects and details are discovered.

Consistently mapping the use case model to objects as the use case model is being developed helps reduce the risk of functional composition. Object modeling and use case modeling each bring unique strengths and weaknesses to the analysis effort. We like to think of the two as "dancing" with each other throughout the requirements analysis.

Following are three example use case descriptions with candidate objects in boldface type.

Use Case: Submit a loan request
Use Case ID: 100
Actor(s): Applicant, loan clerk
Description: The **applicant** submits a **loan request** for processing by the bank's integrated loan processing system. The applicant fills out a **loan application** and submits it to the bank for processing. The system validates information on the loan application and calculates the applicant's **credit score** based on **credit reports** and the applicant's **account history** with the bank. The applicant is contacted for additional information, if needed. The system makes an **initial approval recommendation**. The loan is now ready for the **loan officer's** evaluation, pending any needed manual validation of **credit references**.

Use Case: Evaluate loan request
Use Case ID: 120

Actor: Loan officer

Description: The **loan officer** reviews the online information about the pending **loan request** to determine if the **loan request** should be approved. This information includes the **loan application, credit score, credit reports**, the **applicant's history** with bank, and the system-generated **approval recommendation**. If the loan request is approved, the loan officer marks the loan request as approved and the **loan** is ready to be generated.

Use Case: Process (Book) a new loan

Use Case ID: UC-150

Actor: Loan clerk

Description: Once a **loan agreement** has been signed by the **customer** and returned to the **bank**, the **loan clerk** has the system create a **loan account** based on the agreed upon **terms and conditions**.

The following selected objects are found in these use cases.

- Customer   (role played)
- Loan application   (tangible thing)
- Loan request   (concept)
- Credit bureau   (outside organization)
- Credit report   (tangible thing)
- Account history   (concept)
- Accounts management system   (other system)
- Credit score   (concept)
- Supporting materials   (tangible thing)
- Loan officer   (role played)
- Loan account   (concept)
- Loan agreement   (tangible thing)
- Loan   (concept)

Packaging and Validating the Use Case Conceptual Model

Following is a sample table of contents for the conceptual use case model.

1. Textual introduction
2. Use case and/or context diagram
3. Actor glossary
4. Conceptual use case descriptions
5. Glossary

Conclusion

The outcome of initial use modeling is the creation of a use case model that captured a high-level conceptual picture of what a system will need to do. During this effort, key or primary behaviors of the system are defined, the major actors are identified, and an initial mapping to high-level business objects is performed.

Part 4

Advanced Use Case Modeling Framework: Expanding the Use Case Model

What's in this part?

This part discusses how initial use case descriptions are expanded with more detail and how the increased complexity is modeled.

As described in the last chapter, the outcome of the initial use case modeling activities is a conceptual picture of the role the system will play in the organization. The conceptual use case model describes the system's major responsibilities and the specific actors (people, other systems, and so on) that the system interacts with. The objective of the conceptual analysis is not to focus on the details of these system requirements but to capture an overall understanding of the system's place in its environment.

So far, the major actors and the use cases they participate in have been identified for the system. The use cases and the business event that triggered them have been documented with short descriptions. Key business objects that are within the scope of the system's responsibilities have been identified.

Conceptually, the overall scope and boundaries of the system are starting to become clear. Key decision makers and users have had an opportunity to review and validate the conceptual use case model and provide input. The specifics of each use case, however, are still unclear and ambiguous. For the purpose of discovering and modeling more specific system requirements, we further refine our understanding of what takes place within each use case.

Since a use case describes the set of transactions that occur based on a business event and provides measurable value to an actor, a single use case can contain multiple requirements. A use case is a story, and the story can involve many specific interactions and system behaviors. Each of these interactions and behaviors needs to be identified, alternatives need to be discovered, and behaviors that are common across multiple use case must be modeled. Following are the activities in the "Expand on the use case model" activity group (Figure P4-1).

- Develop base use case descriptions
- Elaborate the use case's flow of events and other related information
- Model extend, include, and generalization relationships
- Map use cases to object models and other analysis models
- Develop instance scenarios

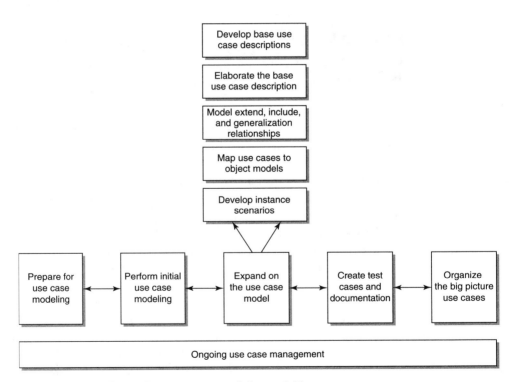

FIGURE P4-1   Expanding use case modeling activities

This activity group is the heart of advanced use case modeling for software systems. Even though the activities in this group are discussed in a specific order, in our experience a tremendous amount of iteration occurs among them. Because these activities are the heart of the use case modeling process framework, each activity is discussed in its own chapter, from Chapter 8 through Chapter 14.

Chapter 8

Develop Base
Use Case Descriptions

What's in this chapter?

This chapter focuses on the definition of base use case representations.

The initial use case diagrams and descriptions provide high-level documentation of the use cases and their relationship to the system. In this activity, the individual use cases are described in more detail. The second level of use case representation is referred to as a **base use case description**. The base use case description identifies the specific behaviors and interactions that take place between the actor and system within the scope of the use case's flow of events. The requirements that are represented in the base use case include the following:

- Specific interactions that take place between the actors and the system during the execution of the use case
- Specific responsibilities of the system within a use case
- Specific responsibilities of the actors within a use case

To discover these details, each initial use case description can be developed into a set of activities that make up a **flow of events**. The flow of events is a description of these activities and order in which they happen when the event that triggers the use case occurs. The flow results in an "end" or postcondition that leaves the system in a specific state. In addition to the flow of events, a base use case description contains supplemental information related to the use case. The primary objectives in developing base use case descriptions follow:

- *Understand the primary interactions between the system and user and the system behaviors that occur as part of the use case.* A single use case can represent multiple interactions with an actor or multiple actors. Each interaction contains or represents requirements of both the system and user. Each interaction can trigger complex system behaviors that need to be understood, modeled, and specified.

- *Document the scope of the use case.* When does one use case end and another begin? What must be true of the state of the system and environment for a use case to be initiated? For a large system there will be many use cases, and each individual use case's role within the system will need to be understood.

- *Start to determine nonbehavioral requirements and assumptions associated with the use case.* A use case naturally describes system behaviors and interactions with actors. However, associated with a use case are other forms of requirements that need to be captured.

- *Document the priority of the use case in the development effort.* It's a good bet that the users and customers will want more than you can provide within the time frame that they will initially specify. The use cases need to be prioritized for development so that the most critical or important system requirements are delivered first.

It is important that these issues are thought out, documented, and then validated with the stakeholders. The system responsibilities will become requirements that the system will need to provide. The interactions that take place will drive the information content that needs to be passed between actors and the system and will highlight the interfaces (e.g., GUI screens and system-to-system interfaces that will need to be built). For each interaction there are other important questions that will need to be defined, including the following.

- How often does the system interaction occur (performance requirement)?
- How many instances of actors will be using the interactions at one time (capacity requirements)?
- What security requirements are associated with the interactions?

To support these objectives, a base use case description needs to provide a complete description of the "normal" or basic set of primary interactions between the actors and the system within the use case. The base use case description continues to use the vocabulary, terms, and activities that are specific and meaningful in the environment or domain in which the system will be built and describes in more detail what occurs when the use case executes. For example, what happens when a customer submits a loan application? How does the loan system respond to this request—what system behaviors are required to service this submission?

Why create base use case descriptions? Why not just start to explore in depth all the alternatives, exceptions, and variations an individual use case can have? The reason has two parts.

First, it takes a great deal of time and effort to document each possible variation and exception. A lot of analysis needs to be performed, and extended discussion with the users and customers needs to occur. This activity will ultimately need to be performed, but now is not the time to get bogged down in the details of all the exceptions and variations that could possibly occur, losing sight of the big picture. Anyone who has been involved in analysis of large systems knows that this can be a concern. That is why in this framework there are separate activities for documenting the basic behaviors and the documenting the exceptions or alternatives. In small-system development, separation of these activities is not so critical, and several can be combined.

Second, as the level of detail of the use case model expands, its understandability to end users and customers can decrease. Concentrating on developing use case descriptions that are detailed, yet still reflect the basic flow, the model, focuses the reviewer's attention on base system behaviors, so they can't get lost in a sea of exceptions. If a use case cannot be successfully reviewed and verified, why bother with the use cases? We return to this topic in Chapter 19 when we discuss the attributes of good use case models.

In the loan management system, we have so far found major actors that interact with the system and captured the key events that trigger the interactions. We have represented these events with the initial use case descriptions "Submit loan request," "Validate loan references," "Evaluate loan request," and "Book new loan." This level of detail provides a high-level conceptual picture of what the system will do. However, we still don't yet understand the specific interactions and responsibilities that occur when a loan is submitted. What does the system do when the loan officer is in the process of evaluating the loan, or what happens when a loan is closed out? The next activity in the use case modeling of the loan system will expand on these short descriptions by fishing out the use case descriptions with detail.

Fields in a Base Use Case Description

The pieces of information captured in a typical base use case description are shown in Figure 8-1, a template for a base use case description. The template in

Use case name:	\<Name of the use case\>
Unique use case ID:	\<Unique identifier for use case\>
Primary actor(s):	\<Names of the primary actor or actors who interact with the system\>
Secondary actor(s):	\<Names of the secondary actor or actors who interact with the system\>
Brief description:	\<Description of the use case\>
Preconditions:	\<State of the system when the use case is triggered\>
Flow of events:	\<Activities and interactions performed when the use case is performed\>
Postconditions:	\<State in which the use case leaves the system in\>
Priority:	\<Relative development priority of the use case\>
Alternative flows and exceptions:	\<Major alternatives or exceptions that may occur within the flow of events\>
Nonbehavioral requirements:	\<Requirements such as performance, security, etc.\>
Assumptions:	\<Any assumptions made\>
Issues:	\<Outstanding issues\>
Source:	\<Meeting, interview, document, etc. the use case derives from\>

FIGURE 8-1   Base use case description template

the figure is based on the use case template defined in the Rational Unified Process (RUP). The template has been modified to include additional information; RUP has been designed to be flexible enough to customize—it is easy to add fields to the template. In any organization or project, don't be afraid to customize templates for your specific needs.

The use case name, primary and secondary actor(s), and brief description have already been captured in the initial use case modeling. The following sections discuss the use of the fields in the template.

Preconditions and Postconditions

It is important to know the scope of a use case's responsibilities and the implications of a complete execution of the use case. When does the use case complete its execution and what are the results of the use case's execution? A use case does not necessarily stand alone; it can represent functionality that is performed within the context of other use cases. Some use cases depend on others, with one use case leaving the system in a state that allows another use case to be able to execute. What other use case(s) is the use case dependent on, and in what state does a use case leave the system? How does a use case fit into the overall use case model? This can be critical to seeing the big picture. For example, in the loan system example, before the "Evaluate loan" use case can take place, the functionality described in "Validate loan reference" must occur. The "Submit loan request" use case leaves the system in the state where a loan request has been validated and is ready for its references to be validated, allowing the use case "Validate loan references" to occur.

The states that define a use case's scope and its place in a larger set of use cases are documented in the use case's preconditions and postconditions fields. **Preconditions** describe the state or status of the system before a use case executes. What must be true in order for the use case to be executed? **Postconditions** describe the status of the system as a result of the use case completing. What is the state of the system after the use case has executed?

Both preconditions and postconditions should be documented at a level of abstraction and with a vocabulary that users can understand. Both conditions should be described with the same level of detail as the use case. If the use case is at a high level, the preconditions and postconditions should also be at a high level. If the use case describes detailed behavior, the preconditions and postconditions should be detailed. For example, if a use case refers to a loan request within its flow of events, then the preconditions and postconditions should be stated at that level of abstraction; if the loan request has been validated, a postcondition might be stated as "The loan request is approved."

It is important to note that preconditions and postconditions apply to the state of the system, not the outside environment. For example, in a use case that models a librarian checking out a book for a borrower, a valid postcondition could be "the book has a status of borrowed"; an invalid postcondition would be "The patron is free to leave the library with the book." For some use cases, such as "Query for book availability," the state of the system remains unchanged.

If they are clearly documented, preconditions and postconditions help define the scope of individual use cases (for example, when the flow of events begins and ends) and identity requirements for the system. A postcondition represents some requirement that must be achieved by the use case. For example, the postcondition of an ATM withdrawal could include "The customer account is debited by [the amount of the withdrawal]. [Firesmith 1999] recommends that each postcondition should be treated as an individual requirement using the traditional "shall" format and be uniquely numbered within the use case model (e.g., "Req 1877—The system shall debit the customer's account by the amount of the withdrawal"). The Firesmith paper, by the way, contains a number of excellent use case modeling guidelines.

Preconditions and postconditions can also help to determine dependencies between use cases. When identifying preconditions and postconditions, remember that they are states that must be true either for the use case to start executing or as a result of a complete use case execution. Some additional guidelines for documenting preconditions and postconditions follow.

- Since preconditions and postconditions can act as requirements, they should be written in a way that allows them to be verifiable and testable.
- A precondition must reflect the state the system needs to be in for the use case to execute.
- Preconditions and postconditions should be written in the present tense.
- Number multiple preconditions or postconditions individually.
- An object model can be used to supplement the description of the system state in preconditions and postconditions

Flow of Events

The flow of events is the "meat" of the base use case. The flow of events in a base use case description describes the basic activities (i.e., behaviors and interactions) that occur during the dialogue between the actors and the use case. The flow of events records the order in which these activities occur, either as a series of steps or as free-flowing text. We prefer steps over free-flowing text in system use cases because this approach helps make use cases easier to follow and modify. The steps can also be easily referenced and mapped into formal requirements documents and other analysis and design artifacts (e.g., system-level transactions, message sequence diagrams, and so on). Note that language here is very important. It should be prose written in user terms, not function call names or tech-speak. Sometimes use case modelers struggle with the right level of formality in the flow of events. For more discussion on this matter, see the Interesting Issue box on page 113.

To develop a flow of events, the activities the actors and the system must perform to satisfy the behavior documented in the initial use case description are determined. For example, in the use case "Submit loan request," ask what interactions are occurring between the actors and the system. What must the system do to respond to these interactions? What measurable value must be provided to the actor? What activities must the system perform when a loan is submitted? Each of

INTERESTING ISSUE: WHAT IS THE BEST LEVEL OF FORMALITY IN A USE CASE?

How formal should the use case be? The use case flow of events can range from free-flowing text to bulleted or numbered steps that may also include conditional and iterative logic. The choice of which method to use will depend on the stakeholders of the use case. The stakeholders form the audience who will read the use cases, so use cases should be targeted at them. The choice may also depend on the domain specified by the use cases. We present three of the more popular textual methods. However, there are many others including some very good formal, nontextual methods [Mitchell 1999]. We recognize that research continues to introduce new ways of describing use cases and that no single method is "best."

- **Prose Approach**. One way of writing the flow of events in a use case is prose. Simply write out in free-flowing text all the paths (both successful and unsuccessful) to the goal that the use case is intended to represent. This style tends to appeal to those writing use cases to model businesses or business processes. It can also be appealing to the software system user community. An advantage of the prose approach is that it yields informal descriptions of the actor's interactions with the system and can be documented quickly. It also tends not to suggest an order or sequence as strongly as a step format. If the step order is unclear or not important, the step format can force the use case into defining an order of execution that does not need to exist or is wrong.

- **Step Approach**. In the step approach, the flow of events is described in an ordered list of the steps. Each step is consecutively numbered and provides a concise description of what happens next. The step approach tends to be less verbose than the prose approach and appeals to software developers.

- **State Approach.** Some domains are most naturally described using state models. The state approach labels each paragraph in the flow of events with a state name. The paragraphs describe the ways to transition out of that state and into a new one. A state transition diagram can augment the use case with a pictorial representation of what is happening. The state approach is excellent for domains that have a lot of nonlinear paths through the use cases—telecommunications systems, for example. Examples of the state approach are presented in Figures 8-2 and Figure 8-3. Important system states are explicit when the state approach is used, whereas they may get buried in the step and prose approaches. States may span use cases (such as a video— on the shelf, reserved, rented) and this should be identified in the flow of events. States are underlined in the use case description to identify them.

The advantage of a more formal description is that the use case clearly specifies the system requirements and points out gaps in the analysis for the user to validate

Continued on next page.

Originate Basic Call

This use case handles responsibilities for the various forms of basic call processing initiated by *customer premise equipment* such as an *ISDN terminal* or *POTS telephone*. A two-party basic call may be broken into a setup and a release phase. The setup phase is designed to establish a call from the time the originating phone begins to collect information to the time the originating and terminating parties are connected. An *active call* is then established. The release phase starts with an active call and proceeds to tear down the elements involved with the connection. The release phase ends with the call at the point the setup phase may begin again. This use case addresses only the setup phase.

Preconditions: The precondition for this use case is that there is provisioned *customer premise equipment* connected to the **switch** and the **switch** is connected to the *telephone network*.

Start of use case: The use case starts with the **switch** in the *NULL* state.

Flow of Events:

Null—When the **switch** receives an indication from the *customer premise equipment* that the originating party (hereafter called the calling party) wishes to place a two-party basic call, the **switch** reacts by creating a **connection** and indicating that it is ready to *collect information*.

Collect information—The **switch** begins to receive the called party's **telephone number** from the *customer premise equipment*. The **telephone number** may be received in the form of individual digits (see "Collect digits" use case) or en bloc. When the **telephone number** is complete, the switch begins to *establish connection*. If the **telephone number** is not complete, the switch continues to *collect information*.

Establish connection—The **switch** passes the **telephone number** to the *telephone network*. . . .

Alerting—The **switch** indicates to the *customer premise equipment* that a **connection** has been. . . .

O Active—The **connection** is now active and the two parties may communicate . . .

Exceptions—The *customer premise equipment* may terminate this process at any . . .

Postconditions: The calling party and the called party may communicate via their . . .

References: The states for this use case were the result of a basic call model analysis by Wakamoton [1995].

FIGURE 8-2   Use case developed using the state approach

---

and/or correct. It also allows the include and extend relationships to be clearly mapped to specific points in the base use case.

For a system of any size we like to start with informal prose use case descriptions and utilize them to elicit more defined requirements from the users. For example, we do a "round" of initial use cases with free-flowing text description,

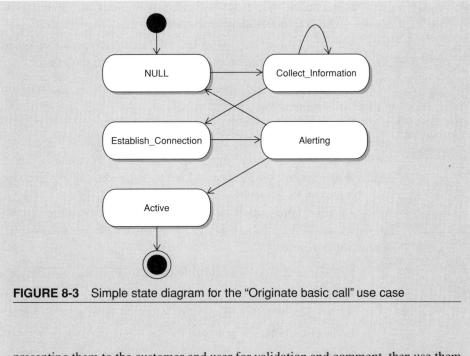

FIGURE 8-3   Simple state diagram for the "Originate basic call" use case

presenting them to the customer and user for validation and comment, then use them as the basis for developing more formal descriptions of the use case interactions. For more perspective on levels of formality in a use case modeling see Cockburn [1997a and 1997b].

these interactions and activities could be documented as follows in a partial flow of events for the "Submit loan request," use case.

1. The applicant completes the online loan application and submits it to the bank via the Internet.

2. In initial preparation for evaluating the loan request:

   2.1. The system validates the information on the loan application, checking that it is correct and as complete as possible. This event includes determining that all mandatory fields are completed and that basic information, such as zip codes, state codes, and account numbers, is correct.

   2.2. The system forwards a request to an external credit bureau for a credit report on the applicant. The request includes the applicant's name, social security number, and current and previous addresses.

2.3. The system retrieves the applicant's account history (if any) from the accounts management system.

2.4. The system calculates the applicant's credit score based on credit reports and the applicants's history with the bank.

When writing the base use case flow of events, focus on defining and modeling the following activities.

Interactions between the Actors and the System. Start with the actor that initiates the flow of events. For example, in "Submit loan request," the applicant actor begins the use case by filling out a loan application. How is this occurring—on the Web, by phone, by paper? By all of the above?

A use case represents multiple transactions between the actors and the system. For example, in the "Submit loan request" use case, we can identify the following interactions.

- Initial interaction—submitting the loan application—between the applicant and the system.
- Interaction between the system and a credit reporting agency.
- Interaction between the system and the bank's accounts management system.
- Confirmation message forwarded by the bank to the applicant that the application has been received and validated, that appropriate material has been gathered, and that the loan request is ready for evaluation by one of the bank's loan officers.

One of the goals of developing base use cases descriptions should be a clear and precise understanding of the user's responsibilities and the system's responsibilities. For the time being, assume that the actors will behave responsibly—that is, they will not input bad data. (Later, when the base use case descriptions are elaborated, consider all the possible exceptions.) It can be difficult to clearly define the actor-system boundary, but as the use case is refined and more details are discovered, the actor-system boundary will become clearer. As the boundary is refined, it is vital to clearly define who is performing or initiating each activity (i.e., the system or the actor), which pieces of an activity are the responsibility of the actor, and which are the responsibility of the system. (Interface analysis is discussed in Chapter 11.)

Key System Behaviors That Are Triggered by the Interactions. Consider whether there are major system responsibilities that need to be performed in response to the interactions. Although these responsibilities may not be visible to the actor, they need to be documented and validated with the customer and users. Use cases are a way of presenting this information to the users within the context of the process in which they take place. But beware: It is very easy to go too far and start a functional decomposition of the system (see the Interesting Issue box on page 120.)

We like to document no more than two or three key system responsibilities for each interaction in the base use case. If there are any issues, concerns, or additional behaviors, document them in the issues field on the template. Note that sometimes responsibilities occur as a result of gathering information from several different interactions. For example, based on the results of several interactions in the "Submit loan request" use case, including submitting a loan application, requesting a credit report and gathering information on the account history with the bank, the system has a responsibility to perform a credit analysis to calculate and create a credit score.

The discovery of system responsibilities may motivate an additional fact-finding effort. Customer and user may need to be reinterviewed or additional requirements workshops may need to be held. The new information captured can also be modeled as part of the object modeling effort and/or documented in formal, traditional software requirements specifications.

Major Manual Activities That Add Context or Understanding to the Use Case. When developing the use case flow of events, do not be afraid to include manual or non-system activities to provide context and enhance comprehension. For example, the statement "User completes the loan application" provides context. However, it is important to clearly define which activities the system performs and which activities are performed by the actors or other entities in the outside environment because a key objective of use case modeling is to outline the scope of the system activities. For example, Figure 8-4 shows the completed base use case for "Submit loan request" where the first activity in the basic flow of events is performed by the actor. Figure 8-5 shows the completed base use for evaluating a loan request by the loan officer. Remember that the goal of system use case modeling is not to model the actor's business or operational environment—that is the objective of business use case modeling; rather, it models the actor's interactions with the system.

Use case name:	Submit loan request
Unique use case ID:	UC100
Primary actor(s):	Applicant
Secondary actor(s):	Loan assistant, credit bureau, accounts management system

FIGURE 8-4   "Submit loan request" base flow of events   *Continued on next page.*

Brief description:	The applicant submits a loan request for processing by the bank's integrated loan processing system. The applicant fills out a loan application and submits it to the bank for processing. The system validates the information on the loan application and the system calculates the applicant's credit score based on credit reports and the customer's account history with the bank. The applicant is contacted for additional information, if needed.
Preconditions:	The applicant has access to a loan request application.

Flow of events:	1. The applicant completes the online loan application and submits it to the bank via the Internet.
	 2. In initial preparation for evaluating the loan request:
	    2.1 The system validates the information on the loan application, checking that it is correct and as complete as possible. This activity includes determining that all mandatory fields are completed and that basic information, such as zip codes, state codes, and account numbers, is correct.
	    2.2. The system forwards a request to an external credit bureau for a credit report on the applicant. The request includes the applicant's name, social security number, and current and previous address.
	    2.3. The system retrieves the applicant's account history (if any) from the accounts management system.
	    2.4. The system calculates the applicant's credit score based on credit reports and the applicant's history with the bank.
	 3. The applicant is informed via e-mail that the loan request has been received, supporting materials are complete, and the loan is in the process of being evaluated.
	 4. The system sets the status of the loan request to "Initial credit check complete."
	 5. The system forwards the loan request to a loan assistant for reference validation activity.

Postconditions:	The loan request is ready to be evaluated.
Priority:	High
Alternative flows and exceptions:	• Based on bank policy, the applicant's credit score is below the acceptable level for further processing, the applicant is so informed by letter, and the loan request is marked as disapproved. • The information on the application is incomplete or incorrect, the application is returned to the applicant for completion, and the loan request process is suspended until the updated application is received. • No external credit information exists for applicant, the loan request is declined, the applicant is notified, and the loan request is marked as disapproved.
Nonbehavioral requirements:	• Only the loan officers and loan clerks of the bank should have access to credit information. • The system should be able to handle 2000 loan requests per day.
Assumptions:	The accounts management system will have current account information on the applicant if the applicant is a customer of the bank.
Issues:	• What are the business rules for calculating a credit score? • What information needs to be on the application to complete the loan request?
Source:	Requirements workshop 123, 5/32/99

FIGURE 8-4 Continued

Use case name:	Evaluate loan request
Unique use case ID:	UC105
Primary actor(s):	Loan officer
Secondary actor(s):	
Brief description:	The loan officer reviews the online information about the pending loan request to determine if the loan should be approved. This information includes the loan application, credit score, credit references, credit reports, and the applicant's history with bank. If the loan request is approved, the loan officer marks the loan request as approved.
Preconditions:	The needed material concerning a pending loan request has been gathered (the loan material has a status of "Initial credit check complete")
Flow of Events:	1. The loan officer asks the system for a set of loan requests that are ready for evaluation. The system presents a list of loan requests for the loan officer's review. The loan officer selects a loan request to review for approval. 2. The system presents the loan information gathered on the customer and the loan application to the loan officer. This information includes • the applicant's credit history (credit report and customer history with bank) • the applicant's calculated credit score 3. The loan officer reviews the material and determines whether the loan should be approved. 4. The loan officer selects the appropriate loan terms and conditions for the loan based on the bank's policy and enters this information into the system. 5. The system changes the status of the loan request to "Approved."
Postconditions:	The loan request is approved (the loan has a status of "Approved").
Alternative flows and exceptions:	• After loan officer review, the applicant's loan request is turned down, the applicant is notified, and the loan request is marked as disapproved. • The loan is referred to the loan committee for their review and evaluation. • Further information needs to be gathered by the loan officer before a decision can be made.
Nonbehavioral requirements:	Only the loan officer or the manager should have access to loan request information and associated material.
	The system should be able to handle 10 loan request reviews by loan officers concurrently.
Assumptions:	N/A
Issues:	N/A
Source:	Interview Minutes memo 123-3

FIGURE 8-5 "Evaluate loan request" base flow of events

INTERESTING ISSUE: BLACK BOX VERSUS WHITE BOX USE CASE DESCRIPTIONS

Should a use case model only the external interactions an actor will have with the system or should it also describe system behavior not visible to the actor? One school of thought advocates describing just the "external" view of the system; another advocates including details on the internal behaviors of the system.

In the **external view approach**, normally just those activities that are directly visible to the external actor are described in the use case. The system is a "black box" that has interactions with the actor, and no description is provided of what the system does to provide or support the interactions. Normally, just the interactions between the system and actors and possibly the manual activities performed by the actors are defined.

For example, if the use case flow of events of an ATM machine providing cash to a customer modeled the customer's interactions with the ATM, the focus would be on the requirements of the customer, such as the request to withdraw cash and deposit funds. Little would be documented on the internal behaviors needed to support this interaction, such as logging the transaction, business rules regarding overdraft limits, and availability of just-deposited funds. In the external approach to use case modeling, the "unseen" system functionality is usually modeled through some other approach, such as object sequence diagrams or static object models.

The rationale for the external view approach is that it allows the analysis to focus on how the actors do their jobs—their interactions with the system—not on the details of system. It also helps to avoid premature design of the system.

The alternative is the **internal view approach**, which includes in use cases some details of the "internal" behaviors of the system (white box). These behaviors are requirements (what, not how) that result from or support the interactions with an external actor. If they are described in the use case flow of events, the use case is "opening the system up"; that is, it is looking inside the system to describe requirements that may not be visible to the actor but are important to the proper execution of the use cases. For example, a use case that looks inside would describe what occurs when a customer withdraws funds: the account is accessed to determine the balance, the funds are debited from the account, the details of the withdrawal—time, amount, and place—are logged, and so on. If this approach is taken, the responsibilities of the system are defined. (It should be made clear that we do not mean that the use case describes implementation, database, or design elements.)

The rationale for the white box approach is that requirements will be missed or will be difficult to validate with the user if the details are not documented in the context of the use case. The proponents of this approach argue that while object modeling is very robust, it can be very daunting to users, many of whom find the use case format much easier to understand and validate.

The advantage of the external view approach is that it focuses on how the actor does the job and how the system fits into the actor's environment to help the actor perform the job. The disadvantage of the approach is that if the use cases are used as the means to understand and document system requirements, the use cases may miss critical requirements, with object modeling not providing the level of understandability needed to elicit and validate the requirements with the user.

The internal view approach captures the key system requirements that are not necessarily visible to the actor and describes them in an easy-to-understand format. The main disadvantage of the internal view approach is that if taken to the extreme, it can result in a functional decomposition of the system.

Selecting an Approach

What is your goal? Is it a high-level analysis of how the actor does the job and how the system fits into it, or is it to understand what the system has to do to successfully complete an interaction with an actor? How knowledgeable is the user about object modeling techniques? Can the user clearly and comprehensively understand object notation and models? Or should more system behaviors be placed in the use case help to elicit, describe, and validate the requirements?

If you choose the external view approach, remember that the use cases will not come close to completely modeling the system requirements. This puts more stress on the understandability and validation of the object models. You may need to provide more formal object modeling training for the users, or more heavily utilize other approaches, such as a text-based software requirements specification (SRS), to validate the analysis results with the user.

If you choose the internal view approach, remember that the use case descriptions could lead to a functional decomposition. Is this what you want? We find that this issue can be mitigated by performing an object analysis in parallel with the use cases. For example, for each level of use case definition (initial, base, elaborated), create object sequence diagrams. This helps to ensure that the behavior in the use case is transformed into an object analysis model. If you are doing extensive use case modeling, do not wait until the use case model is complete to map the use cases to objects. Mapping also has the other benefits: the rigor of developing an object model helps to raise questions about the requirements specified in the use cases, which then can be addressed during the use case modeling effort, not after.

We like to perform a white box use case to document the key internal behaviors of the system that may not be seen by the actor but are key requirements. We have seen too many systems that missed key requirements, because they did not consider the requirements in the use case model. However, we have also seen projects take the white box approach to the point of pseudocode, resulting in a set of use cases that reflect a detailed design, not requirements, as intended. As we progress through the use case modeling process we will return to this issue.

Continued on next page.

Normally, the internal view approach is needed at some point or the developers and testers will not gain significant value from the modeling effort. The external view can be viewed as a complement view; if the system is complex the external view makes it easier for the users to review the use cases.

Approaches that Model Both Black Box and White Box Activities

Several approaches model both black and white activities, while keeping them conceptually separate within the use case model.

Separate Flow of Events Columns for Black Box and White Box Activities

If we want to develop internal behaviors but clearly distinguish between them and the use case responsibilities, an alternate use case flow of events format can be used (abbreviated in the accompanying figure, first proposed by Wirfs-Brock [1993] and also presented in Larman [1998]). This format allows specification of both the user's or external view and the system's behaviors. The two views can be developed and documented in a parallel effort or the user view can be completed first and then the system behaviors completed based on the user behaviors.

Use case: Withdraw funds from an ATM machine

Actor: Customer

Description: A bank customer wishes to withdraw funds from an ATM machine. The customer selects the withdrawal option, the account from which to withdraw the amount, and the amount. The ATM machine interacts with the customer's bank to serve the request.

Flow of events

User view	System view
The customer enters the PIN along with the ATM Card. 　The customer selects the withdrawal option, the account to be withdrawn from, and the amount.	The system validates that the ATM card is active and determines that the PIN is correct for this customer. 　The system, based on the information provided by the customer and the customer's account number, reads the ATM card and determines whether the customer has sufficient funds to make the withdrawal. • The customer account is debited the amount of the withdrawal. • The withdrawal event is logged and includes the time of day, amount of withdrawal, ATM number, and outcome. • The system generates the receipt and dispenses the funds.
The customer receives the funds, a receipt, and the returned ATM card.	The system logs the completion of the event and the ATM is reset for the next customer.

Separate flow of events columns for black box and white box activities

Collaboration Cases

Based on work performed at the Fannie Mae, LeRoy Mattingly and Harsha Rao have presented another approach to address the problem of black box versus white box use case modeling [Mattingly 1998]. In their approach, the use case proper provides only the black box view on the system interactions. The internal behaviors that are triggered in response to a specific interaction are modeled separately using a concept called a *collaboration case* (not to be confused with collaborations as defined in UML). A collaboration case is a separate, use case–like description used to document the details of internal system interaction (the white box details). Collaboration cases are a stereotype of the UML use case concept.

A collaboration case is a text description of the behaviors that occur within the system to accomplish a single task in response to an interaction with the external environment. A collaboration case has similar structure to a use case—it has a purpose (goals), flow of events, and alternate flows. During the use case's flow of events, when an interaction occurs with the actor, a collaboration case is invoked that executes the internal behaviors. A collaboration case is typically linked to one or more use cases and the collaboration case name is referenced in the use case flow of events (see Figure 8-6).

In our experience, collaboration cases provide the following benefits:

- Separation of the internal complex details from the interface of the system
- Improved maintenance of the use case model, since the internal behavior can change independent of the interface. With collaboration cases, the external and internal behaviors are not as strongly coupled as they would be if both interactions and internal behaviors were placed in the same flow of events.

In the Mattingly and Rao paper, design-specific information was also included in the collaboration case examples. We refer the reader to that paper for more details on this interesting approach.

Use case: Withdraw funds from an ATM machine	Collaboration case: Validate customer	Collaboration case: Perform withdrawal transaction
Flow of events (partial) 1 The customer enters the PIN along with the ATM card (see "Collaboration case: Validate customer"). 2 The customer selects the withdrawal option, the account to be withdrawn from, and the amount (see "Collaboration case: Perform withdrawal transaction"). etc. . . .	Flow of events 1 The system validates that the ATM card is active. 2 The system determines that the PIN is correct for this customer.	Flow of events 1 The system, based on the information provided by the customer and the customer's account number, reads the ATM card and determines whether the customer has sufficient funds to make the withdrawal. 2 The system debits the customer account the amount of the withdrawal. 3 The system logs the withdrawal event, including the time of day, amount of withdrawal, ATM machine number, and outcome.

FIGURE 8-6   Base use case and collaboration cases

Guidelines for Developing Flow of Events

When developing the base use case flow of events, keep in mind the following guidelines.

Use numbers or bullets to delineate activities. If there is a natural order to the activity outlined in the flow of events, number each activity. If there are subsets, use lower-level numbering, such as 2.1, 2.2. If there is no explicit order, or if several steps can occur at once, use bullet points or repeat the same number. The description of each activity can vary in length from a sentence or two to several short paragraphs.

Keep the use case flow of events understandable. The base use case should tell a story, and complete, descriptive sentences should be used to convey the actions that occur. To assist in understanding the flow, use the active voice. For example, "Applicant fills out a loan application and submits it to the bank" is more understandable and provides better context than "Loan application is submitted."

Avoid getting bogged down in too much detail. Do not document every detail of the system at this time, and keep each use case at the same approximate level of detail. More details are documented when the use cases are elaborated, as well as during the object modeling efforts.

For now, avoid documenting exceptions or conditional logic unless they are necessary for a conceptual understanding of the use case behavior. Exceptions, alternatives, and extensions will be addressed with alternative flows, extend relationships, and use case instances described in Chapters 9, 10, and 13. When modeling the flow of events, keep in mind the postcondition or end result of the use.

Look for additional actors. As the use case flow of events is detailed, other actors, such as those that interact with the system to provide some service or value to the primary actor or those that receive some information from the system as a result of the use case, will become clearer. These actors may be external entities that help support system responsibilities. For example, in the base use case flow of events for "Submit a loan request," the need to capture a credit report on the applicant is defined. Can the system itself generate the report? No, since it does not contain that information. Since it can't, it needs to be served by another actor, in this example, a credit bureau. The credit bureau will then collaborate with the loan system to provide the service. Add new actors and update the descriptions of existing actors (if needed) with this new information.

The requirements surrounding the system's interfaces with all the actors are often not clearly understood until late in the development process. This late "discovery" of interfaces can cause significant delays in the implementation of the system. Think through this issue early; it will help drive the system architecture.

Watch the length of the flow of events. How long should a use case be? There is no industry standard for the length of an individual use case. Some practitioners favor few but very long use cases, with the flow of events possibly running five or more pages, while others prefer more numerous but shorter use cases. In our experience, to maintain understandability and to manage the complexity of the flow of events, the flow of events should normally not exceed one or two pages. Use cases can be very hard to read and follow if they exceed several pages. Readers get lost in the detail, losing the focus of what the use case is attempting to describe. And, just like other models, the larger and more monolithic use cases become, the harder they are to maintain as the system requirements evolve. It also can be more difficult to map a very long use case to object sequence diagrams. Finally, it is also harder to partition the use case model for iterative or incremental development.

However, shorter, more fine-grained use cases mean a lot of use cases, perhaps hundreds of use cases, instead of dozens of longer, more detailed ones. The use cases must then be grouped by functionality and/or together by their preconditions and postconditions. (Use case model organization techniques are discussed in detail in Chapter 15.) There will also be a need to utilize include, extend, and generalization relationships to structure the use case model.

Whichever approach you take, expect a small number of use cases to naturally fall outside the norm in terms of length. No matter how you decide to structure the length of your use cases, each use case must represent a complete story; that is, it should address the actor's objective or goal in initiating it and should leave the system in a stable state.

Have guidelines in place for modeling the flow of events. However you decide to approach the structure of the use cases, you should have organization standards/ guidelines in place. If the user, customer, and other stakeholders cannot follow, understand, and validate the use cases, there is no point in having them.

Some interesting tips on writing a use case's flow of events are discussed in Jaaksi [1998]. Some of the tips follow.

- A use case flow of events is like a play: the actors must be enabled to "act" in the play by reading the manuscript (use case). If the use case provides the actor with too much freedom, the unpredictable can occur, resulting in ambiguous requirements that can be interpreted in different ways by different stakeholders.

- A use case must be active and clear about what it represents so that everyone who reads it is clear about what it means. Use cases should be written so that customers can sign off on them and use them as a contract. A use case should be written to motivate design and implement testing.

Use Case Priority

In a large development effort, when there is iterative or incremental development of the system or scope needs to be controlled and monitored, the establishment of priority relationships between the use cases is essential. The functionality in some use cases may be more important or critical than that in other use cases. Use case priorities document for each use case its development priority in relationship to the other use cases, and in which iteration or increment it will be developed. Priority is based in part on what the user's priorities are, in part on which use cases need to be developed so that other use cases can be developed. Prioritization normally begins during the initial use case modeling and is revisited and formalized in the base use cases. Priority can be described using such techniques as a straight numerical ranking or the grouping of use cases into priority categories such as high, medium, and low.

Alternative Flows and Exceptions

Although this is not the time to perform detailed modeling of exceptions and alternatives, start to discover and list any major alternatives or exceptions that may occur in a use case flow of events. Quickly document them with a descriptive name and a short description, if needed, so that they are not lost and can be returned to later for more analysis and elaboration. We discuss expanding the major alternatives into alternative flow descriptions in Chapter 9.

Assumptions

In the process of developing use cases, information arises that doesn't fit in any of the predefined fields in the use case template. Use the assumptions field to document important miscellaneous use case issues such as the following.

- Assumptions made about the use case's scope
- Expectations about information available via external servers
- Development issues surrounding the use case, such as the level of effort needed to develop the use case, time frames, and so on

If specific categories of concerns seem to be growing in number as the use case model is developed or are of critical importance to your project, create a new field for them within the use case template and move the already documented assumptions to that field.

Guidelines for writing assumptions include the following.

- Assumptions should be in the present tense.
- Assumptions should be individually numbered.

- Assumptions should not document the state of the system needed to start the use case. Do not confuse preconditions and postconditions with assumptions.

Issues

As the use case is developed, issues will be raised and questions asked. Although some issues will or can be resolved right away, many will either have to be investigated or held until a more pertinent later stage of analysis or design. Don't ignore issues; rather, document them briefly so that they are not forgotten and can be answered at the appropriate time. Sometimes this list is referred to as a "parking lot" where issues can be set aside and picked up later. Following are some guidelines on issues.

- The description of each issue should clearly define the challenge.
- Each issue should be numbered and annotated with priorities or criticality.
- Each issue should be annotated with who is responsible and the date or development phase at which the issue should be addressed.

Source(s)

What is the source of the information from which the use case was derived? Did it come from a requirements workshop, an interview with a customer, or a training manual? Make sure that information that comes from specific stakeholders is referenced explicitly. Traceability is the key. Without traceability, there is no explicit way to validate how or why a use case exists.

Getting Started Creating Base Use Case Descriptions

To develop base use case descriptions, expand and develop each initial use case description with a flow of events, preconditions and postconditions, and, if appropriate, additional actors, and so on (Figure 8-7). A base use case description is usually just a matter of adding more details to the initial use case description. However, as more is understood about the requirements, multiple base use cases may be discovered in the details of a single use case. If an iterative approach to system development is being taken, concentrate on use cases that will be developed in the first iterations.

In moving from an initial level of use case description to the base level of description, we have found that it is efficient to break the use case development team into small working groups. Each working group is responsible for expanding

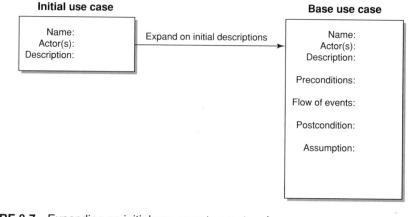

FIGURE 8-7   Expanding an initial use case to create a base use case

a subset of the initial use case descriptions. Ideally, each working group should have one or two use case modelers, and it should have direct access to domain experts, customers, users, and system architects. For example, the "Book a loan" use case base description should be based on specific information from a domain expert or the loan clerks who do the actual booking, and the "Report on loan port-folio performance measures" description should involve input from the loan man-agers, bank policy documentation, and the senior bank executives. The subgroups then reconvene with drafts of their base use case descriptions and walk through them with the entire group.

Before the meeting, the draft base use case descriptions should be available for review by the rest of the team, for example, on a Web site. The rest of the team should review the use cases before the meeting. Plan on reworking the use case model based on the outcome of the meeting, if needed, to make sure that the use cases are on the same level of abstraction (i.e., level of detail), use consistent terms for the same things, and follow the same guidelines. Walking through the use cases with the group will print out the areas that need reworking.

The expansion of the initial use case descriptions normally results in the dis-covery of more actors and additional requirements. Detailed questions will be raised about the particulars of the system behaviors. This is a natural analysis pro-gression, and it is better to answer questions about what the system will have to do now rather than after the system code has been written. For more discussion on documentation, the use case flow of events, see the Interesting Issue box on page 129. Also, don't be afraid to record something as an issue and move on while the issue is being resolved.

INTERESTING ISSUE: WRITING THE USE CASE FLOW OF EVENTS

One of the hardest things to do when writing a use case is to start writing the flow of events. It looks deceptively easy, yet it can be very difficult. Where do we start? In the last chapter, we mentioned that an actor initiates a use case with an event that sets the use case in motion. So how do we describe this trigger in our flow of events? The answer, of course, depends on the style of the use case.

With the step approach, getting started is easy. Simply write the number "1" in the flow of events and describe the trigger that starts the use case. For example,

1. The *calling party* takes the **phone** off the hook.

Make sure that the trigger is unique for each use case. Otherwise the use case may seem to be initiated by a single ambiguous event. For example,

1. The *customer* enters the **video store.**

This event may signal a video rental, return, new membership, or a whole host of other possible goals. (We're assuming that we are not counting people who enter the store to determine some sort of metric information.) Ask yourself if the event definitively signals the beginning of the use case based on the use case name.

Getting started with the prose approach is also easy. Use case writers using this approach often start the flow of events with the phrase, "The use case starts when . . ." For example,

1. The use case starts when the *calling party* takes the **phone** off the hook.

Many of the same rules regarding ambiguity in the step approach apply equally to the prose approach. Many like to start with the step approach to quickly outline the use case, then flex it out in prose, just as they would produce any kind of report, article, or book—first do the synopsis, then fill in the details.

The state approach can be more confusing. While many systems that can naturally be modeled using states have an obvious initial state, others do not. However, we have to start somewhere. If you are having difficulty naming the initial state, try "Initial." If you find a better name (or one exists), you can always change it later. If your domain has a name for the initial state of your use case, use that. For example,

1. *Initial State:* The *calling party* takes the **phone** off the hook.

Finding New Use Cases

As the base use case effort progresses and questions concerning system behaviors are addressed, new use cases are likely to be found. New use cases can be discovered by finding completely new functionality (discovering a new system behavior not related to any of the existing use cases) and by dividing an existing use case into two or more new use cases. Use cases can be divided either vertically or horizontally.

Vertical Division

A single use case should be divided into multiple use cases if major parallel or alternative processes are discovered in the use case's flow of events. These are typically driven by different types of inputs or a different type of actor (e.g., the type of loan, whether the customer is a business or an individual). For example, if you discover two large parallel flows in your base use case that both seem to be "basic," consider creating two use cases, one to reflect each flow (Figure 8-8). For example, as the details of submitting a loan request become clear, the significant differences between a business loan and a consumer loan become clear. In this case, you would "vertical partition" the use case "Submit loan request" into two new use cases: "Submit business loan request" and "Submit consumer loan request." This type of division will become clearer as the use case model is expanded and will continue

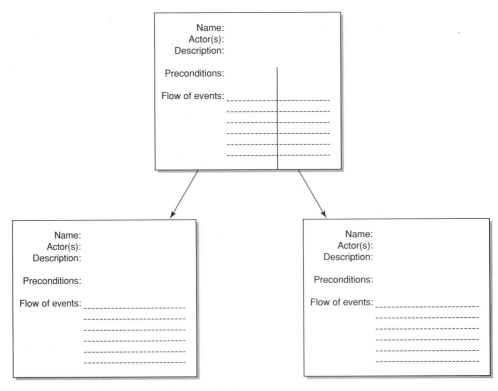

FIGURE 8-8   Use case divided vertically

throughout the use case modeling process. Vertical division can also be done through generalization relationships (Chapter 9).

Horizontal Division

Sometimes a single use case represents a long sequence of behaviors involving many actors. Under these circumstances, it is possible that two use cases are occurring sequentially in the one flow. For example, initially it might seem reasonable to model the entire loan process, from loan request submission to the dispensation of loan funds to the customer, as a single use case with one long flow of events. However, as the flow of events is elaborated, a number of actors are identified that are participating and receiving measurable value.

If a number of actors are receiving value from the system, review the use case and ask the following questions.

- Are two or more business processes being modeled in the use case?
- Are two or more actors participating in the use case?
- Are the sections of the use case separated by time or other actions?
- Would two or more use cases be more understandable to the stakeholders?
- Is the flow of events becoming too long?

If the answers are yes, consider dividing the use case horizontally (Figure 8-9). Create a new postcondition for the first use case and a precondition for the second use case (make sure they match up) and update the existing use case modeling documentation (initial use case, actor glossary, and so on). In addition, the use case flow of events can be divided into multiple use cases. However, be aware that a system use case is a sequence of transactions, not just one. Don't break the use cases down to the point that they are modeling just single interactions or screen inputs with the system, such as entering the amount of a checking account withdrawal.

The need to divide a use case horizontally is rare if the business use cases are done beforehand because each system use case neatly supports each step in the business use case. So the business use cases are the natural guide for the scope of the system use cases. (*Note*: If there is a need to tie the resulting use cases together, see Chapter 16 for information on dependency streams and business function packages.)

Watch for Use Cases that Have To Be Completed by a Certain Time or Date

Sometimes a use case requires execution by a certain time or date. For example, the use case representing the creation of a daily report on loan approvals requires that the report be generated and ready for review at the start of the business day. In

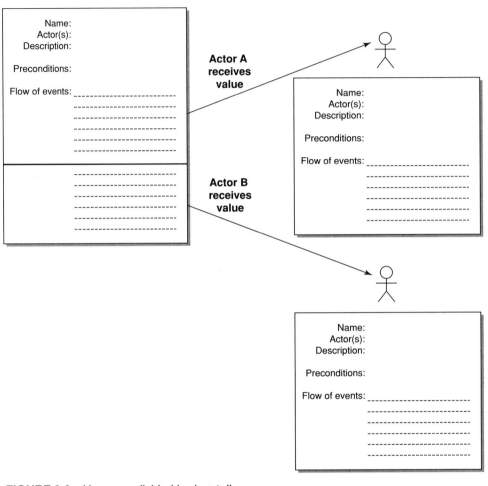

FIGURE 8-9   Use case divided horizontally

another example, in the "Generate standard payment notice" use case, there could be a requirement to follow a billing cycle that completes at a specific time on a specific day of the month. A time requirement is normally stated in the use case description or nonbehavioral requirements section. While it may not be necessary during use case analysis to specify the time a use case should be completed, recording time-based requirements is important. For example, in the use case "Generate loan approvals report," the specific time of the use case may be a design decision, but the fact that the business user needs the report daily is a business requirement motivated by the bank's loan policy, and is a requirement that needs to be captured in the use cases. Note that this requirement mandates when the use case must complete, not when it must start.

In completion requirements, there may not be a requirement that an actor actually initiate the reporting or the billing generation cycles. Or, there may be an explicit requirement that the system initiate the behaviors automatically without user intervention. While an actor obviously has to schedule or set the billing and reporting cycle, once this is complete, the use case executes based on the passage of time without human intervention.

We have seen use case efforts where the use case modelers represented the system itself as an actor. That is, based on a passage of time set up by an actor in another use case, the system initiates the use case. We personally have found that this exception to the rule of actors being external to the system is beneficial in these situations (as long as the intent of this "internal actor" was clearly documented). However, given the generally accepted practice of representing external entities only as actors, a reader unaware of the intent will be confused. If it is an "initiating" actor that is desired, then the use case flow of events can be written to include the behaviors in setting up the time-based cycle and the actual behaviors in the cycle itself. For example, an actor that sets up the report and its execution can be documented this way:

1. A user requests to schedule a report.
2. The system prompts for schedule information.
3. The user enters the time for executing the report and the system stores the request.
4. When the scheduled time is reached, the system starts the requested report.

Some may consider the foregoing to be two separate use cases: setting up a report schedule and generating a report. Whatever style you use in representing use cases, make sure to be consistent and to document your approach. It is important not to forget to consider time completion requirements.

Try to Keep Your Use Cases Concise

When writing a use case there are two things to keep in mind. First, the use case must tell a story and mean something to its readers from beginning to end. The use case must also be complete; there cannot be any holes in the logic.

Second, to ensure that the use case is concise, test each line to ensure that it moves your understanding forward [Cockburn 1997a]. Can we get more information while retaining readability by combining lines or using better words? Keeping the use case concise makes it more likely to be read by its stakeholders. Remember, describing a large or complex system usually requires many use cases.

Creating concise use cases helps to prevent a well-documented problem called use case explosion [Hansen 1995]. One project that experienced use case explosion generated enough use cases to "bury" the engineering group that was supposed to create a new system. Of course, nobody read the entire set—to do so might have taken more time than was allocated to complete the entire project! Besides, all of the information contained in the use cases was contained in another, smaller document. This engineering group chose the logical course—to ignore the use cases.

Circulate the Base Use Case Descriptions for Review by the Stakeholders

After the base use cases are completed, they should be circulated to the other stockholders for review and feedback. It is important to manage the stake-holders'expectations of the level of detail in the base use case descriptions. If you make a formal deliverable out of the base use case descriptions, the users and customers need to understand that this is not the end of the use case modeling effort. Rather, it is way station or checkpoint to make sure that all stakeholders are headed in the same direction. The final validation of the use case model will come later.

In many efforts, the initial use case description and the base use case description are documented in one activity, rather than two separate ones. This is a matter of style, based on such factors as the availability of the key stakeholders (domain experts, users, size of effort, and so on).

Conclusion

The outcome of the base use case activity is a set of base use case descriptions that are a expansion of the initial use case description: the description of each use case is expanded and more detail is added. During this activity new actors may be found and new use cases discovered, along with new system behaviors and requirements. Almost certainly, more questions will need to be addressed with the customer and users of the system, but the ideal and basic requirements of the system are becoming clear.

Chapter 9

Elaborate the Base Use Case Description

What's in this chapter?

This chapter discusses the practice of creating alternative flow descriptions and placing conditional logic in a use case's flow of events.

In the previous chapter we focused on describing the ideal behaviors of a use case in a base use case description. We now discuss techniques for expanding the base use case descriptions:

- Describing alternative flows, which list the flow of events that occurs when an alternative or exception occurs in the use case

- Using conditional logic directly in the flow of events to document exception and alternative processing that occurs during the flow of events

We refer to a use case description that has been expanded in this manner as an **elaborated use case description**.

As discussed in Chapter 8, base use cases typically avoid detailed descriptions of alternative flows and conditional/iterative logic (if-then and while logic). Although this makes sense early in the modeling of the use case, as more elaborated functionality is discovered and documented in the use case model, alternative flows and conditional logic can be a useful approach for capturing the added complexity.

As more information is gathered about the requirements the use case is modeling, a number of choices must be made about how the information will be represented. This chapter first discusses alternative flow descriptions and then describes the practice of placing conditional and iterative logic in a use case's flow of events. It presents two formats for modeling these concepts: text written directly in the use case template and UML activity diagrams.

Describing Alternative Flows

Normally a large number of possible variations, alternatives, and exceptions can occur when a use case is executed. What behaviors will occur if the borrower's credit is bad? What if a customer attempts to withdraw funds from an ATM machine and the customer's account does not have sufficient funds?

Alternative Flow Descriptions

Since these alternatives and variations can represent significant functionality, it is necessary to think through the implications of the alternatives and document them as part of the use case description. One approach to documenting alternatives is through the use of alternative flow descriptions. An alternative flow description documents the specific behaviors that will occur if an alternative or variation from the base flow of events occurs. An alternative can include such things as a different processing option based on user input, a decision taken within the use case flow of events, or an exception condition that results in a different set of behaviors executing.

Alternative flows can be documented quickly and briefly in the base use case description (as discussed in Chapter 8) or, if the details are viewed as representing important requirements, they can be written in separate description templates (Figure 9-1). Remember, however, that alternative flow descriptions are part of the use case, not separate use cases. A sample template for an alternative flow description is presented in Figure 9-2.

An alternative flow description can have many of the same fields as the base use case description. Included in the alternative flow also is a new field that documents its **insertion point** in the base flow of events (where it starts its execution). Although the template contains a number field, it may not be necessary to document simple alternatives in great detail; the key behaviors that will occur and the point in the base flow of events that they will be executed may be enough. An example flow description for the alternative of disapproving a loan request in the "Evaluate loan request" use case is shown in Figure 9-3.

Not all alternatives or exceptions need to be represented with separate alternative flow descriptions. In many cases, it is sufficient to document them in the alter-

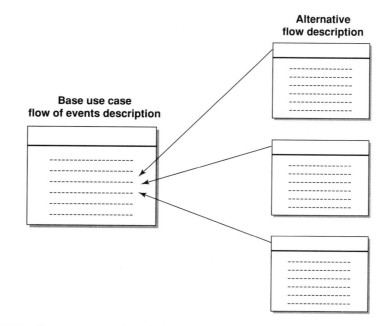

FIGURE 9-1   Base use case description and alternative flow descriptions

native flow section of the base use case description. However, for alternatives that need to be explored in more detail, alternative flow descriptions can be useful. We normally model only the major alternatives to the ideal flow with alternative flow descriptions. If an alternative has requirements that are unclear, unknown, or highly likely to be misunderstood if they are not explored and documented, consider writing an alternative flow description for them.

Adding Alternative Flow Details Directly to the Base Use Case Flow of Events

As an alternative to an alternative flow description, details about the alternative flow can be added directly to the use case flow of events. The advantages include the following.

- By representing the more detailed behaviors in the use case's flow of events, the stakeholder has only one place to look to validate the use case's requirements.

- In-case descriptions are useful for representing situations where there is not really a primary flow and variation but where there are several subflows

Alternative Name:	<Name of use case>
ID:	<Unique identifier for use case>
Actor(s):	<Names of the actor or actors who interact with the system as a result of this alternative flow>
Brief description:	<Description of the alternative flow>
Insertion point	<Point in the base flow of events at which the alternative flow executes>
Preconditions:	<State of the system when the use case is triggered>
Alternative flow of events	<Activities and interactions performed when the use case is performed>
Postconditions:	<State in which the use case leaves the system>
Priority:	<Relative development priority of this use case>
Nonbehavioral requirements:	<Performance, security, etc.>
Assumptions:	<Any assumptions made>
Issues:	<Outstanding issues concerning>
Source:	<Meeting, interview, document, etc., from which this use case is derived>

FIGURE 9-2   Alternative flow description template

within the flow of events that are considered (at least by the customers and users) to be relatively equal in importance.

- Small exceptions or variations that do not warrant a alternative flow description can be captured.

Text-Based Conditional and Iterative Logic in the Flow of Events

Conditional logic can be added directly to the flow of events text to represent the different results that are possible when determining an applicant's account standing. In Figure 9-4, conditional logic has been added to the "Evaluate loan request" use case reflecting alternative processing and exception conditions: The elaborated detail describes what happens if the customer does not have good credit. (Note that the conditional logic could have been represented as an alternative flow.)

Alternative name:	Disapprove a loan request
ID:	UC130-A1
Actor(s):	Loan officer, loan assistant
Brief description:	After loan officer review, the applicant's loan request is turned down, the applicant is notified, and the loan request is marked as disapproved.
Insertion point	Step 3, the loan officer reviews the loan requests.
Preconditions:	A loan request is marked as disapproved.
Alternative flow of events	1. The loan officer enters the disapproval and the reasons for the disapproval into the system. 2. The system generates a letter to the applicant stating that the loan request has been declined and the reasons for the decline. The system also includes in the letter the name and contact information of the credit bureaus from which the credit information was obtained. 3. Electronic copies of the letter are forwarded to the loan officer and the loan assistant and a copy is archived in the system. 4. The status of the loan request is set to be disapproved by the system and all processing on the loan request is stopped. 5. The loan assistant mails the letter to the applicant (manual).
Postconditions:	Loan request is disapproved.
Priority:	High
Nonbehavioral requirements:	• The loan disapproval letter should be generated within 1 hour of a disapproval decision. • The information on the loan disapproval should be available only to the responsible loan officer and loan assistant and to their direct management.
Assumptions:	N/A
Issues:	N/A
Source:	Meeting memo 7865

FIGURE 9-3   Alternative flow description: Disapprove loan request

The use of conditional logic tends to highlight use cases that when described at the conceptual or base level of description seem to represent a set of broad behaviors, but that when elaborated really represent two or more use cases. For example, a single base description might describe the event of submitting a loan request. Then, when the details and conditional logic of the use case are refined, it might become clear that processing loan requests from individuals may be very

Use case name:	Evaluate loan request
Unique use case ID:	UC105
Primary actor(s):	Loan officer
Secondary actor(s):	Applicant
Brief description:	The loan officer reviews the online information about the pending loan request to determine if the loan should be approved. This information includes the loan application, credit score, credit reports, and the applicant's history with bank. If the loan request is approved, the loan officer marks the loan request as approved.
Trigger:	N/A
Preconditions:	The needed material concerning a pending loan request has been gathered (the loan material has a status of "Ready for Evaluation").

Flow of events:	1. The loan officer selects a loan request for evaluation.
	
	2. The system provides the loan officer the information gathered on the applicant's loan request to the loan officer. The loan officer reviews the material for completeness. This information includes:
	  • Loan application
	  • Validated references, such as external bank accounts and repayment sources
	  • Applicant's external credit history (credit report and customer history with bank)
	  • Calculated credit score
	  • Type of loan requested and initial automated recommendation
	
	If further information is needed from the applicant
	
	3. The loan officer enters the request for the needed information into the system, the system generates a letter to the applicant and forwards a message to the applicant via e-mail asking for the missing information. The loan request status is set to "Suspended pending additional information." **Otherwise** the loan officer evaluates the completed loan request for acceptability and adherence to bank policy.
	
	4. **If** the applicant credit status is **acceptable**, the loan is approved. The loan officer determines the appropriate terms of the loans, using suggested loan terms generated by the system. Based on the loan officer's experience and any extenuating circumstances, the loan officer can modify the suggested loan terms, making any needed changes to the loan terms. The status of loan is set to "Approved."

FIGURE 9-4   Conditional logic in the "Evaluate loan request" use case

Flow of events (continued):	**If** the applicant credit status is **not acceptable**, the loan is disapproved. The loan officer outlines and enters the reasons into the system, and the system then generates a letter to the applicant and forwards a message to the customer via e-mail. The status of request is set to "Disapproved."
	If the applicant credit status is **marginal** or the amount of request is outside the bank's loan policy, the loan officer can forward the loan request and related online information to loan committee members for their review and recommendations (see the use case, "Refer loan request to loan committee").
Postconditions:	The loan request has been evaluated (the loan request has a status of either approved, disapproved, or on hold).
Alternative flows and exceptions:	None
Nonbehavioral requirements:	• Only a loan officer or manager should have access to loan request information and associated material. • The system should be able to handle 10 loan officers reviewing loan requests concurrently.
Assumptions:	
Issues:	
Source:	JAD meeting minutes memo 123-3

FIGURE 9-4   Continued

different from processing those of businesses. Different materials need to be submitted with a business loan request, such as financial statements, business plans, market analysis, and so on, which are not required in the case of individuals.

Conditional logic and alternative flows obviously both overlap and diverge in the concepts they attempt to model. In the case of a loan request, a generalization relationship is created by splitting the use case into at least two use cases—"Submit business loan request" and "Submit consumer loan request"—each of which details the unique behaviors associated with the different type of applicant. In fact, one of the advantages of refining a use case flow of events with more details and conditional logic is to identify generalization relationships that would not have been clear without the added level of detail. If the use case is split, remember to update the list of actors to reflect two new actors: the business applicant and the individual applicant. In this instance, the conditional logic that highlighted the differences goes away as two specific and linear use cases are created.

When should you use conditional logic and when should you use alternative flow descriptions? We like to use the following heuristics.

- If the alternative/extension is very complex and long, use an alternative description, since it will clutter up the flow of events if it is placed in the base use case.
- If the variation or exception is very important for the user's understanding and validation of the main flow of events, then use conditional logic.
- If the alternative is short or will occur frequently when the use case is executed, use conditional logic or simply list it in the exceptions section of the use case.
- If multiple paths course through the flow of events and no one path is considered primary or more basic than the others, use conditional logic. However, this condition should raise a red flag, as it may indicate that the use case needs to be split into two or more use cases.
- If the alternatives have different development priorities, then use alternative flows so that each one can be annotated with its relative priority.

This elaboration should be done to help validation efforts. Elaboration should never confuse or obfuscate the issues. This goal will help greatly in avoiding the detailed flowchart-style exposition that sometimes causes a use case to look like a technical design.

In a use case modeling effort, conditional logic, alternative flows and extend relationships can complement each other. Use them when appropriate, and don't be afraid to experiment to see which gives the best results, based on the context in which they are being used.

Iteration in the Use Case's Flow of Events

Sometimes when a use case flow of events is executed, a single activity or group of activities is repeated multiple times. In these cases, it is useful to represent iteration directly in the use case's flow of events. For example, in the use case "Generate loan approval report," a report is generated to summarize the amount of money approved in new loans. The system needs to gather information from each newly approved loan and calculate the total amount of all loans. This behavior could be represented as an iteration over a set of loans to gather the necessary information.

Iteration can be documented either informally or formally. Informally, a statement could be added to the flow of events: "Add and total the amounts of individual loans to calculate the total outstanding loan portfolio." Alternatively, while or repeat loops can be added directly to the use case's flow of events. More formal looping structures are useful when more than one activity is involved. However, remember your users: iteration can be very hard to follow and understand.

If your use case has a large amount of iteration, or if the entire use case seems to iterate—i.e., the flow of events begins with an iteration statement and ends with its closure—ask if the use case can be represented singularly. A use case such as "Generate standard payment notices," which has to cycle through the loan customers and generate and print out monthly bills, might be better represented as "Generate standard payment notice," with the description section of the use case documenting the fact that it needs to do this for all loan customers every month.

Applying Conditional Logic to Use Cases

When developing elaborated use case descriptions, be sure to keep the descriptions and logic at a manageable level of detail. The objective is to understand the requirements, not to write the code. Develop only enough detail for the stakeholders to understand and validate the requirements. If there are many exceptions, list them separately as alternatives in the "Alternatives" section of the use case description or as a separate alternate flow of events of the use case. We find that one level of conditional or iterative logic is normally readable; deeper nesting is very difficult to follow, particularly for nontechnical readers. Develop standards for the structured text, and remember your stakeholders' backgrounds when you do this.

Try to keep the level of detail approximately the same throughout the use case. If a specific activity requires significantly more detail to explain, provide it in an include relationship or alternative flow description.

In moderation, added details can aid the stakeholder's ability to validate the use case and ensure that requirements are not missed. However, as with any technique, it has its limitations. If too much detail is added, the use case's flow of events will become very long, possibly pages and pages, significantly decreasing the stakeholder's ability to follow the flow and validate the requirements. A long flow also makes the use case more monolithic, less capable of being partitioned so that its behaviors can be reused across use cases. For these reasons, we add very detailed logic to the use case carefully, primarily to highlight very important details in the main flow. If there is a lot of complexity that just can't be left out, we use alternative flows, include relationships, or other supplemental specifications.

We try to limit the entire flow of events to one or two pages of text. If there is more than that, ask if more than one use case is being modeled, and consider the use of include or alternative flow descriptions to isolate the details. When adding details to the use case flow of events, strive for a balance between the need for details to meaningfully capture the requirements and the need not to overwhelm the stakeholders with details. If the use case has too little detail, the validation of the use case will not be effective. If it has too much, the customer and users will get lost and the use case will be harder to validate. We have seen both extremes. In one project, the use cases stopped at the base or conceptual level, and the project teams were not able (or willing) to capture and validate the requirements successfully through other means, resulting in "assumed" requirements and, of course, the wrong set of system features developed. In another project, the use case flow of events was too long and the customer rejected the use case model because it was not understandable. Nonetheless, detailed requirements have to be captured, specified, and validated to ensure that there are no surprises when the system is built.

A result of conditional logic within the use case flow of events is that different subflows have different outcomes and different postconditions, complicating the documentation of the postconditions. When modeling alternatives or exceptions directly in the use case's flow of events, determine what effect these alternatives or exceptions will have on the postconditions. In these cases, either generalize the postconditions to reflect the results of both flows or note multiple postconditions, based on major alternatives described in the use case's flow of events. If the postcondition is generalized to reflect both flows, be careful not to lose so much specificity that the requirements become ambiguous.

A danger with using conditional logic in the use case flow of events is that it can look like design—in fact, it can be taken for a design when it is not. A system use case should not tell the designer to iterate through all the approved loan requests in one step instead of keeping a running total of approvals as the approved loan requests come in. That decision should be left for the designer. Make sure the designers know that iterative and conditional logic is used to help model the requirements and validate them with the users, not to design the system.

It is also easy to make conditional and iterative logic extremely complex by trying to document every possibility formally. Unless there is a compelling reason to provide rigorous formality in the use case flow of events, **AVOID IT**! A system use case should not design or code the system.

Using Activity Diagrams to Represent a Complex Flow of Events

When the flow of events is linear—that is, it contains little or no iteration or conditional logic—text is usually sufficient to capture and represent the use case information. However, when there is complex logic in the use case's flow of events, conditionals and iteration can become very difficult to follow. In these situations, consider using UML activity diagrams [UML 1999] as an alternative means to model the use case's flow of events. Activity diagrams

- provide a visual reference for understanding and documenting complex conditional logic within a use case,

- are an excellent means for presenting complex use cases to the stakeholders,
- can be used to understand the dependencies and relationships between the activities in the use case flow of events, and
- can be used to help clarify and model parallel activities using synchronization bars.

Here we present a short introduction to activity diagrams and discussion of their application in documenting the flow of control from activity to activity in the use case's flow of events. In Chapter 15 we look at using activity diagrams to model the flow between multiple use cases. For more comprehensive discussion of activity diagrams, see *The Unified Modeling Language User Guide* [Booch 1999]. For additional discussion on activity diagrams with use cases and examples, see *Use Case Modeling: A Practical Guide* by Geri Schneider and Jason Winters [Schneider 1998] and *UML Distilled: Applying the Standard Object Modeling Language* by Martin Fowler [Fowler 1997].

Activity diagrams (Figure 9-5) are easy to understand and easy to utilize in representing the use case's flow of events. Activity diagrams are composed of activity states, which will map to individual activities within a use case. Each

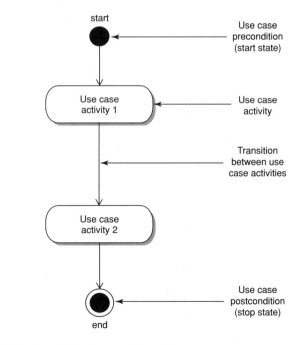

FIGURE 9-5 Simple activity diagram format for use cases

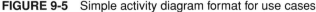

activity in the use case's flow of events is modeled as an activity state and is given a short name to reflect its purpose. The transitions between the individual activities are modeled by directed lines between the activities. Each activity diagram begins with a start state that maps to the use case's precondition and ends with a final state that maps to the use case's postcondition.

A diamond in an activity diagram represents a transition to different branches or paths through the use case (Figure 9-6). The conditions causing a branch should be documented on the directed line leaving the branch.

Iteration and looping can be implemented in a similar manner, with the transition line leaving the branch returning to a previous activity (Figure 9-7). All activities between the previous activity and the branch will be repeated until the condition is satisfied.

Though the use of synchronization bars, activity diagrams provide an excellent means to model concurrency in the use case flow of events (Figure 9-8). A synchronization bar is a horizontal line that models a transition into two or more parallel paths. A synchronization bar is also used when activities sync back into one.

Figure 9-9 represents the flow of events for the "Submit loan request" use case. Note the use of conditional logic and synchronization bars. Figure 9-10 represents conditional logic in the "Evaluate loan request" use case.

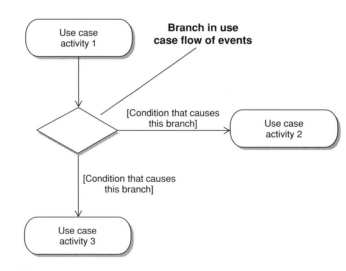

FIGURE 9-6   Branching in an activity diagram

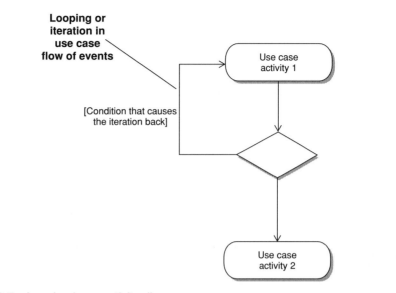

FIGURE 9-7 Looping in an activity diagram

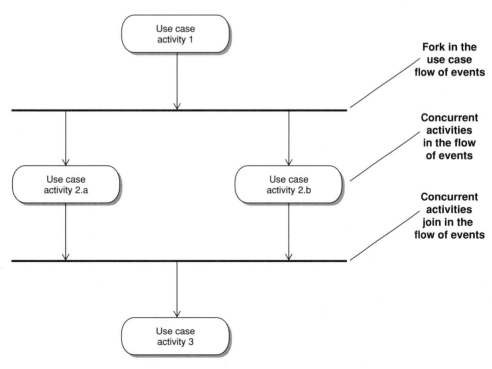

FIGURE 9-8 Synchronization bars in an activity diagram

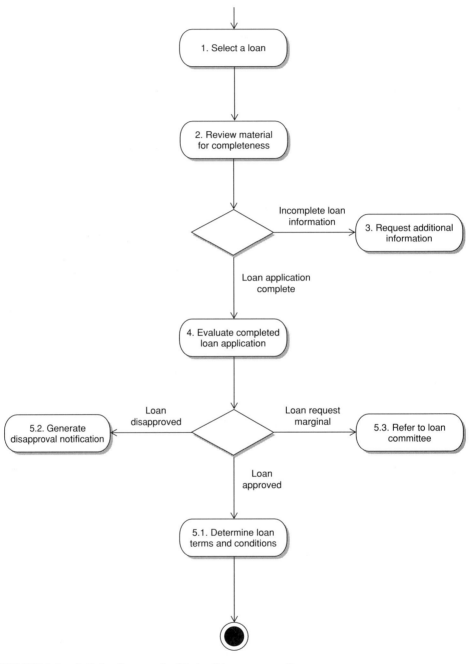

FIGURE 9-9   Activity diagram for "Submit loan request" use case

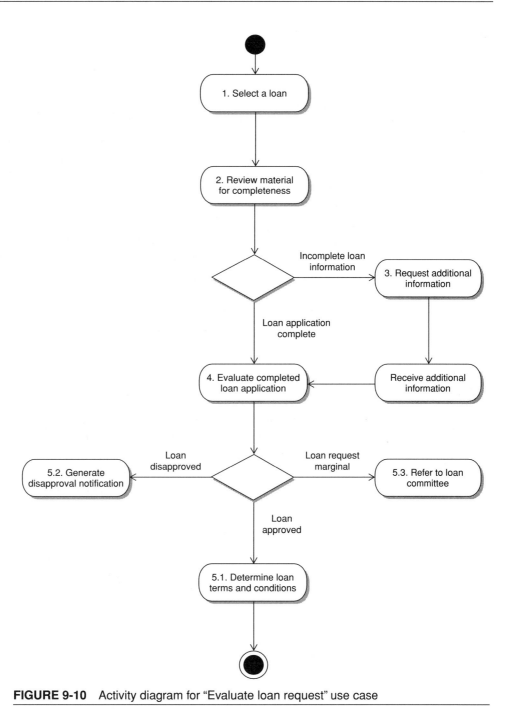

FIGURE 9-10   Activity diagram for "Evaluate loan request" use case

Activity Diagrams versus Detailed Text

Text can provide a level of detail that diagrams cannot. However, activity diagrams show the flow of events in a more precise and readable fashion than paragraphs of text. The strengths of both text and graphics can be combined by mapping the activity steps in the use case flow of events to the corresponding activities in the activity diagram. If a project is using only an activity diagram to document the use case's flow of events, don't forget to capture and maintain the use case information—priorities, actors, and so on. Documenting complete details in both text and activity diagrams can be a maintenance challenge; it probably makes sense to keep details out of the diagrams.

Activity diagrams provide a visual representation of the flow of events through the use case. They are especially useful in representing conditional, concurrent, and iterative logic within a use case's flow of events and can be very beneficial when validating a complex flow of events. In text, deeply nested logic or iteration can be very confusing for readers. If deeply nested conditionals or a lot of iteration is necessary, activity diagrams can be used instead. Activity diagrams are extremely useful in presenting complex use case flows to stakeholders, customers, and users.

Conclusion

When more information on the use case needs to be captured, the base flow of events can be elaborated with alternative flows and conditional and iterative logic. Alternative flows capture the details of the major alternatives. Conditional logic can be described in the flow of events text or represented in an activity diagram.

Elaboration should enhance the ability of the stakeholders to validate the use cases.

Chapter 10
Model Extend, Include, and Generalization Relationships

What's in this chapter?

This chapter discusses the use of extend, include, and generalization relationships for modeling extensions, additional behaviors, and commonality within the use case model.

So far, we have discussed the identification, definition, and description of the behaviors and details of a use case. The base use case description provides an excellent perspective on the overall system behaviors. The addition of alternative flow descriptions and conditional logic helps to define the variations and exceptions within a use case. The use case modeling activities in this chapter explore the relationships between individual use cases.

As the use case model is progressively defined, commonality across the use cases is likely is to be discovered and shared. Possible extensions and other behaviors may also be uncovered and defined. During the execution of use cases, extensions or additions to the base flow of events occur as a result of interactions between the actors and the system. In the loan processing system example, as the base use case descriptions are utilized to elicit and document more detailed requirements from the stakeholders, questions and new requirements may arise. For example, what behaviors will need to occur if the evaluate loan use case is extended to include automatic support for the review of a loan request by the loan committee?

A use case model for a large, complex system needs to represent an equally large amount of requirements information. As with any complex model or documentation, there will be relationships and commonality between the various elements. One can view an individual use case as set of related requirements that are organized based on a business event initiated by an actor. It is the purpose of a system use case model to help the stakeholders clearly understand these requirements prior to creating the final system.

In fact, all requirements analysis models, whether represented using use cases, data flow diagrams (DFDs), or any other modeling approach, share this common set of problems. The goal of a good requirements analysis is to take an amorphous, cloudy vision of a problem and structure it as completely, consistently, and unambiguously as possible. The model needs to be defined at various levels of abstraction to allow the different types of stakeholders to follow it. The model also needs to be structured to support incremental and iterative development.

Fortunately, use case modeling provides a number of constructs that support the clear elaboration of added complexity and detail.

- *Extend relationships* model significant extensions and behaviors that can occur as additions to the use case model.
- *Include relationships* model encapsulated behaviors that can be inserted into a use case and possibly reused across multiple use cases.
- *Generalization relationships* model conceptual similarity between use cases.

Each of these techniques provides an approach to dealing with the increased level of complexity and detail that can appear during use case modeling.

Before we begin the discussion on extend, include, and generalization relationships, the reader should be aware that with the introduction of UML 1.3, a major revision was made to use case relationships. The old UML "extends" and "uses" relationships have been refined into extend, include, and generalization relationships. This is not just a matter of removing the "s" at the end of "extends" or renaming "uses" with "include"; rather, some significant aspects of the relationships have been changed and sharpened.

Extend Relationships

Sometimes when developing a use case model, significant behaviors are identified that extend rather than replace the behaviors in the base use cases. These additional behaviors can be documented using extend relationships. The latest UML document [UML 1.3] states that "an extend relationship defines that instances of a use case may be augmented with some additional behavior defined in an extended use case." (See the Interesting Issue box below: Old Extends Relationship and New Extend Relationship.)

Extend relationships have two main features. First, they allow the use case model to draw out and highlight significant behaviors that can be added to the base use case. Extend relationships help to represent and structure behavior extension in the use case so that the extensions do not clutter up or get lost in the base flow of events. Second, the base use case flow does not have to be rewritten or restructured to reflect this new behavior. As new extensions are discovered during the use case modeling, they can be added to the use case model without disturbing the base flow of events.

In an extend relationship, an extending use case is extended at specific points in its flow, referred to as **extension points**. At these points, under certain conditions, the extending behaviors are executed. Control is returned to the base use case flow of events at the same place in the flow where the extension took place.

More specifically, in an extend relationship the extending use case (also referred to as a client use case) [Rumbaugh 1999] adds behaviors to the base use case by inserting one or more behavioral sequence segments into the base use case flow of events. When the base use case reaches the extension point, a single set of additional behaviors is executed. UML formally defines an extension point as "a location within a use case at which action sequences from other use cases may be inserted. Each extension point must have a unique name within a use case."

Optionally associated with an extension point is a conditional guard (Figure 10-1). If the conditional guard is evaluated as true, the extending use case is executed. If the condition is false, the base use case flow continues to execute as normal and the behaviors in the extending use case are not executed. Note that the

INTERESTING ISSUE: OLD EXTENDS RELATIONSHIP AND NEW EXTEND RELATIONSHIP

The UML 1.3 definition of the new extend relationship differs somewhat from the UML 1.1 definition of extends relationships. The old extends relationship was a generalization relationship between the extending use case and the base use case. The new extend relationship is now one of dependency rather than generalization; the extending use case depends on the base use case. Another difference between the old extends relationship and the new extend relationship is the concept of extension points.

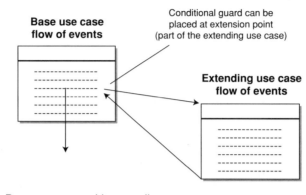

FIGURE 10-1   Base use case with extending use case

base use case does not know about the extending use case, and the conditional guard is considered part of the extending use case.

We refer to the use case descriptions in this relationship as the **base use case** *description,* and the *extending use case description* and to the resulting combination of the two as the *extended use case.* The base use case description contains the main body of the use case and the extending use case(s) describes the extending behaviors that can occur. The extended use case contains both the base and extending behaviors.

Once an extend relationship is specified for a base use case, the relationship is considered part of the use case and the resulting extended use case will always include the extending behavior, whether or not it is executed based on the conditional guard. In Figure 10-2, the dashed lines represent the execution path of the use case if the conditional guard is true. Note that after executing the extension, the execution returns to the same spot in the extended use case from which it was extended and resumes executing the extended flow.

Key to the extend relationship is that control is returned to the same spot at which the extending use case was inserted. Extend relationships are reserved for the insertion of added behaviors, not behaviors that are simple alternatives or exceptions that do not return to the same location at which they were executed.

Jacobson [1992] states that these behaviors are "added" under certain conditions to what is specified in the base flow of events and do not replace existing behavior in the base use case flow of events. Rather, they "extend" the use case to show additional processing that may be needed to perform additional requirements associated with the use case that are not part of the basic flow of events. The rest of the use case execution is as before and should be able to stand alone without the extension.

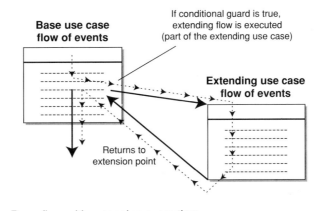

FIGURE 10-2   Base flow with extension executing

As mentioned earlier, in an extend relationship, the behaviors in the base use case description do not know about the extending use case. The base use case should be able to execute with or without invoking the extending use case, depending on the circumstances. For example, in the "Evaluate loan request" use case, the basic flow can be extended with behaviors that refer the loan request to the loan committee under circumstances where the loan request exceeds a certain amount of money and higher level of approval is needed (Figure 10-3).

Organizationally, while it may be important for the loan request to be sent to the loan committee for review, from a system perspective, this is an optional behavior

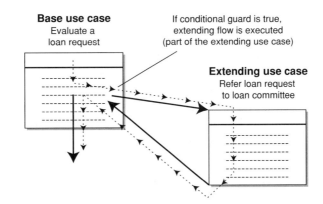

FIGURE 10-3   Base use case and extended use case for "Evaluate loan request"

that can continue to be performed manually at first and added to the system in the future. The basic loan evaluation behaviors can be automated very successfully in an early iteration of development without having to also automate behaviors to forward the loan request to the loan committee for review.

In another example, when the customer accepts the loan, the base use case behaviors require the creation of the loan agreement for the customer to sign. But under certain circumstances, collateral may need to be turned over to the bank to secure the loan (such as title to a car). The activity of entering and recording the receipt of the collateral is an addition to the base behaviors, and does not replace them. Once the receipt of the collateral is entered into the system, the processing of the loan agreement continues as before. When the loan is paid off, the "Loan closeout" use case returns the loan agreement to the customer, marked as paid in full. If collateral is being stored by the bank, the loan closeout use case must be extended to reflect the return of collateral to the customer.

In a more complex case, an extend relationship can involve multiple behavior sequence segments inserted at multiple locations in the base use case flow (Figure 10-4). This allows a use case to be extended by one extend relationship in different locations. There is only one conditional guard for this extend relationship, located at the extension point of the first behavioral sequence. If it is true, all the behavioral sequences will be executed at their extension points.

Multiple extensions in the base use case allow for added behaviors in multiple locations in the use case. The results of a behavioral sequence may change how the later behaviors in the base flow of events will be executed. These changes can be represented in additional behavioral sequences that extend the flow at the additional locations.

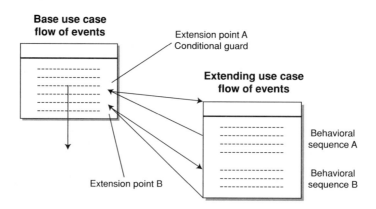

FIGURE 10-4   Sequences A and B will execute at their extension points

For example, in the use case that represents an airline customer making a flight reservation on the airline's Web site, the base flow of events can contain such behaviors as the selection of the flight, the selection of the class of service, the customer reserving the flight, the payment for the reservation, and the generation of the ticket. The base behaviors can be extended by allowing the customer to select a seat assignment (e.g., aisle or window, front or back of plane, Figure 10-5). The base flow of events can first be extended when the customer actually reserves the flight. After the execution of the seat selection behaviors, the base flow of events is then returned to and executed as before, until the generation of the ticket, when it is extended again, with behavior that prints the selected seat assignment on the ticket.

When extending a use case with multiple extension points, make sure that each extension represents significant behavior that needs to be represented in the use case. If there are many extension points, the use case will be very difficult to understand. Extend relationships should be used carefully to represent only behaviors that are significant to the stakeholders and need to be drawn out and highlighted.

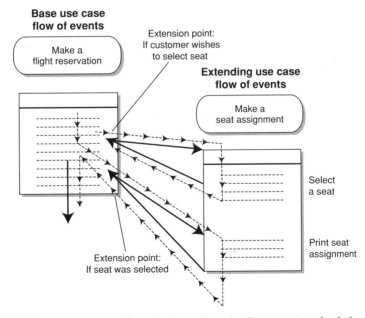

FIGURE 10-5   Base use case with extensions for selecting a seat and printing a seat assignment

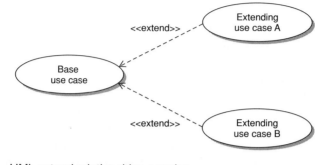

FIGURE 10-6   UML extend relationships notation

Extend relationships have been the focus of much debate. Many practitioners have a difficult time applying extend relationships in a consistent manner, and much misunderstanding and misuse of extend relationships have occurred. (See the Interesting Issue box "Misunderstanding and Misuse of Extend(s) Relationships" on the next page.)

UML Notation for the Extend Relationship

As mentioned earlier in the book, using UML notation, the relationship between the base use case and extending use cases is a dependency relationship and is represented by a dashed directed line with the arrow pointing to the extended use case, as shown in Figure 10-6. Each extend relationship is marked <<extend>>.

In the use case "Evaluate loan request," the flow of events models the approval of the loan. The flow can be extended with flows to deal with additional behaviors such as a request for additional credit information and referring the loan request to the loan committee (Figure 10-7).

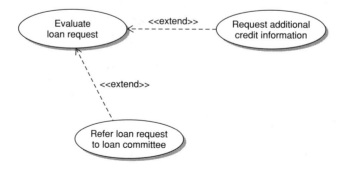

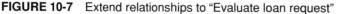

FIGURE 10-7   Extend relationships to "Evaluate loan request"

INTERESTING ISSUE: MISUNDERSTANDING AND MISUSE OF EXTEND(S) RELATIONSHIPS

As stated earlier, Jacobson's original intent was for extending behaviors to be added to the base flow of events under certain conditions, not for them to replace existing behaviors in the base use case flow of events. They should reflect processing that may be needed to perform additional requirements that are associated with the use case but are not part of the basic flow of events.

The original definition has been so "extended" (pardon our humor) that in practice extending use cases sometimes have been used successfully, sometimes in a wide variety of ways. If you asked several practitioners how they have applied extend relationships, you might get many different approaches. For example, some practitioners violate the semantic definition of the extend relationship and use extensions to define alternative flows and exception handling—which do not return control to the extension point. Others extend everything, making the model difficult to understand.

If you see an extend relationship in a use case model, don't automatically assume that it was created with Jacobson's original intent in mind. Typical "nonstandard" uses of extend relationships we have seen include the following.

Modeling the Alternative Flows in a Use Case

Alternative flows contain behaviors that fundamentally change the flow of events in the use case. They are based on a business requirement and are normally the result of some expected actor input. For example, when a loan officer disapproves a loan request, the fundamental flow of the "evaluate loan request" use case is changed; the behavior in alternative use case replaces behavior in the base use case.

An alternative is not an extend relationship because it does not return to the point at which it was inserted. The alternative flow leads directly out of the use case and violates the semantic definition of the extend relationship.

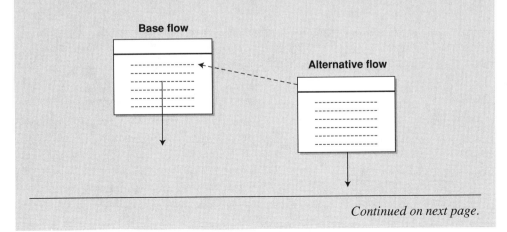

Continued on next page.

Modeling the Exceptions or Error Handling That Occurs When Executing the Use Case's Flow of Events

Exceptions normally occur when something goes wrong (e.g., information is incorrect or missing) or when some condition (such as a bank account not having sufficient funds) occurs. These conditions are requirements that need to be understood and documented. An exception may or may not return to the base use case flow, and if it does return to the flow, it may not return to the same spot in which it was inserted (see figure below). This violates the extend relationship semantics.

An instance of exception handling that does return to the same spot could be represented as an extend relationship. However, the number of exceptions that are possible in a nontrivial use case is so great that extend relationships are usually not the most appropriate means of representing exceptions. While key major exceptions may benefit from being represented with an extend relationship, it is normally better to reserve the use of extend relationships for optimal behaviors only.

In addition to the above examples, we have seen extend relationships used to model situations that are more appropriate for include and generalization relationships, discussed in the next section. We have also seen a number of practitioners "extend" extend relationships to include other approaches. Extending the extend definition has two problems:

1. The model will not mean the same thing to different readers, creating great confusion and misunderstanding among the readers.

2. Extend relationships can be very difficult to "scale up" as the project size increases.

It is tempting to document every alternative, exception, and variation using extends. However, in a large system there will be hundreds or thousands of possible variations, alternatives, and exceptions to the base use cases. Capturing all of them through extends normally will result in too much overhead and will be too difficult to follow.

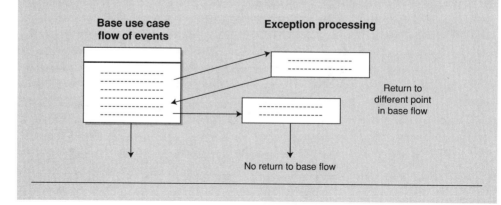

We have seen projects go crazy with hundreds of extends relationships that have extends that have extends that have extends. The user and customers could not successfully validate the use case model, and the use case model was not very maintainable. It serves the modeler well to keep the semantics of extend relationships in mind when applying these concepts. The new "extend" relationship should help to reduce the interpretation problems.

Figure 10-8 represents another example of extend relationship in the loan processing example. In this example, the "Process an approved loan" base use case flow is extended by the extending use case "Enter required collateral" when the circumstances warrant it.

When the extending use case flow has major behaviors with significant details, the details can be captured in the template in Figure 10-9. It may not be necessary to describe every possible extending use case with a detailed extend template. If the extension is self-evident or the issues associated with it are minor or well-known, it can be represented with a use case diagram and possibly a brief text-based description. However, in most cases, since the extending use case represents part of the overall flow that must be implemented, there is normally a need to provide a detailed description. You want to make sure that the state of the system that causes the extension is captured (the conditional guard) as well as the extension points in the base use case. Many of the fields in the extending use case description are the same as those of the base use case description, but several notable differences are as follows:

- *Extended use case name and ID.* These fields refer to the name and ID of the use case that is being extended.

- *Additional actors (not found in extended flow).* If any new actors who are not listed in the base use case are discovered, list them here. Also, update the Actor glossary with information about the new actor.

The extending use case "Refer to loan committee" is presented in Figure 10-10.

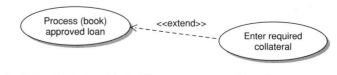

FIGURE 10-8   Extend relationship to "Process approved loan"

Extending use case name:	<Name of this use case>
Extending ID number:	<Unique identifier for extending use case>
Description:	<Description of the use case>
Note: The next three fields are reported for each extend relationship this use case participates in.	
Extended use case name:	<Name of the use case being extended>
Extension point:	<Point of extension in extended use case>
Guard condition (precondition):	<Condition in the extended use case that causes it to execute, i.e., the condition that must be true in the guard condition>
Additional actor(s):	<Any actors not found in base use case flow of events>
Flow of events:	<Activities and interactions performed when the extension(s) are executed>
Postconditions:	<State in which the use case leaves the system>
Priority:	<Relative priority of extend use case>
Nonbehavioral requirements:	<Performance, security, etc.>
Assumptions:	<Any assumptions made>
Issues:	<Outstanding issues concerning the extending use case>
Source:	<Meeting, interview, document, etc., that this extending use case derives from>

FIGURE 10-9   Extending use case template

The new UML 1.3 graphic representation of extension points is shown in Figure 10-11. If the extending use case flow of events has already been defined, each extension point can refer to the specific activity in the base use case at which the extending use case is executed (e.g., 2.1). The numbering of the extension points must be updated if the numbering in the base use case flow of events changes. An example of extension point notation is shown in Figure 10-12.

Applying Extend Relationships

Extend relationships should be used judiciously and the use case modeler should strive to follow the strict interpretation of extend relationships. A use case with two or three extend relationships is much more understandable than one with dozens. One of the chief goals in creating a use case model is to make it understandable for

Extending use case name:	Refer loan request to loan committee
Extending ID number:	Extend-UC105-E1
Extended use case name:	Evaluate loan request
Description:	The loan request is either borderline or exceeds the loan officer's authority to approved. The loan request is referred to a loan committee for approval. The system routes the loan request to the different loan committee members for their review and comments. Communication between committee members is handled online.
Extension point:	Evaluate the completed loan request
Guard condition (precondition):	If the loan request currently being evaluated online is selected by the loan officer to be reviewed by the loan committee.
Additional actors (not found in base flow of events):	Loan committee member
Flow of events:	1. The loan officer has the system forward the loan request and all associated information such as credit reports, financial statements, references, etc., to the members of the loan committee. 2. Each loan committee member reviews the material online, comments on the request, and enters a recommendation into the system. 3. Each loan committee member has the system forward and recommendations to the other loan committee members. 4. Each loan committee member then retrieves, reviews, and provides additional comments (if needed) based on the other member's comments and recommendations. 5. Each loan committee member has the system forward the additional comments to the other members. This cycle continues until consensus is reached (as defined by the loan committee chair). 6. The resulting recommendation is forwarded to the loan officer.
Postconditions:	A loan request recommendation has been determined.
Priority:	Medium

FIGURE 10-10   Extending use case "Refer to loan committee"

FIGURE 10-11   Graphic representation of extension point

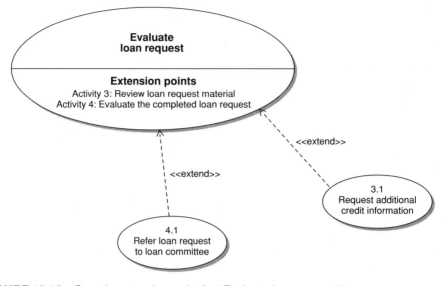

FIGURE 10-12   Sample extension point for "Evaluate loan request"

stakeholder validation. If extend relationships are used to highlight and understand a large number of extensions or are used incorrectly to capture alternatives, their overuse can have the opposite effect.

A good guideline is to use extend relationships to capture only significant optimal behaviors (not exceptions). There may be times when it is critical to capture many, many exceptions with extend relationships, but we have never seen one. Also, remember that the extension should be able to be added or removed from the base use case without affecting the base use case. If the base use case has a dependency on the extending behavior, the relationship is not an extend but an include or a generalization, whichever is more appropriate. Tool support is critical when creating and maintaining extend relationships, since maintaining the extend relationships and keeping them consistent can be a nightmare.

Model Detailed Alternative Flows and Exception Handling.   The major extensions and additional behaviors can be modeled with extend relationships. But what happens to the rest of the alternative and exception logic that needs to be captured?

- It can be documented in the alternatives/exceptions field of the use case in a short description of the alternative/exception with enough information to be able to understand its implications.

- The alternative logic can be represented using conditional logic or with alternative flow descriptions.

- If there is a large amount of detailed logic that needs to be encapsulated, it can be captured using supplemental text such as the activity behavior specifications discussed in Chapter 11.

Be careful with extend relationships: They can grow in number very quickly. Only if the additional behaviors are key to the user's understanding of the use case or if it is determined to be architecturally significant should they be modeled as an extend relationship.

Before jumping in and performing extensive "extending," first be sure you understand the base use case behaviors and alternatives. Modelers need to understand base behaviors first to have a clear understanding of what they are extending. If you are unsure of an extend relationship, document it as an alternative flow (noting your concerns). Later, as the requirements become clearer, reevaluate your decision. If the entire use case flow of events seems to be one variation or the other, consider the use of a generalization relationship, discussed later in this chapter. However you decide to apply extend relationships and/or alternative representations for capturing extending behaviors, be sure to do so in a consistent manner throughout the project.

Reuse Extend Relationships in Multiple Use Cases. The same extending use case can be used in more than one use case. If so, separate extension point documentation will be necessary in each extending use case template. In these cases, consider utilizing an include relationship (discussed next) instead of an extend relationship to represent the behaviors, as include relationships were designed to specifically handle reuse.

Utilize Extend Relationships to Help Manage Incremental Development. Extend relationships can be used to partition out and highlight behaviors to be developed during later development increments. That is, the base use case description can be developed early since the definition of extend relationship provides for the base use case flow to stand alone. Individual extend relationships can be different development priorities that assign them to later development increments or versions. For example, the loan committee review of loan request is a lower development priority than the base evaluation behaviors. Priorities are discussed further in Chapter 11.

Include Relationships

As the use case model continues to be elaborated, it is highly likely that there will be behaviors in one use case that are also used in another use case. Also, there will be behaviors that, for reasons of readability, should be represented separately from the base use case description. The *include relationship* allows one use case to include in its flow of events behaviors specified in another use case. Include relationships provide a way to do the following:

- Capture commonality among use cases
- Manage redundancy and facilitate change within the use case model
- Act as input to the functional architecture by highlighting common logic
- Determine and represent development priorities

The UML 1.3 definition of the include relationship states:

> An include relationship defines that a use case contains the behavior defined in another use case. . . . An include relationship is a directed relationship between use cases, implying that the behavior in the additional use case is inserted into the behavior of the base use case. The use case may only depend on the results of performing the behavior defined in the addition use case, but not on the structure (i.e., on the existence of specific attributes and operations of the addition use case).

An include relationship involves two use cases: the included use case and the use case that includes or uses it (Figure 10-13). Included use cases are simply use cases that are referenced within other use cases.

The include relationship is defined by UML as a dependency relationship. The client use case (base) is dependent on the supplier (include) use case for certain behaviors. The included use case does not know about the base use case in which it is included and can be included in multiple use cases.

The include relationship is represented by a directed dashed line pointing to the included use case (Figure 10-14). This is the reverse of the extend relationship, where the dependency line points to the base use case away from the extending use case.

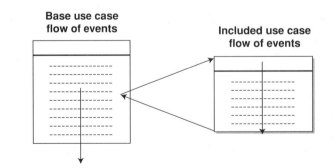

FIGURE 10-13   Base use case that includes the behaviors of an include use case

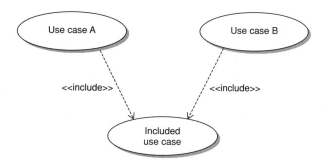

FIGURE 10-14 UML notation for include relationships

The behaviors in the included use case are executed when the inclusion point is reached in the base flow of events. The included behaviors are executed completely and the flow of execution continues at the spot in the base flow of events where the included use case was injected. The base use case does not know or care about the specifics of how the included behaviors are executed. It does care, however, about the results. For example, both the "Submit loan request" use case and the "Offer a line of credit" use case contain a set of behaviors for performing a credit check. Because this set of behaviors will be reused by multiple use cases, the perform credit check behaviors are best placed in an include use case (Figure 10-15). When the "Submit loan request" use case is instantiated and executed, the behaviors in the "Perform credit check" use case are inserted in its flow and executed. Unlike an extend relationship, the behaviors in "Perform credit check" are *not* optional to the base use case's flow of events; the base use case depends on the behaviors in "Perform credit check."

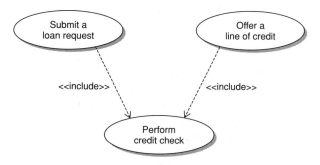

FIGURE 10-15 "Submit loan request" and "Offer line of credit" using the "Perform credit check" use case

INTERESTING ISSUE: OLD USES RELATIONSHIP

It is a common misconception that the include relationship of UML 1.3 is simply a replacement or name change for the uses relationship. The old uses relationship was a generalization relationship between the base use case and the "used" use case. The base use case inherited the behavior of the used use case; the behavior, in a used use case was inserted and used in the base use case flow of events when it was instantiated and executed.

The uses relationship allowed multiple behaviors in the used use case to be inherited and interleaved in the base use case (the new include relationship does not) like a subclass inheriting operations from a superclass in a traditional object model. In the figure below, use case A inherits behaviors from use case B in a uses relationship, resulting in an instantiated use case that has the sets of behaviors of A and B.

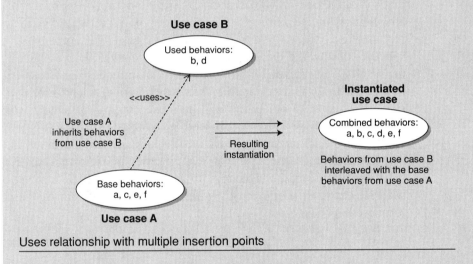

Uses relationship with multiple insertion points

Like the old extends relationship, the uses relationship was perceived and utilized by many practitioners differently. Many practitioners utilized the uses concept as a sort of aggregation relationship, where the base use case was the whole and the used use case(s) were the parts. The definition of the new include comes close to describing how many practitioners were, in fact, applying the uses relationship.

The new generalization relationship now can be utilized to represent shared behaviors, when use cases are conceptually similar to one another. Generalization relationships are discussed in the next section.

The include relationship is different from the extend relationship in a number of key aspects:

1. The dependency relationship in the extend relationship is from the extending use case to the base use case. That is, the extending use case depends on the base use case, and the base use case has no knowledge of the extending use case. In the example of the "Evaluate loan request," the extending use case, "Refer to loan committee," is dependent on a loan being evaluated. However, the base flow of events can execute successfully without the extending behaviors.

2. An include relationship has a dependency from the including use case to the included use case. That is, the including use case needs to know about the included use case and cannot successfully execute its flow of events without it.

3. In an include relationship, no conditional guard is associated with the included use case at its inclusion point, as is so with the extend relationship at its first extension point. (However, this does not preclude the including use case from containing conditional logic that might result in the included behaviors not executing during a particular instance of execution.)

4. An include relationship represents a single segment of encapsulated behavior that is executed to completion when called. There are no multiple inclusion points as there are multiple extension points in an extend relationship.

Utilize Include Relationships to Capture Commonality among Use Cases. The individual use cases in a use case model can share many behaviors. As the use case model is progressively elaborated, common behaviors are noticed in multiple use cases. As shared behavior changes, updating each use case that includes the behavior can be time-consuming and subject to error.

Include relationships can be utilized to help capture the commonality among use cases (one the primary uses of the old uses relationship) and to eliminate the need to describe this behavior redundantly in each use case. The common behavior can be factored out into a separate use case that is used by the use cases that share its behavior.

As stated earlier, in the loan application processing example, when an applicant submits a request for a loan or is offered a credit card, credit is checked in both situations (refer to Figure 10-15). The common behavior, "Perform a credit check," occurs in both use cases. "Perform a credit check" can be removed from the two use cases that utilize it and placed in an included use case that is used by both the use cases. The including use cases need to know only what behavior the included use case is responsible for, not how it performs it. Include relationships can be referenced by the

INTERESTING ISSUES: ABSTRACT AND CONCRETE USE CASES

An abstract use case is one that "cannot be directly instantiated in a system execution" [Rumbaugh 1999]. Both an included use case or an extending use case can be abstract: The included or extending use case cannot be instantiated and executed on its own; rather, it needs to be contained in the execution of another use case. The ability to define abstract use cases is very useful because it allows the definition and representation of behaviors that don't naturally fit the base use case descriptions due to reasons such as reuse or level of detail. A concrete use case, on the other hand, is one that can be instantiated and executed on its own.

Included use cases or extending use cases that are abstract differ from base use cases as there may be no actor participating in them. The behavior described in the included use case can be triggered by an event in the including use case's flow of events. While an included use case does not need an actor, like the including use cases that use them, included use case have preconditions and postconditions.

An included use case can be concrete; that is, it can be instantiated and executed on its own as well as be included in another use case. Although there is nothing to preclude an existing stand-alone use case from being included in another use case (we have seen this a number of times and it just confirms that a use case model is not hierarchical), included use cases do not need to be stand-alone use cases.

base use case's flow of events by annotating the base use case's flow of events to show where the include relationship is invoked. In another example, a "Print the notice" use case is included in the base use cases "Generate standard payment notice" and "Generate late notice" (Figure 10-16). And, in another, the behavior of retrieving loan account information from the account management system is represented as an included use case and shared by four use cases that utilize its behaviors (Figure 10-17).

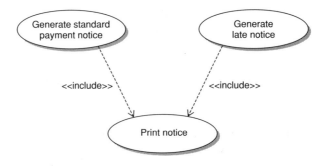

FIGURE 10-16   Include relationships of "Printing notice"

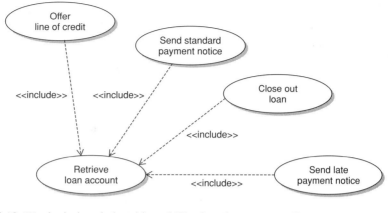

FIGURE 10-17   Include relationships of "Retrieve loan account"

Manage Redundancy and Facilitate Change within the Use Case Model. Like the old uses relationships, include relationships help minimize the number of changes across use cases by isolating common behaviors in single use cases. When iterating across multiple development increments or just progressively building the use case model in an up-front analysis, changes repeatedly occur within the use case model. Managing updates and changes to the use case model is hard enough without the added task of finding all the places in all the use cases that contain the same behavior. Making the same change in multiple places in the model is time-consuming and subject to errors. Even with a good CASE tool this is difficult; without one it is impossible. Changing the common behavior in one including use case helps to keep the use case model in sync with the current requirements. In the loan processing example, since it is anticipated that the system will be enhanced in the future to include the processing of additional loan types, which will all need to check credit as well generate a credit score, the representation of these behaviors with include relationships will allow them to be more easily reused in the future.

Influence High-Level Functional Architecture.   Identifying behaviors that can be developed once and reused in many places can help to facilitate the design and development effort. The high-level functional architecture—the basic design of the system's functionality—can be influenced by include relationships. First, since include relationships represent behaviors that will be used by multiple use cases in the system, the included use cases become a potential starting point for defining reusable frameworks for the system. For example, the behaviors, "Retrieve loan account" and "Print notice" will be used by the system in several ways. It makes sense to investigate the development of a framework to allow its flexible reuse during system development.

Includes can also be used to highlight functionality that may be reused in the future or used in projects other than the current one. In this instance, an included use case does not have to be referenced by more than one use case in the base use case model.

Keep in mind that while include relationships may point out the need for reusable frameworks, the actual design and development of the frameworks is an architectural task that involves the system architects, object designers, and other technical personnel on the project and should not be confused with the primary goals of use case modeling—understanding the user needs.

Determine and Represent Development Priorities. By pointing out the dependencies of multiple use cases on an included use case, include relationships help to show which behaviors in the use cases need to be developed first. If multiple use cases depend on an included use case, a prioritized effort will be needed to develop the included use case. Or, alternatively, the included use case could be "stubbed out" until it is implemented. In either instance, a well-defined interface between the calling behaviors and called behaviors (included use case) is needed.

Discovering Include Relationships

Common behaviors are typically discovered later in the use case modeling process rather than earlier. Occasionally, common behaviors are discovered earlier in the process, especially if the use case modeling involves reengineering of an existing system.

To discover include relationships, begin by reviewing the flow of events of the existing use cases for common activities, and then create included use cases for the significant common behaviors and move them out of the base use cases into the included use cases. In each use case that uses the included use case, refer to the included use case at the point where it is executed (Figure 10-18).

The included use case should contain behaviors that are significant in their own right, so the included use case should be described in detail. A standard use case template can be used. Document only those aspects of the included use case, such as actors, flow of events, and nonbehavioral requirements, that are relevant to the behaviors in the included use case. Remember that an included use case does not know about the use cases that include it. Figure 10-19 shows short description templates for the "Perform credit check" and "calculate credit score" included use case.

Applying Include Relationships

We prefer to have a solid foundation of base use case descriptions and alternative flows before spending a lot of effort on include relationships. Without a good

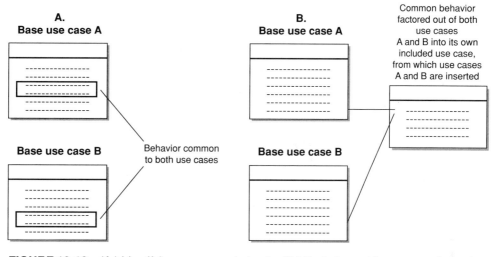

FIGURE 10-18   (A.) Identifying a common behavior (B.) Factoring out the common behavior

grasp of the behaviors represented in the base use case descriptions, it's difficult to
see the appropriate include relationships. Factoring out include relationships too
early normally leads to a lot of needless restructuring of the use case model as
more is learned about the requirements.

Since an included use case can provide behavior to many use cases, it is useful to document included use cases and list which use cases invoke them.
Although the included use case does not need to know which use cases invoke it,
the people responsible for the analysis do. Create or generate an *include relationship use case table* to capture this information (Figure 10-20).

Include relationships are a powerful and useful technique, but just as with
extend relationships, include relationships can be taken to the extreme. We have
seen projects project teams generate hundreds and thousands of includes, many of
which involved trivial behaviors. When applying include relationships to use case
modeling, focus on the following major common behaviors:

- Behaviors that are complex and of such critical importance to the user and
  customer that the user and customer recognize them as important behaviors.
  The use case model should "draw out" those behaviors that assist in the
  stakeholders' comprehension and prioritization of the model. Make sure
  that the included use cases represent significant system behaviors.

- Common or reusable behaviors that are repeatedly reused or referenced by
  the base use cases.

Use case name:	Perform credit check
ID:	IUC-10
Description:	A credit report is requested and retrieved through an automated interface with the national credit bureaus.
Preconditions:	Individual has a social security number or alternative form of ID and their address is known.
Flow of events:	1 Based on the individual's geographical location, the appropriate credit bureau is contacted and the customer's credit report is requested. 2 The customer credit report is received and the information is formatted into the bank's standard credit report template.
Postcondition:	The customer's credit report in standard template form is returned.
Alternative flows:	No credit report found for the individual.

Use case name:	Calculate credit score
ID:	IUC-20
Description:	A credit score is requested.
Preconditions:	A credit report, income information, and financial history available.
Flow of events:	Based on the credit report, income, type of customer (individual or business), and other financial information, a credit score is calculated.
NOTE: The detailed credit scoring criteria and algorithms used in this flow are documented in the Bank Credit Scoring Manual, #8765	
Postcondition:	A credit score is returned.

FIGURE 10-19   Included use cases "Perform credit check" and "Calculate credit score"

Number	Included Use Case	Description	Use cases includes
IUC-10	Perform credit check	Request a credit report from the credit bureau	Submit loan request Offer a line of credit
IUC-20	Calculate credit score	Calculate a credit score for an individual or business	Submit loan request Offer a line of credit
IUC-20	Retrieve loan account	Retrieve the account information for a specific loan	Closeout a Loan Offer a line of credit/send standard payment notice Send late payment notice
IUC	Print the notice	Print out the loan bill	Generate standard payment notice Generate late bill notice

FIGURE 10-20   Sample entries in an includes use case table

- Volatile requirements that will be perceived as changing frequently during the analysis and development process. Consider future requirements and projects when modeling include relationships.

- Perceived shared behaviors that are actually common and aren't likely to diverge in the future.

Again, there is no hard and fast rule, but focus on base behaviors first before trying to create an include relationship for every single common behavior.

Generalization Relationships

With the introduction of UML 1.3, a new relationship between use cases was introduced—generalization. UML describes use case generalization as a relationship between parent and child use cases that "implies that the child use case contains all the attributes, sequences of behavior, and extension points defined in the parent use case and participates in all relationships of the parent use case." If this sounds a lot like classical generalization and inheritance, it is. A generalization relationship between parent and child use cases is one in which the child is a more specialized form of the parent use case. The child inherits the behaviors of its parents and adds new behaviors, and specializes in behaviors inherited from the parent.

For example, when a bank customer elects to withdraw funds from an account, a standard set of behaviors needs to occur, including specification of the account number. However, unique behaviors will need to be performed if a customer chooses to withdraw funds from a saving account rather then a checking account—for example, a check to see whether this withdrawal will exceed the permitted number of withdrawals per month, before a fee is imposed. If the customer wants a credit card cash advance, the credit limit is checked, not the account balance, and a fee based on the amount of the advance is calculated. These use cases share a common conceptual foundation—that of withdrawing funds—and diverge into specialized behaviors for withdrawing the funds from different sources (Figure 10-21).

We have seen this relationship represented using the old extends relationship; the withdraw funds use case was extended with the three alternatives of "Withdraw from savings," "Withdraw from checking," and "Request a credit card advance." We think that generalization helps represent this type of the relationship more clearly and reduces the number of ways that an extend relationship is be applied, clarifying that concept as well.

In the loan processing example, two different types of loan requests can be submitted: consumer loan requests and business loan requests. The two event flows perform common behavior; however, each has specialized behaviors. For a business loan application, the business plans, balance sheets, and other documentation

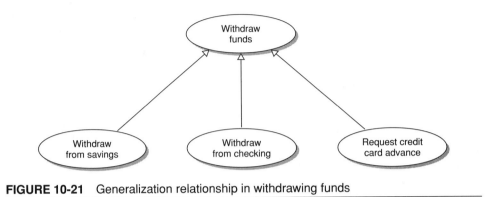

FIGURE 10-21   Generalization relationship in withdrawing funds

are needed; for a personal loan, a simple proof of income is required. The credit analysis behavior based on the different inputs are different. However, the two use cases conceptually share the idea of applying for a loan (Figure 10-22). When generating reports for loan officers, a number of different loan reports can be generated, but they will all share the idea of report generation on loans (Figure 10-23), and generating a loan notice and generating a late notice share the common concept of generating a notice (Figure 10-24).

While generalization is a new concept in use case modeling, we find it very useful. In our experience with generalization, we have noticed a relationship between abstract actors and use case generalization (Figure 10-25). As presented in Chapter 1, an abstract actor is a role that represents shared or common behavior across two or more actors. When distinguishing an abstract actor from the concrete actors that specialize the role, their relationship can point out a possible par-

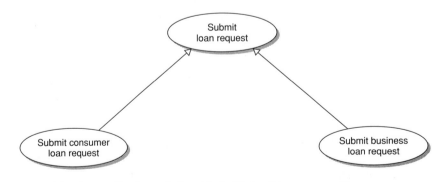

FIGURE 10-22   Generalization relationship in "Submit loan request"

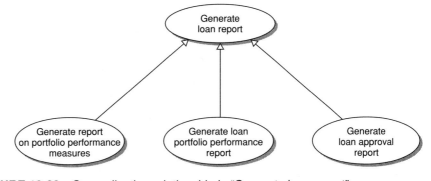

FIGURE 10-23 Generalization relationship in "Generate loan report"

allel use case generalization relationship. As concrete actors are modeled, look for more specialized use cases based on use cases associated with the abstract actor that may be associated with the child use cases. Keeping this pattern in mind makes it easier to discover generalization relationships. The converse is also true: If a use case generalization is discovered, see if it reflects an abstract actor.

Generalization relationships elegantly represent the inheritance relationships between use cases, but when documenting the details of the generalization in the use case's flow of events, things get a little complicated. As stated in the UML 1.3 definition of these relationships, the child use case inherits behaviors of the parent use cases, just as in traditional object modeling. However, in object modeling there is typically no explicit order of execution among the behaviors or operations defined in the parent class; that is, the subclass can inherit the list of operations and add new ones at the end of the list.

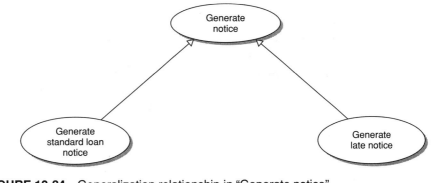

FIGURE 10-24 Generalization relationship in "Generate notice"

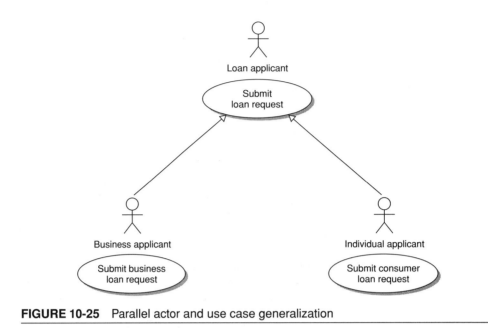

FIGURE 10-25   Parallel actor and use case generalization

In a use case flow of events, a child use case may insert in the middle of the use case flow of events a new behavior that it has inherited, so the order in which the behaviors execute can be important. Without good CASE tool support to manage this aspect, maintaining and documenting generalization relationships is difficult. For example, should only the additional behaviors be listed in the child use case's flow of events? If so, where in the inherited flow of events are they executing? How will stakeholders validate the flow of events if they have a difficult time determining this? How are the new behaviors distinguished from the specialized ones? Is a specific validation based on the child loan request use case or the parent loan request use case?

If the entire flow of events is included, how are the activities distinguished? We think this will require significant tool support to be successful. We suggest that, at least informally, each activity in a child use case flow of events be annotated as to whether it is new, inherited and unchanged, or inherited and specialized. For example, associate with each activity one of the following symbols:

I   inherited and unchanged

S   inherited and specialized

N   new

Along with each symbol, note the activity in the parent and the parent use case ID, if multiple inheritance is used. For example,

(I—Activity 2, UC123)

(S—Activity 4, UC111)

(N)

In the abbreviated use case descriptions shown in Figure 10-26, the parent use case "Send notice" is annotated as an abstract use case. Note that this is the more traditional object modeling use of the abstract concept, not the abstract use case concept used in previous versions of UML and since replaced with include relationships. A child use case, "Send out late notice," is annotated as a child of "Send notice," and each behavior is annotated with its inheritance status.

In traditional class inheritance this would not be necessary as one could just refer to the superclass definition, but a use case's readability is much improved if the inherited activities are included in the child's flow of events. Notation that

Use case name:	Generate notice (abstract use case)
Unique use case ID:	UC130A
Flow of events:	1. The loan system requests loan account information from the account management system. 2. The loan system generates billing statement. 3. The loan system prints the billing statement. 4. The loan clerk mails billing statement to the customer.
Use case name:	Generate late notice (parent is "generate notice")
Unique use case ID:	UC135
Flow of events:	1. The loan system requests loan account information from the account management system **(I—Activity 1, UC140)** 2. The loan system generates the late notice statement with amount overdue. **(S—Activity 1, UC140)** 3. The loan system generates a letter reminding the customer to pay the bill. **(N)** 4. The loan system prints the late notice statement and the letter. **(S—Activity 3, UC140)** 5. The loan clerk mails late notice statement to customer. **(I—Activity 3, UC140)**

FIGURE 10-26   Parent-child relationships in loan request processing use case

documents the specific relationships between individual behaviors in the child and parent use case provides traceability between the use cases, making updating easier (at least when tool support arrives) and making the specifics of the generalization relationship more understandable.

Use case generalization is new, and although it is a powerful concept, its application needs to be investigated by practitioners to learn and share the best practices.

Bringing Together Extend, Include, and Generalization Relationships

Alternative flows describe alternatives in the use case flow of events. Extend relationships model extensions to the base use case flow and always return to the same point in the flow of events. Include relationships document common behaviors in the flow of events. When considering whether to create include relationships, extend relationships, or alternative flow descriptions, different practitioners have somewhat different approaches. We like to ask the following questions:

- Is what is being modeled an exception that does not return to the point of extension? If so, use an alternative flow description.

- Is the behavior utilized in the flow of events of several use cases? If so, remove the description of the behavior from the base use case's flow of events and make it an included use case.

- Is the behavior an addition or extension to the base flow of events, and can the base flow execute without the additional behavior? If so, use an extend relationship. The primary candidate for an extend relationship is a case in which additional behaviors are clearly an extension of the base use case behaviors from the user's perspective. That is, the user would look at the extension relationship and agree that the base is "complete" but can be extended.

- Does the common behavior, detailed behavior, extension, or alternative need to be highlighted for the stakeholders and users?

In any large system development effort, there will be situations where the line is not easy to draw between include relationships, extend relationships, and alternative flow descriptions. In these situations, apply the criterion that the goal is to structure and represent the requirements as clearly and completely as possible. Endless arguing about relationships is a form of analysis paralysis. If necessary, map out the use case using all three approaches and then vote on which is best.

As the complexity of a use case model grows, it becomes increasingly difficult to represent the information in a single diagram. As the extend, include, and generalization relationships are defined, revisit the initial use case diagram (Chapter 7) to see if any of the base use cases or actors have changed. At this point an individual use case may have many relationships. In addition to the initial use case diagram, we like to create a diagram for each use case family—a base use case with all its relationships, a diagram for each major actor to identify the use cases they participate in and a set of diagrams showing how each base use case uses each included use case. (Use case family diagrams for "Submit a loan request" and "Evaluate a loan request" are presented in Figures 10-27 and 10-28.)

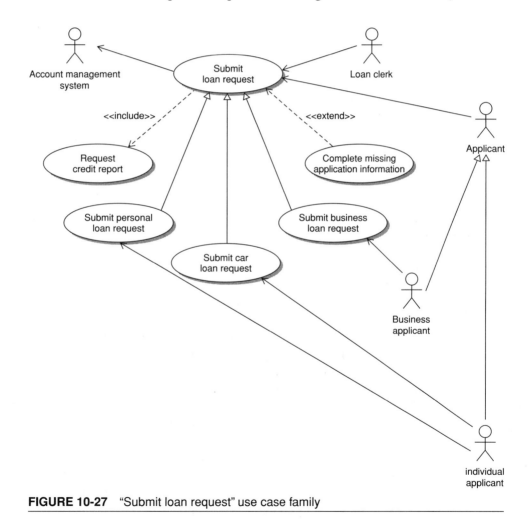

FIGURE 10-27 "Submit loan request" use case family

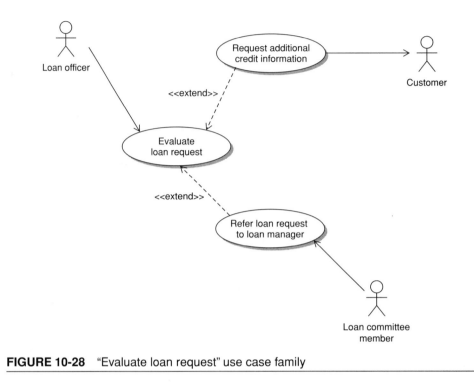

FIGURE 10-28   "Evaluate loan request" use case family

Conclusion

When large and complex systems are being modeled, there will be extensions and additional behaviors associated with the use cases. Some use cases will contain behaviors that are similar in many respects, but will differ in several key aspects. There will be system behaviors that can be shared or reused across multiple behaviors, both within a specific use case and across multiple use cases. When properly used, extend, include, and generalization relationships help the use case modeler manage this complexity. Extend relationships model extensions, include relationships typically model behavior included across use cases, and generalization relationships model the conceptual similarity between use cases. The concepts that have been discussed in this chapter allow the use case modeler to add detail to the model in a variety of ways.

There is not always one right way to use the modeling techniques described in this chapter. Different projects may benefit from different applications of the techniques. However, it is very important to apply these techniques consistently across the entire development project and to follow the UML definitions.

Chapter 11

Add Supplemental Information to the Use Case Model

What's in this chapter?

This chapter discusses the capture of supplemental information documenting use case priorities, nonbehavioral requirements, and detailed business logic associated with an individual use case.

This chapter discusses the capture of nonbehavioral requirements and other information associated with an individual use case through the use of supplemental or additional use case details. Some of these supplemental categories have already been considered, but during a development effort they should be revisited, refined, and reworked to ensure that the use cases capture a complete and updated picture of the system requirements. We focus on two specific types of supplemental use case information in this chapter:

- Use case priorities
- Nonbehavioral requirements
- The capture of detailed business rules and procedures

Use Case Priorities

In a large development effort, when there is iterative system development or scope that needs to be controlled and monitored, the establishment of priority relationships between the use cases is essential [Jacobson 1999]. The functionality in some use cases may be more important or critical to the user than that in other use cases. Also, other use cases may depend on a specific use case, so it will need to be developed sooner rather then later.

Use case priorities document for each use case its development priority in relationship to the other use cases. Priorities can be assigned during initial use case definition, but as the use case model is expanded through extend relationships, include relationships, instance scenarios, and elaborated use case descriptions, priorities may need to be revised to guide the development effort. Priorities are normally assigned based on criteria such as risk, architectural coverage, and business priorities.

When assigning priorities, consider the priorities of the extend and include relationships within the larger individual use case family. For example, an individual base use case may have the same priority as other base use cases; however, its extend and include relationships may have varying priorities. If the base use case has, for example, a high priority, but one of its extend relationships is of low priority, the extend relationship can be developed later in iterative development cycle.

The development priority of an alternative flow or an extend relationship is a combination of the priority of its base use case priority and its own priority in the base use case's family. Assigning a priority to the overall use case can be too "large grain" in an iterative development effort. Some pieces of a use case may be developed in one development increment, other pieces in later increments. When assigning priorities to extend relationships consider the flow or relationship in the context of the overall base use case. For example, in the case of evaluating a loan request, the base use case, "Evaluate loan request," is considered high priority, but not all its alternative and extend relationships are considered high priority (Figure 11-1). The bank may feel it is critical to have a basic loan evaluation system in place quickly that automates the approval and disapproval of a loan request. For less frequent alternatives, such as approving a loan request conditionally or referring the loan request to the loan committee for approval, the bank can continue to perform them manually, with their automation waiting for implementation until the next increment of the system.

The priority of an include relationship is evaluated based on the priority of the other use cases that invoke it. An included use case that is invoked by high priority use cases will obviously have a higher development priority than one invoked only by low-priority use cases.

Priority can be described using such techniques as numerical ranking or categories such as high, medium, and low. Priorities are needed especially if an incremental or iterative development of the system is planned. Of course, the focus is

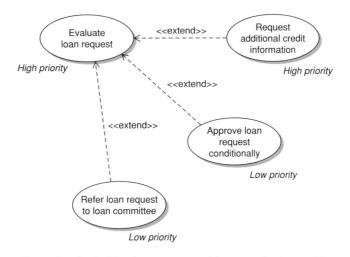

FIGURE 11-1 Example of prioritized use case and its extend relationships

on first elaborating the use cases that are of the highest development priority based on the customer's business need or to minimize development risk.

As a rule of thumb, an included use case should have as high or higher priority than the use cases that include it, since the including use cases depend on the included use case. In situations where the include use case has a lower development priority than the behaviors in the including use case, the included use case will have to be "stubbed in" during development. Extends usually have a lower priority because a project effort tries to get the base functionality in the hands of customers as soon as possible, then it goes back and adds alternative processes.

Nonbehavioral Requirements

Although use cases provide a good mechanism for describing system behavior and functionality, many nonbehavioral aspects associated with an event are not easily captured in the flow of events. Nonbehavioral requirements are not the functions or the behaviors themselves; they are attributes or characteristics of the system behaviors, such as security, reliability, and performance.

Many nonbehavioral requirements specify the global system characteristics, such as portability, overall reliability, maintainability, overall system performance, security, and so on. These requirements should be documented in a global section in the requirements specification. But there can also be nonbehavioral requirements that are specific to an individual use case. They too should be captured and represented as part of the use case description. Like other requirements, nonbehavioral requirements should be business driven and important to the system development effort.

The IEEE [IEEE 1993a] has defined a set of categories for nonbehavioral requirements.

- *Performance.* Once an instance of a use case is initiated, how long will it take to respond to the actor with results? For example, once a loan application is entered into the system, within what time period is a credit analysis expected to be completed? What is the number of transactions performed in the use case? Within what time frame will the transactions occur? What amount of information is to be processed within certain periods for both normal and peak workload conditions?

  The performance requirements may need to be partitioned across the multiple activities and interactions with actors in the use case. Be particularly careful if the use case flow of events contains manual activities, as there may be little control over how fast they execute. Also, the overall performance of a use case depends on how fast automated actors, such as external systems, outside the system responsibility react to requests by the system.

- *Capacity.* How many instances of an actor will need to be supported in the business environment? For example, how many applicants should be able to apply for a loan concurrently? Is there a business need to grow in capacity? This requirement type can also include the number of terminals to be supported and the number of simultaneous users that are expected to be supported.

- *Reliability and Availability.* How reliable does the business need the use case to be? Will the use case be expected to execute correctly 99% of the time? How available will the behaviors in this use case be? Will the use case be expected to execute 24×7? Will regular downtime be needed for system maintenance?

- *Security.* Are there any security requirements unique to this use case? For example, is there a need to log specific events, implement an audit trail, or use certain cryptographic techniques?

- *Design constraints.* Although it is important to avoid premature design during an analysis, sometimes design constraints are unavoidable. For example, the customer may have an existing database or mainframe computer that they require the proposed system to use, or they may have a strong desire to use a Web interface. Only record design constraints that are specific to the use case within an individual use case description. If design constraints are systemwide (i.e., cross multiple use cases), list them in a global section of the software requirements specification (SRS).

While the nonbehavioral requirements are captured in the use cases, their design and realization should be done in the systems architecture. And, as the architecture is defined, more details on the nonbehavioral requirements will emerge. For a good discussion of use cases and system architecture, see Kruchten [1995]. For a great overall work on system architecture, see Rechtin [1991].

See [IEEE 1998a], Leffingwell [2000], Robertson [1999], and Davis [1993] for more information on nonbehavioral requirements. Some nonbehavioral requirements will obviously not be known early in the use case modeling effort. However, be prepared to document them as they become available. A requirements analysis is not complete until both the behavioral and nonbehavioral requirements are known.

Nonbehavioral requirements that apply to multiple use cases—for example, overall loan process performance or capacity—will need to be partitioned across use cases. While the actual partitioning is a system architecture task, this partitioning may impact specific actor needs and other requirements contained in the use case. Dependency streams, discussed in Chapter 15, help to diagram the relationships between the use cases that may point out these cross use case requirements.

Interface Analysis

One of the most critical requirements to capture in system development is the system interface, also referred to as input and output requirements. It is in interfaces that requirements such as capacity and performance are exposed. Interface analysis is an activity that ensures the accuracy and consistency of the interfaces.

In our experience, the lack of well-defined interfaces is one of the major reasons for disappointment down the development road. Without a clear understanding of the interfaces, the successful development of a system architecture is severely handicapped. For each interaction between an actor and the system, consider filling out an interface template (Figure 11-2). These templates will also provide a start in identifying the GUI screens, Web pages, and the system test scripts.

For each interaction between the actor and the system, determine the system's responsibilities and document them as steps in the use case. During requirements capture, key issues to address with the external interfaces include the following:

- Are all the restrictions and constraints defined?
- Are all the performance and other nonbehavioral requirements specified and the limits understood?
- What is the criticality of the interface?

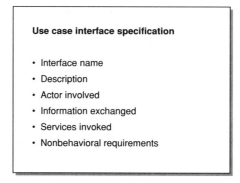

FIGURE 11-2   Simple interface specification

- Are the interfaces testable?
- Have all appropriate standards for the interface been defined (e.g., the use of EDI, XML, and so on)?

A sample template for capturing this supplemental on each use case is presented in Figure 11-3, and an example for evaluating a loan request is presented in Figure 11-4.

Use case name:	
Use case ID:	
Associated nonbehavioral requirements:	
Performance:	
Capacity:	
Reliability and availability:	
Security:	
Design constraint:	
Other nonbehavioral requirements:	
Use case priority:	

FIGURE 11-3   Detailed supplemental use case information

Use case name:	Evaluate loan request
Use case ID:	UC-125
Associated nonbehavioral requirements:	
Performance (Response time)	N/A
Capacity:	The system should be able to handle 10 loan officers reviewing loan requests concurrently.
Reliability and availability:	The system should be available for loan request evaluation during extended business hours (7:00 A.M.–9:00 P.M. Monday through Friday and 9:00 A.M.–5:00 P.M. on Saturdays).
Security:	Only a loan officer or manager should have access to loan request information and associated material.
Design constraint:	N/A
Other nonbehavioral requirements:	
Use case priority:	High

FIGURE 11-4 Example of detailed use case information for "Evaluate loan request"

Focusing on Behavioral Details of Individual Use Case Activities

Sometimes a use case's flow of events becomes very long or complex. Rather than have a lengthy use case flow of events, it may be useful to document the details of a particular activity in the flow of events as a separate description. Separating the detailed behaviors from the main flow of events also allows the details of the behavior to be modified, independent of having to change the base use case's flow of events.

The separate descriptions can occur without a specific motivation to reuse (i.e., the description is not an included use case, referenced across multiple use cases). We refer to these descriptions as **activity behavior descriptions**. They are not use cases that are invoked from the base use case, nor are they subordinate use cases (discussed in Chapter 15). No actor needs to be involved. Rather, they provide more details (or focus) about an activity in the flow of events. They are not necessary for every activity—only for those that are not yet clearly defined in the use case and require further explanation. The activity behavior can be used only once. If that is determined as reuse, change to a standard include.

Use case name:	\<Name of use case this activity is in\>
Activity name:	\<Name of activity\>
Activity step or ID:	\<Activity number within the use case\>
Brief description:	\<Short description of activity\>
Preconditions:	\<Any preconditions associated with activity\>
Detailed description:	\<Detailed description of activity\>
Postconditions:	\<Any postconditions associated with activity\>
Assumptions:	\<Any assumptions made\>
Issues:	\<Outstanding issues concerning activity\>

FIGURE 11-5   Activity behavior description

We don't recommend blindly "decomposing" use cases in this manner in an endless fashion, we do recommend limiting the use of this technique to very large and complex use cases that need further detailing.

Activity behavior descriptions are referenced in the base use case's flow of events by annotations showing where activity behavior descriptions are provided.

We think of activity behavior descriptions as supplemental documentation for representing detailed requirements without cluttering up the use case model. Activity behaviors can have preconditions and postconditions. A sample activity behavior template is outlined in Figure 11-5. For a sample activity behavior description for the "Validate loan application" use case activity, see Figure 11-6.

Documenting Details of Business Procedures and Rules

An area of some debate within the use case community is how to document detailed business procedures and rules that are within the system's scope and will occur as part of the execution of a use case's flow of events.

First, what is a business rule? Business rules are defined as detailed procedures, relationships, and guidelines that drive what the business will do in a particular situation. A system will need to implement these rules if it is to automate the aspects of the business to which they apply. These procedures and rules pinpoint requirements that will need to be captured.

For example, when applying for a loan, what are the rules for determining the interest rate? When evaluating a loan, what are the guidelines governing debt-to-

Use case name:	Submit loan request
Activity name:	Validate loan application
Activity step or ID:	3.1
Trigger:	Loan application received
Brief description:	The customer's application for a loan request is validated to determine completeness and correctness.
Preconditions:	Loan application received
Detailed description:	The system reviews the loan application to ensure that all key fields are filled in and completed • All contact information, such as postal address, e-mail address, and telephone number are complete and in the correct format. • The bank internal account information (if applicable) is correct: the account number is in valid format and the balance is correct. • The credit references (information associated with past and present credit and repayment sources) are complete. • The loan amount is within the broad acceptable limits of the bank for this type of loan and customer. If the loan application is complete, set the loan request status to "Application complete." If the loan application is incomplete, set the loan request status to "Application incomplete."
Postconditions:	Loan application has been validated.

FIGURE 11-6 Activity behavior for validate loan application

income ratio? Including these rules in the use case can clutter the flow, resulting in an overly long flow of events that is hard to read and has lost focus.

However, rather then lose the business rules as they are discovered, document them in activity behavior descriptions or place them in an SRS or other documentation and provide traceability to and from the use case. For a large system with many rules, it can be most efficient to specify them outside the use cases, as these types of requirements can be very detailed and can be used in multiple use cases.

There may be some rules that come from artifacts other than the use case model. For example, the analysis object model and textual requirements not chosen to be modeled in the use cases are possible sources of rules. Although outside the scope of this book, as the rules become associated with domain objects, document this relationship as well. Traceability is then maintained between the use cases, business rules, and domain objects.

When considering whether to break out an activity behavior, consider the following:

- Are there some aspects of the use case that need to be documented at a greater level of detail than others? If so, use activity behavior descriptions to capture the details of the activities.
- Is the use case getting so large and complex with details that it is difficult to follow at one reading?
- Are there requirements within a use case activity that are highly volatile or changeable? To help maintain the use case model, consider placing them into their own activity descriptions.
- Are there detailed business rules associated with the activity that would be better represented outside the use case flow of events?

When using an activity behavior description, leave enough description of the activity in the use case flow of events so that a user can understand what the activity involves. This helps keep the flow understandable. If readers want more specific details about the activity, they can refer to the activity behavior description.

Warning: Use case modeling is not functional decomposition, but taking the concept of activity descriptions too far will result in one. We use activity descriptions only if we feel there is a need to break out a behavior, and we go only one level deep. Doing otherwise decreases the readability of the use cases and therefore the understandability of the use case model and drives the design to a functional decomposition rather then an object decomposition. We prefer to map large amounts of detailed logic into object responsibilities (see Chapter 12) and/or a traditional SRS. Avoiding functional decomposition is also the reason we use the word *descriptions,* not *processes* or *flows.*

Another interesting approach for documenting behavioral detail in a use case model is described by Mark Collins-Cope [Collins-Cope 1999]. In this paper, an approach referred to as RSI is used to partition the use case model into three different types of use cases: requirements use cases, service use cases, and interface use cases (RSI), This approach helps organize and structure the detailed information typically contained in a use case model. Requirements use cases describe business processes (but not detailed functionality), interface use cases describe what is presented to the users, and service use cases provide the detailed description of the underlying functionality of the system (very similar to collaboration cases, discussed in Chapter 9).

Conclusion

Information associated with use cases, such as priorities and nonbehavioral requirements, addresses critical requirements associated with a use case but not easily represented in a use case's flow of events. This information should be captured and documented in associated fields on the detailed supplemental use case information templates. Additional detailed business rules and behaviors can be captured in activity behavior descriptions.

Chapter 12
Map Use Cases to Object Models

The word VALUE, it is to be observed, has two different meanings, and sometimes expresses the utility of some particular *object,* and sometimes the power
of purchasing other goods which possession of that *object* conveys.

—Adam Smith, *Wealth of Nations* [Smith 1937]

What's in this chapter?

This chapter discusses the mapping and integration of the use case model
with a domain and analysis object models. Specific techniques such as CRUD
matrixes, use case to object responsibility mapping tables, and sequence diagrams are discussed.

Use cases are a representation of system behavior that is easy for stakeholders to
work with. However, a complete understanding of a problem also requires that the
analyst consider the static or informational perspective. During system analysis
the things that need to be captured, represented, and manipulated by the system
must also be modeled.

A conceptual or logical object model is used to model these aspects. The
model includes the objects in the domain that the system will be responsible for—
the attributes, business rules, and information associated with each object and the
relationships between the objects. The use case model captures the behaviors of
the system, while the object model describes the static structure.

Davis [1993] describes three characteristics that any analysis approach
needs to provide to completely define what he calls a "knowledge structure"—a

structured collection of concepts and their interrelationships. These characteristics are:

- *Partitioning*. Ability to divide or break a problem into its key parts and understand the relationships between the parts.
- *Abstraction*. Ability to pick out the key aspects of the problem from the more general elements and relationships.
- *Projection*. Ability to view the relationships and interactions of the components from different external viewpoints or perspectives.

Use cases provide the projection aspect very elegantly. And, while some abstraction and partitioning can be represented within the use case model, the use cases do little to represent the structural aspects, such as partitioning and abstracting of information requirements. Concepts such as associations, aggregation, and generalization within the static object model provide another approach to modeling requirements, complementing the use case model and thereby helping to provide a more robust analysis modeling approach. The combination of the use cases and the object model provides a comprehensive means of capturing a complete analysis of what the problem is and what the system will do.

In traditional structured analysis, data flow diagrams (DFD) provided a functional view of the representation and a logical data model represented the static view [Yourdon 1989]. When an object modeling approach is taken, the use cases capture the functionality of the system, and the object model can be used to capture the static or structural aspects (the object model can be used to represent other dynamic aspects as well).

These representations combine to provide a very comprehensive picture of what the problem is and what the system will do.

These two representations of the requirements need to be integrated. Do the objects defined in the object model represent things that participate in the use cases? Are the objects and relationships defined sufficiently in the object model to support the behaviors in the use cases? The use case can be used to both create as well as validate the objects and their relationships.

In this chapter we examine several approaches to integrating two models. This is not a book on object modeling, but it is important to understand the relationship between use case modeling and object modeling during the overall analysis activity.

Analysis Object Modeling

An analysis object model is at a logical or requirements level of abstraction, so it should reflect things and relationships that make sense to the customers and users.

An analysis object model should describe the domain that the system will be responsible for supporting. A distinction is sometimes made between a domain object model and an analysis object model. A **domain object model** is a high-level conceptual picture of the "domain" or business in which the system will operate. An **analysis object model** adds more details to the objects based on specific and detailed system requirements. While this distinction is important during a system development effort, for the purposes of describing the integration of use cases and "logical" object models, we do not make a distinction. We encourage the reader, however, to explore this topic further in a good object development process book [see Jacobson 1999].

In any case, the domain or analysis object model should reflect the customer's business and should use terms that are part of the customer's business so that it can be successfully understood and validated by the customer. The customer should be able to look at the model and say, "Yes, these objects and their relationships represent things about us and what we do." A detailed discussion of object modeling at the analysis level is the subject of a large number of references including Booch [1994] and Rumbaugh [1991]. For discussion purposes in this chapter, we use the following characteristics:

Domain and analysis object models describe the problem domain within the context of the system's overall responsibilities to the business. The classes, their properties, relationships (such as inheritance, associations, and aggregations), and interactions represent the real-world entities. The model is as free from technical or implementation details as possible.

See Figures 12-1 and 12-2 for an example of a partial domain object model for the loan example.

The models and representations used during analysis can be very complex and diverse, and it is difficult to view the pieces from a "flat" or single viewpoint. For example, object relationships and information are represented in the static view of the object model; text-based system behaviors are represented with use cases; and more detailed dynamic aspects can be modeled with sequence, collaboration, and state diagrams. All of this information needs to be integrated and represented. Given this, think of the requirements analysis information as being contained in a large cube with each side of the cube showing a different facet or view of the information (Figure 12-3). For example, turn the cube one way and see the requirements information in its use case form. Turn the cube another way and see it in its static form (i.e., inheritance, aggregation, associations). Turn it yet again and see the object interactions that reflect the behaviors and interactions defined in the requirements. While an analyst needs to be judicious about how much object modeling is performed

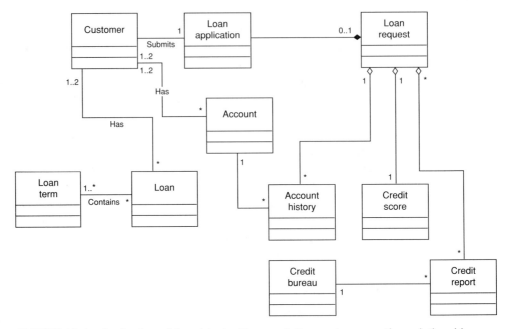

FIGURE 12-1   Static view of the object with association and aggregation relationships

during an analysis effort (to avoid analysis paralysis), the various facets of the cube can help view, understand, represent, and validate the requirements. Object models provide another set of viewpoints from which to judge completeness and consistency. Also, the different views help to alleviate analysis paralysis by providing more than one perspective from which to attack the problem.

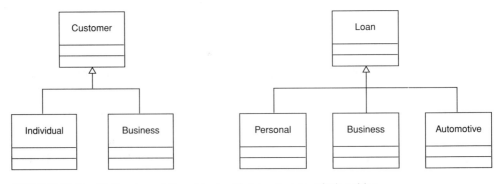

FIGURE 12-2   Static view of the object with inheritance relationships

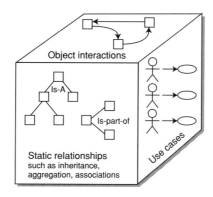

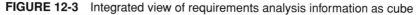

FIGURE 12-3   Integrated view of requirements analysis information as cube

The use case and object models complement each other, with the object model providing the following benefits:

- It provides a representation of the common business abstractions and their relationships that are a responsibility of the system.
- It aids in consistent descriptions of key concepts.
- It balances the functional aspects of the use case model.

Parallel Use Case and Object Modeling

A common practice we have seen is the definition of system requirements using only use cases, with little or no object modeling. Projects, particularly those with inexperienced developers or developers who are under very tight time constraints, are often be tempted to implement the objects without first taking the time to represent them in an object model. The result is a functional design, not an object-oriented one. All good intentions aside, it is important to take the time to perform the translation (Figure 12-4). Our experience has been that if the analysis models do not reflect a solid object-oriented perspective, it is unlikely that the design model will, defeating the purpose of an object-oriented approach; therefore, we like to make sure that our analysis results provide an object-oriented perspective.

The challenge, as mentioned earlier, is to integrate the use case model and the object model and maintain consistency between them. The creation of use cases can help in the discovery of the objects as well as facilitate the definition of their

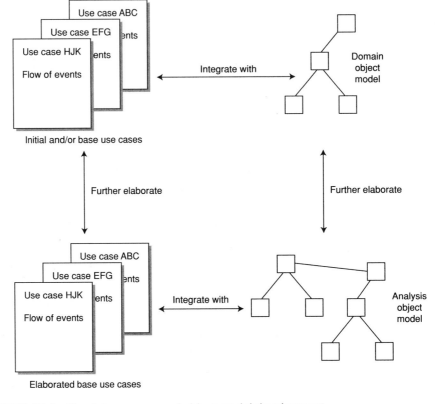

FIGURE 12-4   Parallel use case and object model development

relationships in the static object model in support of the interactions between the participating objects in the use cases (Figure 12-5).

When performing requirements analysis with use cases and object models, a similar mapping issue arises. To ensure that the use cases and the object model stay in sync and that the functionality defined in the use case is reflected in the objects, the following questions need to be addressed:

- Do the objects have the appropriate attributes to support their participation in the use case?

- Do the relationships between the objects—associations, aggregation, and so on—support the interactions that will occur?

- Do the objects have the high-level responsibilities needed to support the use cases they participate in?

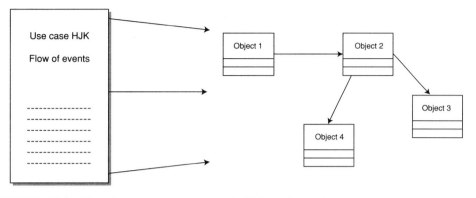

FIGURE 12-5   Mapping a use case to a set of interacting objects

Think of the analysis process as analogous to determining the requirements for a new house. The use cases describe how you and your family will use the house, and the object model describes the things in the house that reflect these needs and their relationships. A description of a bathroom outlines the things that are needed to wash your hands and take a shower, such as a sink and a shower. A description of a kitchen would outline the things needed to cook food, store food, and so on. There are several ways of achieving this use case and object modeling integration, including

- the use of basic CRUD matrixes to provide a simple mapping between the use cases and the object model,
- an expanded form of CRUD matrixes that takes into consideration specific behaviors of the use case that manifest themselves in the object model, and
- if a responsibility-driven analysis approach is desired, the use of UML sequence or collaboration models to map the "strings" of object interactions in a specific use case to the static object model.

Basic CRUD Matrix

In traditional structured analysis, it was typical to develop both a process model and a data model and to map the models through the use of a concept called a CRUD (create, read, update, delete) matrix between the two models.

The use of a CRUD matrix is relatively simple and well tested in the data modeling and functional analysis communities. In a CRUD approach, each use case is analyzed to discover any participating objects; this was first discussed in Chapter 7. A CRUD matrix captures four types of interactions with objects:

- *Create*. Does the use case create an instance of this object?
- *Read*. Does the use case access this object for the purposes of reading one or more of its attributes?
- *Update*. Does the use case update any attributes of the object?
- *Delete*. Does the use case delete this object instance?

In its simplest form, a CRUD matrix is a two-dimensional table with the use cases along the top axis (x) and the objects down the side (y) (Figure 12-6). If an object participates in a use case, note the type—(C) Create, (R) Read, (U) Update, (D) Delete—in the appropriate cell. A partial CRUD for the loan processing system is given in Figure 12-7. For example, the "Book a loan" use case reads information from the loan request object, the evaluation recommendation object, and the loan agreement object, and then creates a loan account object. CRUD matrixes are a simple and effective means of mapping and tracing use cases to objects very early in development. They can also be used to identify the life cycle of objects across use cases.

To create a CRUD matrix, determine the "CRUD" that are performed on each object discovered in the use case. For each unique combination of use case and object, create a CRUD entry in the matrix.

CRUD matrixes provide

- a simple and quick means of mapping objects to use cases,
- help in understanding the basic life cycle of the objects, and
- help in ensuring that the information required for each object by a use case is captured.

	Use case 1	Use case 2	Use case 3	Use case *n*
Object A	C		C	C
Object B		R		
Object C	R			U
Object D			D	

FIGURE 12-6   CRUD Matrix

Use cases/Objects	Submit a loan request	Evaluate a loan request	Book a loan
Applicant	C		
Loan application	C	R	
Credit score	C	R	
Credit report	C	R	
Account history	C	R	
Loan request	C	R, U	R
Loan officer		R	
Evaluation recommendation		C	R
Loan agreement			R
Loan account			C
Loan clerk			R

FIGURE 12-7   Partial CRUD Matrix for several loan processing use cases

Expanded CRUD Matrix

Although a CRUD matrix provides a high level and quick mapping of the relationship between the use case and objects that participate in each use case, which in many cases is sufficient during requirements analysis, it does not address the issues of discovering, capturing, and tracing the responsibilities of the objects. Unlike data entities, objects have responsibilities, and they cannot be captured in a simple CRUD format. For example, when a loan application is validated there is a a lot more going on than a simple read. A CRUD matrix format can be expanded to clearly capture more details of the responsibilities. This in turn helps to identify, highlight, and organize specific requirements. To maintain readability, use cases are rarely thorough enough to capture all the detailed requirements. By modeling this information in formal terms, unknowns can be discussed and addressed. At this level of development, we like the word *responsibility* versus *operation* (the UML standard) to show high-level functionality, not detailed methods, and to help to avoid premature design.

Rather than place a letter (C, R, U, D) in the cell, provide a short description of what object responsibility is involved (Figure 12-8). A responsibility of a loan

	Use case 1	Use case 2	Use case 3	Use case *n*
Object A	\<Responsibility\>			
Object B		\<Responsibility\>	\<Responsibility\>	
Object C				\<Responsibility\>

FIGURE 12-8   Use case object model matrix

request is to determine its status and where it is to be routed based on the status. A responsibility of the credit score is calculating the actual credit score. Place more descriptive text in each cell to describe the way the object is invoked. This helps to map the responsibility of the object in the context of the use case model. The expanded CRUD can be referred to as a *use case object model* (UCOM) matrix.

It is important to remember that the purpose of an expanded CRUD is to help structure the problem and to highlight and define more detailed requirements. Note the responsibilities, and then ask questions. For example, what specific information needs to be validated on a loan application, and why?

A use case object model matrix provides

- traceability to and from the detailed requirements within a responsibility to the objects and use cases they came from,
- a layout of object participation within a use case,
- a more detailed look than a CRUD matrix provides at the responsibilities of each object, and
- a way of organizing and categorizing requirements and their details based on responsibilities.

In the use case, "Submit loan request," a responsibility for validating the information on the application form for completeness is associated with the object modeling the loan application. The object that represents a credit score has the responsibility of calculating the score (Figure 12-9). Again, the objective of a use case object model matrix is to map primary responsibilities from the behavioral representation (use case) to the static representation (object model) to help ensure consistency. When filling in the matrix, new objects that have not yet been discovered and represented in the static object may be found. Update the object model accordingly.

When creating a UCOM, informally review the use case for how an object participates in the use case and what actions are described that are associated with the objects. Create responsibilities based on these actions and place them in the

Use cases/ Objects	Submit a loan request	Evaluate a loan request	Book a loan
Applicant	Initiate the submission of a loan request		
Loan application	Validate application for completeness	Retrieve and present to the loan officer	
Credit score	Calculate credit score	Retrieve and present to the loan officer	
Credit report	Generate evaluation of report	Retrieve and present to the loan officer	
Account history	Generate evaluation of report	Retrieve and present to the loan officer	
Loan request	Create loan request	Update based on loan officer input	Read loan request
Loan officer		Select loan request	Read loan request
Evaluation recommendation		Create an evaluation recommendation	Read loan recommendation
Loan agreement			Generate loan agreement
Loan account			Create new loan account
Loan clerk			Enter loan details

FIGURE 12-9   Partial use case object model matrix for several loan processing use cases

appropriate cells of the UCOM matrix. Then investigate the detailed requirements, business rules, and business logic associated with these responsibilities. If creating the table is difficult—that is, it is conceptually hard to discover responsibilities—perform object sequence modeling (discussed next) to help clarify the various object responsibilities and then fill in the matrix with the results.

Analysis Sequence Diagrams

Object-oriented analysis can be approached from a data-driven perspective, where the static object model relationships are focused on, or from a responsibility-driven approach, where the dynamic relationships are the primary focus. The approach selected is one of style; we have seen good results from both. If a responsibility-driven approach is selected, models to capture the interactions between the objects in use cases are often used. The reason is that while the CRUD and UCOM matrices are very useful and in many, if not most, cases sufficient for requirements analysis, they can miss some key requirements information.

Also, it is sometimes difficult to clearly see and map responsibilities associated with objects without a more formal modeling approach. For example, an object's responsibility is performed in the context of a series of interactions. These interactions may represent business rules and procedures, which influence and help identify more detailed logic that can emerge from a more detailed analysis. In addition, it is sometimes difficult to "see" and describe the requirements in a specific responsibility without explaining the context of how they are used. For these situations, we recommend the use of UML sequence or collaboration models.

One of hardest but one of the most important concepts to understand in an object-oriented analysis effort is the overall flow of control. UML sequence diagrams help make the flow of control clearer. A sequence diagram illustrates how the objects in an object-oriented system interact with one another and how messages are sent and received between the objects. In an analysis effort, a sequence diagram can be used to show the string of object interactions that occur in a specific use case.

Many in the object-oriented community view sequence diagrams as strictly a design tool, not an analysis tool. While we agree that a primary role for these diagrams is in design, they are also a useful tool for responsibility-driven analysis situations where more detail is required. Sequence diagrams also help maintain a balance and integration between the use case view and the object view. For, as we have mentioned several times and related in a number of other experiences (Firesmith [1995] and Berard [1996]), there is nothing inherently object oriented about use cases; the use case model needs to be balanced by the object model.

When developing sequence diagrams, keep in mind that at least three stereotypes or types of object can be defined [Jacobson 1992]:

- Entity (domain or business)
- Interface
- Control

Entity objects, also commonly referred to as business or domain objects, model persistent domain "things" that the system will have some responsibility for. These objects are the focus of the domain object model and elaborated in the analysis.

Interface objects model the specific interfaces that an actor has with system in the context of the use case. Interface objects will ultimately map to the GUI interface, to external systems that interact with the system, or to other interface elements for the specific interaction they model.

Control objects model business rules or processes that cannot be placed neatly in an entity or interface object. They capture processes that are global to the use case and don't nearly fit within a single object. Control objects are the subject of some discussion since they can easily turn into a functional processes. However, their use during analysis helps to understand and represent complex behaviors not associated with any specific entity object. See Jacobson [1992] for additional guidelines.

The objects that participate in a use case interact with each other to perform the behaviors in the use case. These objects pass messages to each other by one object invoking another object's responsibilities (Figure 12-10), where the professor object is asking the student object for its name. When object A invokes object B's responsibility, A is said to collaborate with object B. The invoker object normally waits (in a nonconcurrent sequence) while the invoked object performs its responsibility, perhaps collaborating with other objects. Control is returned to the invoker object when the responsibility has been completed. A string of interactions to perform some behavior is called a sequence (modeled in text by use cases). These interactions are modeled by sequence diagrams [UML 1999].

Format of Sequence Diagram

A sequence diagram has two axes and a single entry point at the upper left corner (Figure 12-11). The order of execution is represented as the vertical axis and is read down. The horizontal axis shows the set of objects that are involved in the sequence. Each object is modeled as a labeled rectangle. Below the rectangle is a dashed line (called the object's lifeline) indicating the object's use during the sequence. Messages between the objects are represented as directed horizontal solid lines between lifelines. Messages indicate requests for a service and are named for the server's responsibilities. Text description of what is occurring can be placed along the left side of the diagram.

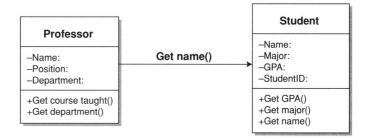

FIGURE 12-10 Professor object sending get name message to student object

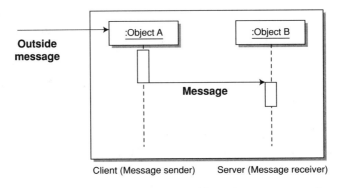

Client (Message sender)   Server (Message receiver)

FIGURE 12-11   Message passing between two objects in a sequence diagram

In a sequence diagram, during analysis, the client object sends a message to the server (collaborating) object. The message name is equal to the receiver's responsibility name. The receiver object then performs its responsibility and may return results to the sender object, as in Figure 12-11. Open rectangles on an object's lifeline can be used to represent when an object has control. The rectangles on the lifeline show the period of time during which an object is performing an action, either directly or through a collaborating object. The top of the rectangle is aligned with the start of the action, the bottom with its end.

A sequence diagram graphically shows the object interactions that result from the execution of the behaviors in a particular use case. An outside message, normally from the actor initiating the use case, invokes a responsibility of object A. Object A kicks off other messages to complete the overall behaviors specified in the use case (Figure 12-12). Object A passes control to object B, and object B must complete the operation, including a message to object C, before returning control to object A.

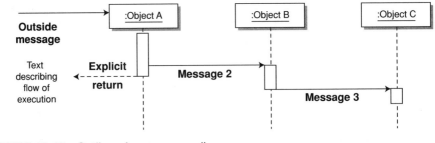

FIGURE 12-12   Outline of a sequence diagram

The first object to be invoked is placed at the far left, and the other objects are placed to its right. Normally, the later the object appears in the use case flow of events, the further to the right it is placed. A vertical dashed line represents the object's lifeline, or its existence over a period of time.

Message Returns

Returns can be either implied—assumed as a condition of the message—or shown explicitly in the diagram. (Tip: Show returns explicitly, but only if it improves the clarity of the diagram; overuse can clutter the diagram.)

Text Description of Sequences

Text describing flow of execution can be placed on the far left side of the diagram. The text narratively describes the illustrated interactions in prose and can include conditionals and iteration. Text can be very useful in improving and enhancing the understanding of the diagrams. When using text, start with the use case flow of events and modify it as new knowledge is acquired during the creation of the sequence diagram.

Preconditions and Postconditions

Just as in use cases, preconditions and postconditions can be associated with a sequence diagram: These conditions can be represented as states in key or important objects in the sequence diagram.

- *Precondition*. What must be true (or needed to have happened for the sequence to be able to execute).
- *Postcondition*. The state in which the sequence diagram leaves the system.

Preconditions and postconditions help to bound or scope the sequence diagram. Start with the preconditions and postconditions of the use case being modeled in the sequence diagram.

Figures 12-13 and 12-14 are sequence diagrams for the submit loan request and evaluate loan request use cases. Remember that the goal of analysis-level sequence diagrams is not design but understanding.

Mapping Use Cases to Object Models Using Sequence Diagrams

The process of sequence diagraming starts with identifying the candidate objects in the use cases. The specific inputs into this process include the use cases and the initial object descriptions. Each use case is replayed (if needed) and the outcome

Precondition: Applicant has access to loan application

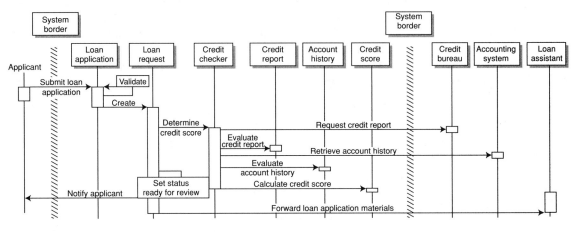

Postcondition: Loan request ready; have credit references validated

FIGURE 12-13   Submit loan request sequence diagram

Precondition: Loan request ready to evaluate

The loan officer selects loan request to review for approval.

• The system presents the loan information gathered on the applicant and the loan application to the loan officer.
• The loan officer reviews the material and determines whether the loan should be approved.
• The loan officer selects the appropriate loan terms and conditions.
• The status of the loan is changed to approved.

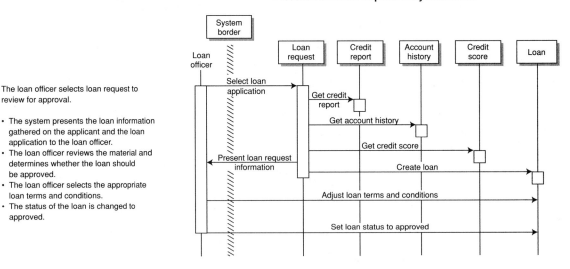

Postcondition: Loan request has been evaluated

FIGURE 12-14   Evaluate loan request sequence diagram

of the processes is a refined set of object descriptions, object sequence diagrams, and a refined or created object model (Figure 12-15).

A brainstorming technique called *role playing* can be used to facilitate responsibility-driven analysis. Role playing helps define objects and their behavior and models the interactions among objects and external users (for example, humans or external systems). With role playing, the analysis team creates object descriptions, traditionally referred to as class responsibility collaborator (CRC) cards [Bollin 1997] [Wilkinson 1995], that document each object's name, description, responsibilities, and other objects with which it collaborates. We like to include object attributes as well, since the role of analysis is to understand the information that will need to be captured.

Role Playing Example

Role playing can be formal or informal, but it always begins by using the initial objects found in the use cases or in other documentation. One approach to role playing would include the following steps:

1. Determine the candidate objects in each use case. Select a set of candidate classes that model the problem. Give each class a name and describe what it is and what it does. For each class, transfer its name and description to a

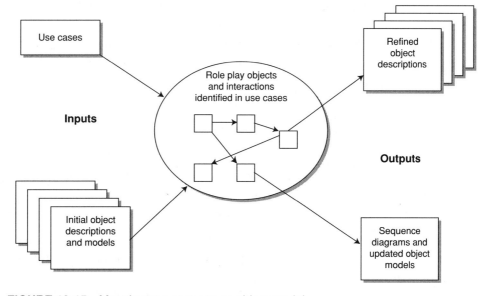

FIGURE 12-15   Mapping use cases to an object model

CRC card or other form of object description, and create a CRC card for each object.

2. Each group member participating in a role-playing session takes a CRC card. The group walks through one use case at a time, simulating collaborations between objects. Each individual plays the role of an object by carrying out its behavior in the context of the use case. As the role playing progresses, object responsibilities and collaborations are identified and documented. On a white board, write down the each class's responsibilities and any collaborators the class uses to accomplish its responsibilities. New objects are created, if necessary, to complete the analysis. Create a sequence diagram to capture the results of the role playing.

3. When a new object is discovered during the role playing, ask if any new associations or other relationships are needed between the objects. In this situation, normally you can wait until after the use case is completely role played and then update the static object model. However, sometimes you get "stuck" creating the sequence diagram and need to explore the object relationships before completing the sequence diagram. In this situation, stop, document the change on the static object model, and then return to the role playing. For each use case, at first focus on the normal flow of events (avoid exceptions and alternatives). Don't try to do all the functionality described in the problem in one use case; rather, break the problem into easy-to-role-play simple use cases.

4. Complete the sequence diagram, and then document any additional detail needed on each object (such as attributes).

5. Copy the sequence diagram from the white board. Erase the white board and start with a new use case.

At the end of session you will have

- a collection of sequence diagrams,
- an updated static object model and object descriptions with high level responsibilities, and
- lots of additional questions to ask the user and customers.

While a sequence diagram emphasizes the time ordering of messages, a UML collaboration diagram emphasizes the structural organization of objects that send and receive messages.

Collaboration diagrams combine elements of the static model and the sequence diagram. While we do not discuss collaboration diagrams in detail here, they can be useful as a complement or alternative representation to a sequence diagram. A good CASE tool such as Rational Rose provides an automated conversion between the two diagrams.

Object Modeling Workshops and Ideal Room Setup[1]

When developing use cases, object modeling, or integrating the models, it is helpful to have facilities and automation to streamline and support the analysis effort. While we have seen very good analysis performed (literally) on a napkin, good automated tool and facility support help the analysis team on a large project with tight delivery times to focus on the important things. Support starts with a good room and equipment (Figure 12-16).

In this room dedicated to the project, white boards line the walls, and static object models can be created and modified on the boards as the team progresses through its analysis. Since the static object model "lives" through time, it has its own dedicated white board(s). The use cases and sequence diagrams are typically developed one at a time. We like to use a recordable white board to create the

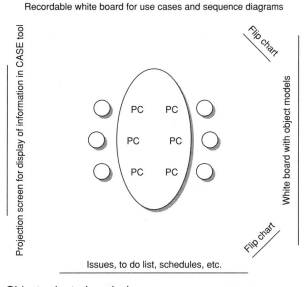

FIGURE 12-16 Object-oriented analysis room

---

[1] We'd like to thank Les Moore of American Management Systems for our interesting discussions on the ideal object modeling room.

sequence diagrams and use cases, print them out, erase the white board, and start again. Project issues, assumptions, and schedule information can be presented on another white board or flip charts.

The results of the session are then transcribed into a CASE tool support. CASE tool support is critical on a large project, although capturing and changing aspects of the object model in a CASE can be difficult during a very dynamic and free-flowing brainstorming session. We like a manual process for the capture, with the results directly entered into the CASE tool.

Issues with Using Sequence Diagrams during Analysis

A sequence diagram provides an effective graphical view of the object interactions in a specific use case's flow of events, along with a means for verifying collaborators, a way to visually identify overly busy classes, and a means for discovering frameworks and patterns. Guidelines for using sequence diagrams during analysis include the following.

- Keep in mind that use cases that represent simple updates and queues normally do not need sequence diagrams. Use cases that represent behavior with complex logic or that needs further clarification benefit most from sequence diagrams.

- The results of a sequence diagram can be placed in a UCOM matrix (or can be automatically generated if you are using a CASE tool that supports the generation of traceability reports between the use case and objects) and each responsibility can then be explored in more detail.

- Sequence diagrams can help find patterns and frameworks in the analysis effort. Factor visual patterns out into include relationships.

- Keep sequence diagrams at the analysis level. Don't get caught up in long design discussions.

- Give each sequence diagram the same name as the name of the use case it is modeling.

- Use the use case flow of events as the default text at the left side of the sequence diagram. It will, however, in all probability become more detailed as the analysis proceeds.

- If arguments occur over where to place a responsibility, ask if it is really a design issue and remember that the goal of analysis is to understand the problem. Select a reasonable object in which to place the responsibility, document the rationale for the decision, and move on.

- Keep the message names informal; the descriptions of the messages should be written to reflect requirements. If there needs to be a description of the operations behaviors, stay away from writing pseudocode, although business rules and mathematical algorithms that express requirements should be documented.

Conclusion

In this chapter, we outlined the rationale and several approaches for creating and maintaining consistency between the use cases and the object models. We discuss several techniques including simple CRUD matrices, use case to object model matrices (UCOM), and UML sequence diagrams. Although this is not a book on object modeling, we outlined key object concepts that can be captured from information in the use cases.

We feel strongly that to effectively clarify, organize, and validate the system requirements, a requirements analysis needs (at least) both the use case model view and a static object model view. Considering the requirements only as use cases will almost always assure that requirements for a large system development will be missed.

Chapter 13
Develop Instance Scenarios

What's in this chapter?

This chapter discusses the concept of use case instances and their use in complementing the use case model. Example approaches discussed include one that is very informal and one that is formal.

We have seen that use cases provide an abstract view of the activities that occur between an actor and the system. When use cases model these activities, however, they do not describe how specific instances of the interactions will occur. Use case instances can be thought of as paper prototypes of how a use case will execute in a given situation. In this sense they can assist in drawing out and validating requirements from the stakeholders. Use case instances are another way of exploring the details, alternatives, and exceptions in the use cases. They are also a nice transition into acceptance and system test cases.

A use case describes the abstract behaviors that happen when, for example, an applicant submits a loan request. In this use case, a generalized description of the behaviors is provided in the flow of events. What the use case does not describe, for example, is what happens when a specific individual applies for a specific loan of a specific amount. The use case does not specify what exactly occurs when Joe Smith submits a loan request for $100,000 on November 10, 2002. This would be considered one **instance** of how the use case would execute under a given set of conditions.

Use Case Instances Model Specific Executions of a Use Case

A use case provides a generalized representation or template of behaviors that occur when a specific event happens. During requirements analysis, documenting system requirements without having to document what would happen in every possible execution of the use cases (an infinite number) can be an advantage. Just as with other modeling techniques applied during analysis, such as conceptual object models, process models, and data models, the specific values or execution normally are not as important to capture as the abstractions of how things occur or what things are.

During analysis, it can sometimes be useful to look at how specific instances of use cases execute, especially in situations when defining the specific instance provides a valuable addition to the use case model. To capture a specific execution of a use case, UML provides a concept called a **use case instance**.

Booch describes an abstraction as a representation of the "ideal essence of a thing," whereas an instance represents a "concrete manifestation" [Booch 1999]. The use case instance is a description of what occurs in a specific situation. UML 1.3 defines a use case instance as a "performance of a use case, initiated by a message instance from an instance of an actor. As a response the use-case instance performs a sequence of actions as specified by the use case, like communicating with actor instances, not necessarily only the initiating one." In other literature and in practice, use case instances are sometimes also referred to as *instance scenarios, analysis scenarios*, or just *scenarios*.

Use case instances can be used during the use case modeling effort to draw out and add more detail to the behaviors in a use case flow of events. Use case instances are also commonly used to capture and understand behavioral variations in a use case. Use case instances can be created in an informal manner or captured very formally with specific input and output parameters.

Use Cases Are to Object Classes as Use Case Instances Are to Object Instances

The relationship between use cases and use case instances is similar to the relationship between an object class and its object instances. An object class is a description of a set of objects (instances) that share the same attributes, operations, relationships, and semantics. So each object instance of a class has specific values for its attributes and relationships. The same can be said for the use case and its instances; the use case is a description of the behaviors, and the instances provide specific executions of the behaviors.

Graphically, UML can be used to represent the relationship between a use case and use case instance as a dependency relationship with the <<instanceOf>> (Figure 13-1). Whereas use cases provide a set of generalized preconditions and postconditions and a flow of events, a use case instance describes what happens if a certain set of input values and environmental conditions occur and a specific set of decisions are made during the execution of the use case. Just as with object classes and object instances, use case instances do not stand alone; they always depend on a use case. Since a specific set of input values will result in the execution of specific path through the use case flow of events, a specific set of output values will also occur. The use case instance can also document these output parameters.

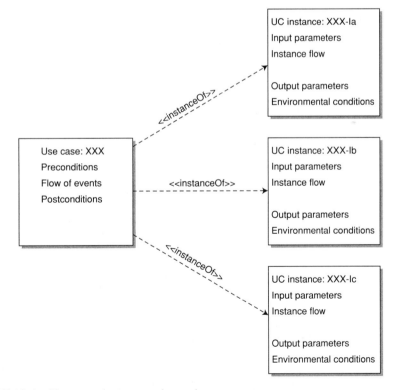

FIGURE 13-1 Use case instances depend on a use case

Why Create Use Case Instances?

Use case instances complement and supplement the use cases in a number of ways.

- They provide a paper prototype of how a use case will execute in a given situation.
- They draw out and validate requirements from the stakeholders.
- They provide another way of exploring the details, alternatives, and exceptions in the use cases.
- They act as a transition into acceptance and system test cases.

Within a use case modeling effort, we have seen use case instances utilized

- in a very informal manner to draw out and validate requirements with the end user and customer,
- in a more formal manner to discuss and document additional details as well as alternates and exceptions,
- as a starting point to develop acceptance and system test cases, and
- as a means to drive incremental development.

In this chapter we discuss applying use case instances both informally and formally. Testing is discussed in detail in Chapter 14. Using them in an incremental development effort is discussed in Chapter 19.

An excellent discussion of both use case instances (referred to as analysis scenarios) and their place in a development effort can be found in *Developing Object-Oriented Software: An Experience-Based Approach* [IBM 1997]. The book states:

> Consider the use case model and analysis scenarios (use case instances) as a complementary pair of work products. The use case model identifies system boundaries, external agents, and top-level system requirements; the analysis scenarios elaborate the requirements and tease out the behavioral variations of the system.

We should state now that there is very little agreement on a "standard" approach to applying use case instances. They are typically applied in a very different manner on different projects. Our intent is not to survey every approach or to specify a standard approach but to present several ways of proceeding with use case instances. Additional information on use case instances and scenarios can be found in a number of references, including Weidenhaupt [1998], Hsia [1994], and Potts [1994].

Use Case Instances Can Be Applied Informally

End users sometimes have a hard time describing or validating behaviors that are too abstract. Users may find it easier to think about and describe what they want in concrete terms rather than in the abstract terms. There is a software development saying that when it comes to defining a system's requirements, stakeholders "know it when they see it." So, developers build prototypes to provide concrete examples to the stakeholders, with the intention of drawing out difficult new requirements early in development. Users and customers often like to express requirements in terms of examples or, conversely, to review and validate the requirements presented as examples. In an informal approach, use case instances can be presented as examples of how a use case will execute.

Figure 13-2 shows an informal use case instance for submitting a loan request. This instance represents one possible execution of the use case. In this example, an instance of the applicant actor named Joe Smith submits a loan request for $20,000 with a "normal" set of circumstances surrounding the loan submission: The applicant's credit is good, all needed information about the applicant is available, and the loan amount is well within bank policy for approval. Another use case instance,

Instance name:	Joe Smith applies for a loan
Use case name:	Submit loan request
Instance description:	An applicant submits a loan request for $20,000, and the loan is granted. The applicant has a typical credit and account portfolio.
Instance flow:	• Joe Smith completes an application for a $20,000 car loan and mails the application to the bank. • The application includes information on Joe's credit references and work references. • The application is received and entered into the system. The system validates that Joe has completed all the required fields including income, address, and work and credit references. • Joe has a checking account with the bank, and the system validates that the account number on the application is correct. • The system forwards a request for a copy of a credit report on Joe along with Joe's social security number and address to a credit bureau. The credit report states that Joe has $2,000 in outstanding debt and no outstanding bad debits. • Joe's checking account history is checked by the system. Joe has $3,500 in the account and has maintained the account for the last five years in good standing. • Based on the credit information, his income of $65,000 per year, and the amount and type of loan, the system calculates a satisfactory credit score on Joe. • The status of Joe's loan request is set to "Ready for review" and the application and all supporting information is routed to Jane Jones, the loan officer, for evaluation. • Joe is notified by mail that his loan application has been received and that it is being evaluated.

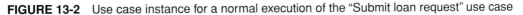

FIGURE 13-2 Use case instance for a normal execution of the "Submit loan request" use case

presented in Figure 13-3, represents a situation where there are specific credit problems. Finally, in Figure 13-4, a use case instance represents the situation of an applicant submitting incomplete information on the loan application.

The informal approach to representing use case instances is useful in both gathering requirements from users and presenting examples to them of how a use case would execute under certain conditions. When taking the informal approach, create a use case instance that represents a normal execution and, if needed, several other use cases instances that represent major variations. Just as in prototyping, focus on areas of the requirements that are unknown or at high risk.

When presenting use cases in this manner, keep the template and descriptions simple and very basic. Remember your audience: If more formal use case instances are needed, they can be documented in another format. Don't overwhelm the user with a large number of informal use cases; the purpose is to present information in a manner that is quickly grasped. Also, be careful in selecting the use cases to be represented in this manner. This technique supplements the use cases; it does not replace them.

Instance name:	Applicant with no credit history submits a loan request
Use case name:	Submit loan request
Instance description:	An applicant submits a loan request for $10,000 but has no credit report with any of the major credit reporting bureaus. The customer's request is rejected due to insufficient credit information.
Instance flow:	• Bob Jones completes an application for a $10,000 car loan and mails the application to the bank. • The application includes information on Bob's credit references and work references. • The application is received and entered into the system. The system validates that Bob has completed all the required fields including income, address, and work and credit references. • Bob has a checking account with the bank, and the system validates that the account number on the application is correct. • The system forwards a request for a copy of a credit report on Bob along with Bob's social security number and address to a credit bureau. The credit bureau responds that no credit history is available for Bob. The system then forwards requests to the other major credit bureaus, which all respond that no credit report is available. • Bob's checking account history is checked by the system. Bob has $100 in the account and has the maintained the account for the last one year in good standing. • Based on automated bank policies, the automated recommendation is to decline the loan based on insufficient credit history. • The status of the loan request is set to "Ready for review."

FIGURE 13-3   Use case instance for an insufficient credit situation of the "Submit loan request" use case

Instance name:	Missing credit information on the submitted loan application
Use case name:	Submit a loan request
Instance description:	John Smith submits a loan request for $20,000 but leaves the references off the application form. The bank asks him to provide the information before the loan request further processed.
Instance flow:	• John Smith completes a loan application for a $10,000 car loan and mails the application to the bank. • The application includes information fields on credit references and work references. • The application is received and entered into the system. The system validates that the customer has completed the required fields for income, address, and work references. The system determines that the credit references are missing. • The system generates a letter notifying John Smith that the references are needed and mails the letter to the customer. The loan request status is set to "Suspended—incomplete information."

FIGURE 13-4   Use case instance for incomplete information on the application of the "Submit loan request" use case

When developing informal use case instances, we find it useful to explicitly describe the flow (at a high level) to help capture the user's focus. Consider using high-level graphics to represent selected use case instances with the users.

Normally, the actual use cases are developed first during the analysis; then, based on this analysis result, selected use cases are chosen to be presented with instances. However, on one project, we developed several informal use case instances first, before developing the actual use cases, since the users felt much more comfortable with this approach and were able to more easily express their needs. We then generalized the use case instances into use cases.

We have also used this technique very, very informally during a use case brainstorming session. We verbally walked through a use case model with different execution paths or instances that could possibly occur. Also, modelers can create instances if they get "stuck" in a use case to help move it along. In these situations, you may not need to write the instances down. This technique proved useful in quickly validating the use cases in a workshop group.

Use Cases Can Be Applied More Formally

While informal use case instances are a useful technique for presenting basic behaviors and attributes to users, a more rigorous approach can be taken for capturing in detail the behaviors, inputs, environmental factors, and alternatives associated with one specific execution of the use case. Use case instances are extremely useful in highlighting and documenting specific details of both the basic use case flow of events and the alternative flows. In this manner they can complement extend relationships, alternative flows, and conditional logic.

We have stressed the pros and cons of capturing a large amount of detailed information in use cases versus leaving them at a higher level (see Chapter 19 for more discussion on this topic). Since use cases are abstract, documenting the details and all the possible alternatives within a use case flow of events or through extend a relationship can be unwieldy. One approach that addresses this problem and provides robustness to the use case model is documenting basic behaviors in the use cases and utilizing the use case instances to flesh out additional details, alternatives, and exceptions. This approach helps keep the use case flow of events "clean" and understandable.

For these purposes, use case instances can be categorized as primary or secondary. **Primary use case instances**, also referred to as "sunny day" use case instances, reflect what normally happens when things go as planned. **Secondary use case instances**, also referred to as "rainy day" use case instances, document what happens when something goes wrong or occurs unexpectedly. For example, what happens if the loan amount exceeds the bank's loan policy guidelines or the credit bureau does not have a record of the customer? Secondary use case instances are used to document alternatives and exceptions.

Layout of a Use Case Instance Description

There is no standard way of representing a use case instance, but several common pieces of information can be captured. These can include the fields described in the use case instance template in Figure 13-5.

A warning on creating detailed instance flows: While they can be very useful for capturing detailed business logic, they can also be very difficult to maintain and keep up to date throughout the development effort. As a tool for drawing out requirements, instances are very effective, but be aware that updating and maintaining a large number of use case instances during a large project development effort can be a nightmare.

Finding and Creating Use Case Instances

The best place to start creating formal use case instances is obviously with a use case. We like to first select use cases that are central to the system and/or that will be implemented first during the development effort. As previously mentioned, the goal is to develop prototypical representations of how the system will execute. As with dynamic or executable prototypes, the entire system is not normally prototyped.

There is no set number of use case instances to create, but keep in mind that there is an infinite number of possible execution paths. It is neither desirable nor

Parent use case name:	Name of the use case that this instance is associated with. This can also include the names of extending or including use cases considered in this instance.
Parent use case ID:	<ID number of the use case this instance is associated with. Can also include the ID of extending or including use cases considered in this instance.>
Instance name:	<Name of this use case instance.>
Instance ID:	<ID number of this use case instance.>
Environmental conditions and assumptions:	• Overall environmental conditions in which this use case instance executes • Specific conditions that must exist for this instance of the use case to execute • Specific preconditions for this instance • Specific nonbehavioral requirements associated with this instance, for example, number of simultaneous users who access the system during the instance, critical system or interface failures, security breach attempts • Other assumptions
Inputs:	<Specific information and values used as input into the use case instance>
Instance flow description:	<What occurs during an execution of the instance. Analogous to a use case's flow of events, except that it describes the specific behavioral paths taken through the use case including the decision points, include relationships and alternatives for this set of input parameters, and environmental conditions.>
Outputs:	<Results of execution of this instance; information produced>

FIGURE 13-5 Use case instance template

useful to document a very large number. We like to target no more than five to seven use case instances per major use case selected for insurance modeling. If significant questions continue to rise after creating several use case instances, you can create additional use case instances to address them. This is not design, so don't try to test every possibility. Look for specific situations that change requirements or are architecturally significant. During requirements analysis, focus on only prototype concrete instances of things that you are unsure of or that carry a risk if they are not defined in detail. Also, if you are performing incremental/iterative development, focus on behavioral sequences that are of the highest development priority.

When developing use case instances in this manner, look at the use case's preconditions and postconditions to determine meaningful examples of inputs, starting with input parameters and environmental factors that are "sunny day." For example, in the "ATM withdraw funds" use case, a sunny day assumption would be that the customer wishes to withdraw $300 from a checking account, that the account currently contains $1,000, and that the customer has not exceeded the daily withdrawal limit.

Do several sunny day instances, focusing on the boundaries—for example, the customer attempting to withdraw all the cash or just the minimum amount. Look for environmental conditions that might impact the execution of the instance.

Then, select several major alternatives/exceptions to model. For example, what happens if the customer tries to withdraw $1,200 from a bank account with only $1,000 in it? What happens if the customer tries the same thing but has overdraft protection? As you can see, the use case instances (see Figures 13.6 through 13.9) can

Parent use case name:	Submit loan request
Parent use case ID:	UC-100
Instance name:	Request is evaluated positively
Instance ID:	UCIS-100-1
Environmental conditions and assumptions:	A "normal" situation is assumed: All the information is available, credit is good, income is sufficient and the loan amount is within the bank's policy parameters.
Inputs:	Loan application for consumer loan of $10,000, credit report
Instance flow description:	• A loan application is submitted by an applicant via the Internet. • The loan application is validated to ensure that all the fields are complete including the amount field. The information on the form, such as address (valid street, city, zip) references, and checking account number and balance, is validated for completeness and correctness. • A system evaluation of the external credit report shows no negative information (no delinquent or late payments). The applicant's credit cards carry a combined average balance of $500. • A system internal credit check determines that the applicant's checking account balance is $3,000 and is in good standing. • Based on the credit information and a reported annual income of $75,000, an automated credit score of 85 out of 100 is calculated and an initial automated recommendation of initial approval is assigned. • The loan request status is set to "Initial credit check complete" and the loan request is routed to a loan assistant for a reference validation.
Outputs:	Initial recommendation for loan request approval

FIGURE 13-6 Use case instance: Positive evaluation of loan request

Parent use case name:	Submit loan request
Parent use case ID:	UC-100
Instance name:	Request is evaluated negatively due to bad credit
Instance ID:	UCIS-100-2
Environmental conditions and assumptions:	The applicant has negative credit, and the system has access to all needed information.
Inputs:	Loan application for consumer loan of $415,000, credit report
Instance flow description:	• A loan application is submitted by an applicant via the Internet. • The loan application is validated to ensure that all the fields are complete, including the amount field. The information on the form, such as address, references, and checking account number and balance, is validated for completeness and correctness. • A system evaluation of the external credit report shows several delinquent credit cards and one account in collections. It also shows a combined average credit card balance of $5000. • A system internal credit check determines that the checking account balance is $100, and four checks have been returned in the last year. • Based on the credit information and an annual income of $65,000, an automated credit score result of 25 out of 100 is calculated, and an initial automated recommendation is to disapprove the loan request. • The loan request status is set to "Initial credit check complete" and the loan request in routed to a loan assistant for a reference validation.
Outputs:	Recommendation for loan request disapproval

FIGURE 13-7   Use case instance: Negative evaluation of loan request

model instances of the submit loan request use case's flow of events and its alternatives. A single use case instance can also model a combination of a use case and its include and extend relationships.

Some developers like to document the major alternative flows with high-level extend relationships or alternative flows and flesh out the details with use case instances. We've also seen developers replace extend relationship and alternative flows entirely with a set of use case instances that model the key alternatives.

What we really like about use case instances is their ability to draw out and model requirements without driving the use case into too much detail. By the way, the UML activity diagrams presented in Chapter 9 can also be used to represent the use case instance.

Parent use case name:	Submit loan request
Parent use case ID:	UC-100
Instance name:	Additional information is needed on the loan application
Instance ID:	UCIS-100-3
Environmental conditions and assumptions:	A loan application is submitted with key information missing.
Inputs:	Loan application with missing information
Instance flow description:	• A loan application is submitted by an applicant via the Internet. • The loan application is validated to ensure that all the fields are complete. It is determined that the account history is missing from the form. • No further processing of the loan request will occur until the applicant provides the information. • The applicant is requested via e-mail to provide the missing information.
Outputs:	Suspended loan request

FIGURE 13-8   Use case instance: Additional information needed

Parent use case name:	Submit loan request
Parent use case ID:	UC-100
Instance name:	Marginal loan case—no external credit history
Instance ID:	UCIS-100-4
Environmental conditions and assumptions:	A loan request is submitted, but no external credit report can be found for the applicant.
Inputs:	Loan application for consumer loan of $8,000
Instance flow description:	• A loan application is submitted by an applicant via the Internet. • The loan application is validated to ensure that all the fields are complete, including the amount field. The information on the form, such as address, references, and checking account number and balance, is validated for completeness and correctness. • No external credit report can be found for the applicant. • No automated credit score is calculated and no initial recommendation is assigned. • The loan request status is set to "Ready for review" and the loan request is routed to the loan assistant for further review to validate the credit and income references.
Outputs:	Loan request marked as marginal. A loan officer will have to make a more detailed evaluation.

FIGURE 13-9   Use case instance: Marginal request of loan request

Conclusion

If use cases tell a broad story, then use cases instances fill in the details based on a specific set of conditions. And, whereas a use case models the abstract, a use case instance describes how specific parameters such as input information, a specific instance of an actor role, environmental factors, and decision points affect the execution of a use case flow of events.

Applying use case instances can be informal, to help elicit and express requirements to high-level stakeholders, or formal, to help model detailed requirements to complement the use cases and/or replace extend relationships when modeling alternatives.

Instance scenarios are a useful tool for understanding the implications of a use case. Instance scenarios can be developed at any time in the use case modeling process to help understand or clarify ambiguous requirements. In addition, use case instances are also a very good starting point for outlining acceptance and system test cases because they document expected input and expected outputs.

Chapter 14
Create Test Cases and Documentation

> Use cases and test cases work well together in two ways: If the use cases
> for a system are complete, accurate, and clear, the process of deriving the
> test cases is straightforward. And if the use cases are not in good shape, the
> attempt to derive test cases will help debug the use cases.
>
> —Ross Collard [Collard 1999]

What's in this chapter?

This chapter presents an integral part of the software development process: testing and documenting the system. Use cases play a fundamental role in driving these activities. When use cases are combined with test cases and documentation, a round-trip vehicle is created to verify and explain the system functionality.

Documentation and test cases are the flip side of use cases. Use cases describe what the system will be like, while **test cases** ensure that the system is all that was promised. **Documentation** describes how systems actually behave. As a system is realized in the software development process, it moves from specification via use cases into testing, and finally into documentation. As you can see, there is a direct relationship between these three areas.

Use cases provide the vehicle for test cases and documentation. They are created early in development, so test and documentation plans can be put in place to coincide with the development schedule. When an incremental approach is used to construct a software system, testing and documentation of the system can be incremental as well. Performing test cases and writing documentation can be distributed over the course of software development instead of being left until the end.

Creating a Test Strategy

Many things can go wrong with a system. Perhaps the easiest to test is the functionality of the system as defined by a use case model. However, if we stopped testing and shipped our product having tested nothing else, we would be doing our user community and our company a great disservice. There are many other things that can go wrong.

Many types of problems occur based upon requirements not found in any use case. Some of these problems stem from the execution platform or interaction with other products, which are beyond the use case model entirely. But many problems represent implicit assumptions in the use case model. These assumptions can be used to test the use case model, as well as the product, for accuracy and consistency.

One problem frequently encountered is the interaction between the use cases. The use case model may have an implied order such as "Submit loan request," "Evaluate loan request," "Generate loan agreement," and "Generate approval letter." This is the natural order of the actions of loan processing. But what if I attempt to generate a loan agreement on a submitted (vs. approved) loan request? How about generating a loan agreement on a denied loan request?

Range checking and error handling of entered values represent another class of problems that the system must be able to handle. What is the maximum dollar amount that can be requested? Does the system handle sufficiently large dollar amounts? How about negative dollar amounts? How large is too large? (Remember that the year 1999 was always considered large enough to handle any system dates that might be encountered.) Ranges must reflect the ability for the system to "grow" over time.

A complete test strategy includes functional testing, interaction testing, testing range/error handling, and many more forms of testing beyond the scope of this book. A complete test strategy requires a plan of attack on the areas that present a risk to the project. Many of these areas are domain specific. Is the project mission critical, graphical user interface-centric, scalable, and security conscious? Answers to these questions will determine the areas that need to be tested to achieve the level of quality desired. We restrict this chapter to the three forms (functional, interaction, and range/error checking) that may be derived implicitly or explicitly from the use case model.

Creating a Test Plan

Once the initial use case model is complete, it is time to begin creating a test plan. The first decision that has to be made is the level of the plan. How many test plans should we build? If the answer is one, it must encompass the entire product and contain test information for each increment. This approach has the following disadvantages [Black 1999]:

- *Communication*. The test plan serves as a communication vehicle for developers, analysts, management, and testers. All these people should review the plan to ensure proper functional coverage and that all of the risks are accounted for. Monolithic documents can be intimidating to start with. A monolithic plan may make it difficult to find the information relevant to the area in which the stakeholder has concern.

- *Timeliness*. If an incremental approach is used to develop the system, timeliness may be an issue. High-priority use cases may be defined in the early increments while detailed descriptions of lower-priority use cases may be delayed until later increments. The result may be a test plan that is waiting for information when the first increments are ready for testing.

- *Goals*. Early test cases need to concentrate on ensuring that the architecture based upon the high-priority use cases will hold together. Prioritizing use cases to reduce risk in the product was discussed in Chapter 4. Test cases may help expose new risks or areas where changes in the architecture must be made to build a more stable product. Test cases in the middle increments focus on functionality. Later test cases focus more on integration and regression as more of the functionality is added. Each of these objectives may deserve its own test plan.

One advantage of the all-in-one test plan is ability to keep the information in a single document consistent. Less cutting and pasting is done, as there is one single document in which the information resides. Even with these advantages, this type of test plan is more apropos to a project utilizing the single-iteration or waterfall approach.

Another approach to test plans is to create one test plan for each use case [McGregor 1997]. Many project plans schedule increments around use cases or scenarios. This approach allows maximum flexibility should use cases be moved from one increment to another as plans change. It also allows traceability back to the requirements model should the requirements change [McGregor 1997]—and one thing you can depend on is requirements and plans changing.

Finally, test plans may be written for each increment of software development. Test plans are kept in sync with the software development project plans, and as the development plans change, so do the test plans. The test plan is partitioned so that each use case has its own section. Changes result in the section being moved from one plan to another, and both plans are updated accordingly.

Each of these approaches has merits. The characteristics of the project and the personal preferences of the managers involved ultimately determine which approach is used.

Elements of a Test Plan

There are many forms of a test plan template ([Black 1999], [Bazman 1998]), including several IEEE standards [IEEE 1998d]. These templates are generally divided into the following sections.

- *Introduction*. The introduction describes the system being tested, purpose of the plan, and objectives of the effort. Elements that differentiate this test plan from other test plans for the same project are discussed.
- *Scope*. This section describes what is to be tested as part of the plan and what is not. An inclusions/exclusions table or section clarifies the range of activities involved. Criteria necessary to enter and exit the test can be included.
- *Schedule*. The schedule determines when the testing effort should start and be completed. As the test relies on development to fix the bugs "blocking" test cases, a certain amount of turnaround time is included. The schedule is naturally contingent on receiving the deliverable from development on time.
- *Resources*. This section describes who will be testing and managing the test effort. Test equipment and other hardware or testing apparatus necessary for the test effort is included in this section.
- *Risks*. The risks section explains events that might keep the test plan from being carried out. Contingency plans, if available, are described in this section.

Use cases make their first impact on the testing process with the test plan. Use case names can be included in the scope section to describe the system uses that will be tested under the plan. When only certain scenarios of a use case are available, the test plan can include one specific scenario while excluding others.

The scheduling section can be directly tied to the use case model. As test cases are directly tied to the scenarios of a use case, test cases can be scheduled by their parent use case. This provides traceability back to the development schedule where the use case was used to schedule the development of certain functionality. Before this section of the test plan can be created, the test cases must be developed to understand how much work is involved.

Creating Test Cases

Although use cases play a small role in the development of test plans, they directly drive the development of the functional test case. In fact, we can create a suite of test cases or **test suite** from a single use case. Each test case represents a scenario in the use case. To see how functional test cases are created from use cases, let's walk through a sample use case, "Evaluate loan request" (Figure 14-1).

Certain steps in the use case represent decision points where the system needs more information from an actor. Following [Collard 1999], we have numbered the steps in the use case to provide a conceptual view of how use cases can be made into test cases. The "A" next to a step indicates the step requires feedback from an actor to be performed; an "S" indicates that the system is performing that action. An "E" indicates that the step is an exception condition and not part of the normal course.

If you do not use the step approach to describing the use case flow of events, you can easily convert your prose description by circling the steps in the description and numbering them in the margin. Or, you can rewrite your prose or state-driven use cases in a step format. Once the steps are numbered, you can create a tree depicting the paths through the use case (Figure 14-2).

Use case name:	Evaluate loan request
Preconditions:	The needed material concerning a pending loan request has been gathered (the loan material has a status of "Credit references validated")
Flow of events:	A1. The Loan Officer selects a loan request to review for approval.
	S1. The system presents the loan application and the loan information gathered on the customer to the loan officer. This information includes • the applicant's credit history (credit report and customer history with bank). • a calculated credit score. A3. The loan officer reviews the material and determines whether the loan should be approved. A4. The loan officer selects the appropriate loan terms and conditions for the loan based on the bank's policy and enters this information into the system. S5. The loan request status is changed to "Approved."
Postconditions:	The loan request is approved (the loan has a status of "Approved").
Alternative flows and exceptions:	AE1. The applicant's credit is unacceptable. AE2. The loan is referred to the loan committee for their review and evaluation. AE3. Further information needs to be gathered by the loan officer before a decision can be made.
Nonbehavioral requirements:	Only a loan officer or manager should have access to loan request information and associated material. The system should be able to handle 10 loan officers reviewing loan requests concurrently.

FIGURE 14-1 The "Evaluate loan request" use case

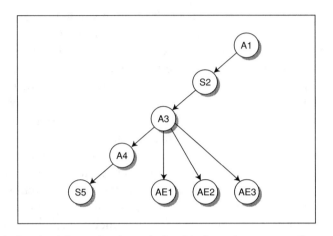

FIGURE 14-2   Graph of the paths through the "Evaluate loan request" use case

The "Evaluate loan request" use case indicates four paths through the system:

A1–S2–A3–A4–S5
A1–S2–A3–AE1
A1–S2–A3–AE2
A1–S2–A3–AE3

Of those paths, the first one leads to a successful outcome while the other three lead to an unsuccessful outcome. Right off the bat, we can create four test cases, one to test each path. We have one **positive test case**, a test case that leads to a successful result, and three **negative test cases**. These test cases are the absolute minimum necessary to test the base functionality of the system.

To create test cases from use cases, we reverse the process by which scenarios become use cases. We replace the abstract entities of the use case with specific instances [McGregor 1999a]. This replacement occurs in the preconditions, postconditions, flow of events, and exceptions. The preconditions map to the setup section of the test case and the postconditions to the teardown section (Figure 14-3).

Each step in the test case must have a status of passed, warning, or failed after the test case is completed. When a step is failed and the next step cannot be run until the problem is fixed, the step that cannot be run has a status of blocked. The overall status is determined by the sum of the status of the steps in the test case. Policies about failed, warning, blocked, and passed steps and their impact on the overall test case should be described in the test plan.

Test case name:	Approve loan request		
Test ID:	TC-105		
Test suite:	Evaluate loan request		
Priority:			
Setup:	• Submit a loan request for Jeff Borrower, Social Security number 178-98-5412, Address 15 Fox Chase Lane, Camden, N.J, 07655,loan principle $500, term 2 years. • Enter validated credit references for Jeff Borrower showing a loan for $1,000.00 paid back on time (12/1/98) with no late payments (positive credit history).		
Teardown:	Remove the approved loan request for Jeff Borrower from the system.		
Step	Description	Result	Problem ID
TC-105-A1	Loan officer1 selects the loan request of Jeff Borrower from the list of loan requests.	Passed	
TC-105-S2	The system responds by displaying Jeff Borrower, a credit history indicating a loan paid back on time, and a credit score of 100.	Passed	
TC-105-A3	Loan officer1 approves the loan.	Passed	
TC-105-A4	Loan officer1 selects an interest rate of 7% and adds no special conditions to the loan.	Warning	MKSys035
TC-105-S5	The system indicates that the loan request has been approved.	Passed	
Status:	Passed		
Tester:	I. Bugs		
Date complete:	12/24/99		

FIGURE 14-3 "Approve loan request" test case

Testing Range/Error Handling

We have examined the various functional paths that software might traverse and created test cases. However, we have not determined that the system will proceed under adverse conditions. We also have done little to test a use case model. To provide better test coverage, we need to look at the inputs to the system, specifically, the circumstances in which the inputs will have an adverse effect on the system.

To understand where the system no longer has control of its information, we again look at the steps where the actors provide information to the system. We need to test the steps to determine if logic is accurately checking appropriate boundary conditions. We are also looking for places where implicit assumptions are made in the use case model.

Implicit assumptions are common to any area where communication takes place. Use cases are no exception. To understand implicit assumptions, we look at those places where decisions are made. Is the system limited in its ability to receive information beyond what is called for in the use case? If so, what is the impact of that information on the system?

A common indicator of these types of problems may be found in the use case path tree. Consider step A1 in the "Evaluate loan request" use case tree (Figure 14-4). What other potential responses could there be? What happens if no loan request applications exist? Obviously, a loan officer cannot select one, so what happens when a loan officer attempts to do so? There must be a missing precondition or system response.

The best way to track implicit assumptions is to look at the actor decision points (nodes marked with an "A"). Are all the possible inputs covered? It is unusual to find a decision point without any potential for errors. That is, there are almost always two or more children representing system responses to each actor response. One is usually the path to success, the others are the failure paths. Failure paths need not remain paths to failure. Corrections may be made that bring the use case back to the path of success.

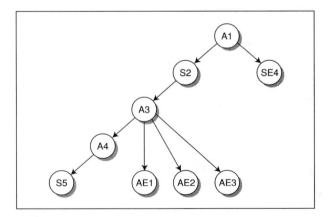

FIGURE 14-4   Missing exception in the "Evaluate loan request" use case

Range checking is another area where the decision points can be exploited. Fundamental business rules come into play at decision these points to ensure that the information given is correct. For example, can a loan officer make a loan at 0% interest? How about a negative interest rate? Range checking involves giving the system potentially damaging data at these decision points to check its response.

The system may prevent some of these types of data from being entered. For example, the entry field for the interest rate may not allow a minus to be entered (it might ignore the minus) as it is invalid information. This must be stated in the use case (as negative interest rates are not allowed) or the system designers will not create the functionality for implementation. If invalid data is allowed to be entered into the system, the appropriate system response must be added to the use case model and the step tree.

Test cases can be written to test the completeness of the validation logic of the system. Boundaries of the data ranges should be tested to ensure that the conditions of the use case are met. These test cases follow the same format used in test cases to test system functionality.

Testing Interactions

Interactions between use cases is one of the most difficult areas to test. This is because of the sheer number of potential combinations formed by even a moderate size use case model. As a result, exhaustive testing of use case interactions is next to impossible. However, we can use certain techniques to look for areas where interaction between use cases is likely to cause problems.

The easiest area is the preconditions of a use case. If a use case has a certain precondition that must be met, is there another use case that leaves the system in a state where that precondition is violated? There are two ways this might happen. The first is when an intuitive step in the process is left out. For example, what if we perform "Submit loan request" followed by "Evaluate loan request," leaving out the necessary credit information provided by "Enter validated credit references"?

The second scenario where the system might enter an awkward state is if an exception condition is met in a use case. What if a loan request is submitted, leaving out the principal? Matching up the use cases that present these types of problems is a simple way to test interactions (Figure 14-5). Once the use cases are matched up, select the test suites corresponding to the use cases. In the test suites, the appropriate functional test cases can be found and combined to form interaction test cases.

Preconditions are one form of interaction that need to be tested; there are other forms of interaction problems. One way of narrowing down interactions is

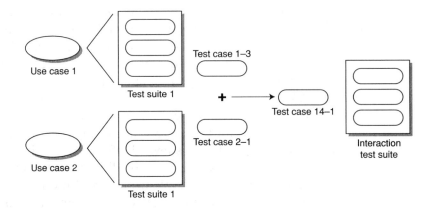

FIGURE 14-5   Combining test cases from different test suites to achieve an interaction test case

to look at objects shared between use cases. In Chapter 12, we created CRUD matrices between objects and use cases. If we combine these matrices, we can see how use cases relate to each other via the objects they touch.

Specifically, we are looking for situations where an object is read, updated, or deleted in one use case and created in another. What happens when the object does not exist? We call this condition "read before creation" and denote it "RC." Another condition we are looking for is when one use case deletes an object that another use case is reading or updating. We call this condition "read after delete" or "RD."

Many interactions are caught using the precondition approach. However, missing preconditions can be found by creating an interaction matrix (Figure 14-6). The appropriate interaction test case is created by combining the functional test cases that involve the "RCs" and "RDs."

	Submit loan request	**Enter validated credit references**	**Evaluate loan request**
Submit loan request			RC—credit history
Enter validated credit references	RC—loan request		
Evaluate loan request	RC—loan request	RC—credit history	

FIGURE 14-6   Use case interaction matrix

There are many other forms of interactions, including those that occur at the subsystem and class level. For an explanation of testing that may be performed at these levels, see McGregor [1999b].

Creating User Documentation

We have seen how easy it is to create test cases given a use case model. Documentation is another area where the use case model can help to structure and scope the work involved. Like test cases, documentation involves much more than use cases. While use cases and test cases can assume some of the details, documentation cannot afford that luxury. This is because users may not be able to ask subject matter experts the kinds of questions that developers and testers can ask during the project. Documentation must be complete, and it must be easy to read.

Traditionally, documentation was structured by product function. Modern approaches to documentation are task-orientated [Hargis 1998]. The task-oriented approach describes how to use the system to do a specific task. This modern approach breaks from the traditional way of structuring documentation by product function.

The first step to writing good documentation is to understand your audience. The audience for the documentation is the people who will use the system. Of course, users are characterized in the use case model by actors. But writing documentation requires a little more than understanding the needs of users. It involves putting yourself in their shoes, understanding their needs, and then communicating how the system meets their needs.

Once an understanding of the audience is achieved, the next step is to examine the tasks they want to perform with the system. This is exactly what the use case model offers. The use case model describes the ideal system. As a result, many details that have been provided through implementation (such as user interfaces) are not part of the use case model. Hence, the use case model provides a task-based outline for the documentation. The technical writer can use the outline to express the value of the system in terms the user can understand.

Software system use cases usually map directly to topics or tasks in the documentation. These tasks, when logically ordered, form a user's guide. Tasks should be placed in the user's guide in the order in which the user will perform them. "Submit loan request," for example, should appear in the user's guide prior to "Evaluate loan request."

Documenting the system can also be a form of system verification. Starting with the use case model as a guide to how the system should work and then performing the task with the actual system often leads to suggestions for usability improvements. Documentation people often contribute a valuable outside opinion that can lead to a polished system.

Conclusion

Many forms of testing must occur to verify a system. Some tests can be based directly on information in use cases; other tests, such as of platforms, interpretability with other products, scalability, and so on, cannot. In this chapter, we discuss test cases based on information in use cases (and some based on the absence of information in use cases). For a full discussion of testing, we refer the reader to the excellent work of John McGregor [2000, 2001].

Documentation, like all communication, is very much an art form. Those skilled in this craft can make technically challenging systems approachable. It is rare to find someone who is capable of understanding a very complex software system and can effectively communicate that understanding to every level of user from novice to power user. For more about task-based documentation, the reader is referred to Hargis [1998].

Chapter 15
Organize the Use Cases

What's in this chapter?

This chapter discusses organizing use cases by business functional packages and by dependencies based on use case preconditions and postconditions. A discussion of various views of the use case model is presented. A wrap-up of key use case artifacts is also presented.

As we have seen, use cases provide an excellent means of modeling and understanding functional requirements. An individual use case captures system requirements based on the interactions between actors and the system. However, in our understanding of system behavior, something is still missing. There are larger system behaviors that will cross multiple use cases. For example, is there a need for the system to perform an integrated process or work flow that will span multiple system use cases? If so, there will be requirements that need to be identified and associated with not just one use case but with a "stream" or grouping of use cases. Particularly in a large system, the use cases can also naturally be grouped into common business functions, such as billing, customer service, accounts management, and so on. Organizing the use cases into these business functions helps improve the understandability of the model, document the scope of each business function, and partition the system for development.

The discovery and modeling of use cases often drives the discovery of additional use cases in each business function. When systems are very large, there may be hundreds of use cases—so many, in fact, that stakeholders need an intermediate level of organization to provide more clarity to the model. If the use cases are presented only as a large list, users and analysts can have a difficult time understanding the "big picture." Although use cases provide an intuitive and natural way to model a system, it can be hard to get a conceptual grasp of a system when it is represented as an unordered set of use cases. This chapter focuses on several ways that the use case model can be organized to facilitate the improved understanding of system requirements.

Although we present these techniques as the last of the major activity groups and in a separate chapter at the end of the use case modeling process (Figure 15-1), the organization of use cases normally occurs as iterative activity spanning the use case model process, from the initial definition of the use cases through their elaboration. We encourage the analyst on a large system effort to organize use cases progressively as the use case modeling process unfolds.

It is usually beneficial to view the set of use cases from a number of different perspectives. We have already looked at several organizational mechanisms such as the use case diagrams that represent the relationships between individual use cases and actors and include, extend, and generalization relationships between use cases. In this chapter we look at four additional techniques to help organize system use cases:

- Business function packages
- Superordinate and subordinate use cases
- Dependency streams
- Use case model views

We use UML concepts such as packages and activity diagrams to help us represent these concepts.

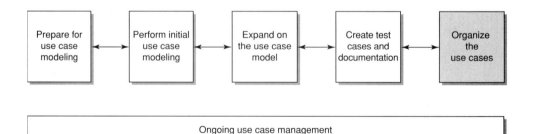

FIGURE 15-1   Many use cases comprise a system

Business Function Packages

The human mind has difficulty understanding and comprehending large amounts of unorganized information. Recall the 7 ± 2 rule that was used when modeling with traditional structured analysis (structured analysis is documented in a large number of references; see DeMarco [1979] and Yourdon [1989]). The guideline was to try keep the number of process bubbles in one data flow diagram at around seven, on the premise that the human mind can most effectively conceptualize and remember about seven major items in a diagram or other artifact. A data flow diagram with 30 process bubbles was a nightmare to read, follow, and remember.

In a very large system, there can be a large number of possible use cases. While use case modeling is clearly not structured analysis, throwing 50 use cases at a customer without any meaningful ordering or organization will be decidedly unsuccessful. Grouping the use cases by actor or by use case family is useful in many situations, but there will be times when a customer may wish to view the use case in different arrangements. In this section we look at grouping the use cases by the larger functions that make up a system.

It is natural for customers and users to think of a system as a set of key business functions or features. These business functions are broad responsibilities of the system and can be viewed from a functional perspective. The business functions are the next level of abstraction down from a system level context or use case diagram. For example, the business functions of a library system might include circulation, acquisitions, inventory, and management reporting.

Use cases can generally be grouped by functionality in business function packages. Each functional business package represents a major business activity supported by the system. In the loan processing system, unique business functions are associated with both loan submission and loan maintenance, and customer care. These are defined as separate business function packages. For a large system, partitioning system behavior into business function packages is critical for understanding the system architecture and effectively defining a development strategy.

Jacobson [1997] has discussed the idea of an overall larger system containing multiple smaller systems with each smaller system containing individual use cases; we will return to this discussion later. During the requirements capture activity, we like to think of these groupings not so much as subsystems, but as groupings of business functionality that the system will be responsible for implementing. The name "business function packages" implies that we may not have decided quite yet how to architect and design the overall system. The system architect may ultimately decide to combine several functional packages into a single subsystem or divide a single functional package into several subsystems. However, the focus during requirements analysis should be on the groupings that make the most sense to the users and customers. The division of the use case model into groups is not a new concept in use case modeling. In addition to Jacobson, a number of references discuss the concept, including Rosenberg [1999], Schneider [1998], and Armour [1995].

During the development of the use cases, look for natural groupings of use cases based on the customer's or user's perspective. Look at such documentation as previously developed business use cases, business process reengineering (BPR) results, and organizational grouping of responsibilities (based on the stakeholder analysis). In most cases, the grouping will become clear as the use case model is created. Name the business function packages in a way that reflects the user's and customer's understanding of the package and the package's responsibilities within the system.

An individual use case belongs to one package, and each package can contain multiple use cases (Figure 15-2). This representation has a number of benefits:

- It represents high-level functionality from a business function perspective.

- It organizes the use cases into logical groups that assist in making the use case model more structured and organized.

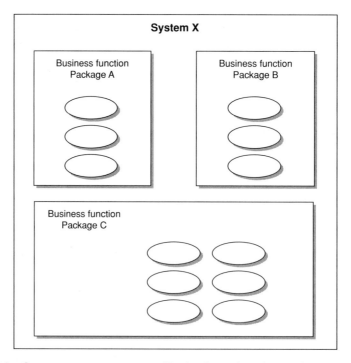

FIGURE 15-2   System use cases grouped by business function packages

- It helps to validate that for each business function the needed use cases exist and none are missing.
- As input into the system architecture definition process, it helps to create the functional architecture.

For example, in the loan processing system, the following business function packages could be defined:

- Loan submission and origination
- Loan account maintenance and care
- Loan portfolio analysis and reporting
- Credit management

Figure 15-3 shows a use case diagram partitioned into these business function packages with selected major use cases. If desired, the actors participating in each use case could also be included in the diagrams.

Developing the use case business function packages for the loan processing system organizes the system behaviors by their functions in processing a loan. The model allows the loan system users and analysts to view the major functions supported by the system and to observe the system's behaviors in supporting these functions. If the system is so large that there are dozens of use cases, consider grouping them into business functions. However, with smaller systems this is probably not needed. Normally one level of business functionality is sufficient, depending on the size and complexity of the system.

Superordinate and Subordinate Use Cases

Sometimes use cases don't fit neatly in a business function package. A use case may be written to describe a set of behaviors that cross multiple functional packages. Jacobson refers to this as a **superordinate use case**.

A single, broadly defined use case may span multiple business functional packages, with the use cases specific to each individual business functional package supporting behaviors defined in the broader use case. Jacobson [1997, 1995c] refers to this relationship as one between superordinate use cases and **subordinate use cases**. A superordinate use case is associated with the overall system and can map to multiple subsystems that contain subordinate use cases, with the individual subordinate use cases partitioned into individual subordinate groupings such as business functional packages. In other words, the different pieces of the each superordinate use case can be partitioned to the individual packages. Jacobson refers to the overall system as the superordinate system and the functionality groups as the subordinate systems. Certain use cases can be

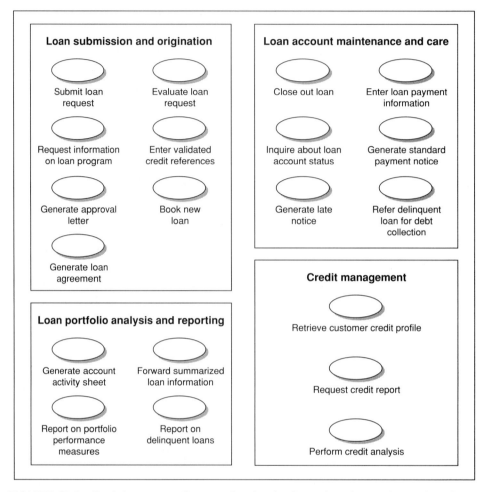

FIGURE 15-3   Partial use case diagram showing business function packages for a loan processing system

associated at both the superordinate and subordinate levels (Figure 15-4). The intent of superordinate and subordinate use case organization is not to design or structure the system; it is to arrange a use case in a meaningful and understandable structure.

Use cases at the superordinate level typically are used to represent overall system behavior and cross multiple subordinate systems. The behaviors in the superordinate use case can be partitioned across multiple subordinate systems as subordinate use cases, with each subordinate use case associated with a single

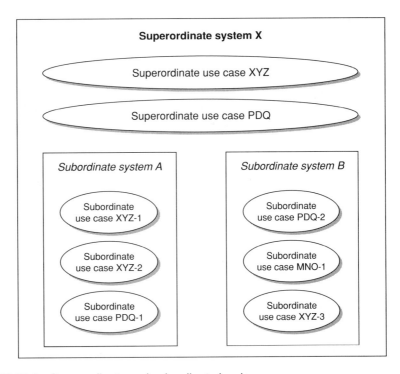

FIGURE 15-4   Superordinate and subordinate levels

subordinate system. Potential requirements associated with the interfaces can then be highlighted between subordinate systems and defined in detail during system architecture. Using this type of division also allows the development of system functionality by subsystems.

One approach is to define the overall superordinate use cases, and as subsystems are identified, develop subordinate use cases for each subsystem based on behaviors in the superordinate use cases. For example, in a large telecommunication system, a superordinate use case "Generate a bill" may involve multiple subsystems, including event rating and pricing, bill presentations and generation, and so on.

While it is not the goal of use case models to architecturally structure the system, for the requirements analysis process extremely large systems will need to be partitioned across subsystems (which can be, in effect, large systems themselves, each of which involves extensive analysis efforts in its own right). The overall requirements of the superordinate system will drive the requirements of the subordinate systems, so the relationship between the two sets of requirements is important to define. For small systems, it makes no sense to partition the system use cases in this manner, since the users who validate the use cases in all likelihood will not benefit from having to know the structure of the system (at least during requirements analysis). In this multilevel representation of use cases, the activities represented in the superordinate use case would be broken down and represented as use cases in their own right.

The relationship between superordinate and subordinate use cases does not have to be as strict as include relationships. The subordinate use cases need to be derived from the requirements modeled in a superordinate use case, but the subordinate behaviors do not need to be strictly included in the superordinate use case.

Using this approach to model the loan processing system, we could document superordinate use cases for such major activities as the loan request submission process (from submitting the request to booking the loan) and the payment process (from generating the payment notice to recording the actual payment). The use cases in the individual business function packages, such as loan submission and origination, would be contained or represented in the superordinate use cases.

Since use cases model requirements, it is instructive to discuss how traditional systems engineering deals with the concept of multiple levels requirements using allocation and flowdown.

Allocation and Flowdown

In traditional systems engineering, two concepts are used when partitioning a larger system into subordinate systems [Dorfman 1997]. In **allocation**, each system level requirement is assigned to one or more subordinate systems. The requirements are, in effect, partitioned across multiple subordinate groupings, as shown in Table 15-1.

The next concept is that of flowdown. **Flowdown** is the actual writing of subordinate system requirements in response to the allocation (Table 15-2). For example, when a system-level requirement is allocated to a business function package, additional requirements will need to be written to reflect the responsibilities of the subordinate business function package. Normally, more than one requirement is

TABLE 15-1   Allocating requirements to subordinate systems

Superordinate system requirements	Subordinate system A	Subordinate system B	Subordinate system C
System req 1	X		X
System req 2	X	X	
System req 3	X	X	X
System req 4		X	

TABLE 15-2 Flowdown of the requirements from a superordinate system to a subordinate system

Superordinate system requirements	Subordinate system A requirements	Subordinate system B requirements	Subordinate system C requirements
System req 1	Sub A req 1 Sub A req 2 Sub A req 3		Sub C req 1 Sub C req 2
System req 2	Sub A req 4	Sub B req 1 Sub B req 2	
System req 3	Sub A req 5	Sub B req 3	Sub C req 3
System req 4		Sub B req 4 Sub B req 5 Sub B req 6	
System req 5		Sub B req 7	Sub C req 4 Sub C req 5

written; each represents detailed functionality. It may be just an elaboration of the higher-level requirement or it can represent new behavior discovered, if new functionality is needed to meet the higher-level requirements. (These requirements are sometimes referred to as *derived requirements*.) When performing this activity, new system requirements will be added, old ones deleted, and modifications made to existing ones.

Use cases can be viewed as requirements for purposes of allocation and flowdown. When modeling requirements with use cases, superordinate use cases are allocated across subordinate systems (in this case, represented logically by business function packages, as shown in Tables 15-3 and 15-4).

TABLE 15-3 Allocating superordinate use cases to subordinate systems

Superordinate use case	Subordinate system A	Subordinate system B	Subordinate system C
Use case 123	X		X
Use case 124	X	X	
Use case 125	X	X	X
Use case 126		X	

TABLE 15-4 Allocating superordinate process loan submission use cases to subordinate systems

Subordinate system/ Superordinate use case	Loan submission and origination	Loan portfolio analysis and reporting	Loan account maintenance and care	Credit management
Process loan submission	X			X

Then the subordinate use cases are created in response to the flowdown (Tables 15-5 and 15-6).

The specification of a flowdown is not a linear process; rather, it is very iterative. Lower-level use cases may be found first and then traced to superordinate use cases as a result of the process. Good traceability should be maintained throughout the process. It should be noted that derived requirements or subordinate use cases do not have to blindly map to the individual activities in the superordinate use cases or high-level requirements. While they should result from them, new behavior may be discovered to support the higher-level use case. Don't force superordinate use cases if they don't naturally exist; in many systems the use cases will naturally fit into individual business function packages.

TABLE 15-5 Use case flowdown from superordinate to subordinate use cases

Superordinate use case	Subordinate system A use cases	Subordinate system B use cases	Subordinate system C use cases
Use case 123	Use case A-10 Use case A-11		Use case C-10
Use case 124	Use case A-12 Use case A-13	Use case B-10	
Use case 125	Use case A-14	Use case B-11 Use case B-12	Use case C-11 Use case C-12 Use case C-13
Use case 126		Use case B-13	

TABLE 15-6 Use case flowdown from "Process loan submission" use case to subordinate use cases in loan processing example

Subordinate system/ Superordinate use case	Loan submission and origination	Loan portfolio analysis and reporting	Loan account maintenance and care	Credit management
Process loan submission	• Submit loan request • Enter validated credit references • Evaluate loan request • Generate approval letter • Generate loan agreement • Book a new loan			• Request credit report • Perform credit analysis

Business Function Package Conclusions

To create a use case business package model, review the use cases, observe natural groupings of functions, and organize the use cases into packages based on business activities. The use case model will then show each package and the use cases that the package contains.

Relationships can exist between use cases in different business function packages. For example, a use case in one package can have an include relationship with a use case in another package. The use case "Submit loan request" in the loan submission and origination package has an include relationship with the "Request credit report" use case from the credit management package.

If there are a large number of relationships between package boundaries, question whether the organization is correct. Ask if the business function packages are defined too narrowly. Revisit the package organization to determine whether they can be reorganized to a higher level of abstraction.

When looking for subordinate use cases, see if there are use cases currently defined that cut across multiple packages. (Hint: A use case provides measurable value to many actors.) For example, multiple actors would participate in the use case "Process loan submission" and a number of them would receive some value from the use case. Consider it a potential superordinate use case. Partition it into multiple subordinate use cases, such as "Submit loan request," "Evaluate loan request," and so on. As more business function packages are found, more detailed use cases will be found. Text usually supplements the information shown in the model to help capture more detail about the business functional packages and to provide an overview of the packages. The text can include the description and purpose of the business function packages and reference to the organization that "owns" the business functionality (if relevant).

Dependency Streams

Within a use case's flow of events, the activities that make up the flow have a relationship with each another. Some activities need to be performed before other activities can be executed, while other activities can be performed in parallel, and some activities can be performed only after another activity. For example, within the "Submit loan request" use case, the activity of entering the loan application into the system has to occur before the activity of validating the loan application can occur (Figure 15-5).

Relationships between activities model important system requirements. If each activity was looked at only in isolation, without regard to how the other activities affect it and how it affects other activities, a large part of the system requirements would be missed. The strength of use cases is that they naturally capture relationship requirements.

But what of the relationships between the use cases? In addition to these extend and include relationships, use cases can sometimes depend on other use cases completing execution before they begin to execute. An individual use case

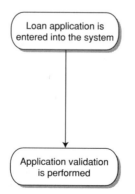

FIGURE 15-5   Dependency between two activities in a use case

can be analogous to a single activity, except on a higher level of abstraction. For example, in a library system, the concept of a returning library material ("Return library material" use case) depends on the patron borrowing the library material ("Borrow library material" use case) in the first place, as captured in the preconditions and postconditions of the use cases. Borrowing a piece of library material is a prerequisite to returning the material.

In most complex systems, there will be use cases that depend on other use cases leaving the system in a certain state. In addition to understanding the individual system interactions documented in each use case, it is useful to understand how use cases depend on each other. We refer to these relationships as **use case dependency streams**. Dependency streams model a stream of use cases that are dependent on each other to perform a larger system process. (Please note that dependency streams are not a relationship defined in UML.)

For example, the activity of processing a loan application involves several use cases, including "Submit loan request," "Enter validated credit references," "Evaluate loan request," "Book new loan," and so on. The relationships between them can be documented with dependency streams. Dependency streams help answer the following questions.

- How do the use cases interrelate to support this activity?
- What use case must execute before another can begin its execution?
- Are there subordinate or superordinate use cases that need to be created?

A dependency stream models the relationship that exists between individual use cases in order to perform some overall system process. In the example of the library system, a patron needs to have borrowed a book before the book can be returned or be overdue. In other words, the "Borrow library material" use case leaves the system in the state "Library material borrowed," which allows the use case "Return library material" to execute. The directed line between the use cases represents a logical dependency that one use case has on another. In this case, precondition of the "Return library material" use case matches or at least contains the postcondition of the "Library material borrowed," defined as the outcome of the "Borrow library material" use case (Figure 15-6). Please note that the directed line points to the use case that has the dependency on the other use case (the reverse of traditional UML representation). This is to display the show through, the dependency, or the overall process it models.

In another example dealing with a library system, for a library book overdue notice to be sent out, the book must have been borrowed, and the borrowing must have been associated with a return date.

Thinking about the requirements in this manner also helps to specify what behaviors each use case needs to have. For example, submitting a loan request needs

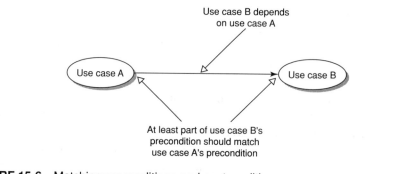

FIGURE 15-6   Matching preconditions and postconditions

to leave the loan request in an initial validation state. The next step in the bank's loan submission is bank validation of the references on the application. Once that occurs, enough information has been collected for a formal evaluation (modeled in the "Evaluate loan request" use case). What information and documentation needs to be gathered to allow its evaluation? What is the final state of the loan request when the "Submit loan request" use case is finished? Does this state allow the validation of references to occur, which then allows the behaviors in the "Evaluate loan request" use case to occur? In Figure 15-7, a dependency stream is presented for a normal flow (a loan request is approved and accepted with no problems).

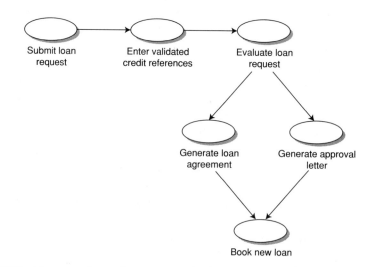

FIGURE 15-7   Use case dependency stream for the loan request submission and approval process

At first glance, dependency streams seem very similar to superordinate use cases. However, they can be applied in a somewhat different manner. First, processes are partitioned into system use case cases, although the processes themselves may not naturally be reflected as use case. Even if a dependency between several use cases is important to understand, it may not constitute an entirely new superordinate use case. Dependency streams help us keep a system use case model as flat as possible, which we like, in order to prevent functional decomposition.

At the same time, dependency streams reflect a strong relationship between use cases; that is, one use case depends on another finishing its execution before it can start executing.

When attempting to organize use cases in dependency streams, look at each use case's preconditions and postconditions. Are there use cases with postconditions that are preconditions in another use case? If so, this may be a signal that one use case may depend on another. Ask questions such as the following.

- Is there a natural dependency between the use cases? If not, don't try to force a dependency between the use cases.

- If there is a dependency, what is its nature?

- Do activities need to occur in the first use case for the second use case to successfully execute?

- How will the important exceptions or variations in the first use case affect this dependency?

- Are there timing requirements across the use cases as well as between the use cases? Is there a requirement that the entire process execute over a defined period of time? How is this larger requirement partitioned to the individual use cases? How soon does one use case have to begin after another one has completed?

If use cases have preconditions that don't map to another use case's postcondition, ask the following questions.

- Are there system activities that have not yet been modeled? If so, what are they? Is the missing activity within an existing use case or is an entire use case missing? Missing use cases may be signaled if a use case's precondition does not match to an existing use case's postcondition. However, not all use cases depend on another use case, so don't force this issue if no dependency exists.

- Are the use cases defined in the use case model at the same level of abstraction? If the preconditions and postconditions don't naturally map together, it may be that they are defined at different levels of detail. If so, rework the use cases.

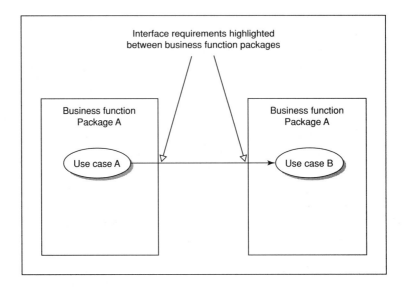

FIGURE 15-8   Highlighting interfaces between business function packages

Dependency streams help to validate preconditions and postconditions. Matching use cases in this manner helps to validate that the preconditions and postconditions are written in a consistent manner and are at the same level of detail. A use case dependency stream can also help to point out where a larger superordinate use case needs to be created or where a large system process needs to be partitioned across multiple system use cases.

If the transition from one use case to another crosses business function package boundaries, dependency streams can help point out package interfaces (Figure 15-8), which in turn point out possible interface requirements that need to be explored during system architecture. However, if an iterative development effort is taken, particularly one that develops the system one subsystem at a time, the interfaces between the subsystem become requirements, and need to identified and modeled.

Activity Diagrams to Model Use Case Dependencies

In Chapter 9, we discussed the use of UML activity diagrams for modeling a complex use case flow of events. We have found activity diagrams to be a useful tool for in modeling use case dependencies, as well.

To model a dependency stream in an activity diagram, each use case is represented as an activity in the diagram. The dependency between use cases is modeled as a transition between the use cases. If a variation in one use case affects the execution of a use case that depends on it, the analyst can use branching and guards to model the relationship.

In a library example (Figure 15-9), a precondition of borrowing is that the borrower is a member of the library, which is a postcondition of the use case "Apply for library membership." The postcondition of the "Borrow library material" use case is that the material is borrowed, a precondition for returning it. The use cases that make up the loan application submission process are modeled in Figure 15-10.

Dependency streams can include conditional logic and iteration, if needed, but we typically use them as more informal tools to help understand the relationship requirements of system. They also make an excellent tool to model the work flow that a system will need to implement. By the way, UML state diagrams can also be used to model dependency streams; each transition between the states represents a use case.

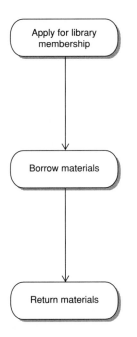

FIGURE 15-9 Simple dependency stream for library system

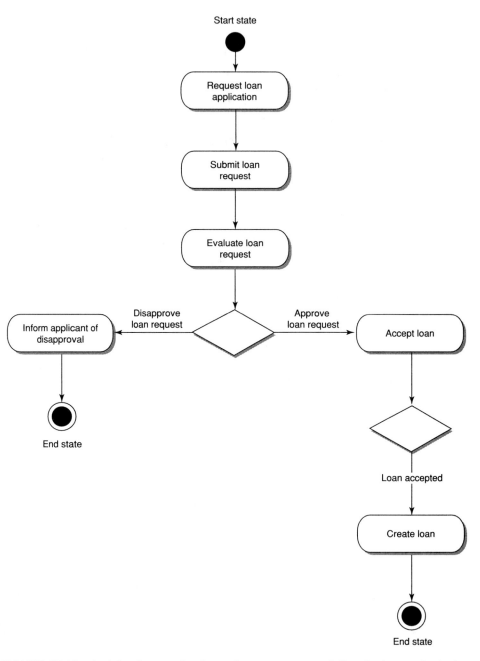

FIGURE 15-10   Activity diagram for dependency stream modeling the loan submission process

Model Views

As you can see, there are a large number of ways to organize use cases. We like to think of them as *views* on the use case model. Depending on the view, use cases can be rearranged for presentation and analysis. In Table 15-7 we outline several views of the use case model. No one view is superior or more right than the others; they are simply alternative means of presenting information. The views can be considered virtual and like the sides of cube, with the use case model inside the cube. The views can be combined, for example, by grouping all use cases by business function package, and then inside each package subgrouping the use cases by primary actor.

TABLE 15-7   View of the use case model

View	Description	Comments
List	List of the use cases	Default organization. Simple, but can overwhelm a reviewer, even if alphabetized or numbered.
Actor	List of use cases in which each actor participates	Useful for presentation to individual system users. Helps to validate how a specific role will interact with the system.
Family	All the details and relationships such as include, extend, and generalization	Useful for validating that sufficient details have been captured on an individual use case family.

Business function package	Multiple use cases grouped by functionality	Good for validation of required coverage of individual business group in the system.
		    Presents customers representing a group responsible for the specific functionality with a good way of seeing what the system coverage will be.
		    Good input into system architecture.

Dependency stream	Use cases grouped by the precondition and postcondition dependencies one use case has on another	Good for "seeing" overall requirements that may span multiple use cases and for finding missing use cases.
Development priority	Use cases grouped by their relative development priority	Useful for helping to organize development plan, resource allocation, and estimation.

The table is not an inclusive list of views; individual developers will no doubt discover additional views that are useful for them. The idea is to think of the use case as a multidimensional model and rearrange it in ways that help to discover, model, and represent requirements.

Putting It All Together in a System Use Case Model

The last 11 chapters have discussed a large number of possible use case modeling techniques and concepts. The use case model "packages" these concepts in a form that represents what the system will do. As a wrap-up, Table 15-8 provides a quick overview of the basic types of concepts and descriptions in a use case model.

TABLE 15-8   Basic types of concepts and descriptions in a use case model

Concept	Description
Actor	Entity that interacts with the system for the purpose of completing a event.
Use case diagram	Represents the system as a black box and modeling the actors and their interaction with the system. It may also be accompanied by a context diagram. The diagram also graphically models extend and include relationships. The diagram grows more complex as more information about the use case relationships is discovered and added.

Note: The descriptions in the following three rows are not different use cases; rather, they are progressively more detailed descriptions of an individual use case.

Initial use cases description	Briefly describes a use case as represented in the use case diagram. Normally is rolled over into the base use cases.
Base use case description	Describes the normal flow of use case. Starts to document other information about the use case including its nonbehavioral requirements.
Elaborated use cases description	Adds to the base use case details about the activities performed during the use case, alternative flows, conditional logic to document exceptions, and alternative processing is split base use case that is too broad into two or more narrowly focused elaborated use cases.
Extend relationship	Specifies how a use case flow of events may be inserted into and therefore extend another use case's flow of events.
Include relationship	Provides a way to model similar behaviors so that they can be used across multiple use cases.

Concept	Description
Generalization relationship	Models the inheritance relationship between a very general use case and more specific use cases that are "sub cases."
Use case instance	Describes how specific parameters such as input information and decision points affect the execution of a use case.
Use case dependency stream	Models a sequence of use cases that depend on each other to perform a larger process (non-UML).
Business function package	Group of use cases based on one broad responsibility of the system, viewed from a functional perspective.
System test case	Cases derived from the use cases and instances to test that the requirements defined in a use case and/or instance scenario have been successfully implemented in the system.
GUI design scenario (discussed in last chapter)	Models the detailed requirements of the user interface, includes individual screens and the flow between screens.

Conclusion

A use case model defines a system's behaviors within the context of the business environment in which it operates; business function packages help group use cases into the larger functions that they will participate in. Dependency streams are used to model how individual use cases depend on each other based on preconditions and postconditions. Finally, use case views can be used to look at the use cases from multiple perspectives for validation and analysis.

Part 5
Additional Topics

What's in this part?

This part presents some additional topics in use case modeling.

Some projects have needs that extend beyond the advanced use case modeling process framework presented in Part 3. In this part, we provide additional topics that may be added to your use case modeling repertoire.

Chapter 16 discusses conceptual user interface modeling. This topic may be of interest to developers who have large, complex graphical user interfaces. Other projects may not require the level of sophistication that this chapter provides. For example, many embedded systems have little or no user interface.

Change is another area that affects some projects more than others. Many management information system projects suffer from "requirements creep," or a rate of change in the requirements that threatens the success of the project. Chapter 17 provides the tools for managing change in the use case model.

Formal process definition is critical to achieving ISO 9001 certification and a requirement for high-ceremony projects [Miller 2000]. Since advanced use case modeling is a process framework, it must be customized to the level of detail necessary to meet the needs of your project. Chapter 18 describes how to identify the pieces of the process necessary for your project. This chapter presents the artifacts most often chosen by projects based on their level of ceremony. It also outlines a documentation methodology called the development case that comes from the Rational Unified Process.

Chapter 19 presents some of the elements necessary for building a quality use case model. Some of the properties of a good requirements document are applied to the use case model to illustrate the best way to ensure their quality. Many of these properties are based on common sense. Creating a quality use case model involves iteration. This model may then be utilized to drive the downstream software development process. The creation of delivery increments is briefly explained with respect to use case prioritization.

Chapter 16
Building User Interfaces

> Until Doug Engelbart began his humanistic approach to computers less than thirty years ago, computer science was not noted for its contribution to the human spirit. That has changed. Designers today realize that our software is more than some static collection of dialog boxes and windows. It affects peoples' lives in powerful and profound ways and we have a solemn responsibility to do everything possible to improve the quality of those lives.
>
> —Bruce "TOG" Tognazzini [Tognazzini 1992]

What's in this chapter?

This chapter presents a method for logical user interface design based on use cases. Use cases are broken down into transactions that are logically grouped together to form screens. Further decomposition may be performed to obtain reuse in the user interface.

A good user interface can make the difference between a software system that is completely intuitive in its use and one that leads to utter frustration. Understanding how to build an intuitive user interface (UI) requires knowledge of aesthetics, the physical elements of user interfaces (controls, widgets, windows, and so on), system content, and the system's users. The best designers balance all these things to produce systems that are so easy to learn that the user only needs to read the documentation to understand the advanced features. Designers accomplish this by building an interface that corresponds to the user's mental model of how the system should behave. However, designing the ultimate UI is perhaps more of an art than a science.

User interface design can be divided into two distinct phases: conceptual (sometimes called logical [Jacobson 1999]) and physical design. During conceptual user interface design, the focus is on the development of the content necessary to reflect the functionality of the system. Content is discovered and initial linkages between logical screens are proposed. The conceptual model reflects the needs of the system and the user in their interaction with one another. A use case model can help in the design of user interfaces based on content and, to some extent, information about the users. Use cases provide an excellent vehicle for deriving the conceptual user interface model.

Separating conceptual and physical user interface design is not new. Most projects concentrate strictly on the physical side. Conceptual design is often performed informally and as a side step through iteration of the physical design. Physical design deals with the aesthetics and selection of actual user interface components rather than with content. This emphasis on the physical side has been exacerbated by the ease of construction made possible through prototyping with user interface builders.

Since most user interface designers concentrate on physical design rather than conceptual design, logical aspects of the UI are often developed through iteration on the physical design until it "fits" the system. This iteration is a necessary part of the user interface development process, but refinement of the physical model should concentrate on usability and aesthetics rather than system functionality. System functionality should be explored in its own phase of user interface modeling, conceptual design. The conceptual design of a system should be explored before physical design is started.[1]

Conceptual User Interface Design

Before starting physical design, it is important to understand what information is needed by the user and the system, and at what time. This idea is the essence of conceptual design. Conceptual design

> involves analyzing users' needs in terms of the activities that need to be accomplished using a system and the objects and operations which a user has to accomplish the tasks. [Benyon 1999]

Use cases, system state diagrams, and the analysis object model can help determine what information the users need and when they need it. These three artifacts can serve as input to the conceptual design process.

Use cases and state diagrams help to provide a logical order to the conceptual design. We have seen in earlier chapters how these two models may be related. Use

---

[1] That is, unless the physical user interface development represents exploration of the system concept. In such a case, the product is so novel or undefined that the users will know what they want only when they see it. The product's use case model cannot be defined until exploratory prototyping is complete.

cases and the analysis object model can provide detail on what information will be needed from the user and the system to accomplish a task. System state diagrams can aid conceptual modeling by describing the state of various parts of the system and the events that may change the state. The analysis object model determines the relationships among objects in the system that contain, and therefore convey, important information.

Use cases naturally play the largest role in the way a conceptual user interface model is defined. Since use cases form the basis for the other two models, we feel use cases best serve as input to the conceptual model.

Creating Conceptual Models from Use Cases

As mentioned in Chapter 4, there is a danger of user interface decisions creeping into use case models. We strongly recommend that use cases remain independent of details regarding the presentation of information. Use cases should focus on uses of the system. The user interface should then be driven by these uses. The use case model should drive the creation of a user interface specification reflecting conceptual design. The physical design may be added to this interface specification later in addition to being captured in a user interface prototype.

We recommend five activities for describing the conceptual user interface model:

- Partition the use case model.
- Decompose the use cases into transactions.
- Determine the information content for each transaction.
- Establish logical screen order.
- Group and lay out logical screens.

Partitioning the Use Case Model

The first step in conceptual user interface design is to logically group use cases in the use case model specifically for user interface design. Two approaches to partitioning can be used, the work model approach and the user group approach. Either or both approaches can be used to start conceptual interface design as they both help to focus on the users as the primary concern.

Grouping use cases determines the potential paths that users will encounter as they proceed through the use case model. It also points out opportunities for reusing the logical user interface designs. When partitioning use cases in the use case model, only use cases with a human actor need to be considered. Separating the use cases that do not contribute to the user interface from the ones that do simplifies the overall user interface development process. It can also bring to the developer's attention missing actors or missing use cases in the use case model. In the loan processing example (see Figure C-4), "Inquire about loan account status" does not have a human actor and so would not require user interface development. However, statistics may need to be recorded on the number of inquiries made. If this functionality were to be added to the system, it would be initiated by the loan manager and a new use case, "Determine inquiry statistics," would be added to the use case model.

Users often expect to find tasks pertaining to activities they feel belong together near each other in the user interface. In the video store example, you might expect tasks related to video rentals to be grouped together in one set of screens and membership tasks grouped in another. The users would look for the function they wish to perform in the "area" that contains user interface representations of similar features. As was discussed in Chapter 15, partitioning the use case model in logical business groupings is called business function packaging. It is also referred to as the **work model approach** [Lif 1999] (Figure 16-1).

Different classes of users often approach the system differently. One class of users might use certain functions of the system every day. Another class of users might use the system occasionally. A third class of users might administer the system. These classes of users usually correspond to one or more actors in the use case model. Therefore, a second way to partition the use case model is by grouping human actors or users (Figure 16-2). This approach is called the **user group approach** [Lee 1993].

A differentiating factor in the user group approach is privileges. One group may have the ability to perform a certain set of functions that another group may not. There are also occasions when a group of even more privileged users is nested in a user group. A common example is management. A manager may be able to

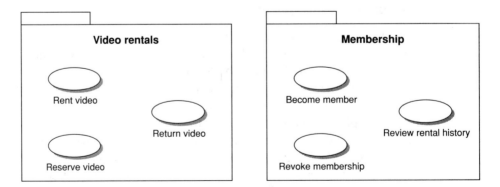

FIGURE 16-1   Work model approach to partitioning the video store use case model

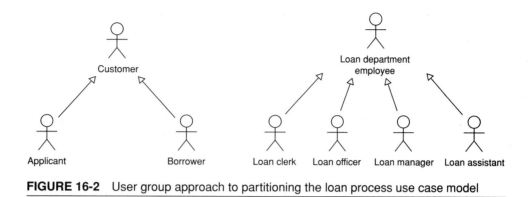

FIGURE 16-2 User group approach to partitioning the loan process use case model

correct mistakes in addition to all the other activities of the user group. If there are several actors that represent different management roles, a new user group may be needed.

In the loan processing example, there are six actors: applicant, borrower, loan manager, loan officer, loan assistant, and loan clerk. We might create two abstract actors, loan department employee and customer, to divide these actors into two user categories or **user groups** (Figure 16-3). Each user group approaches the system differently. A customer will use the system with a lot less frequency than a loan department employee. A customer will have less domain experience as well. As a result, customers will tend to need a simpler user interface than the loan department employees. Customers also should be able to access limited information. They may

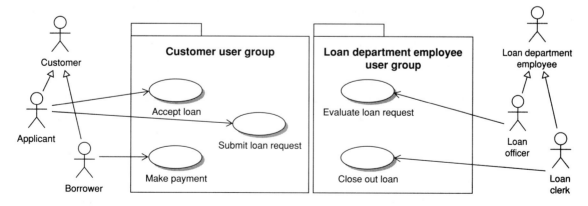

FIGURE 16-3 Partial user group partitioning of the loan process use case model

look at only their own loan records, while the loan department employees may access the information of many customers in the course of their day.

Once the user groups are created, the use case model is partitioned into packages representing the different groups. Some use cases may fall into more than one user group. When this happens, the two user groups need to be examined to see whether they should be combined. More likely, however, the two groups should remain separate; they may do the same sorts of things, but perhaps in slightly disparate ways. A use case may belong to more than one group.

Decomposing Use Cases into Transactions

Once the use case model is partitioned, the use cases themselves must be decomposed. To understand how use cases relate to the user interface, examine this first definition of a use case:

> A sequence of transactions in a system whose task is to yield a result of measurable value to an individual actor of the system. [Jacobson 1995c]

The operative word in this definition is "transaction." A transaction is the section of a use case initiated by an actor stimulus and completed when the use case awaits stimulus from an actor (not necessarily the same as the one that initiated it). Transactions allow us to partition use cases into smaller elements that allow us to determine the minimal information necessary at each decision point. Transactions help determine the minimal content as well as the sequencing.

This definition of a use case is completely consistent with the one given earlier in this book. We need not change our use case model to add the notion of transactions. Instead, we now identify transactions within our existing use case model. This can be done informally by circling the text in the flow of events of the use cases that describes a transaction. In higher-ceremony projects, a new use case model may be formed that formally divides a use case into its constituent transactions. Segmenting the use cases into a set of transactions is similar to segmenting use cases in other fashions (see Chapter 9).

Identifying transactions in use cases varies in difficulty, depending on the style used to describe the flow of events. For the purposes of user interfaces, we view transactions from the user point of view. Thus, transactions from this point of view are the reverse of that of the stystem. These transactions follow the pattern of (1) the system presents information, and (2) the actor does something. This pattern may be repeated many times until the use case is complete. Each instance of the pattern within a use case is a user interface transaction.

The final transaction of a scenario (path through a use case) does not follow this pattern. Usually, the system presents some final information indicating success or failure in obtaining the goal of the use case. In these transactions, there is an implicit user action that indicates that the user has acknowledged the final result, perhaps a closing of the last window, perhaps the clicking of an OK button, perhaps nothing at all but going to the next possible use case. For each of these "hanging" transactions, there should a method of moving to the next logical use case or set of use cases.

Transactions may also be identified in the "Alternative flows and exceptions" section of the use case description. Elements of this section usually fall into one of two categories. The first is an exception where something other than the normal flow occurs and status must be returned. These types of changes represent changes in the state of the system but may not warrant a new screen. In these cases, the exception belongs with the transaction that spawned it. The second is elaborate alternative flows that can yield transactions that follow the same pattern as the flow of events and that therefore should be identified as they were identified in the flow of events. In some use cases, the majority of the transactions may come from alternative flows.

Another area rich in transactions is the included and extension use cases. The transactions from these use cases will need to be evaluated when considering the later steps in the conceptual user interface design process. Included use cases, when involving human interaction, often contain the largest amount of reuse in the user interface. Extension use cases, when not considered in the user interface design, have the greatest potential for causing rework in the user interface.

Each transaction needs to be labeled so that it can be referenced in the user interface specification (Figure 16-4). These labels provide forward traceability between the use case model and the interface specification. Since use cases are not linear (scenarios are), a linear numbering scheme will not work for labels. However, transactions may be named similar to the elements in the flow of events (see Chapter 8). In some cases, names within the flow of events may already correspond to transactions. This correspondence happens most often when the state approach to naming is used.

Determining Information Content

Once the transactions of a use case have been identified, the next step is to determine the information content of each one. This step is similar to what was described in Chapter 12, but the objects should be parsed from the information in each transaction rather than the information in each use case. The information should not be consolidated over the use case model. Rather, each business object should be recorded for its role within a transaction regardless of how many times it may be recorded over the use case model.

Transactions represent decision points in the use case. At a decision point, an actor must be presented with the information necessary to make the decision. This information is in the transaction itself or in prior transactions. After the decision is

Use case name:	Evaluate loan request
Unique use case ID:	UC130
Primary actor(s):	Loan officer

Flow of events:	*Transaction UC130-1*
	
	1. The *loan officer* selects a *submitted* **loan request** from the list of **loan requests** to review for approval.
	
	Transaction UC130-2
	
	2. The system presents the **loan information** gathered on the *applicant* to the *loan officer.* This information includes:
	
	   • *Applicant's* **personal information** (name and **social security number**)
	   • **Terms** of the loan (loan amount and term)
	   • *Applicant's* **credit history** (**credit report** and **customer history** with the bank)
	   • Calculated credit score for the **credit history**
	
	3. The *loan officer* reviews the material and enters the new status of the **loan request** (*approved/denied*).
	
	Transaction UC130-3
	
	4. If the **loan request** is *approved,* the system creates a **loan.** The system acknowledges the new status of the **loan request** and records a **history** (date, loan officer name, changes) for audit purposes.
	
	5. The loan officer adds the appropriate terms and conditions for the **loan.**
	
	Transaction UC130-4
	
	6. The system acknowledges the new status of the **loan** and records a **history** (date, loan officer name, changes) for audit purposes.

FIGURE 16-4   Identified transactions in the partial "Evaluate loan request" base use case

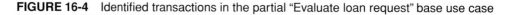

made, information acknowledging the decision is often returned to the actor. The goal of this step, "Determine information content," is to identify the information.

Five classes of information may be found in transactions. The five classes reflect the types of information that may be found in object models. These types are conceptual rather than implementational.

• *Attributes*. Attributes are information elements that make up an object. Attributes are the most commonly displayed class. An example of an attribute is "name" in the "Evaluate loan request" use case. Attributes do not have to be actual data members; they may be derived from the information in the object. Since we have no design or implementation at this point, we cannot assume that these attributes will actually be implemented. For example, a point may have attributes "*x*," "*y*," "theta," and "radius" to reflect Cartesian or polar coordinate representations. Although a point will be implemented using only one of these representations, the other representation is easily derived.

- *Operations*. Sometimes information must be calculated in the context of the use case rather than as a property of an object. This information is not a natural definer of the object, as an attribute would be. It is a genuine operation that must be performed in the context of the use case. An example of an operation is the credit score calculated from the credit history.

- *Business objects*. In user interface design, objects behave in two different ways. Complex objects represent categories of other information elements. These categories help focus the user on logically grouped information. For these objects, the information lies within the object, not at the object level. In the "Evaluate loan request" use case, the object "personal information" contains the attribute "name" and the object "social security number." These objects (name and social security number) will contain the actual information displayed. Personnel information is a composite of other objects. The object "social security number" is a simple object. It behaves, as most simple objects do, like an attribute.

- *State information*. The notion of state in the proposed system has been illustrated throughout this book. State exists at many different levels in the system. System state is reflected through status messages. Objects may also have state. A loan request has at least three states defined by the "Evaluate loan request" use case: submitted, approved, and denied.

- *Relationships between objects*. Objects may be related to other objects in many ways. They may composed of other objects in a whole/part relationship called **aggregation**. They may be simply related to each other in a peer relationship. Relationships (or the lack of a relationship) may be as important as the information contained in the objects. For example, an applicant may or may not have a customer history with the bank. This relationship may not be contained in the customer object, but it must be displayed in the user interface.

These five classes of information must be discovered in the use case model. Missing information is often discovered in the process of mining these classes. This is especially true of attributes, which are commonly left out of the use case model. Conceptual user interface modeling is a good time to find this information, as it is often done very early in software development.

Creating the Transaction Information Model

Now that we have gathered all this information for each transaction, what do we intend to do with it? The answer is to create the transaction information model, which should be recorded in the user interface specification (Figure 16-5).

Recall that there are three areas that must be considered at each decision point in the use case. The first is information delivered to the user in a prior transaction and required by the user in the decision associated with the current transaction. This information is captured in the "Prior information" section. The "Presented information" section recognizes information elements delivered as part of the current transaction. Finally, information elements returned to the system are given in "Returned information." This section lets the system know of the user's decision.

In each area, we can have information from any of the five categories (attributes, operations, business objects, relationships, and state). As we traverse the object model, we often see layering. Layering occurs when elements are contained within other elements. This layering should be reflected in the model by indenting the contained elements. At the lowest layers (most indented elements), we should see attributes, operations, states, and relationships representing the minimal set of elements necessary for the user to make the decision. Elements other than those required to proceed to the next decision point should not be found in the model.

A business object often has many relationships. Therefore, relationships must be spelled out so that they can be understood. For example, the relationship between

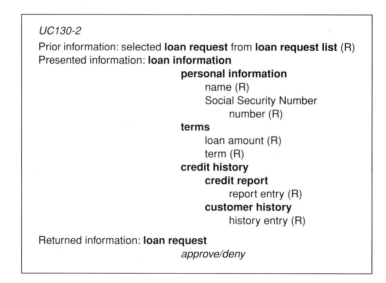

UC130-2

Prior information: selected **loan request** from **loan request list** (R)
Presented information: **loan information**
         personal information
            name (R)
            Social Security Number
               number (R)
      terms
            loan amount (R)
            term (R)
    credit history
         credit report
            report entry (R)
         customer history
            history entry (R)

Returned information: **loan request**
            approve/deny

FIGURE 16-5   Transaction information model for transaction UC130-2

the loan request list and its loan requests is one of selection. Specifying the possible states in which the system or object may be placed must be stated helps to determine the physical user interface component to be used for its representation. It also allows potential validation at the user interface level.

There are several additions to the transaction information model. Objects may be created or destroyed as part of a transaction. A "C" or "D" in parentheses is placed to the right of the object when one of these two operations occurs to recognize a need to change the user interface to reflect new or no longer existing data. Similarly, attributes may be read only, read/write, or write only. When an attribute is read/write, the current value is displayed but may be changed by the user. An "R," "R/W," or "W" reflects the state of each attribute with respect to the transaction.

A precaution: We are using an object-based approach to conceptual user interface modeling. This is consistent with the abstractions that will be found in the domain that the system models. Even so, we must be careful with this approach as it may reflect the programmer's view of the world instead of the user's. A user interface metaphor must be created that provides an intuitive understanding of what is happening in the system. This metaphor must be created through conceptual and physical user interface design. Such a metaphor is the trash can in which files are dumped to signify their detection in some operating systems.

Establishing Logical Screen Order

Once the transaction information model is complete, we can order the potential logical screens. As you might imagine, transactions will drive the development of user interface screens. There is, of course, a natural order to the transactions within a use case that allows us to understand which transactions must be performed before others. The order of the screens derived from the transactions will follow the order of the transactions themselves (see Figure 16-6).

The ordering of these transactions forms a tree in which there are several paths (formed by the constituent transactions) to a successful outcome. The orderings for each use case (with a human actor) in the use case model will lead to a forest of transaction trees.

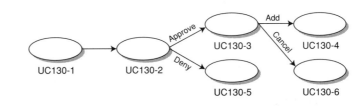

FIGURE 16-6   Logical ordering of transactions in "Evaluate loan request"

Transactions from included and extension use cases should be added to these trees. Transactions from included use cases should be added at the point where the use case logic delegates to the included use cases. Transactions from extension use cases should be added at their extension points. Whole trees from these use cases may often be inserted into the including or base use case.

Grouping Transactions and Layout of Logical Screens

If we combined the models we have built so far in the conceptual user interface process, we'd have a set of transaction trees containing informational elements. These trees would be partitioned by the needs of the user community. Such a model is usually relatively large.

If we created screens for each of the transactions, we would probably have a rather large set of screens. This sounds like a lot of work for our user interface developers. But there is a saving grace. There is not necessarily a one-to-one correspondence between transactions and screens. Multiple transactions may be combined in a single screen, and large transactions may drive the development of multiple screens when real estate (number of pixels on the screen) becomes an issue.

The goal of this step is to produce a small set of trees through consolidation. These trees should map to sequences of logical screens. With this small set of trees we begin the process of developing a physical user interface. To consolidate the trees, we need to find transactions with similar information elements. If we relax the minimal information requirement of the transaction information model, we can usually find places where transactions may be combined. The result is a new tree whose transactions are combinations of transactions from different use cases.

Transactions in the same user partition often have common information elements. Transactions are small enough slices of the use case model that their reuse levels (from an information point of view) can be high. Within the same partition, earlier transactions offer the greatest opportunity for consolidation. Transaction paths often diverge from there.

Perhaps the best example of consolidation occurs in systems that begin with a user logging in. Of course, there will be a use case that separates out this behavior, which will be part of many of the other use cases. Combining trees at this point cuts across partitions but moves the transaction information model to its next consolidation point.

For systems that require authentication, such as a login, the user group approach to partitioning is ideal. The login determines the type of user that is using the system and moves the user to the first application screen. This screen is derived from the consolidation of many of the transactions following the login transactions in transaction trees with the user group. In other words, the first thing a user sees after the login is completed is a screen that is specially made for the appropriate user group. This screen presents the first decisions and information needed to make the decisions based on the type of users. In our loan example, customers are given one screen when they log in, bank employees another.

Consolidating transaction trees is a bit of an art. However, the information content does not have to match exactly. Information elements may be moved off the screen when they are not applicable to all transactions or when real estate becomes an issue. Priorities can also be associated with information elements to determine which elements are less likely to be needed by the user in making decisions.

Physical User Interface Design

Once we have an understanding of the information required by the system and the order in which it is needed, we may begin to lay out the physical user interface. Physical user interface design can be done using paper and pencil. However, the best way to do it is through a graphical user interface development tool such as VisualAge or VisualCafe.

During physical user interface design, we start with each consolidated transaction. The elements are translated into push buttons, entry fields, radio buttons, and other widgets based on their information type. Real estate, aesthetics, and usability become prime concerns during this phase. Prototypes may be made [Bowser 1995] and user interface specifications may be updated using screen shots.

Physical user interface development is a book by itself. We refer the reader to Cooper [1995] for overall physical user interface development and Lee [1993] for information type mappings.

Conclusion

Modern user interface development can be much more than the creation of graphical user interface screens. Technology is available to incorporate sound and other elements for users to obtain the desired experience from a software system. The conceptual user interface methods that we have outlined are designed to transfer information from the user to the system, so they may be extended to different media forms.

Chapter 17
Coping with Change

> No matter where you are in the system lifecycle, the system will change and the desire to change it will persist throughout the lifecycle.
>
> —E.H. Bersoff [Bersoff 1980]

What's in this chapter?

Change is a fundamental part of software development. Software systems often change during and after software development. How we manage and plan for change may decide how successful a system will be.

Change is characteristic of a development project. Whether change is positive or negative depends on the amount of it and when it occurs. The successfully developed system is one whose customers ask for changes or new features after they receive the system. Use of a system will often lead to new ideas or improvements in the system. The fact that users are asking for changes is a sign that they are trying to utilize the system to accomplish some task. In contrast, the poorly developed or unsuccessful system is usually ignored or abandoned.

A certain amount of change during software development is also normal and is the sign of a healthy project. Minor changes, uniformly distributed throughout software development, are part of every software system development process. As long as these changes are managed and the architecture is planned to be able to handle them, the development of the system can proceed, perhaps with only minor delays.

When large changes occur near the end of development, the project is in trouble. The complexity of creating a use case model for a system that is not clear in the users' minds can lead to a constant stream of changes in the specifications. These changes may become a risk to the software development project.

Most changes to software systems can be traced back to the requirements. This means that many changes will need to be reflected in the use case model. One form of changes takes place within the product development cycle. This form represents normal activity associated with the invisibility factor (see Chapter 1), but taken to the extreme, this form could lead to an opportunity for failure. We address this form first. A second form represents future requirements and an opportunity to build a better product. Managing both forms is essential to the success of the system.

Requirements Churn

A software project experiences creeping user requirements syndrome, or "requirements churn," when new requirements are added or existing requirements are significantly modified during the software development process. If requirements churn occurs often enough, a project may be delivered late or may never be delivered at all. In management information systems (MIS), creeping user requirements is the highest risk factor involved in a software development project. One estimate puts 80% of MIS projects at risk [Jones 1994].

During the development of the use case model, change should be allowed to happen freely. The flow of ideas is a vital part of the development process. Once the use case model is complete, it should be reviewed by the stakeholders. This review phase marks the final opportunity to suggest changes to the model before it is declared complete (at least for this iteration). Once the changes from the review are complete, the use case model is presented to the stakeholders for sign-off. This is usually an informal agreement by the stakeholders that the use cases represent the system that is to be built. In rare cases, actual signatures indicate stakeholder approval.

Creating a use case model of the system and obtaining customer sign-off on its content is a good first step toward eliminating requirements creep. The "signed" use case model is a method of managing this risk, but it should not be regarded as carved in stone—sometimes later requirements change is necessary for business or market reasons. A good change control process built into the use case model can ensure that the impact of requirements change is properly planned for.

Planning for requirements change requires a thorough understanding of how change impacts the development of the software solution. When changes occur at the beginning of the project, this understanding is relatively simple. The same process that was used to plan the project in the first place may be reapplied to the new project and the cost or savings of the change can be determined. However, when the project enters software development, replanning the project in this manner is neither cost effective nor desirable.

A software development project in motion carries a certain amount of velocity. Changing the course of the project is easier if the amount of change is small. Large-scale changes often have large impacts and may require substantial amounts of effort. Beyond the economic impact—change almost always costs the project more money—are the people costs. Large-scale changes or even small-scale changes that occur frequently may negatively affect the morale of the development team. Concentration and focus is a large part of developing software, and the interruption caused by a requirements change can be very disruptive to the software development process.

A requirements change may affect the entire product or it may be localized. If a change occurs late in the software development process, some of the parts of the product that are affected by the change may already have been completed. The requirements change for these parts will almost certainly involve rework.

The tendency is to rework the part at the stage of development (analysis, design, construction) where the part is currently, rather than taking it back to an earlier phase. The result is outdated artifacts. This practice can inject errors, in addition to invalidating the work done in the earlier phases. The artifacts may never be updated since few development groups have the discipline to bring all of the artifacts up to date after the project is completed.

Areas of the product that are subject to constant rework can become spaghetti [Brown 1998]. Spaghetti code is a software disease that occurs when software is not designed but rather kludged in. This negative form of software development may become prevalent in a project where change impacts the product requirements but not the schedule. The schedule will not allow the software to be designed nor will it allow the code to be refactored. The result is a part of the product (and in some cases, a whole product) that is unmaintainable.

Source of Change

There are many sources of change in a software system. It is important to recognize the potential areas and examine them for their impact when the vision document is created. They should be revisited when the project is rescoped (perhaps by a change in priority in the product functionality of one of the areas). The following are some sources of product changes.

- *User imagination* [Ecklund 1996]. As the invisibility factor gives way to a concrete implementation, users may realize needs that they had not imagined. Successful deployments are often followed by a stream of additional functionality requests.

- *Technology improvements.* Technology has a remarkable way of shifting the paradigm of the way business is done. A remarkable example is e-commerce. Technological innovation may also be necessary for strategic reasons, such as attracting talent for a software development organization.

- *New or different markets* [Ecklund 1996]. Changes in markets may result from the success or failure of a business to reach its goals in a given market. There may be a desire to expand the role of the system or to change the software to reach a different market.

- *Business process/policy improvement* [Ecklund 1996]. Changes to business processes in which the system is used may affect the system functionality. New business policies may need to be captured by the system.

- *Legislative or regulatory changes* [Ecklund 1996]. When laws or government regulations change, software systems that aid in or automate functions subject to these regulations may have to change as well.

- *Operational betterment* [Ecklund 1996]. To improve operations, changes may be necessary to the software systems that aid in or automate operations. Examples include fully automating a certain operation and reverse automating an operation—that is, bringing people back into the operational loop.

Other areas impact a software system, many of which are industry specific. Brainstorming the types of change that might impact a software system can often lead to surprising results. For this type of brainstorming, it is often wise to include representatives of the many stakeholder groups. Be sure to explain the purpose of the brainstorming. The purpose of the session is not to develop a wish list but to create an understanding of the dynamics of the possible change agents.

Defining the areas from which change may emerge in a brainstorming session can make the difference between short-term and long-term success. Additionally, it can often be worthwhile to understand the perspective of the people making suggestions. They may see future change that others in the project are blind to.

Accelerating Change

In Chapter 19, we describe the use of increments to minimize risk when building a software system. Increments remove some of the "all or nothing" surprise associated with the waterfall approach. With increments, portions of the system materialize sooner so that stakeholders can see what is being built sooner. Increments also allow some of the technical elements, such as architecture, to be tested. A review of a completed increment by stakeholders gives them the ability to "see" if what they are getting is what they asked for. This begins the process of removing the invisibility factor (see the Introduction).

Another method commonly used to visualize software function is prototyping [Bowser 1995]. We have already seen two forms of prototypes: the architectural prototype (Chapter 4) and the user interface prototype (Chapter 13). A third prototype is the functional prototype. This prototype has the sole purpose of demonstrating the functionality of the system. As a result, it is driven by the use case model. Elements of the system may be incomplete, with scaffolding to hard code the dynamic behavior of the system.

Functional prototypes have a single goal: Provide the minimum amount of logic necessary to give stakeholders a visible manifestation of the system in the shortest period of time. The functional prototype is to be thrown away, but its goal is to accelerate the almost certain changes to the front end of the software development process. If there are going to be requests to change the product, we want them as soon as possible to minimize rework.

Managing Change

Some successful projects are built without any requests for change at all. Most projects, however, require a certain amount of it. Changes may affect any of the software development artifacts without requiring a change to the use case model. But since the use case model drives the development of the system and most change requests can be traced back to system requirements, a good number are likely to impact use cases. Change to the use case model must be managed by some change control procedure or the project is likely to erupt in chaos.

What a change control process looks like for an organization usually depends on the level of ceremony. High-ceremony organizations usually have a change control board consisting of representatives of the stakeholders. In low-ceremony organizations, the "board" may be a single person—a manager or architect. The change control board reviews the **change proposal** for its impact on the project schedule, architecture, and system functionality. They also identify the areas and people who will be affected by the change.

We have seen change proposals to the use case model take two forms. One is a revised use case in which the change is made and highlighted. Changes throughout the model are driven by the revised use case. An iteration through the process is performed with the purpose of picking up on the changes. This iteration constitutes rework; the cost of the iteration can be calculated based on experience with previous iterations in the affected area. This approach is ideal for low-ceremony projects.

The second form is a new use case. Change can often take the form of additional functionality or changes to functionality so drastic that new use cases are required. During the use case modeling process, this form of change may result from changes to the definition of the project. During the software development process, these changes may result from an increased scope of the project. When new use cases are written during software development, an architectural analysis must be done to ensure that the architecture will support the new functionality. As we saw in Chapter 4, changes to the architecture during software development tend to have the most serious impact on the software development schedule.

Change Cases

A certain amount of change in a project is inevitable. Predicting *all* the changes that will occur is as difficult as predicting the future. However, predicting many of the extensions that are *likely* to occur may not be as difficult. When we created the vision document (in Chapter 3), we examined the future directions of the domain or industry that we are writing the system for. This type of analysis should give us an understanding of what functionality or technology may be required in the future.

All new functionality needs to be supported by the product architecture. Product architecture changes tend to have the greatest impact on the software development schedule. So, if architecture changes are necessary to support future functionality, the functionality may take much longer to write than if they had been planned for when the architecture was created. In short, it is easier to design a product to be extensible if there is an understanding of the possible extensions to the product in the future [Bennett 1997]. Therefore, possible extensions should be documented when possible as part of the use case model.

New use cases beyond the scope of the current version, revision, or point release in development are called **change cases**. A change case is a use case that represents potential additional, future functionality. A change case lies outside the current development effort. However, the aspects of a change case are like those of a use case. When a change case is incorporated into current development, it becomes a normal use case.

For example, suppose the loan application system presented earlier was extended to become a full-fledged loan processing system. Change cases may be introduced to add loan payment processing. (Figure 17-1) This opens a myriad of new use cases, such as "Process loan payment" by a loan clerk and "Make loan payment" by a Web-based customer using the bank's secure banking system, which would have a definite impact on the architecture.

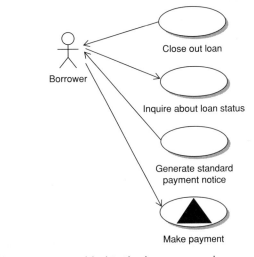

Borrower

Close out loan

Inquire about loan status

Generate standard
payment notice

Make payment

FIGURE 17-1   Change cases added to the loan processing example

Changes to the Use Case Model

It is safe to say that most use case models will undergo a certain amount of change during their lifetime. New versions, releases, and point releases are part of the reality of software development, so there will be changes for a number of reasons, as explained earlier.

Most changes to a case model will not be drastic enough to require an entire rewrite of the use case model. They may not even involve a change case. They will simply occur as alterations in the use case descriptions or use case diagrams. These artifacts (and all artifacts of the software development process) should be under configuration management so that the changes are not lost.

Additionally, each use case should contain a revision history to track its changes, indicated in Figure 17-2 by bars in the left margin. The revision history should contain the date of the change and a short description of the change. This allows use case modelers to understand how the use case has changed over time and can help project managers identify risk areas. Areas that undergo large amounts of change may have to be monitored. If code corresponding to the use case has been written and has undergone similar amounts of change, the code may need to be refactored to ensure that it does not become spaghetti. Artifacts in between use case modeling and the code (analysis and design) may need to be reviewed for accuracy and updated accordingly.

Use case name:	Evaluate loan application
Unique use case ID:	UC-130
Primary actor(s):	Loan officer
Secondary actor(s):	
Brief description:	The *loan officer* reviews the online information about a pending **loan application** to determine if it should be *approved*. The **loan application** includes the *applicant's* personal information, credit score, credit references, credit reports, and history with the bank. If the **loan application** is *approved,* the *loan officer* creates a **loan**.
Trigger:	N/A
Preconditions:	The necessary material concerning a pending **loan application** has been gathered (the **loan application** has a status of *credit references validated*).
Flow of events:	1. The *loan officer* is given a list of all **loan applications** whose credit references have been validated. The *loan officer* selects a **loan application** from this list to review. 2. The system presents the **loan application** and **loan information** gathered on the *applicant*. This information includes: • the *applicant's* **credit history** (credit report and customer history with bank). • a calculated credit score 3. The *loan officer* reviews the material and determines whether the **loan application** should be *approved*. 4. If the **loan application** is *approved,* the *loan officer* selects the appropriate loan terms and conditions for the **loan** based on the bank's policy.
Postconditions:	The **loan application** is *approved* and a **loan** is created. The *applicant* is notified of the approval by e-mail if an e-mail address is given in the **loan application**. Otherwise, the *Applicant* is notified via traditional mail.
Alternative flows and exceptions:	• After *loan officer* review, if the *applicant's* **loan application** is turned down, the applicant is notified, and the **loan application** is marked as *denied*. The *applicant* is notified of the results via traditional mail. • The *loan officer* may be unable to make an evaluation. The **loan application** may *require further evaluation* and is referred to the *loan committee* for review and evaluation. • The *loan officer* may determine that further information needs to be gathered before a decision can be made. In this case, the **loan application** *requires further information*. The *applicant* is notified of the need for additional information by e-mail if an e-mail address is given in the **loan application**. Otherwise, the *applicant* is notified via traditional mail.

FIGURE 17-2   Loan processing use case with a revision history

Nonbehavioral requirements:	Only the *loan officer* or *loan manager* may access a **loan application** and its associated material. The system must handle usage by 10 *loan officers* simultaneously.		
Assumptions:	N/A		
Issues:	N/A		
Source:	Interview minutes memo #123-3		
Revision history:			
Date	**Version**	**Description**	**Author**
12/20/99	1.0	Creation	Frank Armour
1/5/00	1.0	Identification of abstractions, states, and actors	Randy Miller
1/15/00	1.0	Incorporation of inspection results	Randy Miller
1/31/00	1.1	Addition of e-mail or snail mail notification	Randy Miller

FIGURE 17-2 Continued

When changes come in that represent potential future changes (changes that may or may not happen) rather than actual future changes (future changes that are planned for), a revised use case or **use case revision** can be written to track the change. This captures changes too small to be captured in a change case. The use case revision can be assessed for its architecture impact. Should an impact be assessed, the use case revision can be included in the set of use cases that define or redefine the system's architecture (see Chapter 4). This set should include the relevant change cases and the priority 1 use cases.

Use case revisions suffer from the same problems as code modules when multiple concurrent development efforts are underway. The revisions reflecting future, uncommitted changes may become out-of-date as changes occur in the use case model in the ongoing software project. These revisions can be merged into the use case model when they are committed. This is another reason to have the use case model artifacts under configuration management.

Change cases and use case revisions track functional changes to the product. Other possible nonfunctional changes (such as the systems platform—Solaris, Windows 2000, or Linux) need to be tracked elsewhere. The vision document is one place to put these changes. They may also be captured as annotations to relevant use cases or in a separate document.

Conclusion

The use case model will be the subject of many changes over the life of a successful product. Change cases and use case revisions are two ways of tracking functional changes. Understanding potential change is important to the vitality of a system. However, taken to the extreme, it can lead to overengineering or the inability to actually deliver on even a single set of requirements [Abreu 1996]. Like all things in the software development project, balance is critical to the successful use of these techniques.

Chapter 18

Creating Your Advanced Use Case Modeling Process

> In your own groups, if you want to consistently hit your deadlines, you must protect your development team from unnecessary work.
>
> —Steve Maguire [Maguire 1994]

What's in this chapter?

This chapter describes customizing advanced use case modeling to fit a project. The development case, a technique from Objectory (a predecessor of the Rational Unified Process), is used to outline the customized process [Krutchen 1999].

Consider all the activities and artifacts described in the previous chapters. Do you see how each one could be applied to your project? Are you mentally fitting them together into a process? Or perhaps you see the applicability of many of them but do not need all of them in your project. You might even be looking for the smallest subset of these artifacts because your project runs lean and mean. This has certainly been the desire in the modern trend toward lightweight software development processes. Or, you may feel that you do not know which of them would be applicable to your project.

This entire spectrum of feelings is determined by something called **ceremony**—"the practices and rituals that a project uses to develop systems" [Booch 1996]. Ceremony is the greatest influence on our ability to determine which artifacts we will use and which artifacts we should use in our project. Ceremony is the level of specificity required by the organization sponsoring the project (not necessarily your organization) and is determined by numerous characteristics of the project team and the project itself.

Ceremony is a continuum. At one end of the continuum is high ceremony. In high-ceremony projects, the number of artifacts is high. Changing an artifact is often very expensive relative to what is being delivered because of the redundancy (all of which is traced) between the artifacts. Changing one artifact usually requires changing others and may be more expensive than changing the product itself. The changes nearly always require review. The redundancy is built in for a reason: to reduce risk.

At the other end of the continuum is zero ceremony. Zero-ceremony projects have no artifacts. There is simply the deliverable and some independent, heroic workers who make the deliverable possible. All the knowledge associated with the production of the deliverables is in their heads, and the workers are essentially subject matter experts. The zero-ceremony project has one goal: creativity.

In the center of the continuum is medium ceremony. The medium-ceremony project balances risk and creativity. The medium-ceremony project may be the fastest approach for the large projects of today. Obviously, it is more efficient than the high-ceremony project. Less obvious are the advantages this project has over its low-ceremony brethren. Good communication is one of the most important dynamics in the development of today's complex systems. The low-ceremony project communicates informally. This informal technique suffers from economies of scale, becoming less efficient as the project gets larger.

Optimum productivity comes from having the "right" level of ceremony for a project. Finding this level of ceremony can be as much of a learning process as the project itself should be. To find the optimum, start in the ballpark defined by the project and project team and increase or decrease the ceremony as necessary to increase creativity or decrease risk. Different parts of the project may have different levels of ceremony. For example, the process of prototyping requires maximum creativity. Keeping ceremony low for this deliverable is critical.

Effect of the Project and Project Team on Ceremony

The keys to determining the right level of ceremony for your project are its customers, the project itself, and the project team (both engineering and management). This is by no means an exact science. However, the following characteristics of your project can guide you in making this choice.

Project influences

- *Criticality.* Is it "life or death"? How bad is a failure? The worse the result of a failure, the higher you want your ceremony to be. To determine such an impact, look at your industry, government regulations (if any), and competition.

- *Economics*. As you approach the higher end of the continuum, things get more expensive and team members get less productive. Do not assume the contrary. Zero-ceremony projects are not necessarily cheaper, because they may have long-term or intangible costs, such as the costs of rearchitecting, reengineering, or customer dissatisfaction.

- *Culture*. Does your culture favor heroics by individual team members and few rules? Or is there a formal process for each task? Are you ISO-9000 compliant? Attempting a high-ceremony project with a culture that favors low-ceremony can be disastrous. The converse, attempting a low-ceremony project in a high-ceremony culture, causes confusion and team stress.

Project team influences

- *Size*. How many workers are involved in the project? As the size of the project increases, so must its ceremony. The zero-ceremony project cannot be scaled beyond a single team or perhaps as many as 10 workers. On the other hand, high-ceremony projects naturally require larger teams (or huge amounts of time) because of the overhead involved.

- *Locality of developers*. Collocation of workers is necessary for the communication required for lower levels of ceremony. As the team becomes dispersed or if the project spans multiple sites, the level of ceremony must be increased.

- *Experience*. A developer's experience level is determined by how many projects the developer has worked on that have successfully employed use cases to deliver a useful business process, successful software system, or well-designed component system. The lower the experience level of the workers, the closer to the middle of the continuum the project should be. High ceremony and low experience is a recipe for project paralysis. Low ceremony and low experience can lead to a wild ride.

Effects of Artifacts on Ceremony

All major processes actually have two components: an engineering side and a management side. These engineering and management components are subprocesses, since they both have deliverables. Of course, many of us engineers (software, business process, or otherwise) know the management process to be overhead. And many of us managers know that no engineering would get done without our work. Right?

Grady Booch [Booch 1996] called these subprocesses the macro and the micro processes (Figure 18-1). The macro process is the management side and the

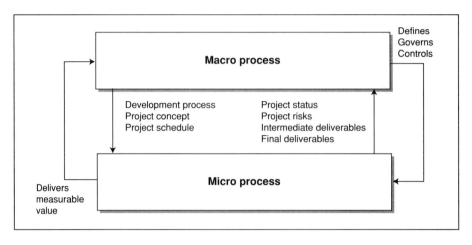

FIGURE 18-1   Micro and macro processes

---

micro process is the engineering side. This is like the yin and the yang. There cannot be one without the other.

Booch wrote:

> Use the macro process to control the activities of the project as a whole; use the micro process to iteratively carry out these activities and to regulate the future conduct of the macro process [Booch 1996].

Is there one macro process for the advanced use case modeling process or one for each phase? As each phase has its own stakeholders, each phase should have its own macro process. The macro process should be governed by those working on (managing and developing) the particular project. One major stakeholder is often the engineering effort upstream. The business process engineers may be waiting for a system that automates an activity of their new process. The software system may, in turn, be waiting for a set of software components.

The level of ceremony and the number of artifacts used on a project are directly related. The higher the level of ceremony, the larger the number of artifacts used. The lower the level of ceremony, the smaller the number of artifacts used. However, which artifacts should be used at which level? The answer to this question depends on the project as well.

The level of ceremony may be different in each phase of the advanced use case modeling process. It may also be different in the macro process (management) and the micro process software development. For example, the management level might be high for a medium-ceremony software development project. The extent to which the ceremony of the macro process influences that of the micro process depends on the ability of the management team to isolate development. If the manager of the medium-ceremony software development project did not isolate the software developers from the macro process tasks, the productivity of the developers in creating and updating artifacts of the macro process might be decreased. A general rule of thumb is to keep the project at a single level of ceremony.

Higher levels of ceremony of the micro process require more progress management than do lower levels. Paralysis is a well-known pitfall of high-ceremony projects. Details that would be glossed over in low-ceremony projects can be the subject of fierce debates in the high-ceremony project. The project plan is ideal for ensuring that the project does not bog down in the details. Lower-ceremony projects can often take off in an unanticipated direction if not properly focused. These projects require the guidance provided by a business or development case (Table 18-1).

Software systems run the gambit of the ceremony spectrum. There are high-ceremony systems (such as an automatic pilot systems) whose failure could mean life or death. There are low-ceremony projects (some small financial systems written for a very specific short-term purpose) whose longevity is measured in days. Most software systems fall in the middle, employing medium ceremony.

Development Case

The development case allows you to customize the development process and its artifacts for your project [Kruchten 1999]. The development case outlines the steps involved in each activity and the creation of artifacts as the result of performing the steps. Key to the definition of a development case is an understanding of the level of ceremony to be used to balance creativity and risk.

Once the ceremony level is determined, the next step is to choose the activities and artifacts that you feel are most important to the success of your project. Since the development case is a macro process artifact, the activities outlined in it will be those to be performed in the micro or engineering process.

What's in the Development Case?

The development case examines each view of the process and its constituent phases. For each phase, activities are defined. If each activity can be broken down into steps, the development case may include them as well. The development case mandates, recommends, or suggests the activities of and artifacts for the engineering process. It also defines the group or the roles of individuals involved with each of the steps. If the role is plural, the step may be the responsibility of a team (Table 18-2).

TABLE 18-1 Suggested artifacts by level of ceremony

Artifacts	High	Medium-High	Medium	Medium-low	Low
Macro process	Business case	Business case	Business case	Development case	Development case
	Development case	Development case	Development case	Project plan	
	Project plan	Project plan	Project plan		
Software system development	Vision document	Vision document	Vision document	Vision document	Vision document
	Requirements tracking matrix	Initial use case model	Initial use case model	Initial use case model	Initial use case model
	Initial use case model	Base use case model	Base use case model	Base use case model	Software architecture document
	Base use case model	Elaborated use case model	Elaborated use case model	System glossary	User interface specification
	Elaborated use case model	System glossary	System glossary	Software architecture document	
	System glossary	Software architecture document	Software architecture document	User interface specification	
	System architecture document	User interface specification	User interface specification		
	User interface specification	System interface specification			
	System interface specification				

TABLE 18-2 Steps in the activity "Find actors"

Use case view—Requirements analysis		
Activity 1: Find actors	**Usage**	**Participants**
Input context diagram from vision document	Mandatory	
Brainstorm actors	Mandatory	Use case developers
Group actors	Recommended	Use case developers
Create inheritance relationships between actors	Recommended	Use case developers
Artifact: Actor glossary	Mandatory	Architect

Three categories of usage may be applied to a step or artifact: mandated, recommended, or suggested. If usage of a step or artifact is **mandatory**, then the use of that step or the creation of that artifact is required. All designated team members must perform the activity and must deliver their contribution to the artifact.

The second category of process element usage is **recommended.** In this category, a process step or creation of an artifact should be completed unless there is a good reason not to do so. Such a reason might be that the step is not applicable, the information derived from the step is trivial, or the same information could be obtained from another artifact (created earlier).

The final category is **suggested**. These artifacts or process steps are optional but are suggested as valuable in clarifying certain project characteristics. Process elements in this category might be applied only to those areas exhibiting these characteristics (examples include artifacts to address concurrency, real-time, or performance issues). Suggested process elements are often footnoted to indicate the type of characteristic.

Activities usually start with some information to be used as a basis or starting point. This information may have been created through another activity or it may be available from other sources in the organization. This information is captured as an input to the activity. Inputs may be mandatory, in which case the information is necessary for the activity to proceed. Recommended inputs should be used whenever possible, and suggested inputs are usually useful.

Each activity in the development case should culminate in the delivery of artifacts of measurable value. The role of each minor step is to add more information to the final delivery. If a step does not increase understanding of the system, the step is misplaced or should be omitted.

The usage of the artifact should correspond to the highest usage of any process step. Thus, a set of mandatory steps should not culminate in a suggested artifact, nor should a set of suggested steps culminate in a mandatory artifact.

The development case need not be elaborate. Each activity should be decomposed only to the level where a single group or individual is responsible for its completion and the same usage level is maintained throughout. Suppose that all three steps under "Find actors" were mandatory and performed by the use case brainstorming team. We could simply note in the development case that "Find actors" was a mandatory step to be completed by the use case brainstorming team.

Don't be afraid to reference process descriptions that are available to the development teams involved (Table 18-3). The intent of the development case is not to write a process book. However, make sure any reference included in the development case is available to all process participants. There is nothing more frustrating than having to track down an obscure reference to understand how to do your job!

Who Should Develop the Development Case?

The development case sets the tone for the project. The development case also enforces the ceremony. The more activities and mandatory artifacts, the higher the level of ceremony. The fewer activities and suggested artifacts, the lower the level of ceremony. The development case is one of the key inputs into the project plan. As you can imagine, a poorly thought-out development case can easily sabotage a project.

Experience is the key to creating a good development case. Experienced developers and managers know when to take risks and when to unleash creativity. They also know when to mitigate risk and when curtail creativity. Key to the development plan is an understanding of the ceremony levels corresponding to the customer and development team. Is it a brand new product unlike any ever delivered before? Is time to market the key requirement? Or is this a mission-critical system whose failure could lead to loss of lives?

Creating a development case should involve the most experienced people on the development and management teams. Achieving consensus is important, and the finished product should reflect the level of ceremony desired on the project, not a set of compromises. No matter how you approach the creation of the devel-

TABLE 18-3   Abbreviated version of an activity using a reference

Use case view—Requirements analysis		
Activity 1: Find actors	**Usage**	**Participants**
Input: Context diagram from vision document	Mandatory	
Find actors (as prescribed in Chapter 7)	Mandatory	Use case developers
Artifact: Actor glossary	Mandatory	Architect

opment case, members deciding which artifacts should be used should be the people who are actively working on the creation of that project's deliverable. Having "skin in the game" is extremely important as characteristics of the project may be discovered that may lead to the need to revise the development case.

Iterative Development and the Development Case

The engineering process defined in the development case should not be performed in a waterfall fashion [Royce 1970]. At least some part of the project should be the subject of an iteration of the process. Iterative development is especially important if the process is new to the organization. Problems with the development process can be detected more readily if it is performed in increments.

The development case is a living document, as are the artifacts it contains. As the project proceeds, changes to the development case may be necessary to reflect increased experience with the subject matter being developed, increased experience with the development process, or the need to increase creativity or decrease risk.

A word of caution before proceeding to change the development case: Ensure that you are changing the development case for good reason. Many developers have changed a development case because they perceived lower ceremony to equal productivity increase. What they got from lower ceremony was lots of rework that actually cost them more in the long run.

One of the biggest reasons to change the development case is changes in the experience level. An inexperienced development team might have started with medium ceremony and learned the value of certain activities and artifacts that they had not expected. They might also downgrade the usage of activities they did not find especially useful. As teams become more comfortable with a development process, they tend to want to change it to reflect what they really do.

The best time to change the development case is between iterations in the engineering process. At this time, the entire process will have been tested for problems. Problems found in the development case can be corrected and these corrections can take effect in the next iteration.

Finally, those of you feeling overburdened by ceremony, take heart. For each of you there is someone who feels that there is not enough and that their project is flying by the seat of its pants. Achieving the right level of ceremony is a difficult undertaking and personal preferences vary.

Conclusion

One size does not fit all when it comes to a development process. This is because each organization and each domain is different. Therefore, each process must be customized. Creating a good development case with the right activities to model your domain and the right level of ceremony to satisfy your customers and development team is challenging. However, getting it right the first time is not necessary. Iterating over the development case as you would iterate any other aspect of the development project will help you zero in on the activities that are right for you.

To help you out in this regard, "typical" development cases for each of the phases of advanced use case modeling are given in Appendix B. To reflect the most common setting, the business process definition development case is high ceremony. The software system development case is medium ceremony, and the component development case is low ceremony.

Chapter 19

Ensuring a Successful Use Case Modeling Effort

What's in this chapter?

This chapter discusses the quality attributes of a good use case model when it is used to represent requirements. The various roles that use case modeling can play within a system analysis effort are discussed as well. Iterative and increment development with use cases is also briefly outlined.

How do you know you're developing a use case model "right"? As we said in Chapter 5, use case modeling can be applied in many ways. Some developers like to do it very formally and comprehensively, while at the other extreme, others utilize use cases as an informal way to elicit requirements from users. In the formal approach, the use case model is large, comprehensive, and detailed; in the informal approach, the use case model is high level and omits cursory details. Some developers like to develop a comprehensive use case model early in project development; others create and implement the use case model iteratively. Which is the correct method? Is there a middle ground? We have seen projects successfully implement systems using each one of these approaches—and we have also seen projects fail with each of these approaches.

What separated the successful from the unsuccessful projects was the planning. The developers of successful projects understand the role that use cases will play in a project. They also understand the strengths and weaknesses of each approach and plan accordingly. For example, if a large project plans to use the use cases as *the* requirements and then creates a high-level, informal use case model, requirements will be missing, incomplete, and ambiguous, leading to a failed development effort. If, on the other hand, a project plans to use the use cases to help communicate the system requirements to the customers and then creates a very detailed, comprehensive model with lots of use cases, with many include and extend relationships, and with lots of logic and business rules in the flow of events, the validation can bog down in the details and the project is most likely to be unsuccessful.

Appropriate Level of Detail and Organization in the Use Case Model

No matter which of the different techniques and approaches for elaborating the use case model are used in a use case modeling effort, the base behaviors of the system must be captured. And, depending on the level of use case modeling ceremony and formality, it is important not to disregard the additional details, alternative flows, and common behaviors associated with a complex information system. It is important that the completed use case model be as comprehensive and thorough as possible to ensure that the user's needs are understood and that the right system is being built. As we've said, the primary cause of system development failures is the lack of a good understanding of system requirements. At the same time, it is important to chose the right level of detail to expand the model. The right amount of detail depends on the complexity of the system being modeled.

Like other analysis techniques, a key to use case modeling is knowing when to stop. Remember that the goal is a good enough understanding of the system's functionality so that the requirements can be captured and validated with the users. At the same time, it is important to avoid overanalysis and unnecessary detail.

How many use cases do you need? What is the proper level of detail? How should the use cases be organized? For large information systems, there may be dozens of base use cases. As extends, includes, and elaborated use case descriptions are created, the number of use cases may grow into the hundreds.

There is much discussion in the use case modeling community about the appropriate level of formality of a use case model. The level of formality of a use case model directly affects the questions of when to stop and what a "good" use case is. Use case modeling efforts can be anywhere on a continuum of formality (Figure 19-1). The key to understanding the role that use case modeling will play on a project is to know the implications of the continuum.

Based on where on the formality continuum a developer decides to model a project's use cases, there will be different development expectations for how the use case model will represent the requirements. The key goal of the project team should be to capture a quality set of requirements that can be successfully specified, validated, and implemented.

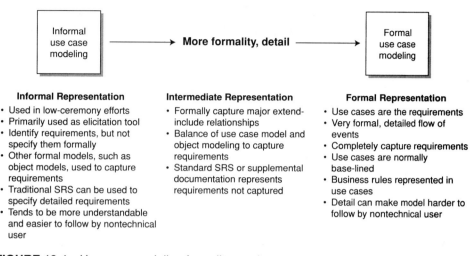

Informal Representation	Intermediate Representation	Formal Representation
• Used in low-ceremony efforts • Primarily used as elicitation tool • Identify requirements, but not specify them formally • Other formal models, such as object models, used to capture requirements • Traditional SRS can be used to specify detailed requirements • Tends to be more understandable and easier to follow by nontechnical user	• Formally capture major extend-include relationships • Balance of use case model and object modeling to capture requirements • Standard SRS or supplemental documentation represents requirements not captured	• Use cases are the requirements • Very formal, detailed flow of events • Completely capture requirements • Use cases are normally base-lined • Business rules represented in use cases • Detail can make model harder to follow by nontechnical user

FIGURE 19-1 Use case modeling formality continuum

Knowing when to stop use case modeling is not a question that can be answered without first knowing the place use cases have in the requirements analysis. No matter what approach a developer selects, careful organization of the use cases as well as maintenance of an appropriate and consistent level of detail are critical to the success of a modeling effort. The following are some criteria for judging whether a system is modeled at a sufficient level of detail.

- Can analysis objects and their behaviors be realized relatively smoothly from the use cases, or are some behaviors difficult to model with objects due to functionality that the use cases failed to model? In these situations, it might be helpful to continue use case modeling until it helps clear up the ambiguity.

- Is the high-priority functionality (i.e., the functionality is expected to be developed in the first increments or releases) modeled to the point where solid, validateable requirements can be derived? If not, more analysis is needed.

- Could system or acceptance test scripts be generated easily from the use cases? If the answer is yes, the use cases are probably detailed enough.

- Can a complete set of verifiable and unambiguous traditional requirements be derived from the use cases?

We prefer to use use cases to capture a broad understanding of the requirements and to keep the very detailed business logic and interface specification out of the use case model. The more detailed requirements, however, are defined and documented in the appropriate artifacts so that they can be traced back to the use cases. Requirements that are in forms difficult to represent in the use cases can also be associated this way. These representations might include spreadsheets, diagrams, report layouts, GUI screens, and so on.

Attributes of a Good Use Case Model When Specifying Requirements

Before we can discuss what a good use case is, we need to understand what a good requirement is. The IEEE [IEEE 1998b] defines a well-formed requirement as

> a statement of system functionality (a capability) that can be validated, that must be met or possessed by a system to solve a customer problem or to achieve a customer objective and that is qualified by measurable condition and bounded by constraints.

If use cases have a place in modeling and representing requirements, it is only proper that we hold them to, and evaluate them based on, the standards to which we hold traditional requirements. A number of quality requirement frameworks are used to evaluate requirements and can be applied and customized for use cases. We choose the quality attributes outlined in the IEEE recommended practices for software requirements [IEEE 1998a] and Alan Davis's book, *Software Requirements: Objects, Functions, and States* [Davis 1993]. These include:

- Correct
- Unambiguous
- Complete
- Verifiable
- Consistent
- Understandable by the customers and users
- Extensible and modifiable
- Traceable
- Prioritized

Requirement quality attributes are also discussed in numerous other references including Davis [1997], Robertson [1999], and Leffingwell [2000]. A good use case model may not have all the attributes, depending on the role of the use case model. However, the quality attributes can be customized for specific use case modeling efforts. They can then be used to help organize use case walkthroughs and review sessions. If the use case model does not have these attributes, it is up to the developer to figure out alternative and/or supplemental means to represent requirements that do.

Correct

A use case model is correct if every use case contained in the model represents a piece of the system to be built; in other words, no use case should contain a behavior or nonbehavioral requirement that is not needed by the system. In addition, simply because a user initially states that the system should do something does not necessarily make that behavior right. It may be that given the resources, time constraints, or other development constraints, the behavior cannot be implemented. It may also be true that one user's needs conflict with other stakeholders' needs. To help ensure correctness, make sure that all the use cases are reviewed and agreed on by all the stakeholders. It may be that the user needs to be helped to "understand the real needs" with the assistance of the use case modelers.

A common mistake made in this regard is when use cases end up modeling the "as is," and not the "to be." It is very easy for users to provide information for the use cases that is based on their current perception of their needs, not what the system will need to do in the future. In one example, a set of users defined use case for reporting that stated that large amounts of paper reports would need to be generated. When we asked the users why, the response was that the information needed to be mailed to a number of other outside organizations. We helped the users understand that their real need was not to print a lot of paper but to distribute information to outside groups and that an electronic means was the best way.

Use cases also age; that is, a use case that represents a correct understanding of what the system should do now may not be correct a year and half from now, when the system is implemented. Changing business conditions, new customers, and users all impact correctness.

To address issues of correctness, ask the following questions.

- To what extent have the users/customers been involved in the use case process?
- Is each use case an accurate reflection of the users'/customers' need? Why or why not?
- Have the users/customers given careful consideration to each use case?
- Are the use cases traced back to their source? Does each use case in the model trace to a business use case, BPR model, interview, or requirements workshop?
- Have domain experts who are independent from the users/customers reviewed the use cases?
- Has the project management determined that the use cases in the model are feasible and implementable?
- Have applicable industry standards, government regulations, and laws affecting the system's functionality been considered?

Unambiguous

A use case model is unambiguous if every use case in it has only one interpretation; in other words, if 10 stakeholders looked at a use case, they would all agree on the system functionality that the use case represents. An unambiguous use case reduces the chances that someone later in development will say, "That is not what I thought the use case did." Ambiguity in requirements is one of the major causes of disappointing system efforts. Many times people read into a use case what they would like the system to do. Although it might appear that the customers and developers agree on what the system should do, in reality they are expecting different functionality. The result is usually unintentional and innocent, but unmet expectations can cause hard feelings and lack of trust to develop between the customers and the development team.

For example, in the use case "Withdraw funds," an activity in the flow of events is written as follows:

- The system shall take appropriate action if the customer attempts to overdraw the account.

The activity would be less ambiguous if it were written as follows:

- If an attempt is made to overdraw an account the system will

  1. cancel the withdrawal.
  2. respond with an message explaining the cancellation.
  3. log the withdrawal attempt.

To address issues of ambiguity, ask the following questions.

- Is there a system glossary that is used in the use case model?
- Are all terms with multiple/unknown meanings defined (e.g., in the glossary)?
- Are use case activities quantifiable and verifiable?
- Can acceptance measures or testing criteria be assigned to each use case?

Complete unambiguity is a big challenge for a use case model. Use cases that are very unambiguous are likely to be very detailed, and they can be very long or have a very deep nesting of includes or subordinate use cases. This can significantly impact readability and therefore understandability. We find that an iterative approach to developing, elaborating, and implementing the use case model is a good way to deal with the situation. We also use supplemental and traditional requirements specifications to document and baseline detailed requirements. When developing a use case model for a large system, it can be a challenge to stuff all the requirements into an unambiguous use case model.

Complete

A use case model is a complete representation of the requirements [Davis 1993] if it includes

- all significant requirements relating to behaviors, performance, design constraints, and external interfaces,
- for each use case, the definition of the system outputs to all actor inputs for both valid and invalid flows,
- full labeling and references on all diagrams, figures, tables, and other documentation, and
- a definition of all terms and units of measure used.

A use case model should normally always try for broad completeness: Does it cover the broad range of behaviors that will be supported by the system? Completeness in terms of depth (i.e., does the use case model capture the detailed requirements?) is more of a challenge.

To address issues of completeness in a use case model, ask the following questions.

- Are any behaviors missing from the use cases? Business processes?
- Do the system use cases map to the business use cases or business processes?
- Do the system use cases map to the domain and analysis object models? Are CRUD or other mapping approaches used?
- Are all the actors participating in the use cases clearly defined?
- Has an interface analysis been performed? Is each interface between the system and the actors clearly defined (including information passed)?
- Are the expected input and output values defined for each actor interacting with the system?
- Are the exceptions and alternative flows documented?
- Are there any TBD references?
- Are there any undefined terms or references?
- Are all sections of the use case model complete?

To check that nonbehavioral attributes are completely specified, ask the following questions.

- Have performance considerations been addressed?
- Have security considerations been addressed?
- Have reliability considerations been addressed?
- Have capacity considerations been addressed?

Completeness in a use case model is not something that typically occurs in a waterfall approach. If an iterative development approach is taken, the use case model will be in various states of completeness. As the iterative development proceeds, completeness needs to be judged within this context.

Verifiable

A use case model is verifiable if every use case stated in it is verifiable. A use case is verifiable if a person or machine can check in a cost-effective way that the implemented system meets the behaviors contained in the use case.

To address issues of verifiability in a use case model, ask the following questions.

- Are there nonverifiable words or phrases in the use cases, such as "works well," "fast," "good performance," and "usually happen"?
- Are use case activities stated in concrete terms and measurable quantities?
- Are the preconditions and postconditions stated in a manner that can be tested?

For example, a behavior in a use case such as "The system takes appropriate action if the customer attempts to overdraw an account" is not verifiable, since what is "appropriate action" is not defined.

If you are unsure whether a use case is verifiable, attempt to create acceptance test cases for it. If you cannot, then the use case is ambiguous and nonverifiable. This does not necessarily mean that the use case is flawed. If informal use case modeling is being performed intentionally, it just means that other techniques will have to be used to represent the detailed requirements.

Consistent

A use case model is consistent if no two individual use cases described in it have conflicting behaviors. Types of conflicts include the following.

- A common behavior specified in two different use cases has conflicting descriptions.
- The characteristics of a behavior or thing conflict. For example, a precondition of use case X implies that behaviors in use case Y must have

occurred, and use case Y's precondition implies that some behavior in use case X must have occurred.

- There is a time-related conflict between two specified behaviors. For example, one use case states that behavior A always has to occur before behavior B, but another use case states that behavior B always has to occur before behavior A.
- Two or more use cases describe the same behavior or object but use different terms.

To address issues of consistency, ask the following questions.

- Is the use case model organized in a manner that encourages consistency? Have include relationships been used to factor out common behaviors? Have business function packages and dependency streams been used to organize the model?
- Do the preconditions and postconditions of individual use cases match up?
- Do any behaviors conflict? Do statements about what a behavior does contradict each other? If two behaviors conflict, are they actually two different behaviors that need to be specified?
- Do any terms have conflicting definitions?
- Are there any temporal inconsistencies?
- Are all use cases modeled at a consistent level of detail with respect to importance?

We have found that inconsistencies are typically introduced in a use case model due to a number of possible situations, including:

- Multiple teams working on the use case model
- Updates to the model that create unseen conflicts
- Updating the model and not taking or having the time to review it for consistency
- Formally not defining terms

It is very important not to skip good review, integration, and validation practices in the use case modeling effort.

Understandable by Customers and Users

Use cases should be self-explanatory. That is, the notations, models, and format of use cases should allow the stakeholders (specifically customers and users) to review, understand, and validate the use cases with a minimum amount of effort. This is obviously where use cases shine. However, to ensure clarity, the use cases need to be written in the customer's and user's "language" using terms that are used in the business domain. The use cases should be grouped, as discussed in Chapter 15, in a way that helps the customer and user see the big picture. If the use cases are too long or have too many extend or include relationships, understandability can be adversely affected. The attribute of understandability can conflict with the attributes of unambiguity and verifiability. The more informal the use case model is, the more it tends to be "understandable" to the customer, but the more it tends to use ambiguous wording and represent system functionality in higher-level, nonverifiable terms (Figure 19-2). Because informal models are ambiguous, they can be hard to validate accurately. Formal techniques can be simplified and made more understandable using techniques such as use case organization (Chapter 15), use case views (Chapter 15), and levels of use case descriptions (Chapters 7 and 8).

Extensible and Modifiable

A use case model is modifiable if changes to it can be made easily, completely, and consistently while retaining the structure and style. The use case model should be robust enough to handle changes or new functionality with relative ease.

To address issues of modifiability, ask the following questions.

- Are there a table of contents, glossaries, and an index?
- Are common use cases or behaviors, such as the same behavior appearing in multiple places in the document, factored into include relationships and cross-referenced?
- Is a CASE tool used to assist in maintaining the use cases?

Traceable

A use case model is traceable if the origin of each use case is clear and if it facilitates the referencing of each use case in future development or in enhancement documentation.

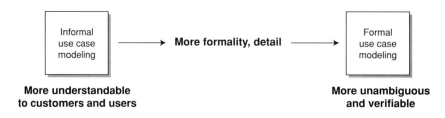

More understandable   **More unambiguous**
to customers and users   **and verifiable**

FIGURE 19-2   Understandable versus unambiguous and verifiable

There are two forms of traceability:

- *Backward traceability (traced).* Each use case explicitly references its source (e.g., memo, law, meeting notes, business use cases, BPR results, and so on).
- *Forward traceability (traceable).* Each use case has a unique name or reference number so that design components, implementation modules, and so on can reference it.

Traceability is facilitated by uniquely identifying each use case, including each extending and included use case. In some situations, each activity within a use case will need to be traced; in this case, the unique ID would be a combination of the use case's ID and the activity step number in the flow of events.

Prioritized

A use case model is prioritized if the relative importance of each use case is understood. A use case is prioritized if it has an identifier to indicate either its importance or its stability. Each system use case may not be equally important. Some use cases may be essential, while others may be desirable.

Example prioritized use cases for an ATM use case model might include

- Withdraw funds, deposit funds (essential)
- Pay bills (conditional)
- Buy certificate of deposit (CD) (optional)

To address issues of priority, ask the following questions.

- Is each use case identified and its priority noted?
- Are the criteria used to prioritize clearly defined?
- How are the use case priorities specified (e.g., essential, conditional, optional)?
- Are the priorities being used to drive schedule and cost?

Incremental and Iterative Development with Use Cases

As we mentioned in Chapter 5, it is neither likely nor desirable for a project to implement its entire set of functionality in one "big bang" approach. Rather, what typically happens is that requirements (e.g., use cases) are defined at a conceptual or base level. Based on project priorities, a subset of the use cases is expanded and developed, and feedback goes into the next increment, where the next set of selected use cases is expanded and realized in design and implementation. Hence, the use case model is in varying states of completeness at different times during iterative development. When discussing this form of development, we like the concepts used by Cockburn [1998] to distinguish between incremental and iterative development.

Incremental development is defined as the development of a system in a series of versions, or increments. A subset of functionality is selected, designed, developed, and then implemented. Additional increments build on this functionality until the system is completely developed. **Iterative development** is planned rework of existing functionality. It is common practice in the industry to use the term *iterative development* to represent both concepts.

There are many possible process models for system development, with no one approach that works best in all situations. We like to develop a complete set of initial use case descriptions up front, validate them with the stakeholders, and, depending on the size and complexity of the system, expand on the initial descriptions to create base use cases as well as major extend and include relationships. Then, based on development priorities, a subset of the base use cases, extensions, and includes is chosen and used to drive the incremental development. These use cases are a scoping mechanism for an increment; the acceptance criteria for an increment are based on the use cases selected to be developed. The use cases that are selected are further elaborated with detail early during the increment. A single increment is represented in Figure 19-3.

In early increments, select use cases to develop that are very important to the users/customers so that you can get feedback early in the development cycle. Also, architecturally significant use cases, such as ones that represent infrastructure that supports or enables functionality present in other use cases, will also be developed in early increments. Throughout this process, plan on different parts of the use case model being in different states of detail and completeness at different times. Also, since use case instances tend to be more specific than the use case

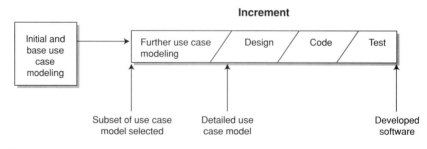

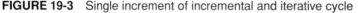

FIGURE 19-3   Single increment of incremental and iterative cycle

they depend on, they can be used to more finely plan an incremental/iterative development effort.

Estimating and incremental definition take place at multiple places in the incremental/iterative development process. First, during or after initial and/or base use case modeling, a high-level master plan laying out the number of increments, their general scope, and the overall project length should be made. Then, when each increment is planned, another more detailed planning and estimating process should occur for that increment. Throughout the development process, the master plan will need be revisited and revised based on the actual results of the increments.

The advantage of an iterative and incremental approach is that it is easier to plan, estimate, and predict several four- to twelve-week increment development efforts than a two-year waterfall project. For increment scheduling, good acceptance criteria—that is, criteria that define what test cases or other evaluative measures will be applied to the completed system to ensure that it has met its requirements (based on the use cases and other requirements specifications)—are critical before beginning an increment. Without good verifiable acceptance criteria, functionality that should be developed in an early increment is intentionally shifted to later increments. The result is that the project subtly falls behind, with later increments becoming burdened with impossible amounts of functionality to develop. A common problem we have seen is that projects don't have good increment exit criteria, so when the time is up for an increment, it is easy to move functionality that was not completed in that increment to a later increment, resulting in the same insidious "scope overload" in later increments. Once stakeholders agree on acceptance criteria early in the increment, the use cases and other requirements for that increment should be "baselined." If the users or customers wish to add functionality after this point, the new requirements should be assigned to a later increment. If the customer demands that new functionality be added to this increment, then the developers must explain that the increment will need to be "broken" and replanned and rescheduled based on the added functionality. A diagram representing a simplified increment cycle is presented in Figure 19-4.

Early increments are typically more focused on requirements definition and testing the feasibility of architectural decisions, and later increments are more focused on code and testing. The amount of time you spend in each step will vary depending on which increment you are in. Additionally, it is dangerous to do too much coding before the majority of the requirements are known.

At the end of each increment, do a postmortem on what worked well and what did not work with the use cases (as well as the other development practices) [Armour 1996b]. Reviews help facilitate process improvement and the learning process. Modify your use case practices according to the lessons learned in the increment. Use case practices should be modified based on input from developers

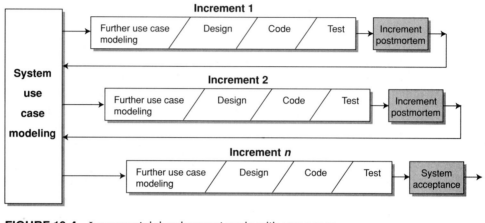

FIGURE 19-4   Incremental development cycle with use cases

and stakeholders. This is an easy step to skip because you will feel pressure to start right in on the next increment. But if you do skip this step, you will pay for it later. The developers, not just management, should be actively involved in the review not only for valuable insight but also for ownership of the changes.

A number of factors affect incremental and iterative development, including architectural decisions, time, functional priority, and resources. We have addressed these issues only as they relate to use cases. For a further discussion of use cases and incremental development, see Rowlett [1998]. For a discussion of iterative development during OO development, see Chapter 4 of Krutchen [1999].

Know When Not to Use Use Cases

Use cases are excellent for capturing behavioral or functional aspects of a system. However, they are not normally as effective in modeling the nonbehavioral aspects, such as data requirements, performance, and security. Additional techniques are required to define these nonbehavioral aspects. For example, object and data modeling can be used in conjunction with use case modeling to capture information needs. Because of this, use cases should be integrated with other models. Maintaining consistency and traceability between the models is important and necessary.

Use cases or specific activities within use cases can be selected for prototyping. Prototypes complement use cases, particularly for behaviors that are difficult to model with use cases alone. For example, prototyping is an effective approach for modeling ad hoc queries, report generation, what-if analysis, and similar activities. Testing the feasibility of a use case can also be performed with prototyping.

Questions to Ask When Use Case Modeling

Following are some questions to ask when planning for a system use case modeling effort.

Goals of the use case model

- What is the goal for the use case model? What is the project attempting to model?
- Based on the goal for use case modeling, what type of use cases are going to be created (e.g., business system use cases, use cases to model the GUI, etc.)?

Use case model approach

- What stopping criteria will be used? How will you know when to stop use case modeling?
- What can't be modeled well with use cases? What other techniques will be used to capture this information?
- How will the nonbehavioral requirements be modeled?
- What will the guidelines be for the length of the individual use cases?
- Are batch processes to be represented with use cases?
- Will iterative and conditional logic be used in the use cases?
- Will the use cases be mapped to traditional requirements? Will both techniques be used on the project?
- How will incremental and iterative development be performed with use cases?
- How are use case dependencies to be modeled?
- Will the use cases be used for non-OO development? If so, what other models will be used? How will they relate to the use cases?
- Will functionality not visible to the user be placed in the use cases?

Use case quality guidelines

- Have walkthrough/review tasks and procedures been formally defined and included in the task plan?
- Are configuration management procedures and tools in place to control the evolution of the use case model? (Yes, it *will* evolve.)
- What templates are being used to specify the use cases? Are the templates based on industry practice?
- What level of use case modeling is to be performed?

- Are there written standards/style guides for the use case model (e.g., a use case writer's handbook)?
- Are the use cases traced back to their source?
- Is there an approach to deal with incompleteness (e.g., iteration, traditional SRS)?
- Are both behavioral and nonbehavioral requirements being specified?

Conclusion

At the beginning of a use case effort, it is critical that the project team determine first what the goals of the use case modeling are and how use case modeling fits into the overall system development goals. The use case modeling can vary from the very informal to the very formal. In any case, if the use cases represent requirements, quality requirements attributes should be applied to them. Iterative and incremental development can be used to expand and develop the use case model. No matter what development approach a project selects, it is critical to organize the use cases carefully and maintain an appropriate level of detail.

The goal of use case modeling is to understand system functionality sufficiently to be able to validate your understanding with users and to motivate the design and implementation, resulting in a system that meets the customers' and the users' expectations.

Appendix A

Use Case Development Review Checklist

What's in this appendix?

This appendix provides a checklist to review when performing use case modeling. The checklist is organized in the order in which use case modeling activities are done.

The checklist in this appendix summarizes the key guidelines for developing use case models presented in body of the book. The checklist is based on the authors' experiences, the experiences of other veteran use case modelers, and other experts in the field. A project, organization, or customer can/should add to or customize the checklist for their specific needs.

Getting Started

❑ A set of use case modeling standards and templates has been selected or created. Appropriate tools are identified and purchased.

❑ The use case modeling process is determined in the context of the overall development process.

❑ If use case modeling experience is low or not uniform (members of the team have done use case modeling in different ways), education or mentoring needs have been identified and scheduled.

❑ All of the stakeholders of the system have been identified.

Scoping the System

❏ The system boundary is clear. Stakeholders understand what hardware/software resides inside and outside the system.

❏ A concept of operation/system concept/vision document has been created to outline the scope of the system.

❏ The business need for the system is clear (possibly defined in a business case).

Identifying Actors

❏ All external entities that interact with the system (primary and secondary actors) have been identified. Consider the external systems (for example, legacy systems, sensors, and so on) as well as the human users and system administrators.

❏ All actors are entities outside the system.

❏ Each actor is an abstraction of a specific role.

❏ Each actor is the most specific delineation of the role possible. No broadly defined, "single" catch-all actor, such as "person" or "computer," interacts with all use cases.

❏ Appropriate abstract actors have been identified when multiple actors share common behavior.

❏ All actors derive observable value from/provide observable value to the system.

❏ Each actor's role in the overall business environment is well understood or has been documented.

❏ Each actor's needs from the system are well understood or have been documented.

Identifying Use Cases

❏ The set of use cases covers all the requirements of the system. Consider both breadth and depth of requirements coverage.

❏ The name of each use case is a verb–noun phrase stated from the perspective of the actor. The verb is in the second person imperative tense, denoting an action that the actor should perform. (Remember that a use case is an event, not a process or information flow.)

❏ The name of the use case reflects the actor's goal in interacting with the system. Test this goal to ensure that the system provides observable value.

Writing Use Cases (General)

- ❏ The names of the actors are consistent with the actor glossary.
- ❏ The terminology of the description is consistent with the system glossary.
- ❏ The use case descriptions can be understood by all of the stakeholders (customers, management, developers, and so on) who will read them. Adequate context is included.
- ❏ Each use case is complete; it provides the necessary behaviors and interactions to satisfy the actor's goals.
- ❏ All observable value required by the interacting actors and described in the use case is consistent with the name of the use case.
- ❏ The use case provides a description from the actor's perspective. It fully captures the actor's expectations from this interaction.
- ❏ The use case is not a scenario. It describes all of the paths that may occur en route when attempting to achieve the goal specified by its name.
- ❏ The use case is initiated by a business event. Users can identify the use case by name or description as a situation they encounter or a task they need to accomplish when playing the role of one of the actors of the system.
- ❏ The use case contains only the functionality that is to be captured in the system; i.e., the system boundary is well-defined. Any context material outside the system but that supports functionality of the system is clearly indicated.
- ❏ All actors associated with the use case are entitled to all the functionality described in the use case.
- ❏ There are no gaps in the system functionality between use cases; that is, each use case completes its area (like a piece of a puzzle). If a gap is found, determine whether a new use case needed or if the functionality is missing from a use case description.
- ❏ The granularity, approach, and style used to write the use case description are consistent with the other use cases (use of prose, step, state, system interaction, and system goal approaches).
- ❏ The use case descriptions are compliant with the standards of the company, customer, and/or project.
- ❏ The use case contains the "right" amount of information to achieve its task.
- ❏ The source of the use case has been documented, if appropriate.
- ❏ If ambiguity exists, the project has an approach for dealing with the ambiguity.

❏ All assumptions about the use case have been documented. Consider assumptions made about the use case's scope, expectations about information available via secondary actors, and development issues surrounding the use case, such as the level of effort needed to develop the use case, time frames, and so on.

❏ If preconditions and postconditions are used (e.g., not used in conceptual use cases), they are documented at a level of abstraction and with a vocabulary that users can understand. They apply to the state of the system, not the outside environment. They are written in a way that allows them to be verifiable and testable. They are written in the present tense.

❏ Alternative flows indicate the triggers that cause deviations from the normal course. If an alternative flow does not remerge with the normal flow, the results of how it differs from the normal flow are stated. If it does remerge, document the point at which it remerges.

❏ Extend relationships are truly extended behavior and not alternative flows.

❏ Significant common behavior has been factored out into a common use case linked by the "include" relationship.

Diagramming Use Cases

❏ The use case diagram is consistent with the conventions of the UML, some superset of the UML, or other well-defined modeling language.

❏ Multiple use case diagrams have been considered/used on a system of any size to partition the functionality. For example, some diagrams may be used to show the relationship between the actors and the system; others may show the base use cases and their extend, include, and generalization relationships. One diagram may be used to show the priorities of use cases based on architectural significance; another may be utilized to indicate the iteration in which a use case will be scheduled to have its functionality designed/developed/tested/documented.

❏ A system boundary in the diagram delineates the functionality inside and outside the system.

❏ All use cases are associated with an actor or are related to another use case (via include, extend, and generalization relationships).

❏ The use cases in a given package are consistent with a single theme or idea captured in the package name.

❏ The diagram is not spaghetti or a mass of relationships. Actors are not too broadly defined and no incorrect (or subroutine) level of use case modeling has been used. (Consider "layering" your use case model, as you would an architecture, so that dependencies between use cases are one-way.)

❏ The priority mechanism (if used) is documented. Priorities can be described using techniques such as a straight numerical ranking or the grouping of use cases into categories (high, medium, and low). Priorities are probably needed if incremental or iterative development of the system is planned.

Organizing the Use Case Model

❏ The use cases are organized in an appropriate manner (e.g., by functional area, by dependency stream, or by actor) making them comprehensible to the stakeholders.

Appendix B

Development Case
for Advanced Use Case Modeling

> Implementing a software development process is a complex task that
> should be carefully controlled.
>
> —Phillipe Kruchten [Kruchten 1999]

What's in this appendix?

This appendix defines a development case for those wishing to integrate the full advanced use case modeling process framework with the Unified Process. This development case contains only elements from advanced use case modeling and should be customized for your environment.

This appendix presents a development case for the advanced use case modeling process framework. This development case is geared toward a high-ceremony organization. In other words, it presents an outline of the entire process. Since advanced use case modeling is a process framework, this development case is meant to be tailored to fit the organization or project that uses it.

A process cannot be presented in isolation; it requires a software development life cycle and methodology. This process framework uses the software development life cycle described by Royce [1998] and the methodology described in this book. It also takes partial input from the Unified Process process framework described in Jacobson [1999]. To allow this document to stand on its own, we present a brief summary of Royce's life cycle. Chances are, your development case (at least the part describing the capture of software requirements and architecture) will be smaller, as life-cycle information is usually contained in other documents.

Software Life Cycle

Royce's software development life cycle forms the basis for the Unified Process [Jacobson 1999] and the Rational Unified Process. Both are iterative/incremental, use-case-driven and architecture-centric process frameworks for object-oriented development. Among other things, these frameworks provide practices, procedures, and guidelines for the entire object-oriented system development life cycle. Like advanced use case modeling, these process frameworks must be customized to fit the level of ceremony of your organization. Each framework is designed to be flexible and modifiable based on specific domain and project characteristics.

Royce's life cycle divides the process of software development into four phases (Figure B-1). Briefly, a phase describes the activities and time between the major milestones. A milestone is a well-defined point where a well-defined set of objectives are met, artifacts are completed, and decisions are made on whether to move into the next phase.

- **Inception**. This phase is where the business case for the project is created and the project's scope is outlined. In addition, success criteria, risk assessment, project estimates, and plans are created.

- **Elaboration**. During the elaboration phase, the problem is analyzed, a system architecture is created, and the description of most of the system requirements is documented. Usually, a part of the system can be created during this phase to validate the architecture by executing significant use cases.

- **Construction.** During the construction phase, the system is created iteratively and incrementally. If the previous phases were successful, much of the activity in this phase involves manufacturing the system.

- **Transition.** During the transition phase, the system is deployed to the user.

The major phases, process workflows, and their mapping across iterations are presented in the Figure B-2. Each iteration goes through different workflows with the focus being different at each phase.

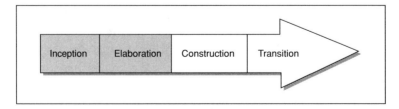

FIGURE B-1   Software system development life cycle [Royce 1998]

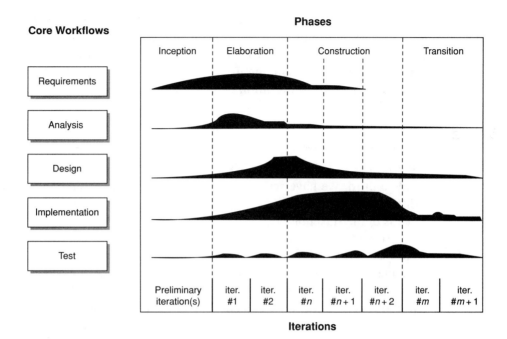

FIGURE B-2   Iterations and workflow across rational unified process phases [Jacobson 1998]

- **Business modeling**. This workflow models the organization or business.
- **Requirements**. In this workflow, the use cases and requirements are discovered, documented, and modeled.
- **Analysis and design**. In this workflow, the system is further analyzed and designed.
- **Implementation**. In this workflow, the software is developed.
- **Test**. In this workflow, the test cases and procedures are created and executed.
- **Deployment.** In this workflow, the final system configuration is documented.

Use case modeling (at a system level) is primarily performed in the requirements workflow, which mainly crosses the inception and elaboration phases. If the use case modeling framework presented in this book was to be customized to fit within the Unified Process, the initial use case model would occur mainly in the inception phase and the remaining use case modeling would occur in the elaboration phase.

As a result, most of the activities of the advanced use case modeling process framework are found in the inception and elaboration phases of the life cycle. However, these activities drive the other phases. Because this book concentrates on the activities surrounding use case modeling, we do not include the details of the construction and transition phases.

Views

Workflows and phases provide two dimensions to the Unified Process; views provide a third. We have seen (in Chapter 16) how stakeholders may require many different ways of looking at a system. Artifacts must often be tailored to meet the needs of the stakeholders.

To address differing stakeholder needs, the Unified Process contains five views. A view allows us to isolate architectural details of a complex system in a manner much like the blueprint of a house [Kruchten 1995]. Isolating the details focuses the engineering effort on the needs of the stakeholders. Instead of attempting to describe the entire system in a single model, views allow us to specialize several models to meet the needs of the various stakeholders. The decisions of the stakeholders can then be captured in the models defined in each view.

Activities within a view may require information from other views. Elements from one view may depend on or be driven by those of another. Moreover, the views may need to be ordered so that the information shared between two or more views remains consistent. This dependency is depicted by an arrow in the view diagram. An exception to this rule occurs with the use case view that appears in all three view diagrams (one for each phase). The use case view has no arrows. Because use cases drive each view, the use case view is in the center of the diagram, signifying the dependence of the other views on it.

Advanced use case modeling defines the elements of the use case view. Since this view drives the others, the methodology also addresses the interfaces between the use case and other views. The methodology does not address all aspects of the other views. For these elements, we refer you to other methodologies that concentrate on these areas.

The architecture of software systems can also be decomposed into five views (Figure B-3). The names of the views are slightly different from those originally defined by Krutchen [Eriksson 1998]. The original names are given in parentheses.

- **Use case view**. The use case view describes the functional requirements of the proposed software system. The functional requirements present the system's functionality or what the system should do. This view describes how the system interacts with the other four views. The use case view also

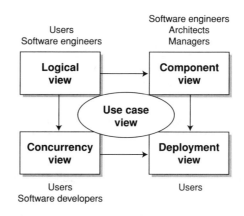

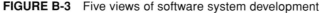

FIGURE B-3   Five views of software system development

shows when a use case occurs relative to the rest of the system. Nonfunctional requirements and constraints on the system, such as performance, reliability, and availability, should be left out of the use case view.

- **Logical view**. This view shows the static and dynamic structure of the system (analysis and design). Functional requirements may be validated by checking them against the operation of the model.
- **Component view** (development view). This view depicts the component and subsystem organization.
- **Concurrency view** (process view). This view provides an understanding of the concurrent elements of the software system.
- **Deployment view** (physical view). The deployment view determines how the system maps to the physical layout (e.g., networked computers) of its environment.

Using the Development Case

This section is divided into life-cycle phases, tasks, views, activities, and steps. Life-cycle phases appear as bold headings. Tasks and views appear as subheadings. Activities appear as table titles; inputs, steps, and outputs appear as rows in the tables. Each input, step, or output may be categorized into one of three usage categories: mandatory, recommended, or suggested. These categories are described in the following table.

Usage	Definition
Mandatory	The use of the step or the creation of the artifact is required.
Recommended	The process step or creation of an artifact should be completed unless there is a good reason not to do so.
Suggested	This artifact or process step is optional but has been suggested as valuable in order to clarify certain project characteristics.

Advanced use case modeling can be used to define the requirements for a software system; other activities, such as analysis, design, and construction, are beyond the scope of this book. The process framework must be customized and placed within the larger software development life cycle that defines the various phases of the software development process. Many companies have defined their software development life cycle to meet the needs of software development in their industry or business. There are also commercially available processes that come with their own life cycle or definition of the development phases.

Inception Phase

The goal of the inception phase is to achieve a consensus on what is to be built, an understanding of the benefits it will bring, and an acceptance of the costs of building it. The activities of the inception phase center on the determination of these three things.

Task: Define the System Scope.   This task defines what is to be built from an external point of view. It also defines who will interact with the new system.

Use Case View

TABLE B-1   Activity: Develop system concept

Inputs, scopes, outputs	Usage	Participants
Input: Detailed business use case model and activity diagram from business process development	Suggested	
Develop a brief textual explanation of the problem to be solved.	Mandatory	Executive manager
Develop a brief textual explanation of why it needs to be solved.	Mandatory	Executive manager
Describe where a solution would be positioned in our business.	Mandatory	Executive manager
Describe the risks involved in solving the problem.	Mandatory	Executive manager

Inputs, scopes, outputs	Usage	Participants
Create a list of future business trends that might affect the project.	Mandatory	Executive manager
Name the project.	Mandatory	Executive manager
Artifact: Product sections of vision document	Mandatory	Executive manager

Note: In our organization, all software development projects are initiated by executive management. For more information about this activity, see Chapter 4.

TABLE B-2   Activity: Identify stakeholders

Inputs, steps, outputs	Usage	Participants
Input: Organizational structure diagram	Suggested	
Describe the sponsors of the system.	Mandatory	System analyst
Describe the various intended users of the system.	Mandatory	System analyst
Describe those involved in the creation of the system.	Mandatory	System analyst
Artifact: Stakeholder and customer or user sections of the vision document	Mandatory	System analyst

Note: The organizational structure diagram describes the anatomy of the organization. If the users of the system already exist (i.e., form precedes function), then the organizational diagram will help identify users and their management. For more information about this activity, see Chapter 7.

TABLE B-3   Activity: Create initial system boundary

Inputs, steps, outputs	Usage	Participants
Input: Partially completed vision document from the previous activities	Mandatory	
Set up context diagram.	Mandatory	Facilitator
List actors.	Mandatory	System analyst
Describe the interaction between actors and the system.	Recommended	System analyst
Artifact: Context section of vision document	Mandatory	System analyst

Note: When setting up the context diagram, draw a large circle and place the system name inside. However, proceed no further. It is the job of the facilitator to solicit information but to remain objective and thus attempt to refrain from joining this activity. For more information about this activity, see Chapter 8.

TABLE B-4   Activity: Review vision document

Inputs, steps, outputs	Usage	Participants
Input: Vision document	Mandatory	
Check accuracy of each section.	Mandatory	System analyst
Check consistency between sections.	Mandatory	System analyst
Artifact: Reviewed vision document	Mandatory	System analyst

TABLE B-5   Activity: Identify actors

Inputs, steps, outputs	Usage	Participants
Input: Context diagram from vision document	Mandatory	
Brainstorm additional actors.	Mandatory	System analyst
Group actors.	Recommended	System analyst
Determine primary and secondary actors.	Recommended	System analyst
Create abstract actors and inheritance relationships between actors.	Recommended	System analyst
Artifact: Actor glossary of the conceptual use case model	Mandatory	System analyst

Note: For more information about actors in general and this activity specifically, see Chapters 2 and 8, respectively.

TABLE B-6   Activity: Discover initial use cases

Inputs, steps, outputs	Usage	Participants
Input: Context diagram from vision document, system glossary	Recommended	
Determine use cases from the context diagram. Associate the use cases with the appropriate actor or actors.	Mandatory	System analyst
For each actor, ensure that the list of use cases is complete and that each use case is properly named.	Mandatory	System analyst
Describe each use case at a conceptual level.	Mandatory	System analyst
Create a use case diagram.	Mandatory	System analyst
Update system glossary with any new terms.	Mandatory	System analyst
Review initial use case model.	Mandatory	System analyst
Artifact: Initial use case model	Mandatory	System analyst

Note: For more information about this activity, see Chapter 8.

Logical View

TABLE B-7   Activity: Create system glossary

Inputs, steps, outputs	Usage	Participants
Input: Vision document	Mandatory	
Brainstorm domain terms.	Mandatory	System analyst
Consolidate list of terms.	Mandatory	System analyst
Define each term.	Mandatory	System analyst
Artifact: System glossary	Mandatory	System analyst

Note: For more information about this activity, see Chapter 5.

Task: Create a Base Architecture.   This task defines what is to be built from an internal point of view. It defines legacy systems with which the new system may be required to interact. Investigations into the technology and patterns necessary to frame such a system should be investigated.

Component View

TABLE B-8   Activity: Document "legacy" system interfaces

Inputs, steps, outputs	Usage	Participants
Input: Vision document, initial use case model, legacy system documentation	Mandatory	
Document the services provided/ needed by the legacy system.	Mandatory	System analyst
Document the interfaces and protocols necessary to invoke/provide the services.	Mandatory	System analyst
Artifact: System interface specification	Mandatory	System analyst

Note: For more information about this activity, see Chapter 5.

TABLE B-9   Activity: Create initial system architecture

Inputs, steps, outputs	Usage	Participants
Input: Vision document, initial use case model	Mandatory	
Find the minimum set of use cases that "covers" the important architectural aspects of the software system.	Mandatory	Architect
Determine the architectural requirements and analysis patterns from the minimum set.	Mandatory	Architect

Inputs, steps, outputs	Usage	Participants
Decompose the system into subsystems.	Mandatory	Architect
Artifact: Software architecture document	Mandatory	Architect

Note: For more information about this activity, see Chapter 5.

Task: Determine System Feasibility (Macro Process). This task defines an initial cost estimate for the proposed system. A cost/benefits analysis is also performed to determine the value of building it.

TABLE B-10   Activity: Determine system feasibility

Inputs, steps, outputs	Usage	Participants
Input: Vision document	Mandatory	
Calculate net value of benefits.	Mandatory	System analyst
Calculate initial net cost.	Mandatory	System analyst
Quantify risks (cost and probability).	Mandatory	System analyst
Determine return on investment.	Suggested	System analyst
Artifact: Business case	Mandatory	System analyst

Note: For more information about this activity, see Chapter 4.

Elaboration Phase

The purpose of the elaboration phase is develop a detailed requirements model, engineer a sound architectural foundation, and identify the tasks necessary to complete a project plan [Jacobson 1999].

Task: Define the System. This task develops the complete and detailed requirements model.

Use Case View

TABLE B-11   Activity: Develop base use case descriptions

Inputs, steps, outputs	Usage	Participants
Input: Vision document, initial use case model, system glossary	Mandatory	
Choose a use case template and approach (prose, step, state).	Mandatory	Use-case specifier

Inputs, steps, outputs	Usage	Participants
For each initial use case, create preconditions, flow of events, alternative flows and exceptions, and post-conditions.	Mandatory	Use-case specifier
Find any new use cases and create initial descriptions for them.	Mandatory	Use-case specifier
Update the system glossary with any new terms.	Mandatory	Use-case specifier
Update the use case diagram.	Mandatory	System analyst
Review the base use case descriptions.	Mandatory	Use-case specifier
Artifact: Base use case model	Mandatory	Use-case specifier

Note: For more information about this activity, see Chapter 9.

TABLE B-12   Activity: Create use case relationships

Inputs, steps, outputs	Usage	Participants
Input: Initial and base use case model	Mandatory	
Identify common behavior in the use cases.	Mandatory	System analyst
Create extension points where necessary.	Mandatory	Use-case specifier
Create abstract or generalized use cases.	Mandatory	Use-case specifier
Update the use case diagram to reflect the new relationships and use cases.	Mandatory	Use-case specifier
Review the revised base use model.	Mandatory	Use-case specifier
Artifact: Base use case model	Mandatory	Architect

Note: For more information about this activity, see Chapter 11.

TABLE B-13   Activity: Elaborate base use cases

Inputs, steps, outputs	Usage	Participants
Input: Base use case model, system glossary	Mandatory	
For each base use case, describe the alternative flows.	Recommended	Use-case specifier
Add more detail and conditional logic.	Recommended	Use-case specifier
Add any new terms to the system glossary.	Mandatory	Use-case specifier
Create activity diagrams.	Suggested	Use-case specifier

Inputs, steps, outputs	Usage	Participants
Update the use case diagram if necessary.	Mandatory	Use-case specifier
Review the elaborate use case model.	Recommended	Use-case specifier
Artifact: Elaborated use case model	Recommended	Use-case specifier

Notes: For more information about this activity, see Chapter 10.

TABLE B-14   Activity: Develop scenarios

Inputs, steps, outputs	Usage	Participants
Input: Elaborated use case model, project plan	Mandatory	
Develop scenarios for any partial use cases scheduled in the project plan.	Suggested	Use-case specifier
Review the scenarios.	Suggested	Use-case specifier
Artifact: Elaborated use case model	Suggested	Use-case specifier

Note: For more information about this activity, see Chapter 14.

Task: Create the Architecture

Component View

TABLE B-15   Activity: Create new system interfaces

Inputs, steps, outputs	Usage	Participants
Input: Vision document, base use case model	Mandatory	
Document the services needed by the new system.	Mandatory	Architect
Document the interfaces/protocols necessary to invoke these services.	Mandatory	Architect
Artifact: System interface specification	Mandatory	Architect

Note: For more information about this activity, see Chapter 5.

TABLE B-16   Activity: Create conceptual user interface specification

Inputs, steps, outputs	Usage	Participants
Input: Elaborated use case model	Mandatory	
Partition the use case model.	Mandatory	User interface designer
Decompose the use cases into transactions.	Mandatory	User interface designer

Inputs, steps, outputs	Usage	Participants
Determine the information content for each transaction.	Mandatory	User interface designer
Establish logical screen order.	Mandatory	User interface designer
Group and layout logical screens.	Mandatory	User interface designer
Artifact: User interface specification	Mandatory	User interface designer

Note: For more information about this activity, see Chapter 17.

TABLE B-17   Activity: Create architectural prototype

Inputs, steps, outputs	Usage	Participants
Input: Architecture specification	Mandatory	Architect
Create an architectural prototype.	Mandatory	Architect
Test the remaining use cases against the prototype.	Mandatory	Architect
Update the architectural specification.	Mandatory	Architect
Artifact: Architectural prototype	Mandatory	Architect

Note: For more information about this activity, see Chapter 5 of Advanced Use Case Modeling.

Logical View

TABLE B-18   Activity: Create analysis object model

Inputs, steps, outputs	Usage	Participants
Input: Initial and base use case model, system glossary	Mandatory	
Add all of the entities from the system glossary that reside within the system boundary to the class diagram.	Mandatory	System analyst
For each use case, add any classes that are missing.	Mandatory	System analyst
Create message sequence charts for the use case.	Recommended	System analyst
Add the relationships embodied in the use case to the class diagram.	Mandatory	System analyst
Review the analysis object model (class diagram).	Recommended	System analyst
Artifact: Analysis object model	Mandatory	System analyst

Note: For more information about this activity, see Chapter 13.

Concurrency View

TABLE B-19   Activity: Verify analysis object model

Inputs, steps, outputs	Usage	Participants
Input: Elaborated use case model	Mandatory	
For each elaborated use case, add any new detail to the message sequence diagram.	Recommended	System analyst
Add any new classes.	Mandatory	System analyst
Add any new relationships.	Mandatory	System analyst
Review analysis object model.	Recommended	System analyst
Artifact: Analysis object model	Mandatory	System analyst

Note: For more information about this activity, see Chapter 13.

Task: Plan the Project (Macro Process)

TABLE B-20   Activity: Create project plan

Inputs, steps, outputs	Usage	Participants
Input: Initial use case model, architectural specification	Mandatory	
Organize use cases into iterations based on priority.	Mandatory	Architect
For each conceptual use case, determine the amount of design effort necessary by subsystem.	Mandatory	Designer
Determine the amount of development effort necessary to implement the use case by subsystem.	Mandatory	Developer
Revise iteration/use case mapping based on effort estimations.	Mandatory	Architect
Add integration effort.	Mandatory	Developer
Add test effort.	Mandatory	Tester
Review project plan.	Mandatory	Stakeholder
Update the business plan.	Mandatory	Executive manager
Artifact: Project plan	Mandatory	Architect

TABLE B-21   Activity: Refine project plan

Inputs, steps, outputs	Usage	Participants
Input: Project plan, base use case model	Mandatory	
Revise project plan with new design estimate based on base use cases.	Mandatory	Designer
Revise project plan with new development estimate.	Mandatory	Developer
Revise iteration/use case mapping based on new estimates.	Mandatory	Architect
Add new integration effort.	Mandatory	Developer
Add new test effort.	Mandatory	Tester
Review project plan.	Mandatory	Stakeholder
Update business plan.	Mandatory	Executive manager
Artifact: Refined project plan	Mandatory	Architect

Summary of Artifacts

Artifacts are the intermediate outputs or deliverables of a process. Completion of part or all of an artifact represents a milestone in the project plan. This section gives a brief description of the deliverables of the advanced use case modeling process framework.

- **Vision document.** The vision (also commonly referred to as a system concept or concept of operation) document communicates the purpose of the application and the need for its existence [Leffingwell 2000]. The document contains a list of users and provides reasons for which product is needed. If applicable, the vision document positions the application with respect to others in the marketplace or business. Finally, and most important, the vision document contains the list of features required in the completed software application.

- **Initial use case model.** An initial use case model presents the high-level behaviors of the system and the system's place in its business environment. A conceptual use case model provides a conceptual or overall picture of what the system will need to do. It provides a high-level model of the system for validation by key stakeholders before a more detailed use case model is

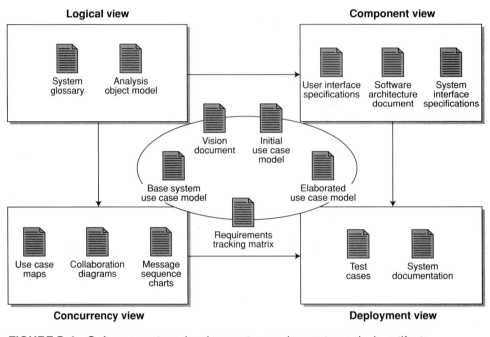

FIGURE B-4   Software system development—requirements analysis artifacts

created. The initial use case model contains the key initial use case descriptions, the major actors, and an initial mapping to high-level business objects. Initial use cases are similar to the user stories of Extreme Programming [Beck 1999].

- **Base system use case model.** The base system use case model describes the uses of the proposed software system at a high level. Uses provide an orderly explanation of how users actually perform tasks with the system. The base use case model provides a cursory explanation of usage, omitting the finer details. The base application use case model also describes how the system interacts with its users and with other systems. This model is described in a combination of text and the Unified Modeling Language.

- **Elaborated system use case model.** The elaborated system use case model describes the uses of the proposed software application at a more detailed level than the base use case model. This finer level of detail achieves greater accuracy in capturing proposed uses of the system.

- **System glossary.** The system glossary is similar to the business glossary in its definition of domain entities. In fact, the business glossary can feed those business entities relevant to the proposed software development system directly into the application glossary. Like the business glossary, the system glossary provides a consistent or standard definition of the names of the elements of the software development system.The goal of the glossary is to provide a name and definition for various elements of the domain. The glossary is especially important if the domain is unfamiliar to the software development team.

- **Software architecture document.** The software architecture document outlines the subsystem layout and other architecturally important features of the software application. Software architecture must be balanced with software requirements and uses. This balance is especially critical in applications that have real-time, performance, or longevity constraints. The software architecture document should be created in parallel with the use case model on most systems.

- **User interface specifications.** The same type of interactions that foster the discovery of the uses of a software application foster user interface discussions. The user interface has been found to both aid and hinder the use of software to create automated or computer-aided solutions. The user interface specification allows user interfaces to be prototyped, captured, and approved by customers and users early in the software development life cycle. The use case model determines the places in the application where user interfaces will be required. User interface specifications may be created with a combination of word processing, screen capturing, and user interface prototyping tools.

- **System interface specifications.** System interface specifications define the interface to other systems. These other systems may exchange data with the proposed application. They may also provide services to or receive services from the application. Definition of the interface between the two systems sets expectations of the relationships between the two systems early in the development. Often, such specifications are used to provide interfaces between new and legacy systems or between two systems developed independently.

Appendix C
Simplified Loan Processing System

What's in this appendix?

This appendix provides sample use case artifacts for the simplified loan processing system.

This appendix brings together the example use cases, diagrams, and actor descriptions for the simplified loan processing system used in the text (Figure C-1). It also includes additional actors and use cases and their descriptions. This appendix contains samples of the following use case artifacts:

- System context diagram
- Descriptions of major actors
- Initial use case diagrams
- Use case diagram showing major use cases and business function packages
- Use case dependency stream and approval process
- Initial use case descriptions with conceptual business objects identified
- Base use case descriptions and diagrams
- Use case description with conditional logic added
- Extend relationships
- Include relationships

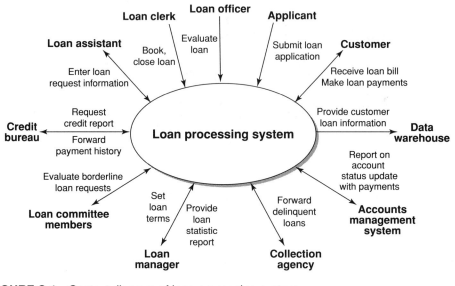

FIGURE C-1   Context diagram of loan processing system

- Generalization relationships
- Use case instances

Major Actors

This section contains a diagram (Figure C-2) and descriptions of key actors in the loan processing system.

Actor Specification
Actor name: Applicant   **Abstract:** <No>
Description: An applicant is an individual or organization who submits an application for a loan to the bank. The applicant will utilize the system primarily to submit loan requests.

Actor Specification
Actor name: Loan officer   **Abstract:** <No>
Description: A loan officer is an officer of the bank who has the designated responsibility of evaluating requests for a loan. A loan officer has the power to grant a loan or, depending on the size of the loan request, refer the requests to the loan committee members for a decision. A loan officer uses the system for such activities as evaluating loan requests and reviewing outstanding loans.

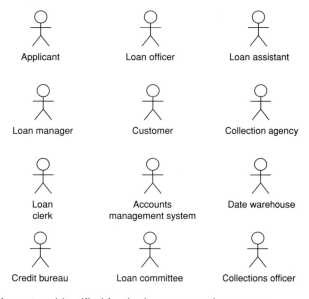

FIGURE C-2   Key actors identified for the loan processing system

Actor Specification
Actor name: Customer   **Abstract:** \<No\>
Description: A customer is an individual or business that currently has a relationship with the bank. For the purposes of the loan management system, a customer is someone who holds an active loan account or has been extended credit.

Actor Specification
Actor name: Accounts management system   **Abstract:** \<No\>
Description: The accounts management system is an existing legacy system that maintains information on the status of a customer's existing accounts with the bank, such as checking, savings, and money market. This system will hold the loan account information for a loan customer that will be needed by the loan management system.

Actor Specification
Actor name: Loan assistant   **Abstract:** \<No\>
Description: The loan assistant is responsible for manually capturing and entering into the system the credit information, including validated references, that is needed for the loan evaluation, as well as initially responding to inquiries by applicants and customers.

Actor Specification
Actor name: Credit bureau   **Abstract:** <No>
Description: A credit bureau is an organization that maintains and provides credit information on individuals and organizations.

Actor Specification
Actor name: Loan committee member   **Abstract:** <No>
Description: A loan committee member is responsible for reviewing loan requests referred by a loan officer that are near or outside the limits of the bank's loan policy.

Actor Specification
Actor name: Loan clerk   **Abstract:** <No>
Description: The loan clerk is responsible for booking (recording and setting up) the loan, once it has been approved, and for entering into the system payments received from the customer.

Actor Specification
Actor name: Loan manager   **Abstract:** <No>
Description: The loan manager directly oversees the loan officers and reviews and evaluates the bank's loan portfolio.

Initial Use Case Descriptions

This section contains selected initial use case diagrams (Figure C-3 and C-4) and descriptions for the Loan Processing system.

Initial Use Case Descriptions

Use case:	Submit loan request
Use case ID:	UC-100
Actor:	Applicant, accounts management system, credit bureau
Description:	The applicant submits a loan request for processing by the bank's integrated loan processing system. The applicant fills out a loan application and submits it to the bank for processing. The system validates information on the loan application and calculates the applicant's credit score based on credit reports and the applicant's account history with the bank. The applicant is contacted for additional information, if needed. The system makes an initial approval recommendation. The loan is now ready for the loan officer's evaluation, pending any needed manual validation of credit references.

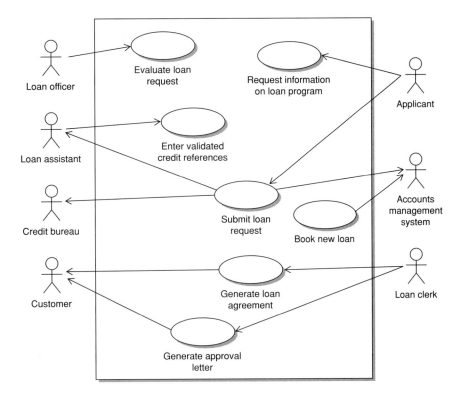

FIGURE C-3   Use case diagram for loan submission use cases in the loan processing system

Use case:	Enter validated credit references
Use case ID:	UC-110
Actor:	Loan assistant
Description:	The loan assistant enters any credit reference information that is needed to be validated manually. This information can include information external bank accounts, and repayment sources (i.e., income) that cannot be validated automatically.

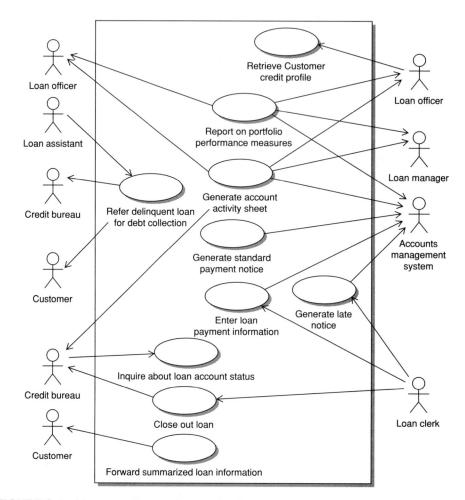

FIGURE C-4   Use case diagram for ongoing loan management use cases

Use case:	Evaluate loan request
Use case ID:	UC-105
Actor:	Loan officer
Description:	The loan officer reviews the online information about the pending loan request to determine whether the loan request should be approved. This information includes the applicant's loan application, credit score, credit reports, and the applicant's history with bank and the system-generated approval recommendation. If the loan request is approved, the loan officer marks the loan request as approved and the loan is ready to be generated.

Use case:	Generate approval letter
Use case ID:	UC-115
Actor:	Loan clerk, customer
Description:	A loan clerk has the system create an approval letter for the applicant, stating that the loan request has been approved and including a detailed listing of the loan's terms and conditions and the period of time the loan offer is available.

Use case:	Generate loan agreement
Use case ID:	UC-120
Actors:	Loan clerk, customer
Description:	A loan agreement is generated based on terms and conditions selected by the loan officer. The loan agreement formally outlines the loan conditions, the obligations of each party, and any restrictions. The loan agreement is presented to the customer for acceptance and signature.

Use case:	Process (book) new loan
Use case ID:	UC-125
Actor:	Loan clerk
Description:	Once a loan agreement has been signed by the customer and returned to the bank, the loan clerk has the system create a loan account based on the agreed on terms and conditions.

Use case:	Generate standard payment notice
Use case ID:	UC-130
Actors:	Loan clerk, accounts management system
Description:	The loan system requests from the accounts management system information on loan accounts that are due for billing. The loan system generates the billings for mailing to the customers.

Use case:	Generate late notice
Use case ID:	UC-135
Actors:	Loan clerk, accounts management system
Description:	The loan system requests from the accounts management system information on loan accounts that are overdue. An automated late notice is generated and sent to customers with overdue accounts.

Use case:	Enter loan payment information
Use case ID:	UC-140
Actors:	Loan clerk, accounts management system
Description:	As payment is received from the customer, the loan clerk enters the information in the appropriate loan account, and the loan processing system for wards the updated account information to the accounts management system.

Use case:	Refer delinquent loan for debt collection
Use case ID:	UC-145
Actors:	Collections officer, collections agency, credit bureau
Description:	The bank's collection officer has the system forward the delinquent loan to a collection agency for outside collection. The appropriate credit bureaus are notified of the delinquency.

Use case:	Close out loan
Use case ID:	UC-150
Actors:	Loan clerk, customer
Description:	The system presents to the loan clerk a loan that has been determined to be paid in full, the loan clerk confirms the paid-in-full status of the loan and marks the loan as paid in full, and paperwork is generated by the system informing the customer of the close-out status. Any collateral certificates are released to the customer.

Use case:	Request information on loan program
Use case ID:	UC-155
Actors:	Applicant, loan clerk
Description:	An applicant requests a hard-copy loan application by mail. The loan clerk enters the applicant contact information in the system and the system generates the application for mailing.

Use case:	Retrieve customer credit profile
Use case ID:	UC-160
Actor:	Loan officer
Description:	The loan officer has the system retrieve and present all pertinent documentation pertaining to the customer credit profile

Use case:	Report on portfolio performance measures
Use case ID:	UC-165
Actors:	Loan manager, loan officer, loan assistant, accounts management system
Description:	The system generates reports on the bank's loan portfolio (set of active loans) for the loan manager.

Use case:	Generate account activity sheet
Use case ID:	UC-170
Actors:	Loan officer, loan assistant, loan manager, accounts management system
Description:	A credit report is generated for every relationship involving new, renewing, or changing loans. Each credit report contains updated information on each loan, current balance, industry information, management information, current financials, and financial analysis to be reviewed at loan committee meetings.

Use case:	Forward summarized data to data warehouse
Use case ID:	UC-175
Actor:	Data warehouse
Description:	Summarized information on the loan submission statistics and payment information is forwarded to a centralized external data warehouse on a daily basis.

Use case:	Inquire about loan account status
Use case ID:	UC-180
Actor:	Customer
Description:	The loan customer can call up online the current status of the loan, including such information as current loan balance and payment history.

Figure C-5 is an initial use case diagram showing key use cases and business function packages. Figure C-6 is an example of use case dependency stream.

Initial Use Case Descriptions with Conceptual Business Objects Identified

Use case:	Submit a loan request
Use case ID:	UC-100
Actors	Applicant, loan clerk
Description:	The **applicant** submits a **loan request** for processing by the bank's integrated loan processing system. The applicant fills out a **loan application** and submits it to the bank for processing. The system validates information on the loan application and calculates the applicant's **credit score** based on **credit reports** and the applicant's **account history** with the bank. The applicant is contacted for additional information, if needed. The system makes an **initial approval recommendation**. The loan is now ready for the **loan officer's** evaluation, pending any needed manual validation of **credit references.**

Use case:	Evaluate loan request
Use case ID:	UC-105
Actor:	Loan officer
Description:	The **loan officer** reviews the online information about the pending **loan request** to determine whether the **loan request** should be approved. This information includes the applicants **loan application, credit score, credit reports**, and the applicant's **history** with bank and the system-generated **approval recommendation**. If the loan request is approved, the loan officer marks the loan request as approved and the **loan** is ready to be generated.

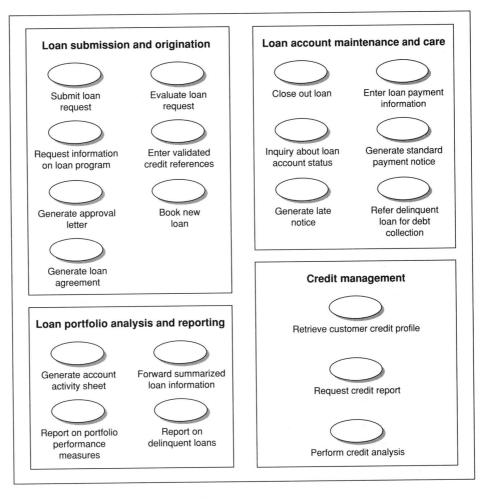

Loan submission and origination

- Submit loan request
- Evaluate loan request
- Request information on loan program
- Enter validated credit references
- Generate approval letter
- Book new loan
- Generate loan agreement

Loan portfolio analysis and reporting

- Generate account activity sheet
- Forward summarized loan information
- Report on portfolio performance measures
- Report on delinquent loans

Loan account maintenance and care

- Close out loan
- Enter loan payment information
- Inquiry about loan account status
- Generate standard payment notice
- Generate late notice
- Refer delinquent loan for debt collection

Credit management

- Retrieve customer credit profile
- Request credit report
- Perform credit analysis

FIGURE C-5   Functional groupings for use cases

Use case:	Process (book) new loan
Use case ID:	UC-125
Actor (s):	Loan clerk
Description:	Once a **loan agreement** has been signed by the **customer** and returned to the **bank**. The **loan clerk** has the system create a **loan account** based on the agreed on **terms and conditions**.

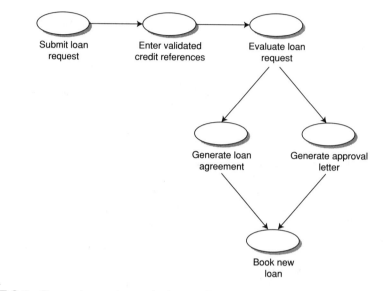

FIGURE C-6   Dependency stream for loan submission and approval

Base Use Case Description

This section contains sample use case diagrams and base use case descriptions for the loan processing system.

Submit Loan Request Use Case

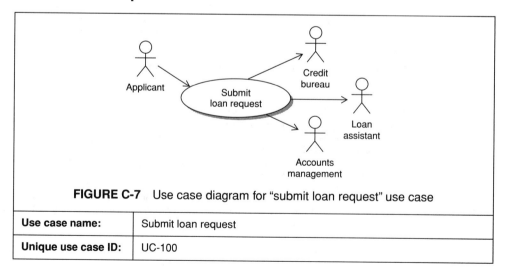

FIGURE C-7   Use case diagram for "submit loan request" use case

Use case name:	Submit loan request
Unique use case ID:	UC-100

Primary actor(s):	Applicant
Secondary actor(s):	Loan assistant, credit bureau, accounts management system
Brief description:	The applicant submits a loan request for processing by the bank's integrated loan processing system. The applicant fills out a loan application and submits it to the bank for processing. The system validates information on the loan application and the system calculates the applicant's credit score based on credit reports and the customer's account history with the bank. The applicant is contacted for additional information, if needed.
Preconditions:	The applicant has access to a loan request application.

Flow of events:	1. The applicant completes the online loan application and submits it to the bank via the Internet.
	 2. In preparation for evaluating the loan request:
	    2.1. The system validates the information on the loan application, checking that it is correct and as complete as possible. This activity includes determining that all mandatory fields are completed and that basic information such as zip codes, state codes, and account numbers are correct.
	    2.2. The system forwards a request to an external credit bureau for a credit report on the applicant. The request includes the applicant's name, social security number, and current and previous addresses.
	    2.3. The system retrieves the applicant's account history (if any) from the accounts management system.
	    2.4. The system calculates the applicant's credit score based on credit reports and the applicants's history with the bank.
	 3. The applicant is informed via e-mail that the loan request has been received, supporting materials are complete, and the loan is in the process of being evaluated.
	 4. The loan request status is set to "Initial credit check complete."
	 5. The system then forwards the loan request to a loan assistant for reference validation.

Postconditions:	The loan request is ready to be evaluated.
Priority:	High
Alternative flows and exceptions:	• Based on bank policy, the applicant's credit history is below the acceptable level for further processing, so the applicant is informed of the reasons by letter and the loan request is marked as disapproved. • The information on the application is incomplete or incorrect, the application is returned to the applicant for completion, and the loan request process is suspended until the updated application is received. • No external credit information exists for applicant, the loan request is declined, the applicant is notified, and the loan request is marked as disapproved.

Nonbehavioral requirements:	• Only the loan officers and loan clerks of the bank should have access to credit information. • The system should be able to handle 2,000 loan requests per day.
Assumptions:	The accounts management system will have current account information on the applicant if the applicant is a customer of the bank.
Issues:	• What are the business rules for calculating a credit score? • What information needs to be on the application to complete the loan request?
Source:	Requirements workshop 123 5/32/99

Enter Validated Credit References Use Case

Loan assistant

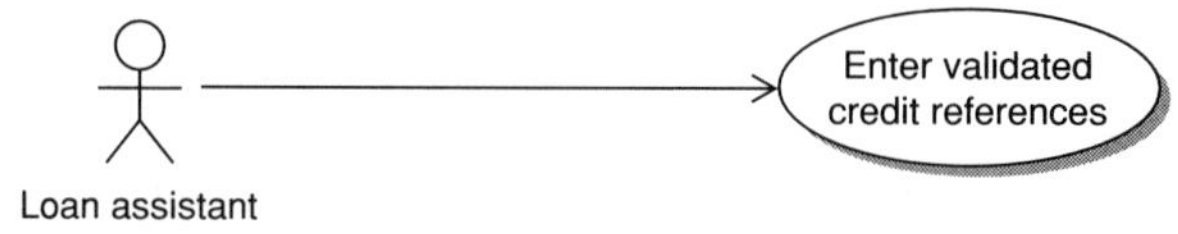

FIGURE C-8 Use case diagram for "Enter validated credit references" use case

Use case name:	Enter validated credit references
Unique use case ID:	UC-110
Primary actor(s):	Loan assistant
Secondary actor(s):	
Brief description:	The loan assistant enters any credit reference information that was checked manually. This information can include external bank accounts and repayment sources (i.e., income).
Preconditions:	The initial credit check has been completed.

Flow of events:	1. The loan assistant has the system present the results of the initial credit check for the loan request.
	2. The loan assistant identifies any unvalidated references, such as bank accounts that are external to this bank and repayment references (such as income for jobs, interest income, etc.).
	3. The loan assistant manually verifies that the credit references stated on the application are correct (the account exists and the balance specified on the loan application is correct). The loan assistant gathers additional information about the applicant's account history.
	4. The loan assistant enters into the system that the repayment references have been validated and corrects any incorrect credit information reported by the applicant on the application.
	5. The loan assistant enters into the system that the repayment references stated on the application are correct and that the amount of repayment income and time on the job have been accurately reported.
	6. The loan assistant enters into the system that the repayment references have been validated and corrects any incorrect repayment information on the loan request.
	7. The loan assistant marks the loan request "Loan references validated."
	8. The system routes the loan request to a loan officer for final evaluation.
Postconditions:	The loan references have been validated.
Priority:	High
Alternative flows and exceptions:	• The loan references cannot be validated and the loan request processing is suspended until the applicant can be informed of this fact and provides correct references.
	• The loan references provided significantly contradict information on credit accounts or repayment sources and the automated credit score needs to be recalculated by the system.
Nonbehavioral requirements:	• Only the loan officer and loan assistant should have access to credit information.
	• The system should support 10 concurrent loan assistants entering reference information at one time.
Assumptions:	None
Issues:	Differences between the reported references and actual references trigger a new calculation of the credit score.
Source:	Meeting with loan assistants, interview memo 2348.

Evaluate Loan Request Use Case

FIGURE C-9   Use case diagram for "Evaluate loan request" use case

Use case name:	Evaluate loan request
Unique use case ID:	UC-105
Primary actor(s):	Loan officer
Secondary actor(s):	
Brief description:	The loan officer reviews the online information about the pending loan request to determine whether the loan should be approved. This information includes the applicant's loan application, credit score, credit references, credit reports, and history with bank. If the loan request is approved, the loan officer marks the loan request as approved.
Preconditions:	The needed material concerning a pending loan request has been gathered (the loan material has a status of "Initial credit check complete.")

Flow of events:	1. The loan officer asks the system for a set of loan requests that are ready for evaluation. The system presents a list of loan requests for the loan officer's review. The loan officer selects a loan request to review for approval.
	2. The system presents the loan information gathered on the customer and the loan application to the loan officer. This information includes
	   • the applicant's credit history (credit report and customer history with bank).
	   • a calculated credit score.
	3. The loan officer reviews the material and determines whether the loan should be approved.
	4. The loan officer selects the appropriate loan terms and conditions for the loan based on the bank's policy and enters this information into the system.
	5. The status of the loan request is changed to "Approved" by the system.

Postconditions:	The loan request is approved (the loan has a status of "Approved.")
Alternative flows and exceptions:	• After loan officer review, the applicant's loan request is turned down, the applicant is notified, and the loan request is marked as disapproved. • The loan is referred to the loan committee for review and evaluation. • Further information needs to be gathered by the loan officer before a decision can be made.

Nonbehavioral requirements:	• Only the loan officer or manager should have access to loan request information and associated material. • The system should be able to handle 10 loan officers reviewing loan requests concurrently.
Assumptions:	N/A
Issues:	N/A
Source:	Interview minutes memo 123-3

Generate Approval Letter Use Case

FIGURE C-10   Use case diagram for "Generate approval letter" use case

Use case name:	Generate approval letter
Unique use case ID:	UC-115
Primary actor(s):	Loan clerk
Secondary actor(s):	Customer
Brief description:	A loan clerk has the system generate an approval letter for the applicant, stating that the loan request has been approved and including a detailed listing of the loan's terms and conditions and the period of time that the loan offer is available.
Preconditions:	The loan request has a status of approved.
Flow of events:	1. The loan clerk has the system generate a letter informing the customer, via e-mail, of the loan request's approval. The letter provides a detailed listing of the loan's terms and conditions, and the period of time that the loan offer is available, as well as any required collateral. 2. The loan clerk reviews the approval and then has the system e-mail copies to the customer and the loan officer who approved the loan. 3. The system saves a permanent electronic copy of the letter for future reference.

Postconditions:	The loan approval letter has been created and forwarded to the customer.
Alternative Flows and Exceptions:	None
Nonbehavioral requirements:	The time between loan approval and notification via e-mail to the customer should be no more then 4 hours.
Source:	Requirements workshop meeting notes 3456.

Generate Loan Agreement Use Case

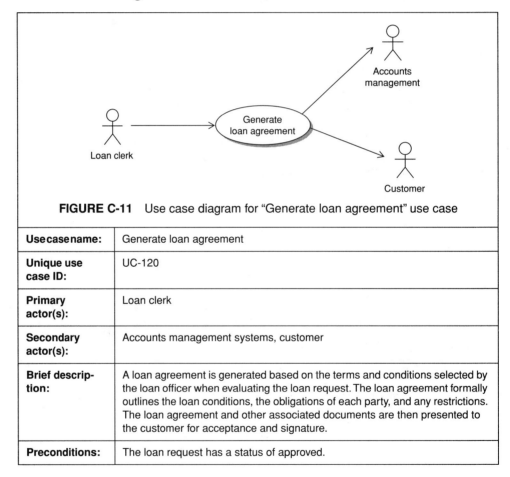

FIGURE C-11   Use case diagram for "Generate loan agreement" use case

Use case name:	Generate loan agreement
Unique use case ID:	UC-120
Primary actor(s):	Loan clerk
Secondary actor(s):	Accounts management systems, customer
Brief description:	A loan agreement is generated based on the terms and conditions selected by the loan officer when evaluating the loan request. The loan agreement formally outlines the loan conditions, the obligations of each party, and any restrictions. The loan agreement and other associated documents are then presented to the customer for acceptance and signature.
Preconditions:	The loan request has a status of approved.

Flow of events:	1. The final terms of the loan are recorded online and the loan agreement is finalized.
	2. The loan agreement is readied for the customer's signature. A loan agreement is generated by the system that outlines the loan's conditions, the obligations of each party, and any restrictions.
	3. The loan agreement is printed out for review (outside the system scope; it is signed by a bank representative and then mailed to the customer for review and signature).
Postconditions:	The loan agreement materials are generated.
Source:	Requirements workshop meeting notes 3890

Book New Loan Use Case

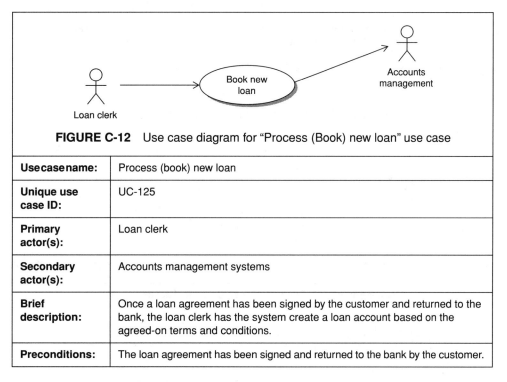

FIGURE C-12   Use case diagram for "Process (Book) new loan" use case

Use case name:	Process (book) new loan
Unique use case ID:	UC-125
Primary actor(s):	Loan clerk
Secondary actor(s):	Accounts management systems
Brief description:	Once a loan agreement has been signed by the customer and returned to the bank, the loan clerk has the system create a loan account based on the agreed-on terms and conditions.
Preconditions:	The loan agreement has been signed and returned to the bank by the customer.

Flow of events:	1. The loan clerk enters the receipt of the loan agreement into the system.
	2. An active loan is created in the loan processing system by the loan clerk. The loan is generated by the system based on the terms and conditions on the approved loan request.
	3. The loan processing system interacts with the accounts management system to create a loan account in the accounts management system.
	4. Funds are transferred to the loan account and a check is generated by the system for the customer.
	5. The system generates a mailing to the customer containing the check.
Postconditions:	The loan is booked and the customer is forwarded the proceeds.
Alternative flows and exceptions:	• When collateral is required, the receipt of the collateral or collateral certificate is entered into the system.
	• Instead of a check being generated, if the customer prefers, a line of credit that can be drawn on is created.
Nonbehavioral requirements:	The time between the receipt of the signed loan agreement and the generation of a check should be no more than one business day.
Source:	Requirements workshop meeting notes 3890

Generate Standard Payment Notice Use Case

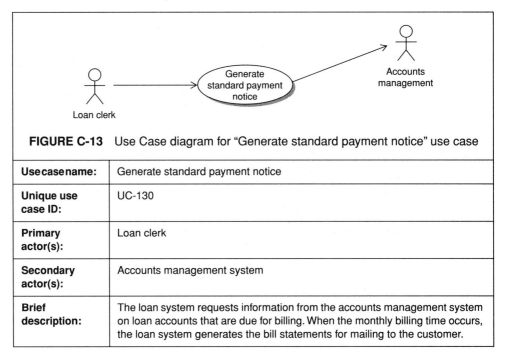

Loan clerk

Generate standard payment notice

Accounts management

FIGURE C-13   Use Case diagram for "Generate standard payment notice" use case

Use case name:	Generate standard payment notice
Unique use case ID:	UC-130
Primary actor(s):	Loan clerk
Secondary actor(s):	Accounts management system
Brief description:	The loan system requests information from the accounts management system on loan accounts that are due for billing. When the monthly billing time occurs, the loan system generates the bill statements for mailing to the customer.

Preconditions:	The customer has an active loan account.
Flow of events:	1. The loan system requests loan account information from the accounts management system. 2. The loan system generates the monthly billing statement based on the loan's terms and current state. 3. The loan system prints the bill statement. 4. The bill statement is manually mailed to customer by the loan clerk.
Postconditions:	The bill is generated and mailed to the customer.
Nonbehavioral requirements:	The system should be able to handle the generation of an average of 3000 bill statements per day.
Source:	Requirements workshop meeting notes 3456

Generate Late Notice Use Case

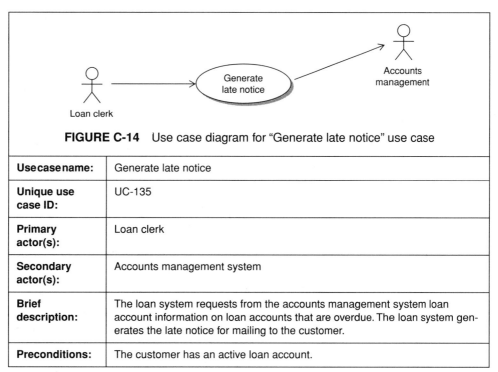

Loan clerk

Generate late notice

Accounts management

FIGURE C-14   Use case diagram for "Generate late notice" use case

Use case name:	Generate late notice
Unique use case ID:	UC-135
Primary actor(s):	Loan clerk
Secondary actor(s):	Accounts management system
Brief description:	The loan system requests from the accounts management system loan account information on loan accounts that are overdue. The loan system generates the late notice for mailing to the customer.
Preconditions:	The customer has an active loan account.

Flow of events:	1. The loan system requests from the accounts management system loan account information on loan accounts that are overdue.
	2. The loan system generates the late notice statement with the overdue amount.
	3. The loan system generates a letter reminding the customer to pay the bill.
	4. The loan system prints the late notice statement and reminder letter for mailing to the customer by the loan clerk.
Postconditions:	The late notice is generated and mailed to the customer.
Source:	Requirements workshop meeting notes 3501

Enter Loan Payment Information Use Case

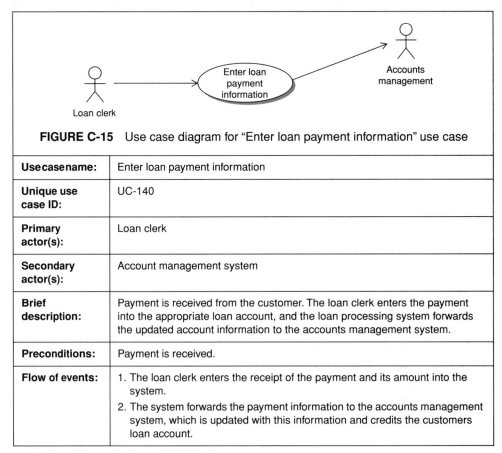

FIGURE C-15   Use case diagram for "Enter loan payment information" use case

Use case name:	Enter loan payment information
Unique use case ID:	UC-140
Primary actor(s):	Loan clerk
Secondary actor(s):	Account management system
Brief description:	Payment is received from the customer. The loan clerk enters the payment into the appropriate loan account, and the loan processing system forwards the updated account information to the accounts management system.
Preconditions:	Payment is received.
Flow of events:	1. The loan clerk enters the receipt of the payment and its amount into the system.
	2. The system forwards the payment information to the accounts management system, which is updated with this information and credits the customers loan account.

Postconditions:	Payment has been credited to account.
Source:	Interview minutes memo 130-4.

Close Out Loan Use Case

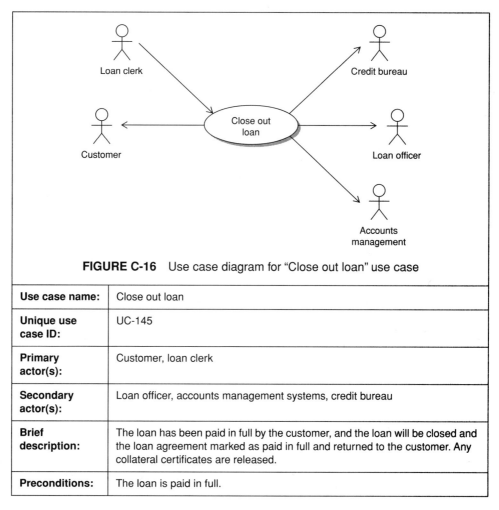

FIGURE C-16   Use case diagram for "Close out loan" use case

Use case name:	Close out loan
Unique use case ID:	UC-145
Primary actor(s):	Customer, loan clerk
Secondary actor(s):	Loan officer, accounts management systems, credit bureau
Brief description:	The loan has been paid in full by the customer, and the loan will be closed and the loan agreement marked as paid in full and returned to the customer. Any collateral certificates are released.
Preconditions:	The loan is paid in full.

Flow of events:	1. The customer's loan account is retrieved from the accounts management system.
	2. The loan clerk reviews the account details and records the payment of the loan by the customer. This includes any information on held collateral that needs to be returned to the customer.
	3. The loan has the system generate and print out a copy of the loan agreement that is marked as paid in full.
	4. The loan clerk has the system alert both the loan officer and the customer that the loan has been paid in full and the loan is closed.
	5. The copy of the marked loan agreement is printed out for mailing to the customer, along with a thank-you letter.
	6. The loan clerk has the system mark the loan account as paid in full and the systems sends this information to the accounts management system.
	7. The system forwards the updated account information to the appropriate credit bureau(s).
Postconditions:	The loan account is closed out.
Source:	Interview with Bob Smith, interview minutes memo 1234

Following is an example of the "Evaluate loan request" use case elaborated with conditional logic.

Use case name:	Evaluate loan request
Unique use case ID:	UC-105
Primary actor(s):	Loan officer
Secondary actor(s):	Applicant
Brief description:	The loan officer reviews the online information about the pending loan request to determine whether the applicant's loan should be approved. This information includes the loan application, credit score, credit reports, and history with bank. If the loan request is approved, the loan officer marks the loan request as approved.
Trigger:	N/A
Preconditions:	The needed material concerning a pending loan request has been gathered (the loan material has a status of "Ready for Evaluation").

Flow of events:	1. The loan officer selects a loan request for evaluation.
	2. The system provides the loan officer the information gathered on the applicant's loan request to the loan officer. The loan officer reviews the material for completeness. This information includes the following:
	• Loan application
	• Validated references, such as external bank accounts and repayment sources
	• Applicant's external credit history (credit report and customer history with bank)
	• Calculated credit score
	• Type of loan requested and an initial automated recommendation
	3. **If** further information is needed from the applicant, the loan officer inputs the request for the needed information into the system, the system generates a letter to the applicant asking for the missing information, and then forwards it to the applicant via e-mail. The loan request status is set to "Suspended pending additional information."
	Otherwise, the loan officer evaluates the completed loan request for acceptability and adherence to bank policy.
	4. **If** the applicant credit status is acceptable, the loan is approved. The loan officer determines the appropriate terms of the loans, using suggested loan terms generated by the system. Based on the loan officer's experience and any extenuating circumstances, the loan officer can modify the suggested loan terms, making any needed changes to the loan terms. The status of loan is set to "Approved."
	5. **If** the applicant credit status is not acceptable, the loan is disapproved. The loan officer outlines and enters the reasons into the system. The system then generates a letter to the applicant and forwards it to the customer via e-mail. The status of request is set to "Disapproved."
	6. **If** the applicant credits status is marginal or the amount of request is outside the bank's loan policy, the loan officer can forward the loan request and related online information to loan committee members for their review and recommendations (see the extending use case: Refer loan request to loan committee).
Postconditions:	The loan request has to be evaluated. (The loan request has a status of either approved, disapproved, or on hold.)
Alternative flows and exceptions:	None
Nonbehavioral requirements:	• Only a loan officer or manager should have access to loan request information and associated material.
	• The system should be able to handle 10 loan officers reviewing loan requests concurrently.
Assumptions:	
Issues:	
Source:	JAD meeting minutes memo 123-3

Use Case Extend Relationships

This section contains sample diagrams and descriptions for several extend relationships.

Sample Extending Use Case Descriptions

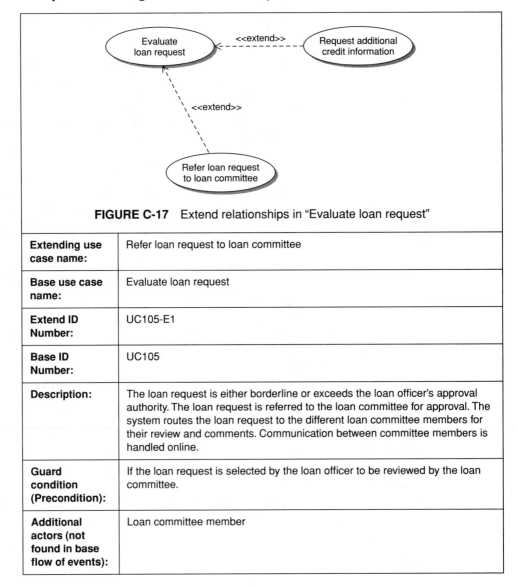

FIGURE C-17   Extend relationships in "Evaluate loan request"

Extending use case name:	Refer loan request to loan committee
Base use case name:	Evaluate loan request
Extend ID Number:	UC105-E1
Base ID Number:	UC105
Description:	The loan request is either borderline or exceeds the loan officer's approval authority. The loan request is referred to the loan committee for approval. The system routes the loan request to the different loan committee members for their review and comments. Communication between committee members is handled online.
Guard condition (Precondition):	If the loan request is selected by the loan officer to be reviewed by the loan committee.
Additional actors (not found in base flow of events):	Loan committee member

Flow of events:	1. The loan officer has the system forward the loan request and all associated information, such as credit reports, financial statements, references, etc., to the individual members of the loan committee. 2. Each loan committee member reviews the material online, comments on the request, and enters a recommendation into the system. 3. Each loan committee member's comments and recommendations are routed by the system to the other loan committee members. 4. Each loan committee member then retrieves, reviews, and provides additional comments (if needed), based on the other members' comments and recommendations. 5. Each loan committee member has the system forward the additional comments to the other members. This cycle continues until consensus is reached (as defined by the loan committee chair). 6. The resulting recommendation is forwarded to the loan officer.
Postconditions:	A loan request recommendation has been determined.
Priority:	Medium

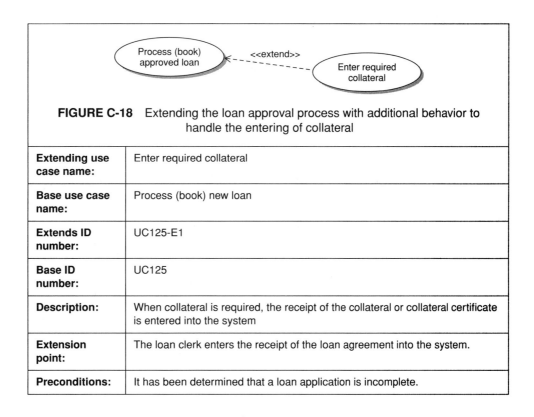

FIGURE C-18   Extending the loan approval process with additional behavior to handle the entering of collateral

Extending use case name:	Enter required collateral
Base use case name:	Process (book) new loan
Extends ID number:	UC125-E1
Base ID number:	UC125
Description:	When collateral is required, the receipt of the collateral or collateral certificate is entered into the system
Extension point:	The loan clerk enters the receipt of the loan agreement into the system.
Preconditions:	It has been determined that a loan application is incomplete.

Additional actors (not found in base case):	Loan clerk
Flow of events:	1. The receipt of collateral is entered into the system by the loan clerk. 2. The loan request is marked by the system "Collateral received"
Postconditions:	Receipt of collateral has been associated with a loan request
Priority:	High

Use Case Include Relationships

This section contains sample include relationship diagrams (Figures C-19, C-20, and C-21) and example descriptions.

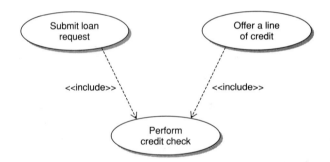

FIGURE C-19   "Submit loan request" and "Offer line of credit" including the credit check use case

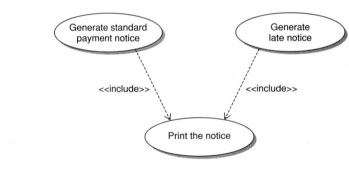

FIGURE C-20   Include relationship for "Print the notice"

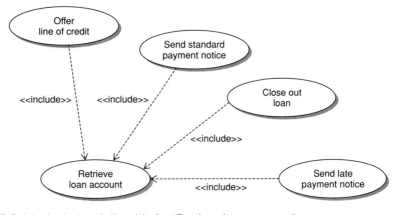

FIGURE C-21   Include relationship for "Retrieve loan account"

Sample Include Use Case Descriptions

Use case name:	Perform credit check
ID:	UC-10
Description:	A credit report is requested and retrieved through an automated interface with the national credit bureaus.
Preconditions:	The customer has a social security number or alternative form of ID and their address is known.
Flow of Events:	1. Based on the customer's geographical location, the appropriate credit bureau is contacted and the customer's credit report is requested. 2. The customer's credit report is received and the information is formatted into the bank's standard credit report template.
Postcondition:	The customer's credit report in standard template form is returned.
Alternative flows:	No credit report for the customer is found.

Use case name:	Calculate credit score
ID:	UC-20
Description:	A credit score is requested.
Preconditions:	A credit report, income information, and financial history are available.
Flow of Events:	Based on the credit report, income, type of customer (individual or business), and other financial information, a credit score is calculated.

Note:	The detailed credit scoring criteria and algorithms used in this flow are documented in Bank Credit Scoring Manual 8765.
Postcondition:	A credit score is returned.
Included use case name:	Transfer loan funds

ID:	UC-30
Trigger:	Loan funds need to be transferred into customer's account.
Description:	For a newly activated loan or an increase in the customer's line of credit, a loan amount is debited to the customer's account. Installment can be extended on a periodic basis, such as in a line of credit.
Preconditions:	A funds transfer has been requested by the loan officer.
Flow of events:	1. The loan officer or loan clerk has the system transfer funds into the customer's loan account. 2. The loan processing system notifies the account management system to transfer the specified amount in the customer's loan account.
Postcondition:	The funds have been transferred.

Generalization Relationships

This section contains sample generalization relationship diagrams and example descriptions (Figures C-22, C-23, and C-24).

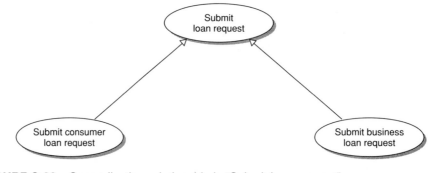

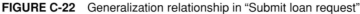

FIGURE C-22   Generalization relationship in "Submit loan request"

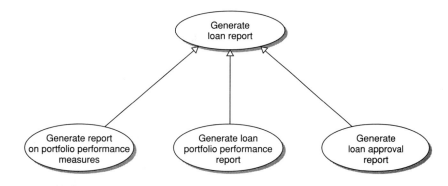

FIGURE C-23   Generalization relationship in "Generate loan report"

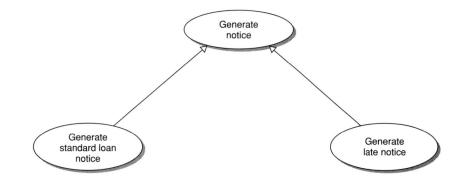

FIGURE C-24   Generalization relationship in "Generate notice"

Use case name:	Generate notice **(abstract use case)**
Unique use case ID:	UC-130A
Flow of events:	1. The loan system requests loan account information from the accounts management system.
	2. The loan system generates billing statement.
	3. The loan system prints the billing statement.
	4. The loan clerk mails the billing statement to the customer.

Use case name:	Generate late notice **(Parent is "Generate notice")**
Unique use case ID:	UC-145
Flow of events:	1. The loan system requests loan account information from the accounts management system (I—Activity 1, UC-140)
	2. The loan system generates the late notice statement with amount overdue. (S—Activity 1, UC-140)
	3. The loan system generates a letter reminding the customer to pay the bill. (N)
	4. The loan system prints the late notice statement and the letter. (S—Activity 3, UC-140)
	5. The late notice statement is mailed to customer by the loan clerk. (I—Activity 3, UC-140)

Use Case Instances for "Submit Loan Request"

Instance name:	Joe Smith applies for a loan
Use case name:	Submit loan request
Instance description:	An applicant submits a loan request for $20,000, and the loan is granted. The applicant has a typical credit and account portfolio.
Instance flow:	1. Joe Smith completes a loan application for a $20,000 car loan and mails the application to the bank.
	2. The application includes information on Joe's credit references and work references.
	3. The application is received by the bank and entered into the system. The system validates that Joe has completed all the required fields including income, address, and work and credit references.
	4. Joe has a checking account with the bank, so the system validates that the account number on the application is correct.
	5. The system forwards a request for a copy of a credit report on Joe along with Joe's social security number and address to a credit bureau. The credit report states that Joe has $2,000 in outstanding debt and no outstanding bad debits.
	6. Joe's checking account history is checked by the system. Joe has $3,500 in the account and has maintained the account for the last five years in good standing.
	7. Based on all the credit information, Joe's income of $65,000 per year, and the amount and type of loan, the system calculates a satisfactory credit score on Joe.
	8. The status of Joe's loan request is set to "Ready for review" and the application and all supporting information is routed to Jane Jones, the loan officer, for evaluation.
	9. Joe is notified by mail that his loan application has been received and that it is being evaluated.

Instance name:	Applicant with no credit history submits a loan request
Use case name:	Submit loan request
Instance description:	An applicant submits a loan request for $10,000 but has no credit report with any of the major credit reporting bureaus. The customer's request is rejected due to insufficient credit information.
Instance flow:	1. Bob Jones completes a loan application for a $10,000 car loan and mails the application to the bank. 2. The application includes information on Bob's credit references and work references. 3. The application is received by the bank and entered into the system. The system validates that Bob has completed all the required fields including income, address, and work and credit references. 4. Bob has a checking account with the bank, and the system validates that the account number on the application is correct. 5. The system forwards a request for a copy of a credit report on Bob along with Bob's social security number and address to a credit bureau. The credit bureau responds that no credit history is available for Bob. The system then forwards requests to the other major credit bureaus, which also respond that no credit report is available. 6. Bob's checking account history is checked by the system. Bob has $100 in the account and has the maintained the account for the last 12 months in good standing. 7. Based on automated bank policies, the automated recommendation is to decline the loan based on insufficient credit history. 8. The status of the loan request is set to "Ready for review."

Instance name:	Missing credit information on the submitted loan application
Use case name:	Submit loan request
Instance description:	Jane Smith submits a loan request for $10,000 but leaves the references off the application form. She is asked to provide the information before the loan request is processed.
Instance flow:	1. Jane Smith completes a loan application for a $10,000 car loan and mails the application to the bank. 2. The application includes information fields on credit references and work references. 3. The application is received by the bank and entered into the system. The system validates that the customer has completed the income, address, and work references. The system determines that the credit references are missing. 4. The system generates a letter notifying Jane Smith that the references are needed. The letter is mailed to the customer. The loan request status is set to "Suspended—incomplete information."

Appendix D
Simplified Loan Processing System User Interface Specification

---

What's in this appendix?

This appendix contains a specification for the user interface component of the loan processing system.

This is the user interface specification for the loan processing system. The intent of this specification is to provide a conceptual model from which a physical user interface prototype, and later a physical user interface, may be constructed. It was derived from the elaborated use case model of the loan processing system (see Appendix C).

Partitions

Using the user group approach, we have partitioned the use case model into two sets of users: customers and loan department employees (Figure D-1). These groups determine the fundamental needs to access parts of the system. Additional information will be accessible on an actor-by-actor basis.

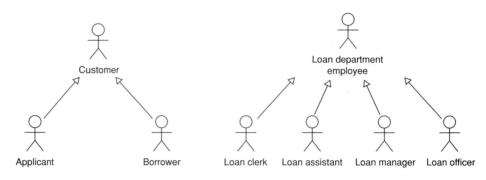

FIGURE D-1   The new abstract actors: Customer and loan department employee

Actor Specification
Actor name: Customer   **Abstract:** Yes
Description: A customer is someone who uses the services of the bank. For the purposes of this user interface, the customer is a loan applicant. A customer does not have the privileges of a loan department employee. As a result, while this actor requires authentication, it does not require the intense security of its counterpart, the loan employee.

Actor Specification
Actor name: Loan department employee   **Abstract:** Yes
Description: A loan department employee is an employee of the bank, more specifically of the loan department. As a result, a loan department employee has access to information (applications, credit history, loans) unavailable to customers.

Identify Transactions in Use Cases

Use case name:	Submit loan request
Unique use case ID:	UC-100
Primary actor(s):	Applicant
Secondary actor(s):	Loan assistant, credit bureau, accounts management system
Preconditions:	The system presents a loan request.

Flow of events:	*Transaction UC-100-1*
	1. The applicant completes the online loan request and submits it to the bank via the Internet.
	2. In preparation for evaluating the loan request:
	2.1. The system validates the information on the loan application, checking that it is correct and as complete as possible. This event includes determining that all mandatory fields are completed and that basic information, such as zip codes, state codes, and account numbers, is correct.
	2.2. The system forwards a request to an external credit bureau for a credit report on the applicant. The request includes the applicant's name, social security number, and current and previous addresses.
	2.3. The system retrieves the applicant's account history (if any) from the accounts management system.
	2.4. The system calculates the applicant's credit score based on credit reports and the applicants's history with the bank.
	3. The applicant is informed via e-mail that the loan request has been received, supporting materials are complete, and the loan is in the process of being evaluated.
	4. The loan request status is set to "Initial credit check complete."
	5. The system then forwards the loan request to a loan assistant for reference validation.
Postconditions:	The loan request is ready to be evaluated.
Priority:	High
Alternative flows and exceptions:	• Based on bank policy, the applicant's credit history is below the acceptable level for further processing, the applicant is informed of the reasons via letter, and the loan request is marked as disapproved.
	Transaction UC-100-2
	• The data on the application is incomplete or incorrect, the application is returned to the applicant for completion, and the loan request process is suspended until the updated application is received.
	• No external credit information exists for applicant, the loan request is declined, the applicant is notified, and the loan request is marked as disapproved.
Nonbehavioral requirements:	• Only the loan officers and loan clerks of the bank should have access to credit information.
	• The system should be able to handle 200 loan requests per day.
Assumptions:	The accounts management system will have current account information on the applicant if the applicant is a customer of the bank.
Issues:	• What are the business rules for calculating a credit score?
	• What information needs to be on the application to complete the loan request?
Source:	Requirements workshop 123 5/3/99

Use case name:	Validate credit references
Unique use case ID:	UC-110
Primary actor(s):	Loan assistant
Secondary actor(s):	
Preconditions:	The initial credit check has been completed.
Flow of events:	*Transaction UC-110-1* 1. The loan assistant has the system present the results of the initial credit check for the loan request. 2. The loan assistant identifies any unvalidated references, such as bank accounts that are external to this bank and repayment references (such as income for jobs, interest income, etc.). 3. The loan assistant manually verifies that the credit references stated on the application are correct (the account exists and the balance specified on the loan application is correct). The loan assistant gathers additional information about the applicant's account history. 4. The loan assistant enters into the system that the references have been validated and corrects any incorrect credit information reported by the applicant on the application. 5. The loan assistant enters into the system that the repayment references stated on the application are correct and that the amount of repayment income and time on the job have been accurately reported. 6. The loan assistant enters into the system that the repayment references have been validated and corrects any incorrect repayment information on the loan request. 7. The loan assistant marks the loan request "Loan references validated." 8. The system routes the loan request to a loan officer for final evaluation.
Postconditions:	The loan references have been validated.
Priority:	High
Alternative flows and exceptions:	• The loan references cannot be validated and the loan request processing is suspended until the applicant can be informed of this fact and provides correct references. *Transaction UC-110-2* • The loan references provided significantly contradict information on credit accounts or repayment sources and the automated credit score needs to be recalculated by the system.
Nonbehavioral requirements:	• Only the loan officer and loan assistant should have access to credit information. • The system should support 10 concurrent loan assistants entering reference information at one time.

Assumptions:	None
Source:	Meeting with loan assistants, interview memo 2348

Use case name:	Evaluate loan request
Unique use case ID:	UC-120
Primary actor(s):	Loan officer
Secondary actor(s):	
Preconditions:	The needed material concerning a pending loan request has been gathered (the loan material has a status of "Credit references validated").
Flow of events:	*Transaction UC-120-1* 1. The loan officer asks the system for the a set of loan requests that are ready for evaluation. The system presents a list of loan requests for the loan officer's review. The loan officer selects a loan request to review for approval. *Transaction UC-120-2* 2. The system presents the loan information gathered on the customer and the loan application to the loan officer. This information includes • the applicant's credit history (credit report and customer history with the bank) • a calculated credit score 3. The loan officer reviews the material and determines whether the loan should be approved. 4. The loan officer selects the appropriate loan terms and conditions for the loan based on the bank's policy and enters this information into the system. 5. The loan request status is changed to "Approved" by the system.
Postconditions:	The loan request is approved (the loan has a status of "Approved").
Alternative flows and exceptions:	*Transaction UC-120-3* • After loan officer review, the applicant's loan request is turned down, the applicant is notified, and the loan request is marked as disapproved. *Transaction UC-120-4* • The loan is referred to the loan committee for review and evaluation. *Transaction UC-120-5* • Further information needs to be gathered by the loan officer before a decision can be made.
Nonbehavioral Requirements:	• Only the loan officer or manager should have access to loan request information and associated material. • The system should be able to handle 10 loan officers reviewing loan requests concurrently.

Assumptions:	N/A
Issues:	N/A
Source:	Interview minutes memo 123-3

Use case name:	Generate approval letter
Unique use case ID:	UC-130
Primary actor(s):	Loan clerk
Secondary actor(s):	Customer
Preconditions:	The loan request has a status of approved.
Flow of events:	*Transaction UC-130-1* 1. The loan clerk has the system generate a letter informing the customer, via e-mail, of the loan request's approval. The letter provides a detailed listing of the loan's terms and conditions and the period of time that the loan offer is available as well as any required collateral. 2. The loan clerk reviews the approval and then has the system e-mail copies to the customer and the loan officer who approved the loan. 3. The system saves a permanent electronic copy of the letter for future reference.
Postconditions:	The loan approval letter has been created and forwarded to the customer.
Alternative flows and exceptions:	None
Nonbehavioral requirements:	The time between loan approval and notification via e-mail to the customer should be no more than 4 hours.
Source:	Requirements workshop meeting notes 3456

Use case name:	Generate loan agreement
Unique use case ID:	UC-140
Primary actor:	Loan clerk
Secondary actor(s):	Accounts management systems, customer
Preconditions:	The loan request has a status of approved.

Flow of events:	*Transaction UC-130-2* 1. The final terms of the loan are recorded online and the loan agreement is finalized. 2. The loan agreement is readied for the customer's signature. A loan agreement is generated by the system that outlines the loan's conditions, the obligations of each party, and any restrictions. 3. The loan agreement is printed out for review (outside system scope; it is signed by a bank representative and then mailed to the customer for review and signature).
Postconditions:	The loan agreement materials are generated.
Source:	Requirements workshop meeting notes 3890

Use case name:	Book new loan
Unique use case ID:	UC-150
Primary actor(s):	Loan clerk
Secondary actor(s):	Accounts management systems
Preconditions:	The loan agreement has been signed and returned to the bank by the customer.
Flow of events:	*Transaction UC-150-1* 1. The loan clerk enters the receipt of the loan agreement into the system. *Transaction UC-150-2* 2. An active loan is created in the loan processing system by the loan clerk. The loan is generated by the system based on the terms and conditions on the approved loan request. 3. The loan processing system interacts with the accounts management system to create a loan account in the accounts management system. 4. Funds are transferred to the loan account and a check is generated by the system for the customer. 5. The system generates a mailing to the customer containing the check.
Postconditions:	The loan is booked and the customer is forwarded the proceeds.
Alternative flows and exceptions:	*Transaction UC-150-3* 1. When collateral is required, the receipt of the collateral or collateral certificate is entered into the system. 2. Instead of a check being generated, if the customer prefers, a line of credit that can drawn on is created.

Nonbehavioral requirements:	The time between receipt of the signed loan agreement and the generation of a check should be no more than one business day.
Source:	Requirements workshop meeting notes 3890

Use case name:	Enter loan payment information
Unique use case ID:	UC-180
Primary actor(s):	Loan clerk
Secondary actor(s):	Accounts management system
Brief description:	Payment is received from the customer. The loan clerk enters the payment into the appropriate loan account, and the loan processing system forwards the updated account information to the accounts management system.
Preconditions:	Payment is received
Flow of events:	*Transaction UC-180-1* 1. The loan clerk enters the receipt of the payment and its amount into the system. 2. The system forwards the payment information to the accounts management system, which is updated with this information and credits the customer's loan account.
Postconditions:	Payment has been credited to account.
Source:	Interview minutes memo 130-4

Use case name:	Close out loan
Unique use case ID:	UC-190
Primary actor(s):	Customer, loan clerk
Secondary actor(s):	Loan officer, accounts management systems, credit bureau
Preconditions:	The loan is paid in full.

Flow of events:	*Transaction UC-190-1*
	1. The customer's loan account is retrieved from the accounts management system.
	2. The loan clerk reviews the account details and records the payment of the loan by the customer. This includes any information on held collateral that needs to be returned to the customer.
	3. The loan clerk has the system generate and print out a copy of the loan agreement that is marked as paid in full.
	Transaction UC-190-2
	4. The loan clerk has the system alert both the loan officer and the customer that the loan has been paid in full and the loan is closed.
	5. The copy of the marked loan agreement is printed out for mailing to the customer, along with a thank-you letter.
	Transaction UC-190-3
	6. The loan clerk has the system mark the loan account as paid in full and the system sends this information to the accounts management system.
	7. The system forwards the updated account information to the appropriate credit bureau(s).
Postconditions:	The loan account is closed out.
Source:	Interview with Bob Smith, interview minutes memo 1234

Determine Information Content for Each Transaction

Transaction	**Information elements**
UC-100-1	Loan request (applicant information)
UC-100-2	Loan request (information message)
UC-110-1	Loan request (credit information, references)
UC-110-2	References
UC-120-1	Loan request (vital information)
UC-120-2	Loan request (credit history)

UC-120-3	Loan request (information message)
UC-120-4	Loan request (information message)
UC-120-5	Loan request (information message)
UC-130-1	Approval letter (vital information)
UC-140-1	Loan agreement (vital information)
UC-150-1	Loan agreement (status)
UC-150-2	Loan
UC-150-3	Loan (collateral information)
UC-180-1	Loan (payment information)
UC-190-1	Loan (current balance)
UC-190-2	Loan
UC-190-3	Loan (information message)

Establish Logical Screen Order

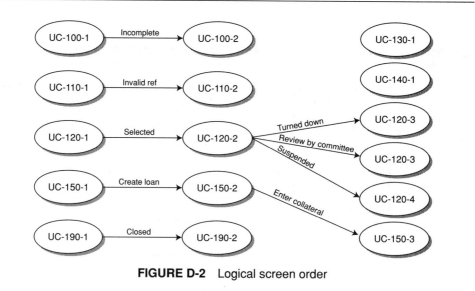

FIGURE D-2   Logical screen order

Group Transactions and Lay Out Final Screens

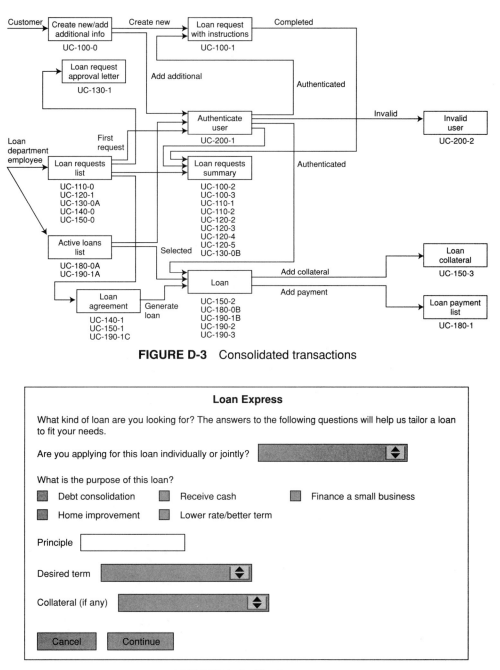

FIGURE D-3   Consolidated transactions

FIGURE D-4   Final screen

Bibliography

[Abreu 1996]   Abreu, Fernando Brito e, Dennis de Champeaux, Brian Henderson-Sellers, Simon Horner, and Granville Miller. "OO Process and Metrics for Effort Estimation," Workshop Report, OOPSLA '96, available at http://www.advancedusecases.com.

[Ahlqvist 1996]   Ahlqvist, Stefan, and Patrik Jonsson. "Techniques for Systematic Design of Graphical User Interfaces (for Highly Usable Systems) Based on Use Cases," Tutorial, OOPSLA '96.

[Ambler 1997]   Ambler, Scott. "The Various Uses for Use Cases," *Software Development* 5(11), November 1997: 69–71.

[Andriole 1998]   Andriole, Steve. "The Politics of Requirements Management," *IEEE Software* 15(6), November/December 1998: 82–84.

[Armour 1995]   Armour, Frank J., and Monica Sood. Workshop paper, "Use Case Modeling for Large System Development," OOPSLA '95, October, 1995, Austin, TX.

[Armour 1996a]   Armour, Frank J. and Marilyn Krause. Experience report, "Experiences Using Mentoring and Other Support Approaches on an Object Oriented Project," OOPSLA '96 Conference, October 1996, San Jose, CA.

[Armour 1996b]   Armour, Frank J., Monica Sood, and Marilyn Krause. "Experiences Using Controlled Iterative Development on an Object Oriented Development Effort," Proceedings of 1996 Pacific Northwest Software Quality Conference, October 1996, Portland, OR.

[Armour 1999]   Armour, Frank J., and Monica Sood Gupta. "Mentoring for Success," *IEEE IT Professional* 1(3), May–June 1999: 64–66.

[Bass 1998]   Bass, Len, Paul Clements, and Rick Kazman. *Software Architecture in Practice*, Addison-Wesley, Reading, MA, 1998.

[Bazman 1998]   Dorgan, Barry. Software Test Plan. Available at http://www.members.tripod.com/bazman/.

[Beck 1999]   Beck, Kent. *Extreme Programming Explained: Embrace Change*, Addison-Wesley, Reading, MA, 1999.

[Bellin 1997]   Bellin, David, and Susan Suchman Simone. *The CRC Book*, Addison-Wesley, Reading, MA, 1997.

[Bennett 1997]   Bennett, Douglas. *Designing Hard Software: The Essential Tasks*, Manning Publications, Greenwich, CT, 1997.

[Benyon 1999]   Benyon, David, Thomas Green, and Diana Bental. *Conceptual Modeling for User Interface Developement*, Springer-Verlag, London, 1999.

[Berard 1996]   Berard, Edward. "Be Careful with Use Cases," unpublished document.

[Berry 1998]   Berry, Daniel M., and Brian Lawrence. "Requirements Engineering," *IEEE Software* 15(2), March/April 1998: 26–29.

[Bersoff 1980]   Bersoff, Edward H., Vilas D. Henderson, and Stanley G. Siegel. *Software Configuration Management*, Prentice Hall, Upper Saddle River, NJ, 1980.

[Black 1999]   Black, Rex. *Managing the Test Process*, Microsoft Press, Redmond, WA, 1999.

[Boehm 1981]   Boehm, Barry W. *Software Engineering Economics*, Prentice Hall, Upper Saddle River, NJ, 1981.

[Booch 1994]   Booch, Grady. *Object-Oriented Analysis and Design with Applications*, Second Edition, Addison-Wesley, Reading, MA, 1994.

[Booch 1996]   Booch, Grady. *Object Solutions: Managing the Object-Oriented Project*, Addison-Wesley, Reading, MA, 1996.

[Booch 1999]   Booch, Grady, James Rumbaugh, and Ivar Jacobson. *The Unified Modeling Language User Guide*, Addison-Wesley, Reading, MA, 1999.

[Bowser 1995]   Bowser, John, Granville Miller, and Thomas Pangborn. "Building Quality into Switching Software.," in *International Switching Software, (ISS)* 1995: 173–179.

[Brooks 1987]   Brooks, Frederick P. "No Silver Bullet: Essence and Accidents of Software Engineering," *IEEE Computer* 20(4), April, 1987: 10–19.

[Brown 1998]   Brown, William J., Raphael C. Malveau, Hays W. "Skip" McCormick III, and Thomas J. Mowbray. *AntiPatterns: Refactoring Software, Architectures, and Projects in Crisis*, John Wiley, New York, 1998.

[Coad 1991]   Coad, Peter, and E. Yourdon. *Object-Oriented Analysis*, Prentice Hall, Englewood Cliffs, NJ, 1991.

[Cockburn 1997a]   Cockburn, Alistair. "Structuring Use Cases with Goals—Part 1," *Journal of Object-Oriented Programming* 10(5), September 1997: 35–40.

[Cockburn 1997b]   Cockburn, Alistair. "Structuring Use Cases with Goals—Part 2," *Journal of Object-Oriented Programming* 10(7), November/December 1997: 56–62.

[Cockburn 1998]   Cockburn, Alistair. *Surviving Object-Oriented Projects*, Addison-Wesley, Reading, MA, 1998.

[Cockburn 2000]   Cockburn, Alistair. *Writing Effective Use Cases*, Addison-Wesley, Boston, MA, 2000.

[Collard 1999]   Collard, Ross. "Test Design," *Software Testing & Quality Engineering* 1(4) July/August 1999: 30–37.

[Collins-Cope 1999   Collins-Cope, Mark. "The RSI Approach to Use Case Analysis," *C++ Report* 11(7), July/August 1999: 28–33, 57.

[Constantine 1995]   Constantine, Larry L. "Essential Modeling: Use Cases for User Interfaces," *ACM Interactions* 2(2), March/April 1995: 34–46.

[Constantine 1999]   Constantine, Larry L., and Lucy Lockwood. *Software for Use: A Practical Guide to the Models and Methods of Usage-Centered Design,* Addison-Wesley, Reading, MA, 1998.

[Cooper 1995]   Cooper, Alan. *About Face: The Essentials of User Interface Design,* IDG Books, Foster City, CA, 1995.

[Coplien 1999]   Coplien, James O. "Reevaluating the Architectural Metaphor: Toward Piecemeal Growth," *IEEE Software* 16(5), September/October 1999: 40–45.

[Davis 1993]   Davis, Alan. *Software Requirements: Objects, Functions, and States,* Prentice Hall, Englewood Cliffs, NJ, 1993.

[Davis 1997]   Davis, Alan, et al. "Identifying and Measuring Quality in a Software Requirements Specification," in *Software Requirements Engineering*, edited by R. Thayer and M. Dorfman, IEEE Computer Society Press, Los Alamitos, CA, 1997.

[DeMarco 1979]   DeMarco, Tom. *Structured Analysis and System Specification*, Prentice Hall, Englewood Cliffs, NJ, 1979.

[Donaldson 1997]   Donaldson, Scott E., and Stanley G. Siegel. *Cultivating Successful Software Development: A Practitioner's View*, Prentice Hall, Englewood Cliffs, NJ, 1997.

[Dorfman 1997]   Dorfman, M. "Requirements Engineering," in *Software Requirements Engineering*, Second Edition, edited by R. Thayer and M. Dorfman, IEEE Computer Society Press, Los Alamitos, CA, 1997.

[Drucker 1993]   Drucker, Peter F. *Post-Capitalist Society*, HarperBusiness, New York 1993.

[Ecklund 1996]   Ecklund, Earl F., Jr., Lois M. L. Delcambre, and Michael J. Freiling. "Change Cases: Use Cases That Identify Future Requirements," *Oopsla '96*, pp. 342–358.

[Eriksson 1998]   Eriksson, Hans-Erik, and Magnus Penker. *UML Toolkit*, John Wiley & Sons, New York, 1998.

[Fairley 1996]   Fairley, R., and R. Thayer. "The Concept of Operations: The
                       Bridge from Operational Requirements to Technical Specifi-
                       cations," S*oftware Engineering*, edited by M. Dorfman and
                       R. Thayer, pp. 44–54, Instititute of Electrical and Electron-
                       ics Engineers, New York, 1996.

[Finch 1998]   Finch, Lawrence. "A Hybrid Approach," *Software Develop-
                       ment* 6(9), September, 1998: 45–51.

[Firesmith 1995]   Firesmith, Donald G. "Use Cases: The Pros and Cons,"
                       Report on Object Analysis and Design 2(2), July/August
                       1995: 2–6.

[Firesmith 1999]   Firesmith, Donald G. "Use Case Modeling Guidelines,"
                       Proceedings of TOOLS USA '99, IEEE Computer Society,
                       1999.

[Fowler 1997]   Fowler, Martin, with Kendall Scott. *UML Distilled: Apply-
                       ing the Standard Object Modeling Language*, Addison-
                       Wesley, Reading, MA, 1997.

[Gamma 1994]   Gamma, Erich, Richard Helm, Ralph Johnson, and John
                       Vlissides. *Design Patterns: Elements of Reusable Object-
                       Oriented Software*, Addison-Wesley, Reading, MA, 1995.

[Gause 1989]   Gause, Donald C., and Gerald M. Weinburg. *Exploring
                       Requirements: Quality Before Design*, Dorset House Pub-
                       lishing, New York, 1989.

[Greenspan 1999]   Greenspan, Alan. *The Federal Reserve's Semiannual Report
                       on Monetary Policy*, Minutes of the Commitee on Banking,
                       Housing, and Urban Affairs, U.S. Senate, February 23, 1999.
                       Also http:// www.bog.frb.fed.us/BoardDics/HH/1999/
                       February/Testimony.htm

[Hammer 1993]   Hammer, Michael, and James Champy. *Reengineering the
                       Corporation*, Harper Business, New York, 1993.

[Hammer 1995]   Hammer, Michael, and Steven A. Stanton. *The Reengineer-
                       ing Revolution: A Handbook*, Harper Business, New York,
                       1995.

[Hanscome 1998]   Hanscome, Barbara. "Components Defined," *Software
                       Development* 6(9), September, 1998: 7.

[Hansen 1995]   Hansen, Todd, and Granville Miller. "Requirements Defini-
                     tion and Verification Through Use Case Analysis and Early
                     Prototyping," OOPSLA workshop—Requirements Engi-
                     neering: Use Cases and More, Sunday October 15, 1995,
                     Austin, TX, http://www.advancedusecases.com.

[Hargis 1998]   Hargis, Gretchen, Ann Kilty Hernandez, Polly Hughes, Jim
                     Ramaker, Shannon Rouiller, and Elizabeth Wilde. *Develop-
                     ing Quality Technical Information: A Handbook for Writers
                     and Editors*, Prentice Hall, Upper Saddle River, NJ, 1998.

[Heritage 1995]   Heritage, Anthony, and Phil Coley. "Use Case Based OO
                     Development at BT," *Proceedings of Object Expo Europe*,
                     SIGS Publications, New York, 1995: 124–130.

[Hsia 1994]   Hsia, Pei, J. Samuel, J. Gao, D. Kung, C. Chen, and Y.
                     Toyoshima. "Formal Approach to Scenario Analysis" *IEEE
                     Software*, 11(2) March/April 1994: 33–41.

[Hurlbut 1997]   Hurlbut, Russell R. "A Survey of Approaches for Describing
                     and Formalizing Use Cases," published on the Web at:
                     http:// www.iit.edu/~rhurlbut/xpt-tr-97-03.html, 1997.

[IBM 1997]   IBM Object-Oriented Technology Center. *Developing
                     Object-Oriented Software: An Experienced-Base Approach*,
                     Prentice Hall, Engelwood Cliffs, NJ, 1997.

[IEEE 1998a]   *IEEE Recommended Practices for Software Requirements
                     Specifications,* IEEE Computer Society, Std 830-1998, Insti-
                     tute of Electrical and Electronics Engineers, New York, 1998.

[IEEE 1998b]   *IEEE Guide for Developing System Requirements Specifica-
                     tions*, std 1233a-1998 Institute of Electrical and Electron-
                     ics Engineers, New York, NY, 1998.

[IEEE 1998c]   *IEEE Guide for Information Technology—System Defini-
                     tion—Concept of Operations Development*, Std 1362-1998,
                     Instititute of Electrical and Electronics Engineers, New
                     York, 1998.

[IEEE 1998d]   *IEEE Standard for Software Quality Assurance Plans*, Std
                     730-1998 Instititute of Electrical and Electronics Engi-
                     neers, New York, 1998.

[Jaaksi 1998]	Jaaksi, Ari. "Our Cases with Use Cases," *Journal of Object-Oriented Programming* 10(9), February 1998: 58–65.
[Jacobson 1992]	Jacobson, Ivar, Magnus Christerson, Patrik Jonsson, and Gunnar Overgaard. *Object-Oriented Software Engineering: A Use Case Driven Approach,* Addison-Wesley, Reading, MA, 1992.
[Jacobson 1994a]	Jacobson, Ivar. "Business Process Reengineering with Object Technology," *Object* 4(2), May 1994: 16–18, 22.
[Jacobson 1994b]	Jacobson, Ivar. "Basic Use Case Modeling," *Report on Object Analysis and Design* 1(2), July/August 1994: 15–19.
[Jacobson 1994c]	Jacobson, Ivar. "Basic Use Case Modeling (Continued)," *Report on Object Analysis and Design* 1(3), September/October 1994: 7–9.
[Jacobson 1995a]	Jacobson, Ivar. "Beyond methods and CASE: The software engineering process and its integral support environment," *Object*, 4(8), January 1995: 24–30.
[Jacobson 1995b]	Jacobson, Ivar. "Use Cases in Large Scale Systems," *Report on Object Analysis and Design* 1(6), March-April 1995: 9–12.
[Jacobson 1995c]	Jacobson, Ivar, Maria Ericsson, and Agreta Jackson. *The Object Advantage: Business Process Reengineeering With Object Technology,* Addison-Wesley, Reading, MA, 1995.
[Jacobson 1997]	Jacobson, Ivar, Martin Griss, and Patrik Jonsson. *Software Reuse: Architecture, Process and Organization for Business Success*, Addison-Wesley, Reading, MA, 1997.
[Jacobson 1998]	Jacobson, Ivar. "Applying the UML in the Unified Process," Presentation at UML World Conference, 1998.
[Jacobson 1999]	Jacobson, Ivar, Grady Booch, and James Rumbaugh. *The Unified Software Development Process*, Addison-Wesley, Reading, MA, 1999.
[Jeffries 2000]	Jeffries, Ron, Ann Anderson, and Chet Hendrickson. *Extreme Programming Installed*, Addison-Wesley, Boston, MA, 2000.

[Jones 1994]   Jones, Capers. *Assessment and Control of Software Risks*, Prentice Hall, Upper Saddle River, NJ, 1994.

[Knuth 1998]   Knuth, Donald E. *The Art of Computer Programming, Volume 3: Sorting and Searching*, Addison-Wesley, Reading, MA, 1973.

[Kruchten 1995]   Kruchten, Phillipe. "The 4+1 View Model of Architecture," *IEEE Software*, 12(6), November/December 1995: 42–50.

[Kruchten 1999]   Kruchten, Phillipe. *The Rational Unified Process: An Introduction*, Addison-Wesley, Reading, MA, 1999.

[Kulak 2000]   Kulak, Daryl, Eamonn Guiney, and Erin Lavkulich (Illustrator). *Use Cases: Requirements in Context*, Addison-Wesley, Boston, MA, 2000.

[Larman 1998]   Larman, Craig. *Applying UML and Patterns: An Introduction to Object-Oriented Analysis and Design*, Prentice Hall, Upper Saddle River, NJ, 1998.

[Lee 1993]   Lee, Geoff. *Object-Oriented GUI Application Development*, Prentice Hall, Upper Saddle River, NJ, 1993.

[Leffingwell 2000]   Leffingwell, Dean, and Don Widrig. *Managing Software Requirement: A Unified Approach*, Addison-Wesley, Reading, MA, 2000.

[Lif 1999]   Lif, Magnus. "User-Interface Modelling—Adding Usability to Use Cases," *International Journal of Human-Computer Studies* 50(3), March 1999: 243–262.

[Lilly 1999]   Lilly, Susan. "Use Case Pitfalls: Top 10 Problems from Real Projects Using Use Cases," *TOOLS 30 Proceedings—Technology of Object-Oriented Languages and Systems*, Institute of Electrical and Electronics Engineers, Los Alamitos, CA, 1999: 174–183.

[Mattingly 1998]   Mattingly, LeRoy, and Harsha Rao. "Writing Effective Use Cases and Introducing Collaboration Cases," *Journal of Object-Oriented Programming* 11(6), October 1998: 77–84, 87.

[McGregor 1997]   McGregor, John D. "Planning for Testing," *Journal of Object-Oriented Programming* 9(9), February 1997: 8–12.

[McGregor 1999a]   McGregor, John D. "Validating Domain Models," *Journal of Object-Oriented Programming* 12(4), July/August 1999: 12–17.

[McGregor 1999b]   McGregor, John D. "Interactions," *Journal of Object-Oriented Programming* 12(6), October 1999: 16–20.

[McGregor 2000]   McGregor, John D., and Melissa L. Major. "Selecting Test Cases Based on User Priorities," *Software Development* 8(3), March 2000: 26–31.

[McGregor 2001]   McGregor, John D., and David A Sykes. *A Practical Guide to Testing Object-Oriented Systems*, Addison-Wesley, Reading, MA, 2001 (publication forthcoming).

[Maguire 1994]   Maguire, Steve. *Debugging the Development Process*, Microsoft Press, Redmond, WA, 1994.

[Miller 1999]   Miller, Granville G., John D. McGregor, and Melissa L. Major. "Capturing Framework Requirements," in *Object-Oriented Application Frameworks*, edited by Mohamed Fayad and Ralph Johnson, John Wiley & Sons, New York, 1999.

[Miller 2000]   Miller, Granville G. "Ceremony: Taking Model-Based Software Development to the Extreme," to appear.

[Mitchell 1999]   Mitchell, Richard. "Analysis by Contract or UML with Attitude," *TOOLS 30 Proceedings—Technology of Object-Oriented Languages and Systems*, Institite of Electrical and Electronics Engineers, Los Alamitos, CA, 1999: 466–476.

[Potts 1994]   Potts, C., K. Takahashi, and A. Anton. "Inquiry-Based Requirements Analysis," *IEEE Software*, March/April 1994: 21–32.

[Pree 1995]   Pree, Wolfgang. *Design Patterns for Object-Oriented Software Development*, Addison-Wesley, Reading, MA, 1995.

[Quatrani 2000]   Quatrani, Terry. *Visual Modeling with Rational Rose 2000 and UML*, Addison-Wesley, Reading, MA, 2000.

[Rechtin 1991]   Rechtin, E. *Systems Architecting: Creating and Building Complex Systems*, Prentice Hall, Englewood Cliffs, NJ, 1991.

[Regnell 1996]   Regnell, Bjorn, Michael Andersson, and John Bergstrand. "A Hierarchical Use Case Model with Graphical Representation," in *Proceedings of the IEEE Symposium and Workshop on Engineering of Computer-Based Systems*, March 1996.

[Robertson 1999] Robertson, Suzanne, and James Robertson, *Mastering the Requirements Process*, Addison-Wesley, Reading, MA, 1999.

[Rosenberg 1999] Rosenberg, Doug, with Kendall Scott. *Use Case Driven Object Modeling with UML: A Practical Approach*, Addison-Wesley, Reading, MA, 1999.

[Rowlett 1998]   Rowlett, Tom. "Building an Object Process Around Use Cases," *Journal of Object-Oriented Programming* 11(1), March-April 1998: 53–58.

[Royce 1998]   Royce, Walker. *Software Project Management: A Unified Framework,* Addison-Wesley, Reading, MA, 1998.

[Royce 1970]   Royce, Winston. "Managing the Development of Large Software Systems," *Proceedings of IEEE WESCON,* August 1970: 1–9.

[Rumbaugh 1991]   Rumbaugh, James, Michael Blaha, William Premerlani, Frederick Eddy, and William Lorensen. *Object-Oriented Modeling and Design*, Prentice Hall, Upper Saddle River, NJ, 1991.

[Rumbaugh 1999]   Rumbaugh, James, Ivar Jacobson, and Grady Booch. *The Unified Modeling Language Reference Manual,* Addison-Wesley, Reading, MA, 1999.

[Schmidt 2000]   Schmidt, Marty J. *The Business Case Guide*. Parts appear at http://www.solutionmatrix.com.

[Schneider 1998] Schneider, Geri, and Jason P. Winters. *Applying Use Cases: A Practical Guide,* Addison-Wesley, Reading, MA, 1998.

[Schwarz 1994]   Schwarz, Roger M. *The Skilled Facilitator: Practical Wisdom for Developing Effective Groups*, Jossey-Bass, San Francisco, CA 1994.

[Smith 1937]   Smith, Adam. *The Wealth of Nations*, Random House, New York, 1937.

[Thorp 1999]   Thorp, John. "Computing the Payoff from IT," *Journal of Business Strategy* 20(3), May/June 1999: 35–39.

[Tognazzini 1992]   Tognazzini, Bruce "Tog." *Tog on Interface*, Addison-Wesley, Reading, MA, 1992.

[UML 1999]   OMG Unified Modeling Language Specification, version 1.3, June 1999.

[Wakamoto 1995]   Wakamoto, Masaaki, Mitsnori Fukazawa, Moo Wan Kim, and Koso Murakami, "Intelligent Network Architecture with Layered Call Model for Multimedia-on-Demand Service," *Proceedings of International Switching Software (ISS)* 1995: 201–205.

[Webster 1999]   *Webster's Tenth New Collegiate Dictionary*, G. & C. Merriam Co., Springfield, MA, 1999.

[Weidenhaupt 1998]   Weidenhaupt, Klaus, Klaus Pohl, Mattias Jarke, and Peter Haumer. "Scenarios in System Development: Current Practice," *IEEE Software*, 15(2) March/April 1998: 34–45.

[Wiegers 2000]   Wiegers, Kurt. "Stop Promising Miracles," *Software Development* 8(2), February 2000: 49–54.

[Wilkinson 1995]   Wilkinson, Nancy M. *Using CRC Cards: An Informal Approach to Object-Oriented Development*, Prentice Hall, Upper Saddle River, NJ, 1995.

[Wirfs-Brock 1993]   Wirfs-Brock, Rebecca. "Designing Scenarios: Making the Case for a Use Case Framework." *Smalltalk Report*, November-December, 1993: 9–12, 20.

[Yourdon 1989]   Yourdon, E., *Modern Structured Analysis*, Prentice Hall, Engelwood Cliffs, NJ, 1989.

Index